Russia in War and Revolution

Brig. Gen. William Voorhees Judson (ca. 1918) shortly after his return to the United States from Petrograd, where he served as chief of the American military mission to Russia and as military attaché to the American ambassador. *Courtesy of the Newberry Library.*

RUSSIA IN WAR AND
REVOLUTI☭N

General William V. Judson's
Accounts from Petrograd,
1917–1918

Edited by
Neil V. Salzman

THE KENT STATE UNIVERSITY PRESS
Kent, Ohio, and London, England

© 1998 by The Kent State University Press, Kent, Ohio 44242

All rights reserved

Library of Congress Catalog Card Number 97-35946

ISBN 0-87338-597-7

Manufactured in the United States of America

04 03 02 01 00 99 98   5 4 3 2 1

Library of Congress Cataloging-in-Publication Data

Judson, William V. (William Voorhees), 1865–1923.

    Russia in war and revolution : General William V. Judson's

accounts from Petrograd, 1917–1918 / edited by Neil V. Salzman.

      p. cm.

    ISBN 0-87338-597-7 (cloth : alk. paper) ∞

    1. Soviet Union—History—Revolution, 1917–1921—Personal

narratives, American.   2. United States—Foreign relations—Soviet

Union.   3. Soviet Union—Foreign relations—United States.

4. United States—Foreign relations—1913–1921.   5. Soviet Union—

Foreign relations—1917–1945.   6. Judson, William V. (William

Voorhees), 1865–1923.   I. Salzman, Neil V.   II. Title.

DK265.7.J83   1998

947.084'1—dc21   97-35946

                                                    CIP

British Library Cataloging-in-Publication data are available.

To
Jean Salzman
Robin Salzman
Aram, Noah, and Gabriel Salzman
and Barbara and Murray Flam

Contents

Acknowledgments

A number of individuals and institutions have been especially helpful in bringing the publication of this book to fruition. Alice Judson Hayes, daughter of Clay Judson and granddaughter of William V. Judson, kindly shared her memories and family memorabilia concerning the life and activities of her grandfather. Clay Judson first took the initiative of making the papers of his father available to the scholarly community more than forty-five years ago, and Alice Hayes has added additional documents and photographs in recent years.

Fairleigh Dickinson University provided released time from teaching to do research and writing and, in addition, awarded grants to defray the many expenses of travel and research. Patricia M. Verost and Jennifer Harris in FDU's Office of Grants and Sponsored Projects were particularly helpful.

John Hubbell, Director of Kent State University Press; Julia Morton, Editor-in-Chief; and Linda Cuckovich and Joanna Hildebrand, Managing Editors, have been a dedicated source of help, along with Will Moore, copy editor, and the rest of the Kent State University Press's skilled editorial and production staff.

Michael Stroble, a history honors graduate of Fairleigh Dickinson University, gave many hours of his patient research to develop the Dramatis Personae that is included in the introductory material. We both hope this departure from the conventions of scholarly publications will contribute to this book's usefulness.

As in all of my teaching and research, I am fortunate to have the encouragement and support of my good friend Robert Ubell, whose ideas and insights have always been a boon.

Walter Cummins, Gary Jaworski, and Peter Woolley, colleagues of mine at Fairleigh Dickinson University, were kind enough to take time from their busy teaching and research responsibilities to read and comment on portions of the manuscript. Their suggestions have made a better book. Dennis Foster and Elizabeth Janelle Russell helped with index proofreading.

Diana Haskell, Lloyd Lewis Curator of Midwest Manuscripts at the Newberry Library in Chicago, along with her excellent staff, have made each of my visits there both pleasurable and productive. At the National Archives in Washington, D.C., Kenneth Heger, at the Civil Reference Branch, and Mitchell Yockelson, of the Military Reference Branch, Textual Reference Division, helped with the challenges of locating Judson's decoded telegrams received by the War College Staff in Washington. The harried and overworked librarians and research staff at the National Archives deserve the thanks and credit far beyond any I can acknowledge here.

Frances Farrell, Lindsay Zano, Jessica Cain, Evangeline Cochrane, and Zhang Zhiguang, whose dedicated childcare provided countless hours that could not otherwise have been devoted to the work at hand, have my deepest thanks and friendship.

Finally, I thank Gabriel for his patience and resilience in sharing his dad with this project—and in sharing the computer with his dad—and my wife Robin for her love, understanding, and support.

Editor's Note

All documents included here are in chronological order and are in the William V. Judson Papers (WJM) at the Newberry Library in Chicago, Illinois, unless otherwise indicated. Most of the documents in chapters 2 through 5 were formulated by Judson for transmittal to his superiors at the War College Division (WCD), or Staff ("Warcolstaff" in Judson's communications), of the War Department, which operated directly under the supervision of the chief of staff. On 26 August 1918, well after Judson's tenure in Petrograd had ended, the War College Staff was replaced by the Military Intelligence Division.

Most of the official communications included here were sent by telegram and in the special code of the American Military Mission to Russia. In most cases these communications are entitled "Paraphrase of Telegram Sent." Almost all of the documents included here, primarily taken from Judson's personal papers, are the original drafts of communications as Judson composed them. The use of the term "paraphrase" in the heading of nearly all official telegrams sent during the period covered in this book reflects the sender's understanding of the variations in syntax that may be produced by encoding and decoding messages. The sender expected that his precise meaning would be communicated, even though his exact words may not. A comparison of Judson's messages sent from Petrograd with those received at the War College Staff in Washington bears out that those expectations were fulfilled. Responsibility for confusion and for differences of opinion about developments in revolutionary Russia cannot be placed at the doorstep of these mechanics of telegraphic communication. One may wish to speculate about the course of events in American-Russian relations had telephone links connected Petrograd with Washington; however, as interesting and even revelatory as such speculations might be, this is neither the time nor the place for pursuing them.

Where possible, particularly in most of Judson's Warcolstaff telegrams, a footnote cites its location at the National Archives. These are the documents that were reconstructed in Washington for dissemination among Judson's superiors. A cross-referencing of the documents in the National Archives with those of the Newberry Library indicates that, with only two or three exceptions, Judson's set of originals of his official communications during his tenure at Petrograd is complete. Since the documents are arranged in chronological order and since the book contains a detailed index of personalities, subjects, places, and events, there is no independent listing of all of the separate documents. Please consult the index to locate a particular document if its date is unknown.

Most cables and telegrams that are reproduced here were given two numbers, as in the following: "Judson to Warcolstaff, 17 January 1918, No. 281-181." The first is the "service number," which represents the number of a message sent by a particular agency, "as Russian [telegraphic] authorities require consecutive numbering" (WCD 10220-D-93, RG 165/NA). The second is the sequential numbering of Judson's own messages. If only one number is cited, it refers to Judson's sequence.

Judson dated his 1904–5 and 1917–18 correspondence and reports from Russia using the western, or Gregorian, calendar. The Julian calendar, thirteen days behind the Gregorian, was used in Russia until 1 (14) February 1918, when the Bolshevik government officially adopted the Gregorian. All dates here are given in the Gregorian calendar, unless otherwise indicated by the use of parentheses as above.

The editorial introductions to each chapter use a typeface different from that of the body of the book. Some portions clearly *within* Judson's texts have been italicized to indicate that, at a later time, Judson himself quoted this passage for use in his "significant quotations from my communications." He compiled this collection of quotations in late February and early March 1918, and he included many of these passages in his forty-eight-page memorandum of 16 March 1918. This document, addressed to the "Chief of Intelligence Section, General Staff" and simply titled "Russian Situation," was Judson's final report, to conclude his formal responsibilities as military attaché and chief of the American Military Mission to Russia. It is included here along with many selections from Judson's "Military Notes" and "Monthly Resumés."

Judson's own emphases in all his handwritten and typed communications were made by single or double underlining or by the use of capital letters. Throughout this book, unless otherwise noted, all parenthetic phrases are Judson's. All writing for clarification within brackets is the editor's. Here, with the exception of archaic spellings and transliterations, we shall follow as closely as practicable all of Judson's own usages. There are occasional variations in the transliteration of Russian names.

An alphabetical Dramatis Personae is included here to provide a brief biographical identification of individuals who appear in the text. The notes and index will deal with specific events and, generally, will not repeat this biographical information.

Information Source Abbreviations

BERR   Shukman, Harold, ed. *The Blackwell Encyclopedia of the Russian Revolution.* New York: Basil Blackwell, 1988.

DADH   Findling, John E., ed. *The Dictionary of American Diplomatic History.* Westport, Conn.: Greenwood Press, 1980.

DRR   Jackson, George F., and Robert Devlin, eds. *The Dictionary of the Russian Revolution.* Westport, Conn.: Greenwood Press, 1989.

GSE   Paradise, Jean, ed. *The Great Soviet Encyclopedia.* New York: Macmillan, 1983.

KEN RAW   Kennan, George F. *Russia and the West under Lenin and Stalin.* London: Hutchinson, 1961.

KEN SAR   Kennan, George F. *Soviet-American Relations: 1917–1920.* Princeton, N.J.: Princeton Univ. Press, 1956.

MG   Gilbert, Martin. *The First World War: A Complete History.* New York: Henry Holt, 1994.

NVS   Salzman, Neil V. *Reform and Revolution: The Life and Times of Raymond Robins.* Kent, Ohio: Kent State Univ. Press, 1991.

ULL   Ullman, Richard Henry. *Anglo-Soviet Relations 1917–1921.* Vol. 1., Princeton, N.J.: Princeton Univ. Press, 1961.

UNT   Unterberger, Betty Miller. *America's Siberian Expedition.* Durham, N.C.: Duke Univ. Press, 1956.

WAW   Williams, William Appleman. *American-Russian Relations.* 1952. Reprint, New York: Octagon Books, 1971.

WJP   William V. Judson Papers. The Newberry Library, Chicago.

WWB   Wheeler-Bennett, John W. *Brest-Litovsk: The Forgotten Peace.* London: Macmillan, 1963.

Dramatis Personae

ALEKSEEV, MIKHAIL VASIL'EVICH (1857–1918): Alekseev was the commander of the czar's armies on the western front in 1915 and, after the czar assumed field command, served as his chief of staff.* It was Alekseev who, in February 1917, persuaded the czar to abdicate. Under the Provisional Government, Alekseev served as supreme commander until May 1917, when he was replaced by Brusilov. Because of his opposition to the Soviets, Alekseev, along with Kaledin, was regarded as a potential savior by the western Allies. He conspired with Kornilov to form an anti-Bolshevik volunteer army and a government under Denikin in the spring of 1918, only to die a few months later. (GSE)

*Since Judson uses the more traditional transliteration *czar,* rather than *tsar* or *tzar,* we have adopted its use throughout.

ANDREWS, JAMES W. (?): A member of the American Red Cross Commission to Russia, Andrews made a number of trips back and forth from Petrograd to Jassy, Romania, on Red Cross business. (NVS)

AVKSENTIEV, NICHOLAI DMITRIEVICH (1879–1943): In 1917, Avksentiev was a member of the Petrograd Soviet and chairman of the All-Russian Soviet of Peasants' Deputies. During July and August of that year, he served as minister of the Provisional Government, eventually becoming a chairman in the Duma. After the Bolshevik Revolution, he actively opposed the Soviets and helped organize the counterrevolution along the Volga and Siberia. (GSE)

BAKER, NEWTON D. (1871–1937): The secretary of war in Wilson's cabinet, who received many of Judson's communications from Petrograd

Note: Years of birth and death are given. The notation "(?)" indicates information is not available. If more than one text is given, the first is primary and the second is supplementary.

and often expressed to Wilson his interest in those communications and in Judson's point of view on Russia. (KEN SAR)

BEACH, MAJ. W. D. (1856–1932): In his position as the chief of G-2 in Washington, D.C. (the Military Information Division, General Staff, U.S. Army), Maj. Beach was the recipient of many of Judson's reports during the Russo-Japanese War. (WJP)

BERKMAN, ALEXANDER (1870–1936): A Lithuanian Jew of an upper-middle-class family, emigrated to the U.S. and became an anarchist in the 1880s. After meeting Emma Goldman in 1889, they became leading speakers and writers in the American anarchist movement and campaigned against the First World War and conscription. Arrested in 1917, they were both deported to Russia in 1919. At first supportive of the Bolsheviks, the pair soon became disillusioned and took the lead in public protest against the Soviets. The two eventually emigrated to France in 1921. (DRR, BERR)

BERTRON, SAMUEL R. (1865–1938): A Wall Street financier, he was a member of the Root Mission to Russia. Along with McCormick, he recognized that Russia was on the verge of collapse, but he did not report this opinion for fear of jeopardizing support for either the mission or the war at home. (WAW)

BONCH-BRUYEVICH, VLADIMIR DMITRIEVICH (1873–1955): An active Marxist since 1892, he emigrated to Switzerland in 1896, where he met Lenin. Working with Lenin, he wrote and published revolutionary literature and Bolshevik newspapers. After participating in the 1905 revolution in St. Petersburg, he once again left his native Russia.

Returning to Russia with Lenin in 1917, he became a member of the Executive Committee of the Petrograd Soviet and commander of the palace district at Bolshevik headquarters in the Smolny Institute during the Bolshevik Revolution. Later, he played an active part in establishing the machinery of the Soviet state and directed the move of the government to Moscow in 1918. (GSE)

BRUSILOV, ALEKSEI ALEKSEEIVICH (1853–1926): Brusilov was the commander of the successful breakthrough of the Austro-German lines on the southwestern front in early 1917. Despite his strong opposition to Kornilov, he took all measures necessary to continue the war, including the institution of capital punishment within his own ranks. After being replaced by Kornilov in June 1917, Brusilov rejected pleas to join the White forces and eventually served in the central apparatus of the Red Army. (GSE)

BUKOWSKI, LT. (?): Served as a subordinate to Judson on the American Military Mission to Russia during World War I. (WJP)

BULLARD, ARTHUR (1879–1929): A moderate socialist in the U.S., Bullard served as an unofficial listening post for Colonel House, President Wilson's key foreign policy advisor, and continued in that capacity while undertaking the new responsibilities described here. Initially an ally in the struggle to open official lines of communication with Lenin, he served in the Russian office of the Committee on Public Information (COMPUB), and later opposed such contact. (NVS)

BURLESON, ALBERT (1863–1937): A personal friend of Judson's, Burleson also held the influential post of postmaster general and was a recipient of many of Judson's letters. Burleson campaigned on Judson's behalf for a Distinguished Service Medal (D.S.M.), recognizing Judson's contribution to the Allied cause while serving in Russia. This campaign, as well as those to bestow a D.S.M. on Raymond Robins and William Boyce Thompson, drew support from many veterans of American service in Russia, who believed that these individuals were instrumental in delaying final approval of the Brest-Litovsk Treaty and winning the war for the Allies. (KEN RAW, NVS)

CHAIKOVSKI, NIKOLAI VASIL'EVICH (1850–1926): After the February Revolution of 1917, he became a member of the central committee of the moderate Popular Socialists. Actively opposed to the Soviets, he established a government independent of Bolshevik power in Archangel following the Allied landing there on 1 August 1918. Following the defeat of Denikin in 1920, he emigrated to London. (GSE)

CHERNOV, VIKTOR MIKHAILOVICH (1873–1952): A prominent Socialist Revolutionary, Chernov served as the minister of agriculture in the Provisional Government after February 1917. After the October Revolution he went on to lead a center of anti-Bolshevik opposition, seeking a reestablishment of the Constituent Assembly. Following Denikin's defeat in 1920, he emigrated to France, where he aided the French Resistance in World War II. (GSE)

CRANE, CHARLES R. (1858–1939): A wealthy American plumbing magnate with a deep interest in Russia, China, and the Arab Middle East, Crane made extensive visits to these regions and contributed financially to related causes, political and otherwise. As a member of the Root Mission, he was pessimistic about the Kerensky government and its ability to fulfill commitments to the western Allies. Crane believed that hope for order rested in czarist military leaders such as Kaledin, Kolchak, Denikin, and Kornilov, and he encouraged David Francis to accept Wilson's offer of ambassadorship to Russia in order to support these conservative and often reactionary leaders. (NVS)

DAVISON, HENRY P. (1867–1922): A former executive with the House of Morgan and a personal friend of William Boyce Thompson, Davison served as chairman of the War Council of the American Red Cross, headquartered in Washington, D.C. He aided Thompson in developing plans for the American Red Cross Commission to Russia as America's instrument for keeping Russia in the war. At the urging of Theodore Roosevelt, Davison included Raymond Robins in the mission, but later recalled Robins when he became concerned about possible "Bolshevik sympathies." In line with Wilson, Lansing, and House, Davison opposed direct communication with the Bolsheviks, frequently placing him at odds with Robins and Judson . (WAW)

DENIKIN, ANTON IVANOVICH (1872–1942): Beginning World War I as the Russian commander of the Romanian front, Denikin was promoted to chief of staff and later became supreme commander of both the western and southwestern fronts. After being jailed along with Kornilov and other czarist military leaders, Denikin escaped to take part in the creation of a volunteer army under Kornilov. Succeeding Kornilov as the head of this army, Denikin would later link with Kolchak and become his deputy, leading in the Moscow campaigns of 1919 against the Bolsheviks. After the defeat of the White forces, Denikin fled Russia. (UNT, ULL)

DIAMANDI, COUNT CONSTANTINE (?): As the Romanian ambassador to Russia at Petrograd, Count Diamandi became involved in the complex problem of German occupation of part of his country and the presence of large numbers of Russian forces. By the fall of 1917, Russia's armies were in a state of deterioration and disaffection, leading to many crises in Russian-Romanian relations. Count Diamandi was arrested by the Bolsheviks in the hope of bringing an end to Romanian attempts to disarm and expel Bolsheviks from Moldavia. After Diamandi's arrest, Raymond Robins and the diplomatic corps at Petrograd demanded and eventually negotiated his release. (BERR, DRR)

DUKHONIN, NIKOLAI LEONIDOVICH (1876–1917): Beginning World War I as regimental commander, Dukhonin eventually became chief of staff of the Russian army in September 1917. Following the Bolshevik Revolution he was commander-in-chief of the eastern front until relieved by Krylenko. After taking part in attempts to create a counterrevolutionary government headed by Chernov and refusing an order of the People's Commissars to open negotiations with Germany, he was relieved of his post and arrested. Against the orders of the Bolshevik Central Committee, a group of soldiers dragged him from his railway car and killed him. (ULL)

DUNCAN, JAMES (1857–1928): The elder vice president of the American Federation of Labor, Duncan was selected as a member of the Root Mission to counteract the possibility that Russian liberals and socialists would regard the American team as conservative and reactionary. (KEN SAR)

FRANCIS, DAVID ROWLAND (1850–1927): After a distinguished political career as the mayor of St. Louis and the governor of Missouri, Francis served as secretary of the interior under President Cleveland before being appointed ambassador to Russia in 1916, at the age of sixty-five. Favoring the Provisional Government, he opposed communication with the Bolsheviks and awaited their overthrow by counterrevolutionary military leaders. Because of his active participation in relief efforts for German and Austrian prisoners of war, his anti-Bolshevik sympathies, and his involvement with Madame Matilda de Cram (who was suspected of being a German agent), he had to withstand Bolshevik accusations that he was fomenting counterrevolution.

Despite efforts by Judson and others to have him dismissed, Francis remained at his post, urging military intervention on the part of the Allies and keeping Russia in the war at all costs. Due to failing health he left for England in 1918 and later served as an advisor to Lansing at the Paris Peace Conference. (DADH, ULL, UNT, NVS)

GOLDMAN, EMMA (1869–1940): A Lithuanian Jew of an upper-middle-class family, Goldman emigrated to the U.S. in 1885. A factory worker in the clothing industry, she became an international anarchist and was active in the United States from 1890 to 1917. After meeting Alexander Berkman in 1889, they became leading speakers and writers in the American anarchist movement and campaigned against the First World War and conscription. Arrested in 1917 for this activity, they were both deported to Russia in 1919. She wrote many books, including *My Disillusionment in Russia* (1923) and her autobiography *Living My Life* (1931), which is the most widely known.

At first supportive of the Bolsheviks, Goldman and Berkman soon became disillusioned and took the lead in public protest against the Soviets. The two eventually emigrated to France in 1921. (DRR)

GUCHKOV, ALEKSANDR IVANOVICH (1862–1936): A Moscow industrialist and leader of the Octobrist factions of the Kadets (the Constitutional Democratic Party), Guchkov first came to prominence when he called for the suppression of the uprisings of 1905 and the introduction of martial law. After being elected to the Duma and serving as its president in 1910–11, he served as chairman of the War Industries Committee and later as the minister of war and the navy under the Provisional Government. Strongly anti-Soviet, Guchkov resigned following the Bolshevik Revolution and helped organize the Kornilov uprising. Since he had become close friends with Judson during the Russo-Japanese War, he was an invaluable resource to Judson during World War I. (GSE)

HARPER, SAMUEL N. (1882–1943): After receiving support and encouragement from Charles Crane in developing his deep interest in Russia, Harper became a professor of Russian history at the University of Chicago. He observed both revolutions in 1917 and wrote extensively about them. Harper personally supplied much of the information on which early Wilson policy decisions were based, and he also advised Ambassador Francis. A proponent of U.S. economic penetration of Russia, he became disgusted at its failure and returned to the U.S. to brief State Department personnel on Russian affairs.

Later he was selected to analyze the authenticity of various documents, including the infamous "Sisson papers" to help determine if Lenin had been a German agent. (WAW, KEN SAR)

HAVARD, COL. VALERY (?): Along with Maj. Montgomery Macomb, Havard was part of the American Military Mission to Russia during the Russo-Japanese War. (WJP)

HOFFMAN, MAJ. GEN. MAX (1869–1927): As the commander of German forces on the eastern front, Hoffman was empowered by the German government to enter into peace negotiations with the Russians in late November 1917 at his headquarters in Brest-Litovsk. Believing the Bolshevik Revolution to be a godsend to the German cause, he showered Russians with antiwar leaflets and encouraged Bolshevik propaganda among the Russian troops.

   At the negotiating table, Hoffman used the threat of continued hostilities to press for the separation of Poland and Lithuania from the Russian empire. This led to much disagreement between the two sides, and—angered that Trotsky had broken off negotiations—Hoffman renewed the German offensive in mid-February 1918. Shortly thereafter, the Soviets signed the treaty under protest on German terms. (KEN SAR)

HORNE, HENRY J. (?): Given the title of Deputy Commissar, Horne was the railroad transportation expert with the American Red Cross Commission to Russia. (WJP)

KALEDIN, ALEKSEI MAKSIMOVICH (1861–1918): Elected as ataman of the Don Cossacks, Kaledin led a cossack counterrevolution in the Don region in the winter of 1917–18. Pledging opposition to the Bolsheviks and loyalty to the Allies, he joined the White armies, though the forces at his disposal were not sufficient to enable him to engage in any serious enterprise. (GSE, ULL)

KERENSKY, ALEXANDER FEDOROVICH (1881–1970): A lawyer and member of the labor faction of the Socialist Revolutionary Party (SRs), Kerensky became the minister of justice in the Provisional Government under Prince Lvov. On July 21, he became the prime minister of the second Provisional Government. As prime minister he was responsible for the summer offensive of 1917, reprisals against worker revolts, and restraining the Bolsheviks. Kerensky supported the war on the grounds of national defense, and, following the Bolshevik Revolution, he fled to the front. There he led unsuccessful armed rebellions in an attempt to recapture Petrograd and overthrow the Soviets. He fled Russia in 1918. (DRR, GSE)

KERTH, MONROE C. (?): As Judson's immediate subordinate, Kerth carried out the missions specified by Judson and his superior, Ambassador David Francis. At this time his official title was Assistant Military Attaché to Petrograd. As ordered by Judson, Kerth registered an official protest against the Bolshevik desire to initiate a separate peace with Germany. This was done without authorization from Washington. Eventually Judson was forced to order Kerth to return to Petrograd, believing his presence in the field was a source of irritation for the Bolsheviks. (KEN RAW)

KLEMBOVSKY, GEN. ———— (?): He was assistant to the staff of the Russian high command.

KNOX, GEN. ALFRED C. (?): During this period of time, Gen. Knox served as the British military attaché in Petrograd. Pro-czarist and a staunch opponent of cooperation with the Bolsheviks, he gave support to reactionary leaders such as Kornilov. Knox regarded Robins as dangerous and opposed Judson's more conciliatory attitude toward the Bolsheviks. Firmly believing that only a military dictatorship by former czarist elements could save Russia and the Allied war effort, Knox encouraged—and would eventually lead—an Allied military intervention at Vladivostok. After observing the accumulation of Allied supplies at Archangel, which could not get to the front because of railroad problems and losses in Russian manpower due to deaths and desertions, Knox became opposed to both American and Bolshevik initiatives for discussions and cooperation. (KEN SAR, UNT)

KOLCHAK, ALEXANDER VASIL'EVICH (1874–1920): The former commander of a destroyer in the Russo-Japanese War and a former polar explorer, Kolchak was first the admiral of the Baltic fleet and later, during World War I, of the Black Sea fleet. Following the abdication of the czar, he was recalled to Petrograd and sent on assignment to England. Accompanying Gen. Knox back to Russia, Kolchak quickly became involved in counterrevolutionary movements. After being appointed minister of war and the navy in an anti-Bolshevik Siberian government, he secured the help of White forces, the Kadet Party, and Allied interventionists in staging a coup that established a military dictatorship in Siberia, the Urals, and the Far East. Following the defeat of the White forces in 1919, Kolchak attempted to flee Russia. He was executed by the Bolsheviks in 1920. (GSE)

KORNILOV, LAVAR GEORGIEVICH (1870–1918): Kornilov, the son of a cossack officer, served as an infantry general in Turkestan during the Russo-Japanese War and as a military attaché to China prior to World War I. During the war he was appointed supreme commander of the Russian army by the Provisional Government in July 1917. In September 1917, Kornilov led an ill-fated uprising to unseat Kerensky and topple the Provisional Government. His hope to establish a counterrevolutionary military dictatorship came to an end when he was arrested and imprisoned. After escaping to join the White Guard, Kornilov was killed during an unsuccessful assault on Red forces at Ekaterinodar in 1918. (GSE, ULL)

KRYLENKO, NIKOLAI VASIL'EVICH (1885–1939): Following the Bolshevik Revolution, Krylenko was a member of the Petrograd Revolutionary Committee, a deputy of the People's Commissars, and the chairman of the Committee on Military and Naval Affairs. Most significantly he was appointed supreme commander of the armed forces, replacing Dukhonin, in November 1917. His appointment paved the way for a separate peace with Germany. After the war and into the 1930s, Krylenko served as the state prosecutor in major political trials. (GSE)

KUHLMAN, RICHARD VON (1873–1947): Counselor of the German embassy in London from 1908 to 1914, he became the German foreign minister and head of the German delegation to the Brest-Litovsk negotiations. (ULL, WWB, MG)

KUROPATKIN, ALEKSEI NIKOLAEVICH (1848–1925): He held the post of minister of war until 1897. Subsequently, he was the supreme commander of the Russian army during the Russo-Japanese War. Beginning World War I as a corps commander, Kuropatkin went on to command the northern front until 1916. Appointed governor general of Turkestan, he advocated armed suppression of uprisings there.

Following the Bolshevik Revolution he rejected repeated offerings of the interventionists and the White Guard to lead them in the struggle against the Soviets. (GSE)

LANSING, ROBERT (1864–1928): Secretary of state in Wilson's cabinet, he was committed to the policy of nonintercourse with, and nonrecognition of, Bolshevik Russia. He ultimately supported U.S. participation in the Allied intervention in Russia. (NVS)

LVOV, PRINCE GEORGE E. (1861–1925): A wealthy landowner and zemstvo activist, he later became the first head of the Provisional Government. Announcing close ties with the western Allies and continued war with Germany as the basis of his policies, he faced much opposition to his regime. Amidst mass uprisings in July 1917 he resigned and was replaced by Kerensky. (ULL, WWB)

LVOV, VLADIMIR NIKOLAEVICH (b. 1872): Lvov was appointed procurator of the Holy Synod by the Provisional Duma Committee of the first Provisional Government in the first week of March 1917. He had served as a deputy in the Third and Fourth Dumas under the old regime. (GSE)

MACOMB, MAJ. MONTGOMERY (1852–1924): Along with Col. Valery Havard, he was a member of the American Military Mission observing the Russo-Japanese War. (WJP)

MCCORMICK, CYRUS (1859–1936): He was heir to the fortune of his father, inventor and industrialist Cyrus H. McCormick, who had created the International Harvester Company. His company built reapers in Russia, and McCormick was enthusiastic about social welfare work there. Recognizing that Russia was on the verge of collapse in 1917, McCormick urged Wilson to act quickly in providing aid and relief to Russia. (KEN RAW, NVS)

MCCORMICK, COL. ROBERT R. (1880–1955): A member of the noted Chicago McCormick family, he was an acquaintance of Judson's and his correspondent on the issue of U.S.-Russian relations. (WJP)

MCCORMICK, ROBERT S. (1849–1919): Before entering into the diplomatic service in 1889, McCormick was involved in his family's reaping machine corporation. Later, as secretary to the legation in London, he became the first U.S. ambassador to Austria-Hungary in 1901. Two years later McCormick became ambassador to Russia and was the liaison between the warring parties and Washington in the Russo-Japanese War. (DADH)

McCULLY, NEWTON (1867–1951): He was a U.S. naval attaché attached to Russian forces during the Russo-Japanese War. (WJP)

MANIKOVSKI, GEN. A. A. (1865–1920): A Russian artillery general, Manikovski became chief of the Main Artillery Directorate and later the chief of the Supply Directorate during World War I. After the February Revolution in 1917 he became vice minister of war in the Provisional Government and was still serving in that capacity weeks after the Bolshevik Revolution. (GSE)

MARUSHEVSKI, GENERAL V. V. (?): A carryover of the czarist military elite, Marushevski was chief of the Russian General Staff in Petrograd before being imprisoned by the Soviets. (GSE)

MICHIE, COL. B. E. L. (?): Member of the Root Mission to Russia in the spring of 1917. (WJP)

MILIUKOV, PAUL N. (1859–1943): Leader of the Constitutional Democrats (Kadets), historian, and foreign minister of the Provisional Government, Miliukov gave assurances of Russian maintenance of the eastern front. This caused a major crisis in the Provisional Government and offered the Bolsheviks the opportunity to rally the antiwar sentiment in their own behalf. (GSE, WWB)

MIRBACH, COUNT WILHELM VON (1871–1918): Count Mirbach headed the German Economic Mission to Russia, which arrived in Petrograd in the last week of December 1917. There he took part in the peace negotiations at Brest-Litovsk and was later appointed the first German ambassador to Soviet Russia. In July 1918 he was murdered by Social Revolutionaries on instructions from Central Committee members who were attempting to provoke continued war with Germany. (ULL)

MOTT, JOHN R. (1865–1955): Social reformer, head of the YMCA, and member of the Root Mission. (WJP)

MOTT, COL. T. (TOBY) BENTLEY (?): Served on the staff of American Ambassador to Russia Robert S. McCormack at Petrograd during the Russo-Japanese War and as a member of the Root Mission. (WJP)

NIESSEL, GEN. HENRI (?): The chief of the French Military Mission to Russia, Niessel made a strong argument for Allied military intervention in Russia based on the fear that the Germans would have control of vast tracts of Russian territory and be able to manipulate the Soviet government. (UNT)

PARKER, MAJ. FRANCIS L. (?): Assistant military attaché serving under Judson in Petrograd. (WJP)

POLIVANOV, ALEKSEI ANDREEVICH (1855–1920): After the disastrous Russian defeat at the Battle of Tannenberg in January 1915, Polivanov was promoted to minister of war. During the civil war, he joined the Red Army and served as a member of the Military Training Board and as special counsel to the commander-in-chief. In 1920 he was the resident military expert at the Soviet-Polish peace negotiations. (GSE)

POOLE, MAJ. GEN. F. C. (?): After a thirty-year career in the British army and serving as chief of the British Artillery Mission in France, Poole arrived in Russia in May 1918. There he was to command all British troops and direct the organization of locally recruited troops as part of the Allied military intervention. Despite his lack of political ability and the fact that the forces at his disposal were woefully inadequate, Poole was able to secure rail lines in and out of Murmansk and was able to put down a coup against the opposition government in Archangel, allowing a successful Allied landing in August 1918. (KEN RAW)

PRINCE, CAPT. EUGENE (?): Assistant U.S. military attaché in Petrograd, serving under Judson. (WJP)

RIGGS, CAPT. E. FRANCIS (?): Riggs served under Judson as the assistant military attaché in Petrograd. He believed the Bolsheviks would accept Allied military assistance and could be induced to request intervention. (ULL)

ROBINS, RAYMOND (1873–1954): Only weeks after the Bolshevik Revolution, Robins assumed command of the American Red Cross Commission to Russia (following Thompson's departure). As part of the Commission, he tried to convince Thompson and others that American national interest required negotiation and cooperation with Lenin and the Bolsheviks if there was to be any hope of keeping Russia from signing a separate peace with Germany. (NVS)

RODZIANKO, MIKHAIL VLADIMIROVICH (1859–1924): An important landowner in the Ekaterina province, Rodzianko served as a deputy in the Duma, becoming president in 1911. During World War I he formed a bloc within the Kadet Party and opposed the influence of Rasputin while becoming president. Although his warnings went unheeded, Rodzianko took the responsibility of warning the czar of the impending revolutionary crisis. Following the abdication of the czar, he served as head of the Provisional Committee. When the Bolsheviks seized power, Rodzianko served under Denikin through the civil war. (GSE)

ROMANOVSKI, VLADIMIR ZAKHOROVICH (1896–1967): The son of a peasant, Romanovski joined the Red Army in 1918 and fought in the civil war as the commissar of an armored train. (BERR)

ROOT, ELIHU (1845–1937): Theodore Roosevelt's secretary of state (1905–1909) and secretary of war (1899–1904) at the time Judson was military attaché and observer of the Russo-Japanese War. Root headed the mission that bore his name, which was one of several such delegations the United States sent to Russia within weeks of its entry into the war to solidify the U.S.-Russian military alliance and to welcome the Provisional Government of Russia into the family of democratic states. (NVS)

RUSSELL, CHARLES EDWARD (1860–1941): Fabian socialist, journalist, and noted author in the United States, Russell was an ally of William Boyce Thompson and member of the Root Mission to Russia. Realizing almost immediately the rising power of the Bolsheviks, he began to campaign against them and pleaded to President Wilson for an understanding of Russian war-weariness, assuring Wilson that "five million [in aid] now . . . may obviate the expenditure of billions hereafter." (WAW)

SAVINKOV, BORIS VICTOROVICH (1879–1925): He was a close associate of Kerensky's, a leader in the Social Revolutionary Party (SRs), and a radical novelist who attempted to challenge Bolshevik control of the Soviets. He later joined the ranks of the Russian émigrés. (GSE)

SCHERBATEV, GEN. ——— (?): Scherbatev, who was the commander of Russian troops in Moldavia, had to contend with the dissolution of order and the disaffection of his forces prior to and following the armistice with the Central Powers in December 1917. The situation was complicated both by the presence upon the battle lines of the Romanian and Russian armies allied against the Central Powers and by Bolshevik propaganda. In a controversial decision, he accepted the help of Romanian forces in disarming and expelling his mutinous forces into nearby Russian territory. (NVS)

SCOTT, GEN. HUGH L. (1853–1934): Gen. Scott was chief of staff of the U.S. Army prior to the outbreak of World War I. (WJP)

SISSON, EDGAR (1875–1948): Sisson served in Russia as the Petrograd representative of the Committee on Public Information (COMPUB), headed in Washington by George Creel. In Russia he initially joined the Robins camp enthusiastically, but later became vindictive toward Robins, Judson, and other members of the mission. As time went on, he became highly anti-Bolshevik, purporting the authenticity of bogus documents that appeared to demonstrate that Lenin and the Bolsheviks were agents in the pay of the German government.

A former newspaperman and publicist, he had been sent to Russia by Washington to evaluate Thompson's propaganda project to influence Russia to stay in the war. Sisson caused long-term damage to Soviet-American relations with his approach to the Soviets, his writing becoming a paradigm for "red scare" rhetoric. (DADH, KEN SAR, WAW, NVS)

SKOBELEV, MATVEI IVANOVICH (1885–1938): A Menshevik deputy in the Duma as a Social Democrat, he left the Duma to become Kerensky's minister of labor in February 1917. Elected to the Executive Committee of Workers' Deputies, he was a delegate to the Inter-Allied Conference on War Aims in Paris. There he represented the defeated Kerensky and pleaded for a revision of Allied war aims toward a negotiated general peace, which would improve the chances of defeating the Bolsheviks and lead to the restoration of the Kerensky government. (GSE)

STEVENS, JOHN F. (1853–1943): Former chief engineer on the Panama Canal, he headed the Stevens Railroad Advisory Commission, which was to have reformed the operation of the Russian railways to meet the extremes of wartime requirements. The commission's scope and duration fell far short of achieving these goals, leaving rail transport as a major problem up to and well beyond Russia's withdrawal from the world war. (WJP)

SUKHOMLINOV, VLADIMIR ALEKSANDROVICH (1848–1920): In March 1909 he became the czar's minister of war, carrying out military reforms until he was dismissed and replaced by Polivanov in January 1915, following the disastrous mismanagement and defeat at the Battle of Tannenberg. In March 1916 he was arrested for treason and later released, only to be arrested and sentenced to life in prison following the Bolshevik Revolution. Rightly or wrongly, he was blamed for Russia's military unpreparedness and incompetence during World War I. (GSE)

SUMMERS, MADDIN (d. 1918): The U.S. consul general in Moscow, Summers requested a transfer from his post because of differences with Raymond Robins and the Red Cross mission. He resigned in 1918 and died in April of that year. He was replaced by DeWitt Clinton Poole. During his service in Russia, Summers opposed recognition of the Bolsheviks and became strongly anti-Soviet. (UNT)

TERESCHENKO, MICHAEL B. (1859–1943): A wealthy philanthropist without party affiliation in czarist Russia, he became the minister of finance under Kerensky. (GSE)

TERESCHENKO, MIKHAIL I. (1862–1939): In the Provisional Government under Kerensky, he served as foreign minister and opposed the publication of prewar secret treaties between Russia and the western Allies, fearing that it would initiate a separate peace with the Central Powers. An apologist for the czar and anti-Soviet, he attended the Inter-Allied Conference on War Aims to plead for greater Allied assistance to the Kerensky government. (GSE, UNT)

THACHER, MAJ. THOMAS D. (1881–1950): Thacher, a New York lawyer who, as a result of his father's reputation and prominence in the New York bar, had access to many influential leaders, including Secretary of Labor Felix Frankfurter, Supreme Court Justice Louis D. Brandeis, and Tariff Commissioner William Kent. The deputy commissioner and the secretary of the American Red Cross Commission to Russia, he was a trusted lieutenant of Raymond Robins and campaigned for recognition of and cooperation with the Bolsheviks. After developing economic plans to restructure and strengthen Russia to the benefit of the United States, Thacher was recalled by William Boyce Thompson in March 1918 to aid the cooperation-campaign efforts at home, only to be rebuffed in Washington. (WAW)

THOMPSON, WILLIAM BOYCE (1869–1930): According to Thompson, a multimillionaire copper magnate, the most significant aim of the United States and her Allies was to keep Russia in the war at all costs. As such, he developed, funded (using up to one million dollars of his own money), and eventually headed the American Red Cross Commission to Russia, arriving there in July 1917.

A strong supporter of Kerensky and the Socialist Revolutionaries (SRs), Thompson, through the Red Cross Commission, supported the Provisional Government until it fell to the Bolsheviks. As part of his plans, he acquired Russian newspapers and printing facilities to distribute Wilson's war messages, and made staggering offers for the purchase of Russian government bonds in an effort to subsidize the Provisional Government.

Because of his staunch support of Kerensky, Thompson was virtually *persona non grata* with the Bolsheviks following their ascension to power. (NVS)

TROTSKY, LEON D. (1870–1940): A Marxist theorist and prolific writer, Trotsky was one of the most important leaders of the Bolsheviks. Both a former protegé and a rival of Lenin prior to 1917, Trotsky was living in New York at the time the czar abdicated, campaigning against World War I. Returning to Russia, he found his views much closer to Lenin's than they had been prior to the war. An energetic organizer and gifted orator, he became the chief spokesman of the Bolsheviks. Allied with Lenin for the first time in over a decade, he quickly became the number-two Bolshevik.

Rumors of a coup prompted Kerensky to crack down on the Soviets, but Trotsky used this to galvanize unity within the party and to win public support for the Bolsheviks, a key to the Bolshevik Revolution. (DRR, GSE)

TSERETELLI, IRAKLII GEORGEVICH (1881–1959): After the abdication of the czar, Tseretelli became an influential leader and a major exponent of Menshevik programs. He attacked and opposed the Bolsheviks and, following the Bolshevik Revolution, served in the cabinet of an independent Georgia until it fell to the Bolsheviks in 1921. (BERR, GSE)

VERKHOVSKY, ALEKSANDR IVANOVICH (1886–1938): While opposed to the Kornilov movement, he became the last minister of war under Kerensky. In this capacity he attempted the reform and decentralization of the army under near-impossible conditions. Following the Bolshevik Revolution, he helped organize anti-Soviet forces and was arrested. Deciding to change his views, he joined the Red Army in 1918. (GSE)

VINAVER, MAKSIM MOISSEEVICH (1862–1920): The founder of the Constitutional Democratic (Kadet) Party, Vinaver was also a prominent member of several Jewish organizations. Serving as the leader and spokesman for this party, he was elected to the Duma when he became an active opponent of Soviet power. After the Bolshevik Revolution he became the foreign minister of the White forces. (GSE, BERR)

WITTE, SERGEI IUL'EVICH (1849–1915): The interior minister, the minister of finance, and the chairman of the Council of Ministers under Czar Nicholas II, Witte was often thought to have orchestrated the Russo-Japanese War as a foreign diversion to the domestic problems that ultimately led to the 1905 Revolution. While serving the czar, he forcefully advocated concessions to the bourgeoisie and an overall policy of accommodation, but initiated punitive military measures in suppressing uprisings. When World War I erupted, Witte expressed the desire for Russia to get out of the war as quickly as possible, foreseeing the conflict as the end to all monarchies in Europe. (GSE, DRR, WWB)

YATES, LT. COL. H. E. (?): An army colleague of Judson's, Yates sought the creation of a separate American military mission in southern Russia. He hoped this would serve as a suggestion of an official U.S. presence in the camp of anti-Bolshevik forces then assembling there for the purpose of political and military opposition to the Lenin government. (NVS)

ZALKIND (1876–1947?): Undersecretary of state in Lenin's first months of leadership and foreign office assistant to Trotsky. (KEN SAR)

Introduction

In his capacity as military attaché, General Judson should have reported
to the United States government on political subjects only through the
Ambassador, or at least with his knowledge and approval. In his capacity
as chief of the Military Mission in time of war, he had a responsibility
to report directly to the Secretary of War on anything he chose.

—GEORGE KENNAN, *Russia Leaves the War*

This collection will provide Judson's eyewitness analyses of conditions under the Provisional Government, beginning in June 1917, three
months after the February Uprising had resulted in the abdication of
Czar Nicholas II. In chapters 2 and 3 we see how Judson carefully exam-
ined the area of his professional expertise: the organization and battle-
readiness of the Russian army. He was particularly concerned about the
breakdown in the command structure and discipline in the Russian army
in the wake of the reforms and "democratization" that had followed the
czar's abdication. Judson meticulously reported on all political developments since these affected the prosecution of the war, the most fiercely
debated issue facing the Russians after the fall of the Romanov Dynasty.
He analyzed the important and growing role of the Soviet of Workers'
(later, Workers' and Soldiers') Deputies and, likewise, the influence of
the Bolsheviks within their ranks through the summer and fall of 1917.
Our understanding of the Kornilov Uprising is enhanced by our looking
through the lens Judson provides. Gen. Kornilov's coup to overthrow
the second Provisional Government of Alexander Kerensky (9–13 September 1917) was a key event, not only in the faltering evolution of Russia's first experiment with democratic government, but in her fragile
relations with her British, French, and U.S. wartime allies.

The major focus of this collection, as seen in chapters 4 and 5, will be
the Bolshevik seizure of power and the U.S. response to the unfolding
events in Soviet Russia; however, to understand Judson himself and his

view of U.S. foreign policy, Russia, and the world, the collection will begin with a brief selection of his earlier letters and excerpts from reports and speeches that relate to these concerns. In the years before the outbreak of World War I, Judson's experiences in Puerto Rico and, particularly, his observation of the Russo-Japanese War in 1904 shaped his outlook on U.S. overseas commitments, imperialism, great power rivalry, and military preparedness. (See chapter 1.) On 2 April 1917 the United States entered the World War, and two months later Judson was again in Russia, this time carrying out his initial duties as military attaché to the special U.S. diplomatic mission headed by Elihu Root.[1] Throughout his tenure the overriding task for him—and for all other U.S. representatives—was *to keep Russia in the war against Germany as a viable and active ally of the United States, Britain, and France.* All of Judson's thinking, reporting and analysis must be understood in this light.

The collection concludes with some of Judson's observations on revolutionary Russia and on U.S.-Soviet relations after his return to the United States in February 1918. Only weeks later President Wilson made the fateful decision to join a British and French military "intervention" against Red Russia. Wilson never consulted with Judson, who had been his senior military representative there, but the president knew full well how strongly Judson opposed such an "uninvited" invasion of a former World War I ally. It is hoped that publication of the Judson papers will contribute to our understanding of both the Revolution and the American struggle to find an appropriate policy to guide our relations with Bolshevik Russia.

William Voorhees Judson built his career by combining his deep interest in science and engineering with his devotion to the United States Army. He gave up successful studies at Harvard after two years when he passed competitive examinations for admission to West Point. From the time he graduated from the United States Military Academy in 1888 to his death in 1923, his career centered on a leadership role in the Army Corps of Engineers.[2]

Judson was born in Indianapolis, Indiana, in 1865. His deeply religious family traced its ancestry to colonial settlers, Puritan on his father's side and Dutch Reformed on his mother's. His teenage determination to study science and engineering met with disapproval. Nevertheless, he persevered, charting his own course then as he did throughout his life. Upon graduation from West Point, third in his class, Judson

Studio photograph of Judson taken on the occasion of his graduation from West Point in 1888. *Courtesy of the Newberry Library.*

earned the honor of admission to three-year, graduate-level study at the Engineer School of Application at Willet's Point, New York.

In 1891, he married Alice Carneal Clay of Lexington, Kentucky. Their marriage was marked by mutual love and devotion, often reflected in their correspondence, some of which appears in the pages of this volume.

Judson applied his engineering skills to harbor and river projects on Lake Erie, on the Mississippi, and particularly in the port of Galveston, Texas. His reinforced-concrete retaining wall and bulkhead in Galveston resulted in the award of a U.S. patent for his innovative design, which was stronger and more economical. Another of his inventions, a floating reinforced-concrete caisson, which could be fabricated, towed to its destination, and submerged into position, was also patented. The Judson Papers (box 1) at the Newberry Library documents that his designs were in use as late as the 1940s. In both cases, he voluntarily divested himself of all commercial rights to these patents in favor of the Army Corps of Engineers.

Judson's firsthand experience with the complexities of U.S. foreign policy began in the aftermath of the Spanish-American War. Initially, Judson had to struggle with his disappointment at not serving in combat in Cuba. Gen. J. M. Wilson, his commanding officer in the Corps of Engineers, was not willing to spare Capt. Judson from his regular duties as recording and disbursing officer for the Board of Engineers. Then, immediately following the war, Judson was appointed to the posts of chief engineer and president of the Board of Public Works of Puerto Rico. The former colony, which the U.S. took from imperial Spain, became the nucleus (along with Cuba and the Philippines) of a new American empire. It was still the age of the European "scramble for Africa," the New Imperialism, the "White Man's Burden," and the drive for sea power to secure overseas possessions.

Judson's work in Puerto Rico centered on planning and supervising road building and public works projects for the alleviation of the economic dislocation left by the Spanish administration. He was also responsible for rebuilding in the aftermath of the destructive hurricane of 1899. Judson's engineering successes matched his organizational achievements. He devised methods for the adjudication of right-of-way for the roads and the water systems being built under his supervision. Judson had to chart a difficult course that was both sensitive to the rights of the citizens and appropriate to tight construction schedules. His work in Puerto Rico was hailed as a paradigm of enlightened colonial administration and imperial initiative. But implicit in Judson's discussions of the overseer's role is the probing question: Was such benevolent "Western" imperial control of the non-European world advisable and necessary as the planet entered the industrial age of the twentieth century?

Judson rejected this conventional wisdom of the McKinley-Roosevelt era and, more specifically, opposed all U.S. overseas imperialism. He maintained that U.S. security depended on America's ability to defend its shores and to minimize its involvement in the great power's colonial competition. The latter goal required a substantial navy; to apply naval resources to the game of overseas imperial expansion was a risky, irresponsible business, since no navy could guarantee victory. In "Strategic Value of Her West Indian Possessions to the United States," we see Judson's own statement of U.S. foreign policy priorities.[3]

He was a realist, fully convinced of the necessity of every major state in the international arena to maintain its military and build an alliance network unmistakably capable of self-defense. The price of any defensive weakness in an expansionist world system would inevitably lead to a loss of sovereignty. But Judson cogently argued that under twentieth-century conditions the United States should not and could not engage in the expansionism and imperialism of that system. The United States's long-term interests would not be served by such a policy; and further, the *national* interests of the dominant imperial powers would also be better served by withdrawing from their imperial possessions, particularly those overseas.

"Strategic Value of Her West Indian Possessions to the United States" was the first of many published expressions of Judson's independent thinking. In this case, there appears to have been no negative repercussions to Capt. Judson's career from his writing a paper in strong opposition to U.S. jingoism. However, this was not so with Gen. Judson's 1917 analysis of U.S. national interests, which led to his initiation of U.S. contact with the leadership of the Bolshevik Revolution, or with his persistent recommendations for discussion and negotiation. These led to his early recall to Washington from Petrograd.

On 8 March 1904, Judson set sail from New York City en route to St. Petersburg, Russia, to carry out his first assignment as a military attaché. He was one of eight officers chosen from a long list of candidates to observe and report on the Russo-Japanese War. He briefly served as military attaché at the American embassy in St. Petersburg, under Ambassador Robert S. McCormick. But Judson, along with three fellow officers, was then assigned to the headquarters of Gen. A. N. Kuropat-kin, commander in chief of Russian armies in the Far East, in the Manchurian city of Liaoyang. (Four U.S. officers were similarly assigned to observe and report on the Japanese forces.)

Judson had specific responsibility for reporting on the areas of his expertise: fortification structure, command organization, bunker design and construction, and troop deployment. He prepared reports on the fortification of Liaoyang at the end of April and was then assigned to the battlefield headquarters of Gen. Zasulich, commander of the Second Siberian Corps. Judson filed his reports from that post to his military superiors and wrote several letters to Ambassador McCormick, appraising him of developments at the front.[4] In July, when Judson succumbed to the dysentery epidemic that was spreading so rapidly among the front-line soldiers, he was forced to return to Liaoyang and then to continue on to Vladivostok for treatment. While in Manchuria, his recovery was never complete. Nevertheless, even after a number of relapses, he persevered at his work.

During the Japanese siege of the Manchurian capital of Mukden (the current city of Shenyang), in February and March 1905, Judson and two of his fellow officers were present to report on the defense of the Russian stronghold. Judson had already filed many reports on the superior numbers and supplies of the Japanese forces. Nine months earlier, on 26 July 1904, he had written of his conviction that, given their obvious advantages right then, a Japanese initiative would have resulted in the swift capture of Mukden.[5] On 9 March, still early in the siege, the three American officers were instructed to leave Mukden before dawn the following morning. Maj. Montgomery Macomb set out as instructed. Judson (still ill) and Col. Valery Havard planned to leave Mukden on the train scheduled to depart that afternoon. Only an hour after Macomb's departure, on 10 March, the Japanese captured Mukden. Havard and Judson were awakened by Japanese soldiers, who detained them as prisoners of war. They were treated well, immediately dispatched to Tokyo, and upon arrival, on 19 March, were released and instructed to return home.

In Washington, D.C., in April, Judson began composing his final report to his superiors. The process was at first inconclusive since his notes had been lost at the time of his capture in Mukden. They were finally recovered, and Judson's complete report was written. On 1 March 1907, it was published by the War Department in *Reports of Military Observers Attached to the Armies in Manchuria during the Russo-Japanese War*.[6]

Most of Judson's seventy-six-page contribution to the volume focused on the areas of his technological expertise, but some of his conclusions went far beyond those narrow limits.

Until 1904 the measure of modern warfare had been the American Civil War or the Franco-Prussian War. The disparity of military power of the adversaries in the Spanish-American War had nullified its usefulness as a guide to modern war. Judson attempted to communicate the profound lessons of the twentieth-century battlefield that he had learned from his observations of Russia's defeat: the limitations of cavalry, the new importance of supply (especially with the encumbrance of the Trans-Siberian Railroad's single track), and the necessity of a more decentralized command structure that allowed initiative at the lower echelons. The most important lessons, because of new weaponry and trench structures, were the great defensive advantages and offensive disadvantages. Judson saw the entire Russo-Japanese War as a vindication of his opposition to Admiral Mahan's "navalism" and to overseas adventurism and imperialism.

Judson's service in Manchuria was significant not only because it provided the evidence to support his convictions about and understanding of U.S. military and foreign policy priorities, but also because it introduced him to Russia and its people and problems and to the military under the czars. He made the acquaintance of a number of Russian officers, particularly Gen. Alexander Guchkov, with whom he established a relationship and friendship. Judson and Guchkov met on the Trans-Siberian Railroad journey from Petrograd to Manchuria. Because of wartime delays, the normally eight-day trip lasted nearly a month. Guchkov's perfect English and the fascination of each man for the other's homeland provided for many days of intense conversation and discussion. These exchanges provided Judson with his first primer on the political parties, social structure, and economic realities of Russia on the eve of the Revolution of 1905.

It was Judson's service in Manchuria, along with the recommendation of Postmaster General Albert Burleson that led to his appointment as military attaché to the Root Mission to Russia in the spring of 1917.[7] When that diplomatic initiative ended, Judson was ordered to remain in Russia to serve as chief of the American Military Mission and military attaché to the American ambassador at Petrograd.[8]

The Root Mission, like the Stevens Railroad Advisory Commission[9] and the American Red Cross Commission to Russia, was initiated only weeks after United States entry into the World War. Each was undertaken to draw the U.S. into closer cooperation with the new Russian ally—the recently transformed democratic Russian ally—that had, through revolution, broken its ties with Nicholas II's ineffectual monarchy, just as the United States' founding fathers had broken theirs with George III. The Root Mission, headed by former Secretary of State Elihu Root and staffed by many American dignitaries, was to cement American-Russian ties and lend "support" to the Russian forces that were then staggering under the successful campaigns of the Central Powers on the eastern front. At the same time, as will be borne out by so many of the communications in this book, the Russian armies were rapidly deteriorating, for lack of supplies as much as the evaporation of discipline in the ranks. Rates of desertion, nearing 30 percent for all Russian land forces, were higher than for any other major world power in any twentieth-century warfare.

Other than expressions of support and solidarity in diplomatic exchanges, the Root Mission had no concrete agenda of negotiation nor a program of proposed military assistance. When Judson was then reassigned to his two new posts, he fully appreciated the emptiness of the Root Mission gesture. He was similarly critical of the failure of the Stevens Railway Commission. Under the Provisional Government, Russia's rail system appeared to be no better off than it had been under the mismanagement of the czar's minister. Given the critical role of the railways in the supply structure of the war effort, especially in a land empire spanning seven time zones, the failure of its effective reorganization was decisive in shaping the outcome of the war.

Millions of tons of supplies were stockpiled by the British, French, and U.S. at the principal Russian ports of Murmansk and Archangel on the White Sea and Vladivostok on the Pacific. Judson's communications throughout his tenure at Petrograd persistently focused on how the shipment of these supplies to the eastern front could be more efficiently organized. After the Bolshevik Revolution, Russian armistice, and the separate peace with the Central Powers, every effort was made to safeguard those supplies. The greatest concern was that they would fall into the hands of the German and Austrian enemies to be used against Allied forces on the western front in the spring offensives of 1918.

The large French and British diplomatic and military missions had been operating in Petrograd since the early months of the war.[10] Judson assumed his two posts, with a combined staff of three assistant military attachés: Maj. Francis L. Parker, Maj. Monroe C. Kerth, and 1st Lt. E. Francis Riggs, who was soon promoted to captain. To further complicate the fulfillment of Judson's responsibilities, no budget mechanism, other than the established salaries of the four officers, had been put in place to fund Judson's offices. Thus hamstrung, he was forced to appeal to his superiors at the War College Staff for funds and personnel at every turn.

At the first opportunity after his return to Russia with the Root Mission, Judson renewed his acquaintance with Alexander Guchkov, who had just resigned as minister of war and of the navy in the Provisional Government of Prince Lvov. Judson arranged a meeting between Root and Guchkov to permit the American elder statesman to learn firsthand the views on Russian democracy of this constitutional monarchist. The record suggests that no Russian had greater influence on Judson's understanding of the military and political crises of revolutionary Russia than did Guchkov. Guchkov's ideological commitments were democratic, but were on the conservative end of the democratic spectrum. He played a founding role in the Octobrist faction of the Constitutional Democratic Party (Kadets) and supported a constitutional monarchy. Judson's high regard and admiration for Guchkov, reflected in many documents in this collection, did not however deter Judson from an openness to discussion and cooperation with the leaders of the Bolsheviks, one of the most radical factions in Russia, after they successfully seized power.

As Judson perceived them, the imperatives of U.S. national interest overrode any personal or philosophical objections he may have had about the Bolsheviks. Judson, the scientist and engineer, was first a pragmatist, particularly when struggling for solutions in the complex matrix of an international war and a domestic revolution with a world revolutionary agenda. He seized the initiative and on 1 December 1917 met with Trotsky. Judson did not believe that the Washington directive banning all official communication between the U.S. government and the Bolshevik government of Russia applied to the emergency issues he wished to raise with Trotsky. As senior American military representative in Petrograd, Judson simply wished to learn from the new Russian minister for foreign affairs whether the U.S. delegation in Petrograd was in any danger of revolutionary retribution and whether there was any basis for discussion and negotiation, official or unofficial, between the Allies and the new regime.

Unlike Raymond Robins, who took on the leadership of the nongovernmental American Red Cross Commission to Russia, Judson was a formal representative of the United States Army and the nation's diplomatic corps. While Robins's contact with the Bolshevik leadership, beginning within twenty-four hours of their seizure of power, could be justified under the "no official communications" directives of Secretary of State Lansing, Judson's could not. So, he raised the question with his immediate superior on the scene, U.S. ambassador to Russia David R. Francis. Judson communicated his plans to meet with Trotsky both orally and in writing. (See chapter 4.) Nevertheless, because that meeting was received with such disfavor in Washington, the ambassador denied either having had knowledge of or having approved the meeting. There had been a serious misunderstanding.

In the weeks and months that followed, Judson's and others' documentation of the crisis in U.S.-Bolshevik relations in 1917–18 strongly suggests the imperative for the appointment of a knowledgeable diplomat as ambassador, as opposed to a political appointment. Sadly, the record of developments in U.S.-Russia relations found here is fraught with misunderstanding, misinformation, ignorance, and incompetence. While disapproving of the policies of the Lenin government, especially its decision to leave the war even if it meant a separate peace with Germany and its allies, Judson persisted throughout his communications with his superiors in his conviction that U.S. and Allied interests necessitated communication and negotiation with the communist government of Russia. Such communication, he affirmed, did not represent recognition of a regime so antithetical to Washington's principles. Keeping Russia in the war as an ally against the Central Powers required contact with the Lenin government.

Judson faced a serious dilemma—and, perhaps, therein lay his failure. He understood that the American ambassador was the senior person in the U.S. chain of command in Petrograd. But after the misrepresentations described above, Judson had lost confidence in Ambassador Francis. Try as he might to observe every nuance of protocol and respect, Judson could not simultaneously support the policies he was convinced were in the United States's national interest and support and serve his immediate superior. The situation was further complicated by Judson's separate responsibilities as chief of the American Military Mission to Russia, which were formally independent of his service as military attaché to the ambassador. (See the Kennan epigraph that begins this introduction.) By not sustaining the full confidence of Francis, Judson's tenure in Russia was threatened and was finally terminated.[11] His last, vain hope was to try to effect a change in U.S. policy toward Russia upon his return to Washington.

The final chapter of this book provides ample evidence of Judson's continued personal involvement in the drama of U.S.-Soviet relations long after he was ordered home from Petrograd. While he was convinced that his recall was a serious mistake and a grave injustice, he carried out his orders to the letter. If the extant written record of *personal* correspondence can be relied upon for thoroughness, he seldom expressed bitterness at his treatment by his superiors.

Judson's first command after his return was the New York Port of Embarkation at Hoboken, New Jersey, where he supervised the departure of more than five hundred thousand American troops for the battlefields of France during September and October 1918 alone. Like thousands of those under his command, Judson succumbed to the deadly influenza epidemic that ravaged many U.S. cities in 1918. He recuperated, but learned only days after the 11 November 1918 armistice in Europe that he suffered from a seriously enlarged heart. Following the hospitalization required by that diagnosis, Judson learned that he would be honorably discharged from the national army and revert to the rank of colonel in the Army Corps of Engineers. His commission as brigadier general was in the national army in time of war, which was considered "Federal Service other than the Permanent Establishment."[12]

Now, with his office in Chicago, Judson resumed his post as division engineer in charge of river and harbor improvements on the Great Lakes. The storms of international politics and world war were replaced in Judson's daily work by those of America's inland seas, and his bulkhead and caisson designs resisted the deluge. But his heart condition necessitated long hospitalizations in 1922 and no longer permitted him to lead a normal life. He was forced into early disability retirement in August 1922. Judson died at Winter Park, Florida, on 29 March 1923 at the age of fifty-eight.

Gen. William V. Judson was one of the most thorough, astute, and informed eyewitnesses of the Bolshevik Revolution and of the initiation of U.S.-Soviet relations. Judson, like Raymond Robins and William B. Thompson of the American Red Cross Commission to Russia and like many other Allied representatives, was convinced of the critical necessity of direct discussions and negotiations between the government of the United States and the Lenin-Trotsky government following the Bolshevik Revolution. However, from the first, President Wilson and the three conservative Republican administrations that succeeded him, chose a different course for U.S. policy toward Russia. It is only now, in the 1990s, under the drastically changed circumstances of an end to both the Soviet Union and the Communist Party of the Soviet Union, that we are witnessing the first stages in a new cooperative and constructive U.S.-Russian relationship. Could such a partnership, like that envisioned by Judson and his allies in 1917, have come to fruition sooner?

The purpose of this volume is to make available to the scholarly and general audience a carefully considered selection of the letters and reports of William V. Judson during his simultaneous tenure as military attaché to the American ambassador at Petrograd and as chief of the American Military Mission to Russia.[13] Included here are Judson's detailed eyewitness accounts of the trials of the Provisional Government and of the Bolshevik Revolution. Published for the first time is Judson's documentation of his 1 December 1917 meeting with Trotsky, the first official face-to-face discussion between a leader of the Bolshevik government and a diplomatic representative of the U.S. government. The concluding chapter focuses on the challenges in the U.S.-Russian relationship during the early months of Soviet power, as Lenin steered his government toward a separate peace with Germany and the Central Powers, which were still at war with the United States.

Judson's reports, observations, innovative recommendations, and diary entries were indefatigably prepared, day by day, responding to all consequential events for months before and following the Bolshevik seizure of power. This body of documentation has provided a key source for more than a dozen scholarly accounts of the Russian Revolution and the United States' response to it.[14] The materials collected here are taken primarily from the singular archive of Judson's personal papers in the manuscripts collection of the Newberry Library in Chicago, Illinois. It was the availability of these Judson Papers that led the noted scholar of the history of American foreign policy, William Appleman Williams, to begin work on a major biography of Judson, about whom he wrote: "I have become not only attached to but an admirer of the image I see rising from my research notes."[15]

The revolutionary transformations in Russia in the 1990s, along with the opening of one Russian, Soviet, and C.P.S.U. archive after another—many dealing specifically with Bolshevik foreign affairs—suggest the appropriateness of publishing a volume of the writings of Judson. Given Judson's role as chief of the American Military Mission and an "on-the-spot" decision maker in U.S.-Russian relations, his eyewitness accounts will also have great significance for the student of this period.

The works of two scholars, George Kennan in *Soviet-American Relations, 1917–1920* and William Appleman Williams in his 1950 doctoral dissertation, "Raymond Robins and Russian-American Relations, 1917–1938," have provided the definitive foundation for exploring the nascent Soviet-American relationship. Jane Weyant's doctoral dissertation, "The Life and Career of General William V. Judson, 1865–1923," provided the first biography and monograph on Judson's important role in the inception of U.S.-Soviet relations, but it is only available as an offprint from University Microfilms International Dissertation Information Service. Recently, Neil Salzman's *Reform and Revolution: The Life and Times of Raymond Robins* and David McFadden's *Alternative Paths: Soviets and Americans, 1917–1920* have explored the communications, initiatives, discussions, and proposals of both official and unofficial U.S. and Soviet representatives from November 1917, the Bolshevik Revolution, to November 1933, when the Roosevelt administration opened diplomatic relations with the U.S.S.R. The third chapter of *Alternative Paths*, entitled "Judson, Trotsky and Bolshevik-American Military Collaboration, 1917–1918," reaffirmed the conclusions of earlier scholars regarding the importance of Judson's role, documentation, and analysis of events in Petrograd during 1917–18. However, nowhere other than in his own writings can we fully appreciate the evolving thoughts, insights, and initiatives of Judson himself.

The Russian-American relationship has been the single most important international relationship in the post–World War II era. With few exceptions (most notably the World War II alliance and the post-Soviet present), that relationship has been adversarial and confrontational, characterized more by grave misunderstandings and misperceptions than by clear communication and sometimes close to the brink of nuclear war. Yet the telling origins of the Soviet-American relationship in the weeks and months following the Bolshevik Revolution of 1917 have not received the scholarly attention they require and deserve. It is hoped that this collection of Judson's papers will help draw that attention and further our understanding of this important relationship.

1 | **Formative Experiences**
Puerto Rico and the Front Lines
of the Russo-Japanese War

In all of Judson's career, entirely devoted to military service, only four posts involved international responsibilities: public works administrator in Puerto Rico, attaché in the Russo-Japanese War, attaché to the Root Mission to Russia, and the combined posts of attaché to the American ambassador to Russia and chief of the American Military Mission to Russia. Each assignment was politically sensitive, and each provided lasting lessons that shaped Judson's outlook on the role of the military in modern industrial society and within democratic political systems, and on the foreign policy priorities of the United States.

The U.S. victory in the Spanish-American War, especially in light of public opinion and its manipulation by the press, gave pause to thoughtful critics of the United States's New Imperialism and overseas adventurism. Judson's service as chief engineer and president of the Board of Public Works of Puerto Rico, from July 1899 to August 1900, gave him on-the-spot experience in a U.S. colonial dependency, which influenced the anti-imperialist ideas expressed in his first published scholarly paper. We begin this book with excerpts from this 1902 Judson article, "Strategic Value of Her West Indian Possessions to the United States."

The ideas expressed in 1902 also have application to the Russian experience with retrenchment, which Judson uses effectively in his paper, and territorial expansionism. Only two years after this article appeared, Russia was engaged in a war with Japan that had disastrous repercussions for the Romanov Dynasty. Territorial loss was compounded by a curtailed Russian influence and power in both east Asia and the international arena generally. Given the centuries-old European world hegemony, Russia could no longer have been considered one of the world's great powers after its defeat by an Asiatic state. To this was added the Revolution of 1905. The economic and political crises of czarist Russia at the turn of the twentieth century, which was to have been alleviated by a remunerative and victorious war against a "weak"

Japan, reached flood tide soon after the war. Judson's advice to U.S. policy makers about far-flung territorial acquisitions, like that of Nicholas II's finance minister, Sergei Witte, was ignored.

STRATEGIC VALUE OF HER WEST INDIAN POSSESSIONS TO THE UNITED STATES[1]

If "in time of peace we must prepare for war," it becomes necessary also in time of peace to contemplate the dangers to which we may be exposed in war, for only thus shall we make our preparations adequate, and along the right lines. If in the following article emphasis is laid upon the dangers rather than the advantages of certain conditions, it is but to bring out forcibly the means by which the dangers may be averted, as well as the advantages reaped.

In its broadest sense, strategy deals with all acts, diplomatic or political, civil or military, that make ultimately for a nation's strength in war. The accepted leaders of our people expect the policy of expansion in the West Indies and elsewhere to yield great increase of trade and new opportunities for the profitable use of the American capital. It is generally believed that this policy will increase our national prosperity and our influence for the world's good in the council of nations.

. . . Prior to 1898 the United States was the strongest of all nations <u>on the defensive</u>. Our population was self-sustaining and could not be reduced to submission through blockade. On account of the difficulties of ocean transport no army could land and sustain itself for a successful campaign within our borders. . . .

Notwithstanding our great defensive strength we should have been in a very embarrassing position if at that time we had been called upon to enforce the Monroe Doctrine as against Germany, France or Russia. These nations were each superior to us upon the sea, and where else against either one of them might we even have attempted a hostile blow? We must admit that our <u>offensive</u> military strength, except as against England in Canada, was insignificant.

When we acquired possessions beyond the sea, we lost in great measure our splendid defensive strength, while we added to our power to strike offensive blows. At the same time that we increased our ability to sustain the Monroe Doctrine, and thus reduced the probability of war due to its violations, we increased the probability of war due to other causes, for we entered into contact with the world's great powers at a greatly increased number of points.

Whether the gain of offensive and also of defensive strength leave us with a balance to the good is, in a measure, an indeterminate problem, the unknown quantities being indicated in the following questions:

1. Who will be our antagonists?

2. What preparations shall we make, in peace, to reap advantages from our new conditions?

In a war today with a great commercial power, equal or inferior to us in naval strength, we should undoubtedly find our acquisitions a distinct gain. But in a war with a power of considerably greater naval strength we should find that we had but acquired points vulnerable to attack, and several burning problems now agitating the public mind would be speedily solved by our opponent.

The relation of sea power to overseas possessions may be briefly stated in the light of history and of European policies. Of the five great European powers Russia alone has pursued a policy that enables her to ignore the command of the sea. With unorganized and inferior peoples upon her eastern and southeastern borders, she has been able to extend her limits by the absorption of contiguous continental territory whose inhabitants are quickly assimilated. Why did Russia part with the Kurile Islands in 1875, and with Alaska in 1867, if it was not to divest herself of distant possessions, recognized as sources of weakness to a nation whose military strength lay upon the land? And what isolated possessions does she now maintain vulnerable to British attack? It seems written upon the wall that, when land communications between Russia and India shall possess military advantages over water communication between Great Britain and India, the day of British rule in India shall pass. . . .

. . . In closing we may sum up the case as follows: The possession of distant islands weakens the United States defensively. So also would the construction of an isthmian canal without the building of an adequate navy. For offensive operations as bases for our mobile force— the navy—distant islands, properly located, increase our strength materially. The construction of an isthmian canal would also add to our offensive strength in that it would tend to facilitate the distribution and concentration of our offensive arm.

The main point is that no possible good, in war, can result from a canal or our West Indian possessions unless we possess an adequate navy.

Dearest Father:[2]

I have been awfully bad about writing to you as I have written you but one letter since you left. I saw something in the paper some time ago which said that you had gotten to Liao Yang. I expect by the time you get this letter it will be about time for you to come home again.

Now I will tell you about school and some other things that are happening here. . . .

. . . I guess you are doing all kinds of things there going around with Generals, Princes, and all sorts of fellows.

I have gotten about 30 postal cards from you and the stamps are just fine. You must not forget to save me some coins.

I saw a picture in Colliers the other day. Its name was "Attachés Bottled up in Tokyo." Aren't you glad you went with the Russians. I wish I could think of something interesting to say but I can't and so I guess I will have to stop.

> Goodbye
> Your loving son,
> [signed] Clay Judson

P.S. Excuse pencil writing but then it is so much easier.

July 26, 1904, Liaoyang [Manchuria]

Dear Ambassador McCormick,[3]

. . . Thus far the operations have been more favorable for the Russians than could reasonably have been expected.[4] It was hardly to be supposed that they would emerge from the period of numerical inferiority with so few losses, and with such a hold left on the railroads. In 2 or 3 weeks they will have nothing to fear from Japanese offensive operations, except of course at Port Arthur. But they will have a bitter campaign against the Japs, in prepared positions, when they (the Russians) start to take the initiative.

The rainy season has not yet begun but is expected daily. We had hard rains for 8 to 10 days the end of June and the beginning of July, but since July 6 the weather has been fine but very hot. The rains we have had demonstrated the impracticability of operations on large scale during a rainy season of ordinary character.

The health of the troops is not as good as two months ago, there being considerable dysentery—still it is remarkably good if the conditions be considered. The hospital service of the Red Cross, both at the permanent hospitals and on the railroad are most excellent and have not yet been taxed. I can imagine that a big battle, or extended dysentery during the approaching rains, might give them more than they could do.

The war is not popular among the troops—officers and men are discontented. But this is not a serious condition, and when the autumn comes and the Russians advance, it will disappear I think.

The Russians are treating the Chinese very well—a fine crop is being raised this year. If a camp is formed, even over night, in cultivated land, the farmer is fairly recompensed, as he is for every thing taken or purchased. Nevertheless the Chinese rejoice at Jap victories. I can explain it only as a matter of racial pride. The conditions of war here are remarkable because of the fact that the neutrality of the population is observed (generally) by both sides. It is difficult to find a parallel case in history.

As to atrocities such as killing and mutilation of wounded, I should say it is in betting parlance a "stand off"—Both sides have indulged in the practice, although the high authorities on both sides of course discountenance it.

To recapitulate, the Russians have nearly reached the crest of the hill—Unless they act quickly the Japs will have lost their opportunity for successful offensive tactics against General K. [Kuropatkin]. The failure of the Japs to do more in the post is inexplicable. At least they could easily have won important successes and be now in Mukden [Shenyang]. If the rains come now, they will have to look to their laurels when the fine weather returns.

During the rainy season I am going to visit the army of the Ussuri, and the vicinity of Vladivostok, returning for the fall campaign. We are all well. I write by the light of a miserable little candle, with no table— I hope you can decipher this.

x x x x x x x x[5]

I hear McCully is unable to see much at Port Arthur and is therefore unhappy. I tried hard to get them to let me in Port Arthur, both before and after the investment,[6] but without success. If Vladivostok is invested (improbable) I shall probably be inside. I am only permitted now to go to the vicinity of V. [Vladivostok] with promise that I can go in "if the place comes to possess military importance."

With kind regards to yourself, Mott, Schuyler and the others—

I am very sincerely yours,

SOUTH OF MUKDEN ABOUT 10 MILES—OCTOBER 25, 1904

My Dear Mr. [Ambassador Robert S.] McCormick—

. . . The two armies confront one another upon the line of the Scho Ye—about 15 miles south of Mukden. Both seem to be entrenching—conditions are so near an equilibrium it is useless to prophecy—I am afraid to attempt a description of the situation in detail, as it might not be considered proper by the censor. The recent fighting has as yet settled nothing—The Russians did not succeed in pushing back and defeating the Japs, but their morale (the Russian morale) and their conditions are very good. Every day we can see the Japs at work across the river, and there is generally some desultory artillery practice in evidence at different points of the line. We are living in Chinese "fanzas" (farm houses) which of course hereabouts are deserted (by the Chinese—not by insect tenants). The weather is now beautiful—clear and frosty—ice forms nearly every night.

We are all well and happy, but those of us who are married would like to see some prospect of a conclusion of hostilities—even if the prospect were a distant one. Referring to previous letters, the whole of the 5th, 1st European, and 6th Corps are here now, as you probably know—A division of Don Cossacks has been arriving recently—and the 8th Corps will soon begin to put in an appearance (to be followed by the 13th Corps).

Very Sincerely and Respectfully,

DECEMBER 20, 1905

Mr. Chairman and Gentlemen of the Society of Colonial Wars:[7]

I am permitted to respond to a toast, dear to my heart. "West Point, the Alma Mater of the professional soldier, who succeeded the citizen soldier of colonial days" . . .

Last year I was in the presence of war, where two nations clashed, each with three quarters of a million men that had been patiently trained for years. I saw one battle in which the slain Russians outnumbered the Union dead on twelve of the greatest battlefields of the Civil War. And I knew that we could not fight upon land any of the great powers of the earth with the remotest prospect of success. Yet our popular brand of sham patriotism leads us to believe we can whip the earth.

Perhaps you would like to hear some facts about that Russian army I was campaigning with. It was not popular with war correspondents because it was too hard to reach, and life was too onerous with it.

In the first place I wish to emphasize the fact that Russia's unfortunate expansion to the Yalu and the Yellow Sea was [a] political and commercial enterprise, involving dangers which her professional soldiers understood and pointed out. The special military preparations that could alone have neutralized this folly were in large part lacking, and Russia's professional soldiers knew they were lacking. The military efficiency of the great Siberian railroad was sacrificed to the building of the magnificent commercial cities of Harbin and Dalny, and innumerable well built towns in Siberia and Manchuria. Insufficient funds were provided for the fortifications at Port Arthur, and a great undefended port, with every facility for the handling and storage of supplies and the unloading of troops was created at Dalny, to serve any enemy as an ideal base of operations. Sidings on the Trans-Siberian railroad were so far apart, that when war began, troops could be transported only at a rate of say 30,000 men per month. Moreover, Russia was fairly carrying out her agreement to evacuate Manchuria, and the troops and supplies the world preferred to believe were there, had been largely withdrawn.

When war came, Russia had the trained and equipped soldiers, but they were thousands of miles away. And she had the military sagacity, with professional soldiers in control, to more than treble the transportation facilities of the Trans-Siberian railroad in six months time, and to accomplish with a single track railroad what all experts had pronounced impossible. . . .

The lesson to be learned is that under present conditions of war, when two countries are reasonably well prepared, the result is so near a draw that war is extremely unprofitable even to the nominal victor. This is a splendid fact, as it makes for peace, and eventually it will lead to disarmament. But countries which will not prepare for war, while others insist on preparation, are the countries who are so acting as to retain war in the scheme of civilization. It was a professional soldier who said that "War is Hell."

I beg you to believe that the good soldier is a good citizen.

West Point exists to create good soldiers. The material reward she offers her sons is small. Her ideals may be attained only through discipline, self-abnegation and sacrifice.

I commend to you the sentiment she loves to inspire in the American professional soldier:—Duty, Honor, Country.

SUBJECT: REPORT ON RUSSO-JAPANESE WAR, FEBRUARY 15, 1906
MAJOR W. D. BEACH,
CHIEF OF 2ND (MILITARY INFORMATION) DIVISION,
GENERAL STAFF, U.S. ARMY,
LEMON BUILDING, WASHINGTON, D.C.

Major:

I have the honor to transmit herewith, in duplicate, my report upon the Russo-Japanese war as observed by me while Military Attaché with the Russian Army.

It is my intention to submit a supplementary report at some future time, as I hope to receive certain data from my Russian friend Sarubaiev, and from Captain Edlund, the Swedish Attaché, which will make available data already in my hands.

REPORT OF CAPTAIN W. V. JUDSON, ATTACHÉ WITH THE RUSSIAN ARMY IN MANCHURIA DURING THE RUSSO-JAPANESE WAR.[8]

PART I

Account of the campaign, including description of railroad, etc.

We are never surprised, in reading history, when war begins. We see that it is the inevitable consequence of what has gone before.

The completion of the Siberian Railway and the acquisition of ports in Manchuria gave Russia tremendous advantages over Japan for the commercial exploitation of north east China. It was not so much that the advance of Russia was threatening the territorial integrity of Japan, as that it was interposing a wedge between Japan and what she considered her legitimate prey. Japan struck when she did because of the Russian naval situation. Five or six battle ships were approaching completion in the Baltic. Russia was pursuing the policy of strengthening her eastern fleet as fast as ships came from the stocks. At the beginning of 1904, it was apparent to Japan that the time was slipping by when she could make war with the balance of advantages on her side. That she was ready to take the initiative, and that she did take it at this propitious moment, is evidence of the greatest military wisdom. . . .

While I was with the Russians, nothing impressed and surprised me more than to discover, as time went on, that here was a race more like our own than any other in all the world. . . . Circumstances have indeed given the Russian an entirely different political and industrial environment from our own. The law of self-preservation has compelled them thus far to retain autocracy. Military efficiency is almost impossible of attainment by a people of the Russian (or American) temperament under democratic institutions, and the position of Russia has demanded military efficiency.

The time appears to have arrived when the Russian people are no longer willing to sacrifice their ideals of political liberty and their hopes of industrial development under more liberal institutions to the maintenance of military strength, with its consequences of an assured national unity within Russian territorial possessions, and of an ultimate vast expansion both in Europe and Asia.

The recent eagerness of Russia to lessen the importance of the armed strength of nations, through extensions of the principle of arbitration, and through conventions designed to lessen the probability of war, may be readily understood if one admits that the czar and his advisers have for some time anticipated the necessity for, or the advisability of, a relaxation from autocracy.

It is necessary to understand the Russian people and to appreciate the state of eager expectancy pervading all classes at the beginning of the war with Japan in order to see clearly many important influences that were at work in Russian councils before the war began; in the Manchurian Army through its continuance; and in the mind of the czar during the peace negotiations. Until the pains asserted themselves that were premonitory of the birth of popular government, Russia's territorial expansion was planned with great military sagacity; but of recent years, a new element has been introduced. Expansion must first of all be made popular. . . .

Finally it may be said that when, under present conditions, two countries reasonably well prepared make war, the result is apt to be so near a draw that even victory is extremely unprofitable. This is a splendid fact, as it makes for peace, and may eventually lead to partial disarmament by international convention. But countries which will not prepare for war, while others insist on preparation, are the countries who are so acting as to retain war in the scheme of civilization.

DESCRIPTION OF A MODERN BATTLEFIELD[9]

... Now it occurs to me that I have as yet given you no adequate idea of what the details of war are. In the first place they are utterly unlike the conceptions formed from familiar pictures, or even from the fanciful accounts of war correspondents. Nine-tenths of the soldiers in battle never see the enemy. And the great belt nearly two miles wide between hostile armies in battle, except in isolated sections, is a barren and deserted waste. There are indeed fierce charges and melees hand to hand, but nearly always these occur at night, and afford no spectacles. The romance of war is gone. The killed and wounded are stricken by agencies unseen. The greatest hardships are those of the march. Burdened by 60 pounds of equipment and ammunition the men must often struggle on until the last spark of vitality is gone, and many fall, with staring, glassy eyes, and perish from exhaustion. There are many forced marches in the shifting of troops on a battlefield, and the men shrink from the tortures of these even more than from the perils of the enemy's bullets. Death comes as a blessed relief to many who have been a week or two in battle. The wounded never groan or cry out, and their faces are for the most part peaceful and contented. I doubt not the wounds are often not unwelcome.

If what follows is prosaic and devoid of startling incident, it is simply because, to the individual observer, a battle cannot be otherwise truthfully described.

During the progress of a battle let us approach the front from Army headquarters, which may be from 12 to 15 miles in rear of the firing line. The road by which we advance is filled with a constant stream of ambulances bringing in the wounded, to be placed in cars and sent by rail to base hospitals. These hospitals are from 20 to 500 miles in rear of headquarters, and from 600 to 800 cars are waiting on sidings, equipped with rude mattresses and stores for the transportation of the wounded. Accompanying us to the front are many caissons of the artillery pa[?]ks carrying ammunition forward, and thousands of carts and wagons bearing food for men and animals. Occasionally we overtake a battalion of infantry wearily plodding forward, or a battery of artillery that has recently arrived. 6 or 8 miles from the front we are delayed an hour by a passing column of all arms, crossing our road and moving from one point to another where conditions are more threatening. Here also we pass through great herds of cattle waiting to be slaughtered to meet the requirements of the army. 3 or 4 miles from the front we come upon a village, and notice the headquarters of a Corps commander who is in charge of operations in this portion of the field. Encamped about the village are 4,000 or 5,000 troops, which the Corps commander may rush forward to any portion of the 5 or 6 miles of his front that may show signs of weakness. In the same village are dozens of Greeks selling sausages and tea and cigarettes from carts. And here also are the divisional hospitals, where the wounded await transportation to the rear. Into this village lead several telegraph lines from Army headquarters, and a dozen more radiate toward the front, connecting the Corps commander with his division commanders and important parts of the line. . . . A mile or so in advance of the village is a hill to which we proceed for our first glimpse of the battle. From the beginning of our journey we have heard the artillery. At first it was like thunder, not very distant, and rolling continuously. Now it has become deafening, and each individual explosion is like the barking of some fierce and gigantic dog. Close by a balloon is ascending. We see some of our own guns, a mile or two ahead of us, but in rear of the low hills, and concealed by them from the enemy, spitting out shrapnel which pass in curved flight over the hills and burst in the far distance. . . . Here and there, a few hundred feet above the ground, little white spheres of smoke form out of nothing, and are blown along with the wind and gradually dissipated. They are of very innocent appearance but we know that from each soft smoky ball hundreds of bullets have issued to sweep the ground over an area half that covered by this building.

We are glad to see that for the most part these projectiles are wasted. Our troops are not moving about and very few of them can be seen, except the batteries I have mentioned. For the low hills in front have been honey-combed with trenches and shell-proofs, and the troops are awaiting the enemy's infantry in relative safety, either squatting in the trenches of the foremost line, or huddled in ravines on the rearward slopes of the hills. Our front extends 50 miles toward our right and nearly as far toward the left, everywhere marked by the bursting shrapnel. But except in our immediate front we cannot distinguish our own from the enemy's projectiles. . . . There still seems to be no concentrated effort against the trenches in our front, and we can creep forward through winding and intricate cover-ways seeing nothing until we reach the very front. Here cautiously raising our heads we take chances as to the unaimed bullets dropping occasionally and view the country between the hostile lines. Not a Japanese can we see, and the lower ground in front of us is as bare as a new plowed field. Not a house is standing, nor a tree, nor an animal, nor a human being, and the hills nearly 2 miles away appear perfectly naked. But we know that the Japanese infantry is on and among those hills with its cannon behind them, although the trenches are as invisible as the troops that man them. We take great satisfaction in the thought that we are equally invisible. . . . Evening is approaching, and as we are preparing to retire from the hills, we hear an ominous barking of guns, increasing to a steady roar, and the position in our vicinity is deluged with shell and shrapnel. . . . There is nothing for the soldiers to do but preserve their lives, their vitality, and their courage till night-fall, so that they may repulse the Japanese infantry that will surely approach under cover of darkness. . . . We are relieved when the fire slackens for a moment, and we mount and very soon determine the relative speed of our animals. We spend the night at Corps headquarters, hearing the news of the day. Our dinner would not please a gourmand, but we have music from a regimental band. Then we lie down in our blankets upon the earthen floor of a wretched Chinese hovel and to the sound of the guns and the rattle of distant infantry we go to sleep comfortably, with very little thought of the poor fellows we left in the trenches.

NATIONAL RESPONSIBILITIES AND MILITARY PREPAREDNESS[10]

There have been a great many expressions from persons not especially trained in strategy and the military art as to how world-peace might best be promoted; and there have been many expressions from military (including naval) authorities as to how our country might be protected from the evil consequences of war from whatever cause war might result.

Our great national policies have been adopted by persons commercially, philanthropically or politically interested, for the most part without professional advice as to the military consequences of these policies. Not only has such professional advice not been sought, but when volunteered the expression of it has often been condemned and nearly always ignored or forgotten.

Our geographical situation, our natural resources, our commercial and industrial possibilities and ambitions, the character of our government and people and our national policies and doctrines all are factors determining the chances of war, and determining as well the character and extent of the defensive or potentially aggressive measures which it is essential our country should adopt.

What military situation do all of these factors create?

How might the military situation be altered by changes in our national policies?

Are such changes practicable as would improve our military situation without sacrifice in other directions which would be out of proportion to our gain?

Accepting the fact that our people are pacific and non-military by disposition and strongly desirous of promoting peace among the nations, and especially between our own and other nations, can not due allowance be made for this fact in the formulation of our military policy?

Is there no room in the discussion of all these questions for the professionally educated soldier? Is it not indeed his duty to discuss them, so that the people who have educated him and whom he is trained to serve with the utmost devotion, may have the benefit of his judgment, or at least have opportunity to weigh that judgment and determine whether it is of value to them?

We know now that our military situation is unsatisfactory. We desire to improve it, and at the same time we desire to promote the cause of peace. We do not wish to improve it by abandoning anything which is worth more to us than military security, if indeed anything can be set above the security of the state; and having an aversion to nonproductive expenditures and economic waste we naturally desire to improve it at the least cost. . . .

The very fear on the part of others that we might be driven to abandon our defensive policy, and the very ease with which behind the protection of it we could without the consent of any other nation alter that policy, would be other elements lending us strength to prevail in peaceful negotiations.

The adoption of a strictly defensive attitude is but wisely to take advantage of the splendid geographical isolation which is or rather which once was, our greatest military asset. In large measure we have cast it aside, but it is still possible to recover it.

Perhaps it is intended that some day one nation shall come to exercise imperial dominion over all other nations. Many have tried to do this in the past and have failed.

If one nation shall succeed in this establishing itself, in the nature of things let us hope that such establishment in itself will be a demonstration of its capacity for world dominion. And in proportion as such world-empire is wisely and justly administered, there may be established justice and peace throughout the world. Perhaps some such imperial nation will in the end perform the functions of that "international court" and "international police" of which so many dream. Perhaps wars are but the natural processes of evolution that shall finally establish such a planet-wide imperial power in proper hands. Perhaps then at last the summum bonum of so-called international relations will be reached. And who knows but that nations which suppress their imperial instincts, refraining from such responses to them as war, are but neuters withdrawing from the strife which is a part of natural evolution, thus making such evolution more prolonged and perhaps of a less perfect consummation?

I am not possessed of any such fanciful theories; but I do firmly believe that if for any reason the public opinion of our country holds that imperial doctrines and practices are good, or that we cannot ethically divest ourselves of certain responsibilities because of their moral nature, then in justice to our country's very existence we should not shirk the effort and the cost which are their logical accompaniments.

ADDRESS BEFORE THE GENTLEMEN OF THE UNIVERSITY CLUB, CHICAGO, 1915

. . . We as a nation, are as proud of our recently acquired international importance as a small boy of a new gun. And we keep looking down the barrels, and fooling with the mechanism in the serene belief that it isn't loaded. But it is loaded, and the powder is a highly explosive mixture of Monroe doctrine, and isolated island possessions, and a fortified Panama Canal.

If we continue to live in ignorance . . . we may well acquire the title of the idiot nation of modern times. It is time we persuade our 4th of July orators to cease enacting the role of the fool that rocks the boat.

Please excuse this mixture of metaphors.

When any sane person speaks a word against this situation, if he be prominent enough, he immediately becomes the target of the . . . the daily cartoonist.

The American professor Burgess who recently assaulted the Monroe doctrine in Berlin has met with this misfortune.

One of our Presidents negotiated a treaty with England looking to the neutralization of the Panama Canal, but the treaty could not be ratified, as the newspapers demanded that we have the right to fortify our possession. What this really means is that any hostile nation has the right to seize the canal if it can, and is offered a prize for making successful war on us, while we on the other hand would be handicapped in war by the special dispositions we should have to make to defend Panama.

Let us consider the little disagreement we are now having with Japan. Of course no one expects it to result immediately in war. But there is a very considerable chance of war with Japan so long as we own the Philippine Islands. Japan would never make war on us if she had to assail us by invasion of the Pacific states, but as matters are now, she could force us to carry on the war at a disadvantage in the Far East, and if she won she could take the Philippines. It is a shame to place such temptation before any nation.

Just prior to 1898 the United States was the strongest of all nations *on the defensive*. Our population was self-sustaining and could not be reduced to submission by blockade. On account of the difficulties of ocean transport no army could land and sustain itself for a successful campaign within our borders. The European power with which most frequently we had serious complications in the past, and which most of all nations possessed means to annoy and harass our coasts, was deterred from any hostile undertaking through fear of losing Canada. At this period the Monroe doctrine was by no means as great a peril as it is now. President Cleveland could be reasonably sure that his Venezuelan message would provoke no war.[11]

But now that we have offered hostages to fortune in acquiring isolated foreign possessions it is a different story. Having chosen to live in a glass house we must stop throwing stones. It is impossible to regard the Monroe doctrine as anything but an unfriendly or at least discourteous announcement to other nations. It increases the probability of war, but worse, it affords any nation the opportunity of forcing us into war at its own selected time, whether we are ready or not. Again there is the constant menace that our newspapers may stir the people into a foolish demand for war on some pretext that the Monroe doctrine has been violated, when in reality our State Department may have assented to the action of the foreign power complained of. There is likely to come a time when a political party will attempt to obtain power through hysterical claims that an administration has permitted the Monroe doctrine to be violated.

Of course one may say that we should maintain such an army and navy that no other power can threaten us, however offensive or foolish our policies.

And so there are some people who think all governmental expenditures wasted, unless they result in battleships. We shall have less need of the latter if we abandon policies that are narrow, grasping and arrogant. And so also we shall regain our strength and ability to maintain the right against the strong.

2 | The American Military Mission to Russia

Petrograd, June–July 1917

Judson began his 1917 service in Russia as military attaché to the Root Mission, under the leadership of Elihu Root, the former secretary of state. Root had been secretary of war from 1899 to 1904, at the time Judson was a military attaché and observer in the Russo-Japanese War. There were three U.S. delegations sent to Russia within weeks of the U.S. entry into the war. The Stevens Railway Commission arrived in Petrograd on 12 June 1917, only one day ahead of the primarily diplomatic Root Mission. Two months later, more than thirty American men arrived to take up their duties as the American Red Cross Commission to Russia. Each delegation, ostensibly with its own specific area of work, was charged with the task of helping Russia in her war effort against the Central Powers. In each case the initiative for the delegation came from Washington and not from the Provisional Government of Russia.

The situation was complicated by the fact that David Francis, the United States' ambassador to Russia, and a number of other high-ranking State Department officials already at their posts in Russia did not look favorably at the prospect of the preemption of their responsibilities by the special commissions.[1] The ambassador and his staff viewed the personnel of the various commissions as Johnnies-come-lately and as too inexperienced to understand either the political complications of the Revolution or the Russian military's failures on the eastern front. Judson was one of the few members (if not the only member) from any of the three missions with prior firsthand experience of Russia and wartime. Therefore it did not come as too much of a surprise when he was asked to remain in Petrograd with his new responsibilities after all of the other members of the Root Mission had returned home. Chapter 2 documents Judson's analysis of two central concerns of U.S. decision makers: Russia's political fate and its war-fighting capability during June and July 1917. Like most of his colleagues in Petrograd, he was convinced that the developments in Russia would determine for the Allies either victory or defeat in the world war. On both political and

30

Military and naval attachés in Russia at the time of the Russo-Japanese War, 1904. Judson, in the broad-brimmed hat, stands fourth from the left. *Courtesy of the Newberry Library.*

military considerations, Judson began his analysis by drawing upon his 1904 experience as an observer of the Russo-Japanese War. This first memorandum, on Alexander Guchkov, was prepared for his superiors just prior to his departure for Russia as military attaché to the Root Mission.

APRIL 21, 1917, BALTIMORE, MD.

MEMORANDUM AS TO ALEXANDER GUCHKOV,[2]
NOW RUSSIAN MINISTER OF WAR AND OF THE NAVY[3]

In the spring of 1904 I was appointed Military Attaché at the American Embassy at St. Petersburg and with the Russian Army in Manchuria. After a short stay in St. Petersburg I was permitted to start for the Far East to join the staff of General Kuropatkin. On account of interruption to traffic upon the Trans-Siberian Railroad, incident to the war, the journey to Liaoyang, where the Russian Army was concentrating, occupied nearly a month.

Upon the same journey, in the same cars with myself (for we changed cars several times) was a Russian gentleman; out of uniform, which distinguished him from nearly all of his fellow travelers; about 50 years old; with a short beard streaked with gray; of a pleasing and most open and intelligent countenance; of medium height and sturdy figure; erect but limping somewhat, as though one leg were slightly shorter than the other.

I very soon met and as the journey wore on became intimately acquainted with this gentleman, whose name was Alexander Guchkov. In many respects I found him like a well educated American of the type that achieves leadership in almost any direction. It was obvious to me that he was interested in the fact that I was an American as well as in my mission. He spoke English perfectly, as did a much younger man, _____ Von Meck, by whom he was accompanied. Often our trains would stop for several hours, and Mr. Guchkov and I would walk about near the train talking of his country and of mine.

He told me that the czar was a man as to whose intentions Russian liberals entertained great expectations, believing him to be thoroughly convinced that Russia should at once receive a constitution. The trouble the czar had, Mr. Guchkov said, was to determine how much power could safely be lodged with the people at the start, so that the inauguration of liberal institutions might not be accompanied by a breakdown of government. The czar, he said, had no selfish desire to retain power for himself and was disposed to go just as far and as fast as circumstances might permit.

Frequently we would stop where some peasant-soldiers had left the train to engage in such a frolic as was their custom in their home villages. Their plaintive songs, their dances and their simple natures reminded me of the plantation negroes [*sic*] of our southern states. Mr. Guchkov, watching them, would often characterize them as "splendid fellows," but often in the same breath he would describe them as "utterly simple and untrained, like big, faithful animals".

Mr. Guchkov bitterly regretted the outbreak of war with Japan, as he felt that such a war might give a decided setback to the movement for a constitution. He spoke of the czar's initiative, shortly before, in securing international conferences at the Hague, and said that one of the motives of the czar in thus promoting the cause of international peace was to lessen the importance of war in the lives of nations, in as much as he (the czar) feared that Russia, liberalized, might be less efficient than formerly to carry on war and thus might fall a prey to her neighbors. At that time Mr. Guchkov feared Great Britain most. In fact he showed a bitter antipathy toward that nation. Mr. Guchkov was a great idealist, and his hatred of Great Britain, as well as his sentimental regard for the weak and (as he judged) oppressed, had led him during the Boer War to proceed to South Africa, where he had fought on the side of the Boers as a private soldier, receiving in his leg a bullet which he still carried and which caused him to limp as I have described.

We talked much of the then recent Far Eastern adventures of Russia. He condemned utterly the whole fabric of them, and for them he seemed largely to blame Witte. In order that some favored Russian capitalists might prosper he thought the Empire had risked a quarrel with Japan which promised to be without favorable issue to Russia. He thought that Russia was entirely too weak in the Far East to permit her at that time to expand so aggressively, as was being attempted, under the very nose of Japan. He believed that Russia should not have felt safe in the Far East until it had double-tracked the Siberian railroad. With but a single track road more than 5,000 miles long, he felt that Russia could not operate an army in Manchuria as large as Japan, so near at hand, could maintain there. He had feared that the situation would tempt Japan to hostilities. On the other hand he thought a tremendous mistake had been made in seeking to defend the eastern flank of the Empire with sea power. Mr. Guchkov pointed out that, except as to the small matter of Saghalien [Sakhalin Island],[4] Russia's territory lay all together in one body, with no sea routes necessarily to be traversed, and he believed that Russia should never have taken nor should take in future any action which would make any sea route of vital importance. He said that a navy smaller than the navy of one's opponent was worthless and a waste; and that Russia neither could hope nor should attempt to outbuild the navies of her probable antagonists. Mr. Guchkov believed that Russia should spend no money whatever on seapower. (Several years later when Mr. Guchkov was chairman of the Committee on National Defense he opposed the construction of naval vessels and his efforts and influence for a time prevailed).

Mr. Guchkov in his journey to the seat of war represented the zemstvos, and especially the zemstvos of Moscow.[5] He had a remarkable commission from the czar, which permitted him, in his discretion, to exercise a very large measure of authority. Under this commission, soon after his arrival in Manchuria, he assumed complete control of Red Cross operations east of Lake Baikal, and under the Russian system the Red Cross did most of the work which with us is done by the Army Medical Department. Mr. Guchkov, at the close of the battle of Mukden, fell into the hands of the Japanese, as did the writer of this memorandum; and I last saw him arranging for the care of the Russian wounded who had been taken prisoners.

Alexander Guchkov is now Minister of War and of the Navy in the Russian Provisional Government.

Acquainted with these facts as to Mr. Guchkov I have set them down with the thought that a knowledge of them may possibly be of service to those high in authority.

EN ROUTE, ST. PAUL 6 HOURS BEHIND[6]

MAY 17, 1917

Dear Angel (my dearest wife)—

I have time, almost two days out from Washington, to write you a letter at some leisure.

In the first place my neuritis improves and I no longer fear that it will accompany me to Petrograd—

I have a stateroom and am travelling very comfortably. In the other staterooms of this car are Mr. Root, Mr. Mott, Mr. Bertron, Mr. Russell, Mr. Duncan, Gen. Scott, Col. Michie, Col. (Tobby) Mott, and myself. Also (I had forgotten) Admiral Glennon. The latters and a ? medical doctor, together with 8 or 10 clerks, messengers etc. are in an adjoining special car. Mr. Cyrus McCormick meets the mission at Seattle and Mr. Crane at Petrograd.[7] Several attachés are now in Petrograd and will join us at Vladivostok. We leave Seattle on arrival at 8:30 P.M. Saturday on the S.S. Buffalo, a naval transport. I am writing with an indelible pencil and the train moves and mars my otherwise beautiful hand-writing.

Michie is aid to Gen. Scott. Mott is aide to the Special Ambassador, i.e. "chef de mission", Mr. Root. I am "Military attaché to the special diplomatic Mission to Russia from the United States of America"[8]— You see—I have much the best of it—no personal attentions to pay. Michie ranks me and I rank Mott. All are very agreeable, and excellent traveling companions—mission and officers as well.

Mr. Root is most affable and frank. He has a sense of humor I did not suspect him of—He is 72, but he has not failed at all and still the biggest, brainiest American. Mr. Bertron is a New York banker and broker who is odd enough to be a democrat. He is a handsome clean-cut man of about 50, with excellent manners and much savoir faire—He seems to

have plenty of "savy" and is a gentleman. I like him very much. I think his common sense is greater than that of some of the others. . . .
Faithfully,

My Dear Boy:[9]

I have just been writing to your mother, and have told her to send you my letters—they are really to you both. Although often I'll be repeating in my letters to you.

We have had a great lesson in geography—Have traversed the Bering Sea, are now in the Sea of Okhotsk and tomorrow cross the Gulf of Tartary and the Sea of Japan. It was our shortest course, and safest also as the Navy people had word of a German raider further south. It has been bold and stormy with much fog and some snow, but I have savored every minute of it, feeling a release from responsibilities and . . . work which has permitted me to sleep 10 hours a day—And how much I have read! About nothing am I more anxious to hear than about your camp experience, whether you have found it beyond your endurance and if not how it has all impressed you and affected your spirits and your philosophy. It is great that Elizabeth and her husband are there.

I am glad too that you hate the Germans so comfortably.

I don't believe the war will last 6 months longer, and soon will have had—we all shall have had—most interesting experiences to look back on. We are due at Vladivostok Sunday morning. Write me "in care State Department, Washington, D.C., attention of Mr. Long."

Such prayers as heathens pray I pray for my dear son and wish him all happiness.

Goodbye for today—
Faithfully yrs.

Dearest:[10]

We're coasting along Siberia southwestwardly, slowly, so as not to arrive in Vladivostok till tomorrow, Sunday, morning. We of course do not know what arrangements have been made for our departure thence to Petrograd. I suppose we'll get off rather quickly on a special train. Thus we may arrive in Petrograd any time from June 12th to June 18th. Mr. Root talks of the possibility of a short stay in Russia, perhaps only 10 days. Nobody can tell of course. But I should hate not to stay long enough to get plenty of military information—especially Emjmcee? dope. Maybe I'll try to arrange to stay behind a while. Everything of course is very uncertain till I get oriented at Petrograd. It will be a great temptation of course to go home with the party—perhaps via Japan if not Peking—and see my angel soon again. I suppose I will get one of the "conscripted 500,000" [undecipherable] regiments there ought to be about 16 of them and they'll be starting about the time I get back. I don't think they will ever get any further than training camp—where for 6 or 8 months you can be with me. That will be fine—

Now I'm going to write Clay and one or two other letters and then pack up.

How entirely to exclusion of every thing else and every other thought and sentiment I do <u>love my angel sweetheart wife.</u>

Faithfully Billy

This will be mailed in the ships post office. My best love to Miss Sally.

On Trans Siberian (moving train)
June 5, 1917, Tuesday

Dearest:

We left Vladivostok Sunday after being welcomed by the local Committee of Soldiers' and Workmen's delegates. Yesterday we passed through Harbin which is now a beautiful and thriving Russo-Chinese city. The vacant spaces were piled high with packed grain which cannot be moved for lack of transportation—while they starve in other parts of the world. They sent on for us the former emperor's train. I have the boudoir and bed of the Grand Duchess Tatia and in the reception room of our dining car it was that the czar signed his abdication. I found in that room in the card table a score kept by the czar of his last game of cards—He wrote his own name "Nic" and evidently they let him win. We are having a wonderful journey. Once at Petrograd they say we are to inhabit the Winter Palace. It is almost impossible to write the train wobbles so but I wish to mail this to my angel to say how happy I am and that I am quite well of necessities and every thing else.

We are going through a great rolling prairie country (steppes) that would support millions of cattle and all day yesterday the farms looked like Illinois. What a marvelous country this will be some day!

Love to every body, Your own,

Billy

I am writing on a beautiful maple table on a dainty blue leather portfolio, feeling sorry for the sad and beautiful Tatia.

PETROGRAD— JULY 9, 1917
SPECIAL DIPLOMATIC MISSION OF THE UNITED STATES OF AMERICA

My Darling Wife—

This is the morning of the last day the Mission will remain in Petrograd— Tonight it starts for the Pacific—and the present outlook is that I shall remain behind a while.[11] It is very important for us to have someone here of at least my rank to look out for the needs of Russia in the way of money and war materials, to be obtained in America. The British and the French each have a General and a large staff on this duty. If I stay I'll write you more about it. The reason it is uncertain is because we (the Military contingent) only got back late last night from a two weeks visit to the front, and the arrangements for leaving one behind are complicated.

I am writing on what promises to be a very busy day, before breakfast, so that I may send the letter by some of the party who are returning to the states. I do not allow myself to think of the regret I feel not to return with the rest and the heartache it gives me to think my seeing you will be delayed. I never shall consent to be away from my angel a minute "when this cruel war is over." Tonight I probably leave the Winter Palace and go to the abode of Riggs (our former military attaché who will be one of my assistants). Riggs and a secretary of our embassy are occupying the Polovtsev Palace (on the edge of town—belonging to the richest man in Russia and a marvelous spot) in order to care for it during these parlous times which of course means rent free.

We had a most remarkable journey from here to and along the front. We were most lucky in being at places at the right time. Some time I'll write the history of the two weeks at great length but now I can only sketch it in with few words.

We lunched with the great Generals (Brusilov and the rest)—we saw a remarkably successful and spectacular battle. (Very different from the old Manchurian days in that our side was winning, which permitted us to observe to advantage). We saw what is left of Rumania and lunched with the king and queen—we received "decorations" to wear at our collars because we had "assisted" at the great affusion—and we arrived back on time as Mr. Root had given "orders" to be back by the 8th. I think we as Americans had no right to accept our crosses and ribbons but Gen. Scott took his and no one else could explain of course.[12]

The queen of Rumania is one of the most beautiful and attractive women I ever saw—Had long talk with her. She reminds me of my angel—

Am having my stuff I left on the "Buffalo" sent to you in Ky.

Love to Clay—I am so anxious to know how he is getting on. And I send a world of love to my darling—

Your own

JULY 12, 1917 (THIS LETTER IS INCOMPLETE)

My Darling Wife:

In a day or two I shall be able to send this by some one—I don't know who—

I am living comfortably at the Villa Polovtsev as the guest of Riggs (one of my assistants) and 2 secretaries of the Embassy. It is in the country a short ways and places me under too great obligations to the others for automobiles so I shall soon look about for some more of a pension arrangement and if I could find a French one it would help me in my studies of French, which I wish we had kept up. I have 3 assistants and shall have more. They really ought to send out a general officer to take my job. And now good bye my Angel—I am sure when I get my office fixed up and my new jobs started I shall find time to write you longer and more interesting letters. Am in hopes of hearing from you in a few days, and for the 1st time since leaving America.

With all my love, I am yours always.

[Letter continues.]

. . . I saw Mr. Guchkov but twice, as he was leaving town to visit the front. I brought him and Mr. Root together to their mutual advantage I think. It was Mr. Guchkov, by the way, who went to the czar and demanded that he sign his abdication—requiring some nerve I should say. Mr. G. believed that a revolution was inevitable and that civil war would occur unless the abdication were signed. He did hope however that the upper (i.e. competent) classes would secure the state—That the socialists have done so is something he believes will be followed by very evil consequences—

In any other country so weak a government as now exists here would be accompanied by disorders and anarchy. There are nearly two million people in Petrograd—and no police force. There are 150,000 soldiers, but there is little discipline; and any where else the soldiers themselves, under the conditions, would be a menace to order. Some volunteer militia are supposed to be policing the town but they are not in evidence. Soldiers and sailors depose their officers and select others as suits their fancy. There is very great pessimism among the more conservative classes. The great point so far as we are concerned is <u>will the Russians undertake an offensive.</u> If they had done that this summer the war would have been brought sensibly nearer a conclusion—They have enormous numbers of men and very acceptable quantities of munitions—But they are tired of fighting. Every thing is uncertain yet yesterday I visited an interesting training camp, in the country, for engineer officers. They have a war-course of 8 months. I got many photographs and text books, new ones, to take home with me.

Tomorrow, Monday, we expect to leave for "Stavka" (field headquarters)—and from there inspect the front in spots. A lot of us will go—Gen. Scott, Michie, Parker (now Mil. Att.[aché] here—just up from Rumania where he saw nothing) and two officers who are observers, besides myself.

We live very well at the Palace but the people here are having a hard time. They spend hours standing in line, with tickets to get a little bread or milk, or a pair of shoes—Prices are enormous and I do not see how the populace will get along. There is plenty to eat in Russia, elsewhere, but their transportation system has broken down.

Yesterday I entertained here at luncheon—the French and British attachés etc. who had been so good to me. The air is full of a million church bells. (It is Sunday) and the heat is really terrific. It doesn't have time to cool off—when the sun never sets. Col. Michie and I have a large sitting room about 40 feet square between our bed rooms—and off our private hall is a large bath room.

Still we must walk a mile, nearly, through a labyrinth of passages to reach our apartment. . . .

. . . Maj. Parker I shall send to "stavka" (General headquarters). Maj. Kerth I shall send to some corps as observer. Riggs just getting his captaincy, who has been attaché here for some time, knows some French and Russian. I shall keep with me as assistant and reimbursing officer. Am trying to get funds, clerks etc. Have a nicely located office on the Quai looking out over the Neva (which is a river bordered by beautiful palaces). My principal duties are with the Russian Commission procuring munitions and other things from abroad with the money we loan Russia.

The Ambassador, Mr. David R. Frances of St. Louis, is a typical old southern politician (72 years old) with plenty of money. And much homely wisdom. He is getting along very well with the Russians. I dined with him last night and then he took me out to play bridge where the company was interesting and the stakes low. Tonight I dine with our naval attaché Crosley and wife—nice people.

It is most interesting here. The Provisional Government is composed of conservative socialists who are for continuing the war. The Bolsheviks or extremists want exterior peace but seem not to fear internal trouble. The Army has surprised every one by its offensive, still in progress. We hope that success will encourage those behind the front. Transportation difficulties are immense, and it looks like short [rations?] in Petrograd for food and fuel this winter. There may be disturbances here any time. It is a most interesting situation, as the government has relatively little power and is of course inexpert—I have asked the government to furnish me with an automobile and one is promised—That will add much to my comfort and efficiency—For the moment I have no clerk, no messenger, nothing—but I'll soon get fixed up.

3 | Cooperation with the Provisional Government

The fall of the Romanov Dynasty in 1917 came after many disastrous defeats on the eastern front of World War I and unprecedented civilian suffering. The February Revolution (March in the Gregorian calendar of the West) brought about the czar's abdication and led to the creation of a new government—the Provisional Government. It was based on the center and left parties of the Duma, a quasi-parliamentary body that had been forced on Czar Nicholas II in the aftermath of the Revolution of 1905. At the same time grass-roots committees of workers, or Soviets of Workers' Deputies, which also had origins in the Revolution of 1905, were in many ways the more effective center of organized political and military power after the end of the Russian monarchy.

The fundamental aim of all U.S. representatives in Russia after the U.S. entry into the war was to assist its ally in the prosecution of the war. The Provisional Government of Russia, first under Prime Minister Prince George E. Lvov, and then under Alexander Kerensky, was the focus of U.S. and Allied attention. Both the Lvov and Kerensky administrations pledged their commitment to honor Russia's treaty obligations in the World War. However, of great concern to Judson and his colleagues was the stability of this government and its war-fighting capability. The first Provisional Government of Lvov lasted less than five months, and was marked by a deterioration of Russia's military position on the eastern front. Kerensky became prime minister on 21 July 1917, amid the turmoil of the July Uprising, a left-wing attempt to replace the Provisional Government with a radical, antiwar, socialist regime.

Chapter 3 begins with Judson's reports and his "Military Notes Re. Present Disorders in Petrograd." He was preoccupied by the prospect of an antiwar government coming into power. Such a government, signing a separate peace with the Central Powers, would have allowed all the German and Austro-Hungarian forces serving on the Russian front to be redeployed on the western front to fight the British, French, and newly arrived Americans. Yet even if such a disastrous course of events were averted, Judson's observation of the Russian armies gave him much reason for concern. Discipline had evaporated. The chain of command in many units had been "democratized," and war-fighting capability—for a host of reasons—was nil. As chief of the American Military Mission and American military attaché to the American ambassador, Judson was the senior U.S. representative responsible for helping the Provisional Government solve these critical *military* problems. Even more vexing were problems of political instability.

JULY 17, 1917. MILITARY NOTES RE. PRESENT DISORDERS IN PETROGRAD[1]

Yesterday the four Kadet (Conservative-Bourgeois) Cabinet Ministers resigned. It is understood that this action resulted from the favorable attitude assumed by the Provisional Government toward autonomy for the Ukraine. Last night there were considerable demonstrations by the radicals, including unorganized bands of soldiers and other armed men, in the course of which many shots were fired, and according to report, from two to twenty men killed.

This morning the demonstrations continued. Shops are closed. The trams are not running. There are occasional isolated outbreaks of rifle and machine gun fire. The city is in the hands of the Maximalists. A very rough element, armed, is in evidence, going about in small groups. Automobiles, commandeered, are going about with machine guns pointing to the rear and with men bearing rifles and drawn revolvers. The Bolsheviks (Maximalists) appear to feel some responsibility for preserving order.

Mr. Harper (at Embassy, 3:30 P.M., says that Provisional Government and Council of Workmens' and Soldiers' Delegates are at one on the question of rescuing Petrograd from anarchy. They can, they say, probably count on the loyalty of three regiments in Petrograd, and propose to clean up the town, if they can, today. It is 5:00 P.M. and there is now no sign of the cleaning up process.

There were great parades all day of workmen, soldiers and sailors, mingled, many armed, and many bearing red flags with more or less anarchistic inscription.

It is reported that 10,000 came from Kronstadt.

It is understood that efforts were made to arrest Kerensky last night, which failed because of his having departed from Petrograd some twenty minutes previously.

The Ambassador has not been able to communicate with the Government. Apparently Tereshchenko is also out of town. Miliukov and Guchkov are away.

It is reported that the Petrograd Food Commission resigned yesterday, and that the food situation is bad.

JULY 19, 1917. MILITARY NOTE RE. DISTURBANCES IN PETROGRAD.

Yesterday the situation was as follows: trams not running; bridges closed, except the one by Winter Palace; no cars rushing about with armed men, etc: situation appeared well in hand.

On evening of July 17th, battle on Liteyni Bridge between Bolsheviks and Cossacks: 20 Cossacks killed, 60 wounded; a number of encounters during evening of July 17th and during night.

Many of the mutinous soldiers abandoned the Bolsheviks. Yesterday it was reported that one corps from front would start for Petrograd last night.

Today still no trams: Palace Bridge alone open in early morning. Lenin's house taken, some firing: Lenin said to have escaped. Troops came in from rear, crossing Palace Bridge. At about 11:00 A.M. Troitska Bridge closed: loyal troops crossed: Bolsheviks holding Peter and Paul[2] surrendered. Apparently the disturbances are well over, and if there be proper punishments, the government may have gained prestige.

JULY 19, 1917. TO: CHIEF, WAR COLLEGE DIVISION, GENERAL STAFF. NO. 1175.[3]
SUBJECT: ORGANIZATION OF OFFICE

Referring to my assignment to duty as Military Attaché to the American Embassy, Petrograd; Chief of the American Military Mission to Russia; Observer in connection with Military operations in which Russia is engaged, and the Military Representative of the U.S. Government in all matters connected with the supply to Russia of materials and personnel for use during the War, as set forth in letter of instructions addressed to me by the Chief of Staff, U.S. Army, a copy of which letter has already been furnished, I submit the following remarks upon the duties which it seems essential this office should assume, and as to certain reasons therefore.

The British have more than sixty officers, and the French more than half as many, performing similar functions. Their labors have great moral effect in keeping before the Russian Military Administration in most trying times the circumstance that Russia has Allies upon whose support and advice she can rely, and whose eyes and ears are present to appreciate and receive immediate information as to Russian conditions and Russian needs. . . .

We must undertake these functions also, not merely for the dignity of our Country, but to support its vital interests. If Russia should withdraw from the war, releasing more than 150 enemy divisions for service on the other fronts, how can we hope to win the war in any decisive fashion?[4]

The Russian department most concerned and organized to have liaison with the Allies of Russia in respect to foreign orders . . . is the Russian War Department, a branch of which is the Michelson Commission.[5] The latter coordinates all demands from all Russian departments for foreign purchases and determines relative urgency. . . .

For several months the matter of American military representation on the Michelson Commission had been urged by the Russians and by the Allies here. I have just assumed the duty of such representation.

We have come into the War so late that it will not be necessary or desirable to form as large an organization for our work in this connection as have been inaugurated by the British and French. Nevertheless, I must be prepared to act as a useful member of this very important Commission, which has assigned me certain offices for the work, but which provides neither office furniture, stationery, nor clerical assistance. Under present arrangements, Captain Riggs will assist me in this connection, as well as in Embassy and Military Control work hereinafter described. Very many questions of transportation arise in connection with the Michelson Commission work, and to assist in this work, as well as to disburse for this office, I have asked by cable for an officer of the Q. M. [Quartermaster] Corps. This request I renew. In the meantime, under authority conferred by the Chief of Staff . . . I have designated Captain Riggs as Disbursing Officer.

The present Russian General Headquarters (Stavka) are at Mogilev. Each of the Allies is represented by several officers at Stavka, and there exists there one of the greatest clearing houses for military information which the world has ever seen. Information from Stavka is constantly needed among other things to inform me as a member of the Michelson Commission, for example, as to the relative tactical values of different guns, the purchase of which may be under consideration. . . . It is essential that we have some one at Stavka, and under present arrangements that will be Major Parker.

From my own observations and from reliable report it appears that there is one field in which we can probably cooperate with the Russians to great advantage. The length of the Russian front and the scarcity among the Russians of airplanes indicates that American aero units (the material and personnel for many, many squadrons) could be utilized along this front with the maximum of military result for a given amount of tonnage. . . . I recommend that there be assigned here for duty as soon as possible an aviation officer.

Someone must be at the front, to keep this office informed as to the morale of the troops, to make tactical observations, to report, from the viewpoint of the front, what material in general is most needed and how that in hand is used. Under present arrangements Major Kerth will observe near the front. . . .

The Embassy at Petrograd has constantly before it many general and special questions of a military nature, as to which it constantly solicits the advice of the Military Attaché or his action before the Russian military authorities. This Embassy work is important and can not be neglected.

The French, British and Italians each maintain here Military Control Sections, with officers furnished by the Russians in the building which houses the General Staff. Each of these Sections maintains a considerable personnel in Petrograd and has inspectors . . . at important frontier points. The anti-war propaganda and espionage, carried on most energetically in Russia by the Germans and by German sympathizers renders very important the counter-espionage work of the Military Control Sections, which work in close accord. All who are familiar with the facts are demanding American cooperation. There is a well defined belief that the movement of persons into Russia from America is especially large and possesses great elements of danger.[6] There is so insistent a demand from Russian and Allied sources for us to do our part in this work, that the Ambassador is contemplating an early inauguration of the work with civilian inspectors, my office to furnish liaison between the civilian personnel and the Russian and allied authorities. This work should, for efficiency and to conform with the methods pursued by the other Allies, be made completely military as soon as practicable. . . .

. . . Ambassadors Root and Francis and Gen. Scott on July 9, 1917, joined in a cable requesting that $25,000 from the Emergency appropriation be placed to credit of Capt. Riggs, Disbursing Officer, to carry on the work of which I have written above. I have as yet heard nothing as to action on this request. Meantime, I am obliged to assume that such action will be favorable and to incur certain expenditures.

Mr. Root, Gen. Scott and Col. Michie took with them to America copies of a memorandum on the military activities here that should be started at once by this office, at least on a reduced scale as hereinbefore outlined. . . . It is assumed that this memorandum is now in the hands of the War College.

It is respectfully urged that there be inaugurated a Russian Section of our War College, or at least that some one be detailed to give Russian questions immediate attention and to serve as a clearing house between this office and the various agencies that may act in Russian matters, or that should be advised as to conditions or demands arising here.

I cannot too urgently represent the absolute need of immediate action along the lines herein requested. . . . No ordinary standards can be applied to present conditions here. For example, during the past week the City has a part of the time been in the hands of Bolsheviks (extreme radicals), Anarchists, mutinous soldiers and German propagandists. Pitched battles occur daily between bodies of loyal troops and other forces, with considerable blood shed. The food supply in the City is reduced to the lowest proportions, and no one can say now when the supply will be renewed.

JULY 19, 1917. PARAPHRASE OF TELEGRAM SENT
TO WARCOLSTAFF, WASHINGTON:[7]

This is telegram No. 22 from this office. The creation of a board here is recommended for the purpose of qualifying fit American residents for reserve commissions in important local services. . . .

The detail of one officer of the Quartermaster Corps at Petrograd is requested. . . . One aviation officer's detail is also requested. Both of these officers, if possible, should speak French. Unless there is started immediately essential military Mission features here, including the very important Michelson Commission work on foreign orders for Russia, in collaboration with other Allies, a bad impression will at once result here. This has a real bearing in helping Russia remain in the war. . . .

Please inform me whether the $25,000 requested by Francis, Root and Scott have been placed to Riggs' credit. . . .

JULY 20, 1917. PETROGRAD

Dearest,

We have had a very exciting week. On Monday night rioting began all over town. On Tuesday morning, in the country 5 miles, we found our car disabled and had to walk to town. The city was in the hands of the Anarchists, "Bolsheviks" (which means extreme reds) and mutinous soldiers. They were going about town in seized automobiles, with rifles and revolvers cocked, and with machine guns. The Government did not know what troops were loyal, if any were, and was apparently paralyzed. All day Tuesday there were "scraps," with firing, all over town. In a battle between loyal cossacks and Bolsheviks the cossacks were worsted. There were in the several days more than 500 casualties. I got tired walking in and out 10 miles and Wednesday moved in with a Lt. Hagood, who has a small apartment in town and a good cook. Apparently, for the time being, the Government has restored order. The food situation is very bad—and growing rapidly worse. The Embassy has several lorries out for food and I hope will get along some way.

(Sunday July 23—) The Government has restored order although as late as last night before last there was a pitched battle in front of our house which kept us awake all night. The music of machine guns has been in the air constantly until yesterday. Now the mutinous soldiers are submitting to disarmament and are being sent to the front. The soldiers already at the front, in a very recalcitrant frame of mind, will not be improved I am afraid by such arrivals. In fact from what we hear they are in a bad state of mind already and the Germans have had some marked successes.

Hagood's house seems very satisfactory but I may move nevertheless to a quaint apartment belonging to two ladies of the (former) court—sisters, and have my office in the place. Two good servants go with the place and every thing is "fo[?]d."

I have taken an [?]chick by the month—a nice looking rig, and feel more comfortable. My government machine was seized by the Bolsheviks and I assume it will be a month before I get it.

I'm going to write a bit from time to time—as opportunity arises.

This Sunday I had lunch with the Ambassador's secretary, Mr. Francis Parker and Kerth [was?] there. Parker and Kerth go out to "Stavka" (Headquarters) and the front in a day or two. I wish I could go too—I will when I get things straightened out.

Wednesday, July 25. The Government has gotten the upper hand and has quieted things down in Petrograd—By the way you can <u>stop shipment of the eatables.</u> I have managed to get some from the Army authorities. And the Ambassador is having some shipped from America.

The Russians are having a bad time near Tarnapol, where we spent so hopeful a time watching the beginning auspiciously, of the Russian advance. The Germans have broken through and there is no telling when or where they will be stopped, as the Russian soldiers apparently are not obeying their officers.

It is interesting that the most important recent Russian successes and now this disaster are in the locality I visited and became somewhat familiar with.

August 1. The Russian disaster has spread near Tarnapol. There are signs however of a stronger government being instituted and of an attempt to restore discipline.

Last night I dined with the Ambassador at Riggs's house and went to the Memorial Service to raise funds for the widows of the Cossacks who fell in cleaning up the town recently. The cossacks had a very impressive funeral Saturday.

Last Saturday-Sunday I spent a very pleasant week end at Tereyoki in Finland. The Ambassador and I went and we visited Count and Countess Nostitz. The latter was an American—very beautiful and attractive—Somewhat of an adventurer but nevertheless a very good sort. They have loads of money, a pretty villa by the sea at Tereyoki and others here and in the Crimea. They were close to the Court in the old regime. Met a lot of interesting people—mostly swells. They have sea bathing, tennis, etc. Hope I'll be asked again. The Ambassador is a good old sport. Tomorrow Hagood and I are moving to a wonderful palace where we have not the whole place but more than we need. We get it cheap as they want diplomatic protection. The office I shall move there too in a few days. Then I'll describe it too you.

I hope my angel is not unhappy.

I feel it in my bones that all our separations and worries will soon be over. The old world certainly must be tired of war and nearly ready to stop.

Love to Clay—I suppose you send him my letters—I have so many official ones to write that they wear me out with the mere composition of them—

> and love to all and to Clay.
> Your own
> Billy

no letters since as of June 11

JULY 27, 1917. PARAPHRASE OF TELEGRAM SENT TO WARCOLSTAFF, WASHINGTON: NO. 23.[8]

The cooperation of America with the Military Control Sections against espionage of the British and French is deemed essential by all concerned here. The American Ambassador, owing to the lack of military personnel, is initiating with civilians for the present, direction and the necessary liaison being furnished by this office. For such duty six reserve officers are needed immediately. The Allies are not using civilians and they are not as satisfactory. For reserve commissions the fittest men are now here / however it is suggested that as Chief of Section John Wilkie, formerly Chief of U.S. Secret Service, be commissioned and sent.

PETROGRAD, JULY 31, 1917.

CONFIDENTIAL MEMO FOR THE AMBASSADOR:

I have the honor to advise you that the enemy offensive approaching Czernowitz may later compromise the Rumanian front and compel evacuation of Jassy. I would suggest that you now request the Russian Government, if emergency arises, to offer the Rumanian King courtesies and facilities similar to those enjoyed by the Belgian King in France. It is conceivable that assurance of such treatment might assist Rumania to avoid a surrender and peace.

AUGUST 1, 1917. MEMORANDUM TO:
CHIEF, WAR COLLEGE DIVISION,
GENERAL STAFF. NO. 1186.

SUBJECT: ESTIMATE OF RUSSIAN MILITARY SITUATION
AS OF ABOUT AUGUST 1, 1917.[9]

. . . Until the existing war began, no nation (unless perhaps Germany) realized the fact that the very character of war might be modified by the employment of artillery projectiles in previously unheard of quantities.

The Russo-Japanese War seemed to have demonstrated indeed that battles between the armies of great military powers would be of long duration, on greatly extended fronts, with more or less indecisive results. These results seemed to follow from the facts that the practice of conscription produced large numbers, while the development of arms and the resort to trenches enabled relatively few men to defend a considerable front.

Of course the weak points of all lines have been the flanks. But when lines are greatly extended, the relative importance of the flanks is diminished. Thus when a line was but five miles long, a successful flank attack soon set the whole line in confusion and a rout often followed. . . . But when a line was eighty miles long, even though it possessed assailable flanks, as in Manchuria, a tactically successful flank attack produced no rout and no decision by reason of the great length of the line compared to a day's march. . . .

The Manchurian war seemed also to have demonstrated that a proper trench system was practically invulnerable to frontal attack, for it did not appear to be within the bounds of reason to suppose that as a financial, transportation and manufacturing proposition it would be possible so to blanket with projectiles the ground occupied by a trench system as to render the latter practically untenable. . . .

The quantities of munitions they would require were, before this war began, unsuspected alike by Russia, by England and by France. At the start Russia was fairly well provided to begin a war which would be waged in accordance with precedents. In the beginning, in 1914, she did very well, especially in Galicia. But as the modified character of present-day war revealed itself, she found herself unable to meet the new conditions. . . . To keep her armies supplied, Russia would not provide munitions fast enough either by manufacture, or, for several reasons, from abroad. The disastrous operations of 1915 were a natural result. By

1916, as a result of extraordinary efforts to manufacture munitions at home and to secure them from her allies, Russia was able to resume the offensive and the very successful Brusilov advance occurred. In this advance, if results be measured by casualties inflicted or by ground taken, the Allies have thus far in the war obtained their most marked success.

The fall of Rumania toward the end of 1916 much increased the difficulties and responsibilities of the Russians. With Rumania neutral, the Russian front from Riga to the Rumanian frontier was . . . some 700 miles long. By the Spring of 1917, as a result of the Rumanian disaster, the Russian front became nearly 50% longer.

Nevertheless, the Russian military situation early in 1917 was extremely favorable. Russian manufacturing capacity had reached the following figures per month:

```
3" guns............................................................. 360
4.2"    :
4.5"    :
4.8"    :
5"      : guns...................................................... 80
6" guns and How................................................ 20
8" to 12" guns and How.......................................3
Rifles................................................128,000
Machine Guns...............................................1,260
3" shells...............................................2,865,000
Shells between 3" and 6"...................... 450,000
6" and up, shells........................................553,780
S. A. [small arms] Ammunition....166,000,000
```

Russia's allies had made a careful study of her requirements from abroad and had made a program for supplying the more urgent of them.

The following table of monthly rates of Russian ammunition expenditure during the periods stated is inserted here for purposes of comparison:

During 1914:

```
S.A.A.............................................76,000,000
3" shells............................................. 464,000
Shells between 3" and 6"...
6" and up, shells...................................17,000
```

During five summer months of 1915:

```
S.A.A. .............................................56,500,000
3" shells...............................................811,000
```

Shells between 3" and 6"...
6" and up, shells...............................33,000
During five summer months of 1916:
S.A.A...140,000,000
3" shells...2,229,000
Shells between 3" and 6"...
6" and up, shells...............................152,000

The manpower of Russia was practically inexhaustible. In the reserve battalions, to replace casualties, were a greater number of men in training than were actually in divisions at the front. It was well understood that the British and French would undertake a great offensive in 1917. Certainly, as I have previously remarked, the situation early in 1917 seemed most promising.

At this point I insert the most reliable figures I can obtain as to Russian mobilization. They apply, however, to June, 1917, after the situation had lost the very hopeful character above described.

Effectives.
Before mobilization............................1,300,000
After mobilization..............................4,300,000
May 1, 1916...7,650,000
July 15, 1916.......................................8,500,000
June 20, 1917...(at least)...................10,000,000
Losses to June 20, 1917.
(Mean of Russian and French estimates)
Killed or died of wounds.................. 1,075,000
Wounded beyond recovery for
further military service 2,025,000
Prisoners..2,550,000
Total..5,650,000

On June 20, 1917, the whereabouts of the Effectives was approximately as follows:
235 Divisions of Infantry................... 2,700,000
50 Divisions of Cavalry..........................200,000
Services and works at front
(not in divisions)............................ 2,200,000
Effectives in the interior....................3,400,000
In a state of desertion.........................1,500,000
Total.. 10,000,000

It now becomes necessary to describe certain conditions that followed or resulted from the Revolution of March, 1917, which overthrew the Czar and placed the direction of affairs in the hands of a Provisional Government.

For several months prior to the Revolution of March, 1917, its near approach was distinctly felt in Russia, and efforts were made by the best and most competent of the Duma and Zemstvo people to be ready with a provisional government and a program which would enlist the support of all classes interested in the inauguration and preservation of orderly and liberal government. But the revolution, largely because of bad food conditions in Petrograd, came on with the unexpected suddenness. There was scarcely any resistance to the overthrow of the old regime, but there had not yet been well organized the forces that might most efficiently have directed events during and after the revolution.

The demonstrations in Petrograd accompanying the revolution were rather sympathetically viewed by nearly all classes, but doubtless the anarchists, advanced socialists and extremists generally were much in evidence and probably then and thereafter plumed [preened] themselves upon the thought that they were the real and effective agents of the people in overthrowing autocracy. During the demonstrations, while disorder, anarchy and civil war threatened to engulf the country, Mr. Alexander Guchkov, one of the most intelligent and competent of the Duma leaders, who had been among those endeavoring without entire success to prepare a proper organization to take over the functions of the government from the old regime, interviewed the Czar in behalf of the more conservative liberals and endeavored to persuade him to abdicate in favor of his son, the Czar's brother Michael to be regent. Influenced by his dislike of separation from his son, the Czar embraced the latter with himself in his abdication.

The original Provisional Government, with Miliukov and Guchkov as its stronger members, was unsatisfactory to the more radical elements and had not a sufficiently organized support throughout the Country. After about two months Miliukov and Guchkov found the actions of the Provisional Government so contrary to their theories and themselves so out of sympathy with the forces most in evidence in Petrograd that they resigned, and the reorganized Provisional Government assumed a more socialistic aspect.

On June 14th I had a long interview with Mr. Guchkov, the lately retired Minister of War and of Marine, and found him in a most pessimistic mood. He said that the affairs of Russia were "approaching a precipice along four different paths: one military; one financial; one industrial; and one as concerns food supply." He was of the opinion that Russia must go through a period marked by most acute suffering before she would rise again, when ready to accept a government of sufficient strength to perform properly the various functions of state.

Soon after the Revolution there had been formed a "Council of Workmens' and Soldiers' Delegates," which claimed to be the real repository of Russian sovereignty, and the new Provisional Government in a measure recognized this claim in appointments to fill the places of the retiring ministers, and has since recognized it in various ways which it is not now necessary to describe. In this Council above mentioned nearly all of the members were socialists or near-socialists. The "left" consisted of the so-called "Maximalists" or "Bolsheviks," who were extreme radicals, opposed to the Provisional Government; opposed even to the socialist members of the Government; opposed to continuing the War; opposed to a democracy such as we have in America, alleging that it was capitalistic and objectionable; without constructive ideas, and with many leaders supposed to be in the pay and employ of the German Government. Associated with these Bolsheviks were anarchists, German spies and a great number of very ignorant or flighty persons. The Bolsheviks were principally in evidence in Petrograd, but by assiduous propaganda they very generally poisoned the minds of the troops, among whom their peace plans and their announced programs for a redistribution of the land were received with great favor.

Taking advantage of political crisis which arose about the middle of July on the question of the autonomy of the Ukraine, incident to which four of the more conservative Ministers resigned their portfolios, on the evening of July 16th the Bolsheviks inaugurated a series of disorders which for a time left them apparently in undisputed possession of Petrograd. The Bolsheviks in armed motor cars patrolled the City, and there were frequent collisions with much rifle and machine gun fire. Many soldiers of the Petrograd garrison took part in the disturbances. It was difficult to determine what troops were loyal and whether a sufficient number could be depended to restore order.

With the aid of troops, especially Cossacks brought from out of town, but not until July 19th, order was finally restored.

The discipline of the Army following the Revolution was reduced to the lowest ebb. Capital punishment was abolished. Soldiers ceased to salute their officers. Military organization chose committees of soldiers who very frequently dismissed their officers. Such conduct received the direct or implied sanction of the Provisional Government, the members of which were either ignorant of the necessity of discipline in armies or felt too weak to oppose the troops. About 1,500,000 soldiers proceeded to their homes or wandered about in a state of desertion, encumbering the railroads, upon which they demanded and received free transportation. The men at the front in large numbers fraternized with the enemy. A number of officers in the highest positions resigned for one reason or another.

The position of the Russian officer became pitiable in the extreme.

. . . The test began in the last days of June about 25 miles immediately west of Tarnopol. . . . Great quantities of artillery ammunition had been accumulated during the long period of inactivity. There was but little reply by the enemy. On July 1st troops from the VI Corps began the infantry attack, which, as well as the preliminary bombardment, I had opportunity to observe in company with General Scott and other American officers. . . . 8,000 Austrians surrendered and 17 guns were taken the first day.

Thus auspiciously began the delayed 1917 Russian offensive. The Russian objective was Lemberg. The plan seems to have involved a forward movement by the left of the XI Army, west of Tarnapol, directed straight upon Lemberg; and [the] advance of the VII Army . . . all movements to converge upon Lemberg. . . .

. . . The complete failure of the VII Army seems to have determined the whole matter. Most of the troops who might under ordinary circumstances have been faithful to their duty, were in no state of mind to sacrifice themselves when perhaps more than half the troops were holding back mutinously.

Meantime the enemy was bringing up troops from the French front and elsewhere, and about the middle of July began a counter offensive. The disorders in Petrograd of July 16th and the following days, became speedily known to the Russian troops. What little fighting power they had left departed. The VII Army retreated precipitately; the left of the XI Army did likewise, and the VIII Army, whatever might have happened to it otherwise, was forced to retreat rapidly from Stanislaus and vicinity to avoid being flanked. The retreat developed into a rout.

During these occurrences the Russian officers have for the most part conducted themselves with great heroism. In unheard of proportions they have been killed and wounded, and often, I understand, their own men have slaughtered them. The practical abolishment of discipline by the highest authorities left the Russian Army, as it probably would have left any other, without serious military value. . . .

I am writing this communication with many interruptions. It is now July 28th, although I shall not be able to close before a subsequent date. From the standpoint of July 28th the situation is almost as bad as possible. Major Parker reports from Stavka that "everyone here seems depressed and discouraged and some frankly express the belief that the situation is hopeless. . . ."

. . . If Czernowitz is taken, the Rumanian front will be seriously compromised. But one line of rails would connect the Rumanian front with Russia. . . .

. . . To conclude, the Russian situation is not now hopeless, but it may readily become so.

. . . If all of Rumania comes into enemy hands, it is conceivable that, to start a peace movement, Rumania may be tempted with the offer of very favorable terms. The situation in Russia is such that no very attractive asylum can be offered there to the remaining Rumanians.

AUGUST 4, 1917. PARAPHRASE OF TELEGRAM SENT TO
WARCOLSTAFF, WASHINGTON: NO. 27.

5 P.M. The new Commander-in-Chief, Kornilov, who has replaced Brusilov, has a reputation of great firmness, and to restore discipline there is apparently no one better fitted. The desirability of making at once every effort great and small to show the desire of America to cooperate with Russia and America's sympathy for Russia is evident from the present military, industrial and political crises here.

AUGUST 7, 1917. PARAPHRASE OF TELEGRAM SENT
TO WARCOLSTAFF, WASHINGTON: NO. 27.

That coming events may take Russia out of the war within the next few months seems at present at least an even chance. Our larger war plans should be made accordingly* and our efforts to retain Russia redoubled and I so recom-

---

*Here, and throughout Judson's writings, the italicized text indicates that at a later time Judson quoted this passage for use in his "significant quotations from my communications." Judson's own emphases, in his handwritten or typed communications, were made by single or double underlining or the use of capital letters. Here, we shall follow as closely as practicable all of Judson's own usages. In this quotation from the 7 August 1917 cable, Judson took some liberties to eliminate stylistic awkwardness. See "Editor's Note" in the introductory material of this book.

mend. From the present outlook Kerensky will for a time, nominally as the head of a commission of five of his own choice, remain a weak dictator. Possibly he will alienate his old socialist friends; most others are supporting him only to a fall. There are many opinions regarding him. The best opinions have been spread widely; the worst is that he is an impractical hysteric. In connection with his acceptance of post as Commander-in-Chief, Kornilov has imposed conditions to which Kerensky has not as yet assented. The army today is practically without a chief. Every hour the situation changes. Increased political, industrial, food, fuel, and military difficulties are probable as a result of increasing disorganization of railways. There is a report of a German undertaking against Petrograd by way of Finland.[10]

AUGUST 9, 1917. PARAPHRASE OF TELEGRAM SENT TO WARCOLSTAFF, WASHINGTON: NO. 29.

A Recommendation made by the French Aviation Mission is as follows: American combat planes in the number of 300 for the Russian front, including general depot and six groups, of which two in strategic reserve, all in complete units with personnel. Each group to consist of three squadrons and park and to be provided with special railway train. Assistance with a number of French officers, pilots, etc., has been offered. It is believed by the French that the planes should be adapted to cold; double seated; standard rotary motors; ease of assembly and transport. The French also believe that the United States should furnish without personnel about 700 aeroplanes which are needed by Russian Army corps squadrons, but that there is no urgent need for bomb-dropping machines. Will furnish further information if the United States will offer to send aerial units and matériel.[11]

AMERICAN EMBASSY, PETROGRAD
AUGUST 10, 1917

Dearest—

For the first time since I left home I feel nearly settled down with ordinary conveniences for living and working. Hogard is a fine chap and a good housekeeper. We have a good cook. We have some accumulations of food. We have luxurious quarters in a palace. My office is moved to the same place. And both are but a block or two from the Embassy. I am making enough friends to play bridge and pass the idle hours with. I'll tell you about the palace, which was formerly the Spanish Embassy.

You enter a marble hall with a grand stair case. At the door a Persian in native garb takes your hat. You turn to the left into our billiard room with beautiful smoking room attached. Further on to the left you enter our apartment proper. A dining room about 30 feet square beautifully furnished. Beyond are our large and luxurious 2 bed rooms baths etc. Up stairs is a salon about like Mr. Belmont's in Washington, several smaller salons etc. all beautiful and a conservatory. In front of our dining room and over the billiard room are two library rooms I use as offices and a wonderful oriental room where I tell Riggs he will have to receive the lady spies. Riggs is a fine chap—nephew of Miss Jarvie[?]—not a graduate of West Point but of Yale—He has been in the field artillery for about 7 years and is just getting his captaincy. He is popular socially—very English—and I am afraid somewhat spoiled. He has been here nearly 2 years and knows French very well and Russian some. I am brushing up my French and studying Russian.

A great lot of people have just arrived as a Red Cross Commission. Includes Dr. Billings of Chi[cago]—Mr. Harold Swift of same—a Mr. Thompson, multimillionaire of NY, who found the Government was not responding properly to my requests for funds and has told me to draw on him for $5,000 a month up to $15,000—

I forgot to say I have some flour and sugar put away (about 700# of former and 160# of later) and we have grub coming from America. Hope we shall not be looted.

I do not pay the house servants by the way. Only our cook and maid etc.—The rent is very cheap as they wish us here for protecting of their property. We do not pay for heat light or telephone. So in spite of big expenses for some things I think will get along very well. Meat is nearly $1 a pound and most people can get flour and sugar only once a week on the basis of 1# sugar per person per month and I don't know how little flour. We've laid in 6 dozen boxes of sardines too, by the way. The people will suffer for food and warmth. There is no coal and wood is nearly 200 roubles per cord. The rouble is ordinarily worth 52 cents but now only 21. Our proprietor lives with his wife, who is a Circassian beauty (literally) in a part of the house. His name is Melikov. He comes from the Caucasus and is an oil magnate. By reason of his magnetism we expect him to get the oil to keep the palace warm, as his furnace burns oil.

The Ambassador is a good old sport—I lunch with him today—Kerensky will be there—the most interesting and most important man in the world today.

August 14—The luncheon gave opportunity for a study of Kerensky but I do not like to set down much in letters.

Saturday to Monday I spent again at Terjoki in Finland with the Count and Countess Nostitz—It was a large house party and we had wonderful swimming and dancing. Most every one was high in the circles of the old regime. I was interested in Countess Keller especially as I knew the old Count K., her father-in-law, in Manchuria, where he was [serving?]. She is a pretty pathetic little thing, just married, with her husband at the front. Countess Orlov—a divorcé whose former husband is having an affair with her now was another guest—a very bright and beautiful woman. Next Saturday I go out to the Merserves—who also have a place at Terjoki—where I shall see the same people. Merserve runs the American bank here and has a very pretty daughter whom they call the glorieuse be'be'—He is a Harvard man.

August 21 Gave a dinner dance the other night. Everybody had a bully time. Spent Sunday at the Merserves (Terjoki) and had another bully time.

Saturday had a congratulatory telegram indicating my promotion to Brig. General. Hope it is true but shall not let myself feel good till I get it officially. I would so like it just for your sake and Clay's.

Soon I hope to run down to the front again—

Your letters are fine. Am writing Crowder.

Your own.   Billy

AUGUST 16, 1917. <u>MEMORANDUM FOR THE AMBASSADOR:</u>

I recommend that the following cable be sent:
Secstate, Washington.
For Secwar and War College quote I request cables be sent Judson of sailings for Russian ports with principal cargo items. Judson as member Michelson Commission now obliged to get such information. . . . Judson should also be furnished information from time to time as to probable future tonnage allotments and sailings America to Russia. Also Judson

or Embassy should have frequent cabled information as to military preparations in America. Russians continually demanding such from him as for example whether America building 100,000 aeroplanes as per newspapers and if so why none coming to Russia.

AUGUST 16, 1917. <u>MEMORANDUM FOR THE AMBASSADOR:</u>

I suggest the following cable be sent and that every effort be made to expedite it:

Secstate, Washington.

Copy for Secwar and War College

Evacuation Rumania likely in near future gives rise great problem.[12] Rumanian troops about 300,000 feel situation due largely Russian treachery. Under circumstances difficult to persuade them to withdraw to Russia if worst happens and Rumanian Army may disintegrate. Rumanian Government would be exiled in inhospitable Russia without army funds or credit. Enemy could then form de facto government in Rumania with some claim to de jure and conclude separate peace. Situation may be bettered if I can be immediately authorized to offer credit to Rumanian Government of ten million dollars per month on hypothesis carefully worded by me that essential war expenses Rumania, including support of army, will require and be met by approximately that amount. Russia will be correspondingly benefitted as otherwise she has Rumania as present and future liability and United States would use good offices to secure deliveries supplies, etc. No time now for arranging details with Russia, other Allies or Rumania. Offer must be made Rumania now or everlastingly too late. Immediate answer of vital importance.

AUGUST 22, 1917. PARAPHRASE OF TELEGRAM SENT
TO WARCOLSTAFF, WASHINGTON: NO. 31.

Am cabling following to Pershing. "This is telegram number 1 dated August 21st. Due to German and radical propaganda in ranks the Russia line is everywhere very soft. Probably the enemy could advance at almost any point if determined. If given time Kornilov may be able to restore discipline. The Southwest and Rumanian fronts are now receiving his special efforts.

From Stavka Parker reports Rumanian and general situation very discouraging. Russia may not feel able to remain in war long if morale cannot be restored. In all respects the situation is very unstable and uncertain."

With reference to your telegram number 8, Friede is not desired as assistant to Military Attaché here.

AUGUST 23, 1917. MILITARY NOTE IN RE. POLITICAL PARTIES IN RUSSIA[13]

Beginning at the Left: At present the Bolsheviks are composed of the most radical members of the Social Revolutionary and Social Democratic Parties hereafter described. Joined to the Bolsheviks are the anarchists. The Bolsheviks desire an immediate realization of a socialistic program and an immediate peace. The Bolsheviks are also known as Maximalists. The conservative members of the Social Democratic Party are known as Mensheviks or Minimalists.

The Social Revolutionary Party remains from ante-revolutionary times when it constituted the extreme Left. There are two divisions of this party, one which believes in the nationalization and the other in the division of the land. The Social Revolutionary Party is at present hardly as radical as the party next described.

The Social Democratic Party is composed of followers of Karl Marx. They are completely socialistic in accordance with the ordinary definitions of the word. They would not only nationalize the land, but all industry. The more conservative members of the Social Democratic, as well as the Social Revolutionary Parties are disposed to progress reasonably and slowly toward the consummation of their economic and political ambitions. The Social Democratic Party also remains from ante-revolutionary days.

The K.D. (Constitutional Democratic Party), now known as the Kadet Party, remains from ante-revolutionary days. Its principal leader in the Duma was Miliukov. This body was in the Duma affiliated with the two parties previously mentioned in opposition to the government. It is at present very strong, having gained adherents from those of the parties yet to be mentioned. It practically constitutes the Right, at least all of the Right that is active. Its program has been and is probably now a constitutional monarchy with the utmost power lodged in a parliamentary unit to which the Ministers alone would be responsible.

The Republican-Democratic Party—formerly the Progressive: This party, enduring from the ante-revolutionary period, is in its principles practically identical with the Kadet Party. It is not affiliated, however with it, and differing in some respects from the K.D. Party, is occasionally engaging in great controversies with it. This Party has recently lost numbers to the Kadet Party.

In the last Duma the four parties above mentioned constituted the liberal block. They are in the minority, however, until not long before the Revolution, when they were joined by the Octobrists, the assistance of the latter giving the liberal block the majority.

The Octobrists were so named because they supported the program laid down in the Government's manifesto of Oct. 17, 1905. This program proposed gradual progress toward a parliamentary government, as it is understood in England for example. Until the death of Stolypin, the Octobrists supported the Government. The Octobrists are not now an active party seeking adherents, but their leaders are active. Among the principal leaders are Rodzianko and Guchkov. In the old days the Octobrists constituted the Center and generally held the balance of power.

The Nationalists and Reactionaries constituted the remaining parties in ante-revolutionary days. The Nationalists differed not much from the Reactionaries. The Nationalist Party is not now active.

The Reactionary Party, composed of those who opposed parliamentary reforms in all directions, believed that Russia would best be governed by an autocracy. The Reactionaries are not now politically active, but would be the leaders in any counter-revolutionary movement that may develop and would probably support a military dictator should one arise.

The present Provisional Government may be said to occupy the present Center, with very little support from the two active wings, that is to say, from the two Socialistic groups (Bolsheviks) on the Left, or from Kadet Party on the present Right.

In its immediate program the Provisional Government is to strengthen itself through the Army. It does not however, believe itself strong enough to take such measures as abolishing the Committees of the troops, which must be done before the Army can be redisciplined. It is the special duty of Savinkov, the Acting Minister of War, to get the Army in line behind the government and to make it amenable to the government's orders. At present Savinkov is rather discouraged. He says that if he can not accomplish his purpose he will resign. Savinkov is said to be a very strong man, very courageous and determined, and a man of information and judgment. He was formerly a terrorist and a bomb thrower. Savinkov's duty is to act as a bond between Kornilov and Kerensky. It is understood that there is some jealousy of Kornilov existing in the Provisional Government. They probably fear that he will become a military dictator. A few days ago the Cossacks, through a representative Committee, demanded of the Provisional Government that Kornilov be appointed perpetual Commander-in-Chief and given power remote from the front. This demand of the Cossacks has not been published by the government.

I am informed that the General most completely possessing the confidence (political) of the Provisional Government is General Shcherbachev, now commanding the 9th Army. He was a young Colonel at the beginning of the war and is said to be "making his career," i.e.: pretending to liberal principles which he may not really possess.

AUGUST 23, 1917. MILITARY NOTE IN RE PRESENT FRONT COMMANDERS.

The Northern Front is commanded by General Lechitsky,[14] who recently relieved Klembovsky. This is said to have been a good change. Lechitsky is a steady, reliable man with much experience in war, he having been a commander of a division in Manchuria. At the time of the Revolution Lechitsky refused to stay with the Army by reason of his loyalty to the previously established order. He resigned with tears in his eyes. He has been induced to come back by Kerensky.

The Western Front is now commanded by General Denikin, successor to Gurko. He is an excellent man. Gurko, it is said, will be exiled. A few days ago the Provisional Government provided for the exile of certain dangerous characters, and it is supposed that Gurko will be the first to experience the effect of this law. It is supposed that many Bolsheviks will follow him.

The South-Western Front is now commanded by Baluev, a good man.

There has been no change in the command of the Rumanian Front. General Shcherbachev is still acting. For the propose of commanding the Rumanian units of that front Shcherbachev is Adjoint to the King of Rumania.

AUGUST 24, 1917. PARAPHRASE OF
MESSAGE SENT CHIEFWAR 1 DATED 23RD AUGUST
COPY FOR WARCOLSTAFF, WASHINGTON.

Regarding the situation on the Rumanian front we are now awaiting the issue of the fighting which is now in progress. The element of strength there is the Rumanian troops. I am informed by Kornilov that he hopes to stop the enemy offensive on the Southwest front, but it still seems probable that Rumania will be evacuated. The enemy offensives at Fokshany and Okna still continue but at least temporarily, seem slackening. . . .

. . . Projected enemy operations via Finland are persistently reported here. The most demoralized of all the troops are on the North Front. A campaign would be difficult between Riga and Petrograd due to the rains which are soon expected.

A continued demoralization of the Russian Army due to Bolshevik and peace propaganda *is the salient fact of the present situation.* Almost anywhere a determined enemy attack probably would be successful. *The Government apparently fears to take all the necessary measures thus obstructing efforts to re-discipline the Army.* It is rumored that there is jealousy of Kornilov. Unpublished demands have been made by the Cossacks on the Government that there be a great increase in Kornilov's powers. The plans of the enemy may be, first, to occupy the line of Pruth or Dniester and, second, start an offensive further to the north in an effort, before the winter, to induce a separate peace with Russia. The long endurance of the present Russian Government is not certain. A struggle may follow between the radicals and a military dictator. The interests of the United States, if such a struggle arises, would apparently be on the side of the military dictator, who probably would continue the war. No one can foretell.

AUGUST 24, 1917. MILITARY NOTE IN RE KORNILOV
AND THE REDISCIPLINING OF THE ARMY

This morning there is announced the resignation of Savinkov, which, however, has not yet been accepted. Savinkov is evidently urging strong measures for redisciplining the Army, Kornilov obviously concurring with him. The Provisional Government evidently is not yet ready to adopt proper measures to strengthen the hands of Kornilov.

There is published this morning a resolution adopted by the Council of Cossacks on the 22nd inst., which contains substantially the following:

(1) The Council of Cossacks does not recognize that the Council of Workmens' and Soldiers' Delegates has the right to interject itself into the matters of their organizing of the Army by General Kornilov.

(2) General Kornilov ought not to be replaced. He is the real popular chief, and according to the opinion of the majority of the population, he is the sole general capable of reestablishing the strength of the Army and of leading the country out of the painful situation in which it finds itself.

(3) The Council of Cossacks declares that the replacement of General Kornilov would have a very bad effect upon the morale of the Cossacks, showing them the uselessness of any further sacrifice in view of the hesitation of the government to take measures for the safety of the Fatherland, the honor of the Army and the liberty of the people. The council considers it its duty to declare to the Government and to the people that they reject all responsibility for the front and the rear if General Kornilov is replaced.

(4) The Cossacks strongly assure the hero of the Army, General Kornilov, and the hero of the Revolution, Kerensky, of their complete submission and their aid without limitation.

AMERICAN EMBASSY, PETROGRAD
AUGUST 27, 1917

Dearest:

I am so glad you stayed in Chicago—and Milwaukee as long as you did. It must be hot in Lexington and I wish my beautiful angel to get the good of part of a summer in the cool north. It is most exasperating not to hear oftener from home and have later news from there. Is Clay an officer, I wonder? I have written to Crowder and would like to have Clay detailed in his Dept. if possible. It would be better for him to keep thus a little in touch with the law. I have not yet given up hope that he will be a great lawyer some day.

I have heard nothing more about the Brig. Generalcy since the one telegram of congratulations. I hope it is true of course but am not permitting myself to feel too good about it yet. There may be some mistake.

Parker, who has been at Stavka, has been called back to Washington. I am sorry, but he has wanted to go from the first. He has been appointed Colonel in the National Army.

I wish you would send me 3 suits of big [country?] flannel pajamas, in the pouch from State Department. Put them in 3 separate packages and mail at different times.

They are having a big conference at Moscow of all Russian factions. I hope it will result in a stronger government and in measures to restore discipline in Army. Things look a little bit better for the Russians just now. I pray that improvement may continue. The great bulk of the Russians are like plantation negroes [*sic*] in development. And only force exerted from above the masses can control them.

I send my angel my very best love "and a thousand kisses"—and the same to our boy—

Faithfully yours,

AUGUST 29, 1917. MEMORANDUM FOR THE AMBASSADOR:

The crying need from the standpoint of the Allies, whomever they may be and wherever they may be conducting operations, is the reestablishment of discipline in the Russian Army—one might say the recreation of an army, from the heterogeneous mass of humanity that remains mobilized but that is not an army at all because it lacks the very breath of life of an army: to wit, discipline.

In my opinion the complete reestablishment of discipline can be accomplished substantially as follows:

(1) Restore the death penalty throughout Russia for military crimes which are ordinarily punished with death in the armies of all civilized countries, including the crimes of desertion, disobedience in the presence of the enemy, conspiracy, mutiny and the use of violence against a superior officer under certain circumstances, etc.

(2) Abolish the Committees composed of members of the various units.

(3) Abolish the Commissars.

(4) Restore the marks of respect and subordination, such as the salute.

(5) Restore generally those practices and penalties which formerly prevailed in the Russian Army and which now prevail in the armies of all nations.

(6) Support the authority of officers from top to bottom. Demand of them that they exercise a rigid control over their men. Also at all times demand of them that they train the men of their commands intensively;

and again and always support the officers in all measures necessary to be taken in this connection.

(7) Place under the command of the Commander-in-Chief all mobilized men and units throughout Russia. The measures adopted for the promotion of discipline should, like the authority of the Commander-in-Chief, be coextensive with Russia.

I have no doubt that the opinions of all the trained officers of all the Allied Armies would be in substantial accord with my own as above expressed.

The present time seems to mark a turning point in the history of the Russian revolutionary movement. It seems to me that Mr. Kerensky, returning from the Moscow Conference, must contemplate with the utmost seriousness and many doubts the path he will pursue in the immediate future with reference to the Army. It seems easy to prophesy that unless a rigid discipline is soon restored the country will drift into anarchy, which would eventually be followed by strong government of the old autocratic type.

I suggest that this opportune moment the most earnest representations be made to Mr. Kerensky by all of the Allied powers that the measures suggested above be adopted at once.

The other Allies are faithfully performing their respective parts in carrying on this war. They have been sacrificing the lives of their men and the material well-being of their peoples to give time to Russia to make the military readjustments that have been necessarily incident to the Revolution.

It does not seem fair for Russia to require her allies to make further sacrifices to give time for readjustments of which the necessity must not be obvious to all. It is not fair to Russia herself. It is not fair to humanity thus to prolong the World War unnecessarily.

It is not fair to the cause of democracy so to conduct affairs as to lead to the discrediting of democracy.

It seems to me that the utmost pressure, present, continuous and simultaneous, should be exerted in this matter.

AUGUST 30, 1917. MEMORANDUM FOR THE AMBASSADOR:

The following thoughts occur to me in connection with my memorandum of yesterday in re the redisciplining of the Russian Army.

It seems that America could make an especially strong plea on the ground that it is peculiarly interested in having no failure of democracy occur in Russia.

The Provisional Government has already discovered and now admits that it was in error in abolishing the death penalty. In the same way it will discover, perhaps when it is too late, that the other measures taken subversive of discipline represent mistakes. In this matter it certainly seems safe to accept the experience of all armies in all countries and at all times. Certainly the present condition of the Russian Army as to fighting power, in the presence of a strong and locally victorious enemy, indicates that if errors are committed they should be on the safe side, that is to say, the advice of experts should be accepted and the voice of Russia's interested Allies should be heard in this matter.

If Russia fails, through a neglect to rediscipline her army (and she can fail in no other way), the war may be lost. And if the war should be lost the pains of defeat would fall principally upon Russia of all the larger powers. America certainly would be immune from such pains and penalties by reason of her geographical isolation, her fleet and her natural resources. Russia would offer to Germany the greatest available prizes of territory and commercial and industrial dependence. And Germany would certainly foster in Russia the creation of a government satisfactory to herself and not considered dangerous as an example to the democratic elements of her own people. A victorious Germany would surely remain a non-democratic Germany for at least a generation.

AUGUST 31, 1917. MEMORANDUM FOR THE AMBASSADOR:

With reference to the question of the reestablishment of discipline in the Russian Army, as to which I have sent you several memoranda, it seems fitting to submit the following:

I spent more than a year with the Russian Army in 1904–05 during the Japanese War. I lived always in closest contact with the troops, with regiments, brigades and corps. I had every opportunity to observe the relations existing between officers and men and the state and character of discipline throughout the Army.

I desire now to bear witness not only to the high character of that discipline but to the manner in which the officers exercised control. I never saw a Russian officer raise his hand against a man, or abuse him orally, or behave in a tyrannous manner, or abuse his authority in any manner whatsoever. I made note of the fact that the relations of officers to their men were of a fatherly character; that the men were often addressed by affectionate diminutives; that the officers were universally solicitous of the comfort and well-being of their men; and finally that the men regarded their officers with great respect and frequently with affection, and that obedience to authority was rendered in a fashion at once complete and cheerful.

Now any state of discipline is almost entirely lacking. I do not attempt to give instances such as have abounded in the daily press. They are well known to everyone. But I venture to quote as follows from a very recent report by an American officer at the front:

> "the evening of Aug. 14, in the Sharp-shooter Division of this Corps, the men of the regiment in reserve murdered their Colonel and one of their Captains. Some six other officers were so threatened, they fled to these Hdqrs. The two murdered officers visited these Hdqrs. the day before their death. The Colonel was a young officer, on duty with the regiment since the war began, enthusiastic and able, whose promotion to command the regiment was acceptable to the men. The Captain also was an excellent young officer with whom I had some conversation in French. The Col. reported that the men were becoming surly — saying the replacing of the death penalty in the Army Code was an attempt on the part of the officers to bring about the old pre-revolution conditions. Nothing done to date to punish the guilty troops, but an Inspector (semi-military official with title 'Commissar,' from Army Hdqrs.) came today to investigate. Have not heard result of same."

There may indeed be evidences of temporary improvement here and there if half-way measures are adopted. But one of the most serious elements in the situation is this: that the corps of professional officers is rapidly losing its morale. Nothing can arrest the constant and inevitable deterioration of the officers as a whole, but the adoption of such measures as I suggested in my memorandum to you of Aug. 28th. If the professional officer is practically lost to the Army, the latter will be beyond the possibility of regeneration even if the proper measures be later adopted. It is by reason of this fact that efforts to secure discipline should be made without delay.

AMERICAN EMBASSY, PETROGRAD
SEPTEMBER 1, 1917

Dearest:

I am writing to you before anything else is thought of today, because I want to congratulate you and Clay upon my having become a Brigadier

General. I have just received the official cable to "wire my acceptance," which is rather a joke, isn't it?

I know it will seem a whole lot better for you to be Mrs. General Judson—And I know it will fill the soul of Clay with joy—And why shouldn't you and he have a little good luck for a change. As for me I have been lucky enough in life to have such a wife and such a son.

Last night I had the Wrights to dinner—and the Marshalls—the former the Counselor of the Embassy and the latter nice English people—also a Mr. Bau, a N.Y. banker who knows Frank Van W——— and a member of the Red Cross Commission. After dinner Count Keller and his wife and a number of others came in and we danced in our fine room to the phonograph. Whirled and had a bully time—I showed them your sweet picture and Clay's and confessed I wouldn't have whirled in the presence of the latter—

September 5—Have been terribly busy. Organized a movement to get the Ambassador to demand the redisciplining of the Russian Army—That is the burning question now. The jig will soon be up if the army is not regimented. The earlier step[s] demoralizing the army were taken by the socialists-radicals because they wished to lessen the authority of officers lest there be counter-revolution. The officers have had a h_ll of a time behaving gallantly however. The men shoot them— put them out—don't obey them—The army is like a brick house without mortar. It is perfectly "soft" when the Germans hit it. Like a prize fighter who is groggy and nearly knocked out. Kornilov could probably restore the army if given a show by the Government—They are afraid to give him the proper support because the radicals would object and the others might use army for counter-revolution, and there you are. Meantime Riga is taken and the Germans are heading this way at the rate of 10 miles per day, the Russians interposing little resistance.

Went to a Russian party last night—big banker—big palace—after dinner in the Turkish room over the coffee the older woman embarrassed the younger ones by playing a sort of game in which each woman or girl had to reply (facetiously) to the query whether she would rather be ravished by a German or a Bolshevik. There was great fun—some said they would have to try both before they could reply—some begged the question by expressing preference for a British officer (several being present) or an American (out of compliment to us).

Such freedom of speech is a sign of the hysterical condition of all Russia.

September 10 later. News just received of Kornilov's declared dictatorship—civil war looms up—Shall probably not go Jassy tonight.

I enclose a Kodak of General Scott and some of the rest of us.

September 11. Don't go to Jassy. Kerensky-Kornilov troubles may lead to anything—or may be compromised.

I close hastily as hear of pouch and am so busy, no time for ages.

SEPTEMBER 3, 1917. MEMORANDUM FOR
THE AMBASSADOR:

I respectfully submit these further observations upon the subject of the vital and immediate need of Russian Governmental action to support the military administration in redisciplining the Army:

Half-measures bring great danger in their train. The mere reestablishment of the death penalty, for example, without proper machinery to enforce it, may readily serve only to provoke trouble. Apparently many of the men believe that the death penalty has been restored at the insistence of the officer class and for its own gratification. Alleging this very thing men have killed their officers. The administration of this law is not apparently in the hands of the officers themselves but of the Commissars, who are irresponsible political agents in greater practical authority than the Army Chiefs themselves. The whole procedure further discredits the authority of officers. And as essential part of the reestablishment of discipline is a restoration of authority to the military chiefs and to officers generally.

The great trouble with Russia today is the lack of discipline everywhere; on the railroads, in the factories and at the mines as well as in the Army. Careful study will show that if the Government cannot use force in the last analysis, it cannot impose discipline and order anywhere. And the Government cannot use force unless it has a disciplined Army. Without the latter it cannot protect foreign interests in Russia. It cannot even continue long to assert its right to exist as against the forces of disorder. Along whatever path one seeks relief for the troubles besetting Russia (and throughout Russia, her Allies), one always arrives at a disciplined Army as a point of departure.

SEPTEMBER 3, 1917. NO. 1208
FROM: THE MILITARY ATTACHÉ, PETROGRAD, RUSSIA.
TO: THE CHIEF, WAR COLLEGE DIVISION, GENERAL STAFF,
WASHINGTON, D.C.
SUBJECT: MONTHLY RESUME.

. . . During the early part of August the enemy salient . . . .projecting
toward the . . . Dniester was widened toward the south. Czernowitz fell
on August 3rd, and practically all of Galicia and Bukovina were recovered by the enemy. To the north of the salient above referred to Brody
and vicinity were taken.

The utter demoralization of the Russian Army during the period of
its retreat from Galicia and Bukovina has been dwelt upon in press accounts. It is only necessary to say that with a few notable exceptions the
Army revealed itself to be an undisciplined horde which retreated for
the most part more rapidly than the enemy pursued. In this connection
I enclose two press accounts of the horrors of Kalushch and Tarnopol.

It is fair to say that the officers behaved with heroism and devotion.

. . . I am convinced that the war question of greatest and most immediate
importance today at once to the Allies and to the Central Powers is the state
of discipline in the Russian Army. Believing this I have handed a series of
memoranda to our Ambassador, urging that the Government be pressed by the
Allied ambassadors one and all to take at once the steps it must take sooner or
later if the Russian Army is ever to have its fighting strength restored. I am
taking up this same subject with the military representatives of the other embassies. I enclose copies of these memoranda. . . .

. . . The Moscow Conference, called by the Provisional Government,
was attended by representative of nearly all elements interested in the
welfare of Russia. There was some thought that the Conference might
endeavor to take matters into its own hands, perhaps forming a new
government. On the whole, however, the Conference seems to have lent
stability to the existing government. . . .

SEPTEMBER 7, 1917. PARAPHRASE OF TELEGRAM SENT
TO WARCOLSTAFF (WAR COLLEGE STAFF),
WASHINGTON: NO. 34, SIXTH.

Since September 1st the Germans have been reenforced near Riga with
three divisions and the arrival of more is reported. Among those arriv-

ing are two Guard Divisions; the reinforcements include one from French front and two or more divisions from near Tarnopol. On the evening of September 2d the withdrawal of the last Russian troops at Riga began. On September 4th the German advance reached east of Riga an arc with a 40 verst radius. Offering little resistance the Russians are in rapid retreat. Between Riga and Pskov there are several good lines but their successful occupation may be prevented by demoralization. To seize the Reval peninsula and occupy the line Pskov to Dvina near Dvinsk may be the aim of the Germans. There is an increasing bad effect on Petrograd morale.

Following July 1st the German plan was apparently to take Rumania and then turn to northern operation as a demonstration against Petrograd. A halt on account of the lateness of the season was induced in the Rumanian movement which was not completed in order that the second step of the plan might be carried out. Evidently the Germans desire, even at great risk elsewhere, to take advantage this summer of the demoralization of the Russian Army. After halt in northern operation now in progress the Rumanian operation may be resumed.

If given free hand by Government Kornilov thinks he could regenerate army, but government is afraid to shock radicals by vigorous measures and also afraid to yield power to the chiefs of the army lest there occur a counter-revolution. Kornilov, according to a statement by Kerensky, has a free hand, but former says latter agrees with him in principle only not supporting by measures of a practical nature.

There is a multiplication of reports of a probable German descent on Finland near entrance to the Gulf of Finland. Assistance from the Finns, who are seriously disaffected, is hoped for by the Germans. In Finland the Russian troops mostly lacking in training and discipline number about 50,000. Training is neglected and discipline is absent from most Russian units.

SEPTEMBER 10, 1917. MILITARY NOTE.
IN RE SUGGESTIONS TO AMBASSADOR FOR USE
IN URGING COMPROMISE.[15]

The trouble with Russia as an ally has for several months resided in lack of the morale and discipline of her army.

The men for the most part have not wished to fight; they could only have fought well if disciplined and under the control and direction of intelligent men educated in the art of war and accustomed to command. It is not necessary to know why measures were adopted and policies followed which destroyed discipline and undermined the authority of the officers. Perhaps these measures and policies were born of political necessity. The motives inspiring most of the authors of them may well have been good and patriotic.

Today, however, is not the time to investigate motives any more than it is the time to consult political expediency.

Arrayed on one side are those who would regenerate the Army, including practically the entire officer class. Arrayed on the other side are those who wish for peace and those who desire the successes of Germany, even if also there are those who honestly but mistakenly believe that if the Army Chiefs are defeated the Army can be regenerated from a mass of peasants wishing to stop fighting, with no trained officer class to lead and control them.

The conditions are such that if the Army Chiefs lose in the present conflict with the Temporary Government anarchy will result with the utmost certainty. Russia will remain at war indeed, but not with the common enemy. The Kaiser will have won and Russia will have lost everything, including the peace that so many cherish.

Her allies foresee that if the present conflict is not compromised while there may yet be time Russia will necessarily cease to be a factor in the present war. She will have betrayed her Allies, including America, who was so much impelled by sympathy for Russia to become her comrade in arms.

The result of the war perhaps hangs in the balance.

If you persist with such results impending, where in the future will be found nations daring to be the friends of Russia? What nation would dare associate itself with her? Only Germany, whose slave Russia would become financially, industrially and commercially—nay, also politically.

We demand, in the name of her Allies and in the name of Russia herself, whose destiny, if you do not yield a little, appears but too plain to our calmer and less heated vision, that at once you compromise these differences, either through our mediation or that of a patriotic Russian Commission.

We demand at once an armistice and an amicable arrangement—which alone will enable Russia to endure as a nation and to resist the common enemy until she can through an appropriate body frame her new organic law.

Surrender personal opinion, personal ambition—surrender personal and official dignity, or the moment draws near perhaps when Russia, having disgraced the name of nation, will disintegrate and die and become an offensive thing. The people of Russia do not deserve the fate that would await her and them. Prove by yielding that Russians can compromise and so are fit for self government.

Do not let Russia become a reproach in the mouths of Pole-French men and Belgians whom she will doom to the German yoke; not a repulsive thing to men and women everywhere, from Canada and New Zealand across the Americas to Italy and Serbia and Rumania; nor a mere laughing stock of the enemy nations who would tear her rotten carcass to pieces.

SEPTEMBER 10, 1917. PARAPHRASE OF TELEGRAM SENT TO WARCOLSTAFF, WASHINGTON: NO. 35.

Between Kornilov, who has assumed virtual military dictatorship, and Kerensky, has developed a conflict. Kornilov has been relieved by the latter, and Klembovsky, now commanding the Riga front, has been assigned to his vacancy. It is said that General Klembovsky refuses to accept. Kerensky is said to have failed to adopt measures to reestablish discipline in the army, and to restore order, which is the principle reason for the present situation. The troops of Kornilov are reported to be on their way to Petrograd, but the line is cut. It is reported that Kornilov is to be supported by practically all of the Conservative and intelligent elements in Russia, including some of the strong men of the original revolutionary cabinet, also by the Army Chiefs and the officers of the Army in general, and probably by most of the few remaining reliable troops, including the Cossacks. Supporting Kerensky are those who have formerly been in favor of peace, and the Radical Socialists, and also a portion of the soldiers who have been opposing discipline, and who are in favor of peace. Under the conditions stated, if Kornilov does not win, anarchy will probably result. The aims of Kornilov have not been published, but they apparently include the reestablishment of discipline in the Army, internal order generally, and the continued prosecution of the War, followed by a Government to be chosen by the Russian people. Kornilov is making some efforts to reach a compromise, but he probably has no hopes along these lines, and merely expects to demonstrate that he deserves to be supported.[16]

Unless compromises are soon arranged, there is an immediate prospect of civil war, and a temporary increased weakness against the foreign enemy.

It may be that in the foregoing some sacrifices of accuracy have been made to promptness, but I will soon cable further. I have changed my plans about going to Rumania, as the Ambassador has detained me here.

SEPTEMBER 10, 1917. MILITARY NOTE.
IN RE KORNILOV MOVEMENT.

Last night at a social gathering I learned from newspaper writers (Russian) that Kornilov had declared a dictatorship and was sending troops to Petrograd. In the morning (Sept. 10th) this was verified by an edict of Kerensky's. . . . I immediately visited the Ambassador and urged him to get in touch with the Allied Heads of Missions, visit Kerensky, and urge a compromise. He arranged to visit Tereschenko at 12:45. He was told there that the two sides were of about equal strength and that Kerensky would defend his Government. The British and French Ambassadors had been in communication since the night before and were at the Foreign Ministry at the same time with our Ambassador. The British Ambassador (but not ours) had been warned to leave Petrograd; on the ground that there might be fighting and disorder there. He called a meeting of the heads of foreign diplomatic missions for 5:00 P.M. At such meeting it was determined that the missions would not leave town. There followed a meeting of the heads of Allied Missions, when there was adopted a resolution offering the Temporary Government their good offices to mediate the differences between Kornilov and the Temporary Government. Tereschenko received this offer with apparent pleasure and facilitated a telegram to Stavka to Allied military representatives making the offer of mediation known to them. The Military Missions at Stavka had previously informed their Embassies that Kornilov had suggested to them that they advise, through their Embassies, that the Temporary Government offer no resistance.

It is understood that Kornilov offered to make Kerensky Minister of Justice, to keep Nekrasov, Tereschenko and one or two others of the old Government and submitted names for the proposed new members of a government, presumably under himself. This was refused. Some of the Ministers have resigned. . . .

Guchkov's secretary tells me Guchkov has joined Stavka. Rodzianko is at Moscow and may help there to form a new "facade" of civil government; which may be located at Moscow or nearer front.

I have today sent long telegrams on situation to War College Staff and to General Pershing in France.

Nearly all officers are with Kornilov.

Later refused to vacate Commandership in Chief. Klembovsky, Commander of Northern Front, refused to accept when appointed. So has Alekseev, who came to Petrograd for conference.

Line to Mogilev reported broken near Peterhoff and Kornilov's troops reported en route and at Luga here it is said certain artillery surrendered to them. R.R. reported broken between Petrograd and Moscow at Chuboro, above points about 120 and 100 versts out, respectively.

No disorders in Petrograd or signs of trouble. Several infantry regiments, cavalry, artillery and Cossacks reported for Kornilov.

Kornilov troops advancing include R.R. troops, Cossacks, "Wild Division"[17] and 4 brigades of artillery.

SEPTEMBER 11, 1917. TUESDAY. MILITARY NOTE IN RE. KORNILOV MOVEMENT.

Petrograd troops a short distance out (say 15 or 20 versts) reported holding line from Gulf of Neva. It is said that they will not fire on advancing Kornilov troops. Latter have Narva, thus cutting all lines but Finland and Vologda.

Kerensky said Kornilov had sent Lvov to him with his proposition. Kornilov denies this and says Lvov came to him as agent of Kerensky....

It is said that Alekseev and Likomsky furnish largely the brains for the Kornilov movement.

It is said that Kornilov's coup-d'etat was to have been sprung tomorrow (St. George's fete day) when troops would be here from out of town parading. For some reason it was started prematurely.

It is said that 5,000 officers in Petrograd have formed a machine gun brigade; that 2 divisions of Kumanski Cossacks are approaching Petrograd from Finland.

The Ambassador says that Tereschenko in reply to Missions' note of last night has declined mediation, saying it "was not time" or "was no time" for same. Tereschenko said Government would not publish offer of mediation, as in its form it seemed to place Kornilov and Provisional

Government on equal terms. Tereschenko telephoned Ambassador, who had called him up to ask whether reports of compromise were correct that everything was going very well for the government; that a division approaching Petrograd had deserted Kornilov for Keresnky. All quiet in Petrograd. Both sides claim all front Commanders except Denikin, who is out for Kornilov.

SEPTEMBER 11, 1917. MEMORANDUM FOR THE AMBASSADOR:

I suggest following cable be sent:
Secstate, Washington, Copy to Secwar. Following from Judson quote Referring 1674 September first from Sec State critical situation Petrograd causes Ambassador retain me here. Without visiting Rumania I submit following on Rumanian situation:

Existing Rumanian Government will in all probability continue war if physically possible. Germans could probably now or after taking Moldavia form complaisant government within Rumanian territory and make peace with same if they so desire for morale effect, but may prefer to annex Rumania to Bulgaria and Austria. I think Germans would prefer the peace. Russia at least temporarily weakened by present crisis may conceivably make peace. Kornilov if he wins against Kerensky has still to secure activity and support of great inert peace inclined Russian masses which now unorganized and behind no one. Rumanian situation largely swallowed up in present unresolved Russian situation. Rumania out of it if Russia makes peace. If Russia continued war, present Rumanian Government and Army, subject to extreme contingencies of war, will continue also. Present intentions and spirit Government and Army reasonably satisfactory, but if to remain so, especially under conditions which may reasonably be expected, including evacuation Rumania, help must be afforded now by us. Rumanians look on Russia as broken reed.

Referring 1675 September first from Secstate. From Russia can be obtained certain food stuffs including grain products and perhaps depending on changing war conditions horses, some small arms, guns, ammunition and miscellaneous articles; from United States such essentials for carrying on war as cannot be obtained in Russia. . . .

Suggest all purchases in United States be supervised by our government there as is understood to be done with purchases for Russia.

Practically all purchases in Russia would be from Russian Government which now purchases all grain from producers. . . .

Present Russian Government says is making no discrimination in supplying its own and Rumanian armies; perhaps true but result is Rumanian army which is only reliable large body of troops on this front is not nearly as well supplied as could be under arrangement proposed and which its relative quality deserves in interest of Allies. Not satisfied to remain thus at mercy of Russian Government. Extent and character of backing by United States will largely determine character and numbers of Rumanian army of future. Russia now charges England and France each one third cost of supplies furnished Rumania. Thus credit to Rumania would benefit Russia, France and England as well as United States, latter as partner in conduct of war. End quote.

SEPTEMBER 12, 1917. MILITARY NOTE.
IN RE KORNILOV MOVEMENT.

Reports are that Guchkov and Denikin arrested; also many others.

From this point of view it looks bad for Kornilov this morning. "Novoye Vremya" and "Russkoye Slovo," the 2 best papers in Russia, suppressed by Kerensky. Papers full of lies (such as that relating to action of Ambassadors). Nine-tenths are on fence and if either side can make its own success seem assured (by lies or fact) it wins.

All wires reported closed from midnight Sept. 10–11.

1:30 P.M. called to Embassy. Ambassador just from Foreign Office with British, French and Italian Ambassadors. Informed by Tereschenko that he was in session with Alekseev all last night (till 2 A.M.) trying to persuade him to accept Command-in-Chief. At 3:30 A.M. Kornilov presented offer to surrender (resign?) by hand of Captain Muravyev. At 8:30 Kerensky telephone Alekseev and latter accepted. A military man to be Secretary of War and another Secretary of the Navy. Evidently a compromise in some degree, as Alekseev and Kornilov represented same issue—redisciplining of Army. Alekseev has greater intellect, but less force, they say, than Kornilov.

British Military Attaché believes failure of Kornilov means Russia done for during this war. French Attaché believes in waiting 2 weeks before giving up hope, giving new conditions time to reveal themselves. Allied Missions' attitude toward Kornilov and Kerensky as revealed in their offer to mediate, was greatly misrepresented in press by statement indicating their opposition to Kornilov.

SEPTEMBER 13, 1917. MILITARY NOTE.

Saw Countess Keller at her home. Alekseev stayed there during his recent visit here. He left for Stavka last night. Countess Keller said Alekseev refused to accept Command in Chief for long time (2:00 A.M.), saying he wished to see Kornilov first, but finally accepted at 8:30 A.M. by telephone to Kerensky, without seeing Kornilov. Kornilov surrendered (or gave up post?) at 3:30 A.M. Threats of arrest, promises, lies used with Alekseev; 3 Cossack deserters used to impersonate a Committee from Kornilov's soldiers anxious to surrender and to know what to do with their officers; misrepresentation of position of Ambassadors. . . . Alekseev very hopeless as to situation, seeing how officers have been discredited. (Rumors of murders of officers by men). Alekseev demanded immunity for all.

Kerensky to be Commander-in-Chief and much at Stavka; North Front, Ruzsky; S.W. Front, Dragomirov.

Plan October—Bolshevik uprising—Kornilov to Petrograd to subdue same—Coup d'etat. Hand forced by Lvov, emissary from Kerensky; asked Kornilov to act as one of 5 to form Government with Kerensky. Kornilov refused. Lvov may have misrepresented Kornilov to Kerensky. Kerensky telephoned Kornilov and relieved him. Kornilov refused to give up post. Kornilov apparently not yet arrested. Military Missions asked to leave Stavka. Many arrests, including Guchkov. 50,000 workmen around and on line in front of city with certain troops apparently.

Germans concentrating troops about Riga, apparently for grand offensive.

SEPTEMBER 14, 1917. (NIGHT). MILITARY NOTE.

This morning at 2:00 A.M. while Kerensky with his old associates was trying to form a new Ministry and was about ready to announce one, a delegation from the Soviet told him (it is understood) that no Kadets could enter the Ministry if S.[ocial] Democrats were to hold portfolios. Cabinet meeting broke up in some excitement.

It is understood that the Soviet was formed Militia subject only to its own orders, of some 50,000 armed workmen.

Tereschenko said he made his acceptance conditional upon; (1) postponement of internal reforms till end of War; (2) restoration of discipline in Army; (3) punishment of murderers of certain officers.

General Krimov committed suicide after interview with Kerensky yesterday. Krimov was Tereschenko's friend. They had plotted together with another man to kill the Emperor on March 5th last. I saw Tereschenko today with the Ambassador.

The resolution of the Allied Missions, offering mediation between Government and Kornilov, which was sent to Belgian General at Stavka for presentation to Kornilov, informally, was so presented and was accepted by Kornilov on Tuesday before 7:00 P.M. (He "surrendered" at 3:30 A.M. Wednesday.)

This resolution was distorted and given out here in Wednesday morning's papers so as to make it appear that Allies condemned Kornilov.

Allied Missions met today at call of our Ambassador and discussed very serious situation, which points to anarchy. They meet again at 3:00 tomorrow.

About 15 1/2 Div. Infantry and 4 1/2 Div. Cavalry now on Riga Front. Secret agents say big German offensive begins tomorrow, with object in 2 weeks of taking Pskov.

Q. M. Gen. Potopov asked if we had heard anything about Sweden—many German officers entering same. German expedition against Finland (30,000) postponed till near end of Pskov offensive.

Many officers being killed or committing suicide.

SEPTEMBER 15, 1917. PARAPHRASE OF
TELEGRAM SENT TO WARCOLSTAFF WASHINGTON: NO. 37.

It seems that General Alekseev accepted his post under considerable pressure, which included threats, and that he has not much hope. He was very close to the Kornilov movement, which failed because it was a few days premature. The soldiers are now murdering many officers. By a vote of 279 against 115 the Soviet makes the following demands. There are to be no Kadets in the Ministry, the land is to be nationalized without compensating the owners, the workmen are to have control over production and distribution, there must be an immediate offer of a democratic peace to all nations now engaged in war, capital punishment at the front to be abolished. There must be freedom for political agitation and organization in the Army, and the latter must be freed from all leaders considered counter-revolutionary. Local units are to elect the Commissars, and so forth. The Soviet and Socialists use the term Counter-Revolutionary to include all political opposition. The 40,000 armed Bolsheviks and workmen, who were used by the Government against the Kornilov movement, now constitute a militia under the Soviet. There is a revolution against the Government under General Kaledin, but it is impossible to make an estimate of their strength. Kerensky does not seem inclined to yield to the Soviet. As he made use of the forces of the Soviet against Kornilov, I think it doubtful whether he can now use the Army to resist the Soviet forces if a conflict arises. The strength of the Bolsheviks is apparently increasing. Social as well as political revolution is desired, and the situation is approaching anarchy.

According to reports the Germans are sending reinforcements to the North Front with the apparent idea of renewing operations in that vicinity. The Russian General Staff are reported to be uneasy about the attitude of Sweden. The arrest of Romanovsky[?], chief of the General Staff and many others, including Kornilov and his chief of staff, has been announced.

The expedition of the enemy against Finland has been delayed apparently in order to continue further Finnish propaganda. The temporary Government now provisionally consists of five men, including Kerensky, Tereschenko, one admiral and one general. The departments are under administrative heads.

SEPTEMBER 15, 1917. MILITARY NOTE.

A day of surprises.

In the morning we had information of the action of the Soviet, 279 to 115 adopting an extreme socialistic program. Later in the day Tereschenko told our Ambassador that the Soviet had told the soldiers not to obey Kerensky and had summoned the Baltic Fleet to Petrograd. Tereschenko sent for Blair, the British Attaché, and told him to tell the other Attachés to ask for such guards for their Embassies as were thought proper. The French asked for one immediately. We asked for a small guard to be sent when the Petrograd District deemed it necessary. The British asked for 2 orderlies but got their own men in (they have perhaps 40 officers and 20 men in town).

The British have 2 barges chartered and we tried to charter 1 for our colony.

At 7:30 P.M. Prince telephoned that the Council (Soviet), by a close vote, supported Kerensky. Has Kerensky yielded or has the Soviet been bought up?

SEPTEMBER 17, 1917. PARAPHRASE OF
TELEGRAM SENT TO WARCOLSTAFF WASHINGTON. NO. -38-

. . . The joint session of the Executive Committees Workmens and Soldiers Deputies, and Peasants Council rejected the Radical resolution referred to in my number 37, and adopted a substitute calling a convention of all the Democratic and Radical elements for September 25, "to decide the problem of organization of a Government to lead the country until the Constituent Assembly," and favouring democratization of the Army, and changes in the higher commands. Kerensky has decreed a Republic, and confirmed the Government of five men referred to in my number 37, thus some evidence of compromise. The Ministry of Foreign Affairs says that Kerensky will insist on a Coalition Ministry, while apparently Soviet and later Democratic Convention or Congress will demand responsible Socialist Ministry. The government has expected a Radical uprising in Petrograd the last few days, and has offered and sent a guard to the Embassy. The Government will probably go to Moscow in a short time, accompanied by the Embassies, etc.

Kerensky has gone to the Stavka at Mogilev.

The present situation is that the Government is very weak, as effective support by any aggregation of strong forces seems uncertain.

The Germans have reinforced the 8th Army operating in the Riga district, from 8 1/2 infantry and 3 1/2 cavalry divisions on August 29, to 15 1/2 infantry and 4 1/2 cavalry divisions on September 12. Fighting is in progress 30 miles East of Riga along the river Aa.

The German attack is indecisive as yet. . . .

AMERICAN EMBASSY, PETROGRAD
SEPTEMBER 19, 1917

Dearest:

Have just been reading your sweet letters and one from Clay—to Aug. 3. I suppose Clay is a 1st Lieutenant now and I doubt not will soon be a

Captain if he is the top of the list in his regiment—someone will doubt-less drop out. It is splendid that he so enjoys and profits by his present life.

Since I last wrote the Kornilov movement has been suppressed. It was sprung prematurely I have learned—and had trouble getting started—although its adherents claim they had with them in hope and sympathy the great bulk of the intelligent people. Kerensky is now Commander-in-Chief of the Army—with Alekseev as Chief-of-Staff. Alekseev seems to have represented all that Kornilov did. The great task remains to discipline the army.

Meanwhile the radical wing of the Soviet (or Council of Workmen and Soldiers) seems to be growing and a conflict looms up between Soviet and Kerensky. There is fear of a Commune here any day.

I am going to hand this to Mr. Crane of Chicago who leaves for home tonight. It won't be very long as I have so many things to do.

Parker has gone to the States—Kerth is back here from the front. I hate to think of going away from Petrograd if the Government shall move (as is talked of) to Moscow (this is confidential). We are so comfortably installed.

I play bridge a good deal with the Ambassador and others and "play round" enough on occasional evenings to keep from getting stale. Last night dined with the Crossleys (naval attaché). Tonight dine with Count and Countess Keller—and then early to the Embassy to talk with Crane before he starts away. Tomorrow night I am going to a dance at an old Countess Beabodskys.—Saturday night dine with some enormously rich Russian banker—

If only my angel were here I am sure she would enjoy many things—but I am <u>mightily</u> glad she is safe at home.

The two or three American women here are in more or less continual terror—About once a week there is an alarm and they prepare to fly to Moscow—then conditions change for the moment and they have a day of peace.

Good bye my sweetheart—Love to Clay and the Clays.

Your own,

SEPTEMBER 21, 1917. MILITARY NOTE.[18]

This morning the Allied Military Representatives were called by the new Minister of War, General Verkhovsky, to his office. There were present the Minister of War and an officer of the Russian Army, General Janin and Colonel Laverne of the French Army, Colonel Blair, Acting British Military Attaché, the Japanese and the Italian Attachés, two of the latter, and myself.

Gen. Verkhovsky then made, in French, a most important statement to the Military Representatives. The Minister's statement was as follows:

As a result of the Kornilov plot, there has been a complete breakdown in the relations existing between the officers and the soldiers. Alekseev says he cannot cope with the present situation. He will be replaced by either Cherimetseif or Dukhonin. Each of these officers now commands an army. Cherimetseif was once Quartermaster General of the South-Western Front and later commanded that front for a time. There is to be a complete reorganization of the officer corps of the Army. Many of the old ones of high rank must go. They are accustomed to doing their work in old fashioned ways in accordance with the methods of long ago, and did their duty largely through loyalty to the Czar. They are unable to comprehend and accept new political conditions. They will be replaced by young men of proper inclinations. There are many excellent young officers who do recognize existing political conditions and conform to them. These young men after all furnish a large part of the brains of the Army. (In response to a question by me, the Minister of War said that it would be a reasonable estimate, although it was impossible to state exactly, that half of the existing brigade and division commanders and those higher in rank must go). The old officers do not possess the confidence of the men. New officers must be chosen that will. The Committees and Commissars must remain, but will be gradually relegated to unimportance and extinction (after a few months), as the new officers come to exercise command and to possess the confidence of the men. The administration of military justice will be placed in the hands of the officers as soon as it can be done. The Committees of the soldiers are with the Soviet, but the majority of the Soviet and the Government will work together. The great importance of restoring discipline in the Army was thoroughly recognized by the Minister.

The Russian people are in great misery and their economic condition is at a very low ebb. There are 12,000,000 men mobilized in the Army. Only 2,500,000 are at the front. If the whole 12,000,000 were at the front properly conducting war, a point might be strained and all might be kept at work, for the country is determined to go on with the war. As conditions exist, however, it becomes ridiculous to continue a situation where so small a percentage is really effective. It has been decided, therefore, to demobilize a portion of the Army. The plans for such demobilization have not been completed, but certain elements of the plan have been resolved upon. All over 40 years of age are to be released. 60 recently formed infantry divisions, now without artillery, etc. are to be broken up and the men used largely to build up organizations at the front. A large number of reserve regiments and a great part of the militia are to be demobilized. Such a demobilization will not increase disorders, but diminish them, inasmuch as the men are more disorderly in their military organizations than they would be scattered in the country. (I am not sure, but as I remember it, the Minister of War stated that from 400,000 to 600,000 men would be very quickly demobilized and that plans to release others were in contemplation.)

The above is as near as possible a verbatim account of the Minister's remarks. Very few questions were asked by the Allied Representatives and no opinions were requested from them. At the end it appeared that the Minister of War had an appointment to which he had been summoned, which compelled him to leave rather abruptly.

PETROGRAD. SEPTEMBER 22, 1917

Dearest:

A pouch tonight—in a few minutes—

Am well and reasonably happy—and send my love to you and Clay—Did I enclose a photo taken on the boat coming over? I do now anyway—

Have just bought a fur coat for 260 roubles—a bully "Shuba"—lined with young sheep-skin. It is getting colder. The white nights are being followed by gray days—and soon it feels as tho' they would be white days.

Had a long interview today with the new Minister of War. It gave me much business of writing dispatches etc.

"Time's up—"

My angel has all my love—

SEPTEMBER 23, 1917. NO. 1216. FROM: THE MILITARY
ATTACHÉ, PETROGRAD
TO: CHIEF, WAR COLLEGE DIVISION,
GENERAL STAFF, WASHINGTON.
SUBJECT: SUPPLIES TO RUSSIA, ETC.[19]

The following communication relates to the control of American supplies to Russia and especially to the coordination of American supplies
with supplies from Great Britain. . . .[20]

. . . To recapitulate: (1) this letter should be placed where it can
receive immediate attention; (2) there should be formed an American
Section to deal with Russian supplies; (3) I should be furnished with
1 Quartermaster and funds as above described as quickly as possible;
(4) I should be furnished with the information hereinbefore requested.

In addition to its work upon orders the Michelson Commission handles all tonnage to Russia, in the sense that it prepares monthly lists
indicating the priority of shipments, which lists are followed by the
shipping agents abroad. If the Michelson Commission thinks that certain orders in the U.S. should not have been placed, it refuses priority
for the shipment of such orders, with the result that factories in America during war time have been allowed to work upon articles which
will lie perhaps through the period of the war upon the docks at the
ports, unable to find their way to Russia, encumbering space, tying up
capital, and wasting the productive capacity of manufacturing plants.

When the Root Mission returned to America, one member of it, Mr.
Samuel R. Bertron (Care of Bertron, Storrs and Griscom, Wall Street,
New York City) told me that he had especially charged himself with the
matter of supplies for Russia and tonnage for same, and that he would
place before the proper authorities in the U.S. the need for the creation
of the proper machinery to handle this matter in the U.S. and here. I
suppose that Mr. Bertron has done the best he could, but as yet I have
not even been advised as to who would listen attentively to such a
communication as this; have not received sufficient funds and officers
to enable me to attend to the matter and effect the proper organization at this end, nor have I been informed that there has been created
in America an American Section on Russian supplies, corresponding
to that which has been found essential in Great Britain. I am writing this communication to the Chief of the War College Division because I know not to whom it should be properly addressed and in the

confident hope that the War College will place this very important matter in the proper channel to receive prompt attention. In this connection I would suggest correspondence with Mr. Bertron. . . .

. . . Due to the overshadowing influence of changing political conditions upon military matters in Russia and to such needs as preparation for evacuation of Petrograd by the American Colony in case of pogroms or communes always to be expected, I am obliged to keep in close touch with the Embassy and with many matters not ordinarily falling to Military Missions or Attachés.

Armenians, Poles, Lithuanians, Ukrainians and other nationalities within Russia desire to form separate armies. Thousands of Russian officers desire to offer their services to America. The physical work of handling these questions is obstructive to business and requires the attention of a number of people. . . .

SEPTEMBER 23, 1917. PARAPHRASE OF TELEGRAM SENT TO WARCOLSTAFF WASHINGTON. NO: -42.[21]

My present opinion is that the policy announced by Verkhovsky for the Army, is the only one opportune under the difficult existing political conditions, but not likely to result in an effective Army. The War Minister, Verkhovsky, is a well educated soldier, radical, intelligent, forceful, nervous, ambitious, and 34 years of age. He believes in decentralization throughout the Army administration essential in which I concur.

The so called Democratic, but practically Socialist, Convention, called for September 25, may by its complexion and action determine or affect many vital Russian problems. It may not accept Kerensky, who may not feel strong enough to fight it, and who may be succeeded very soon by a Socialist of the Moderate wing, perhaps Tseretelli, with the Ministry responsible to a Convention or Soviet. The more Radical members, advocating a peace policy, would probably be dangerous opponents of such a new Government. The latter probably will not last long.

The Soviet contains no representative of the Kadet or other parties, similarly conservative to the principal parties of the U.S. which it, the Soviet, would regard as Bourgeoisie or counter revolutionary. The latter two terms are becoming synonymous.

General Dukhonin succeeds General Alekseev as Chief of Staff. The reports as to the former are rather favorable.

On a large scale the Germans are attacking apparently with success along the Dvina in the Jacobstadt district.

Dearest:

We live at such high tension that ordinary letter writing seems almost impossible. Nearly every day I compose a long telegram to the War Department and another to Pershing. I have to watch not only military but also political and economic developments—and report upon them frequently and—of course accurately.

At present it looks as though Kerensky would not last long but be superseded by a socialist ministry responsible to the Council of Workmen and Soldiers—Nor would such a new government last long.

The situation here is most discouraging in every respect. And the situation here may readily influence the termination of the war. There are already peace rumors drifting in from England and France, if we are correctly informed.

Night before last I attended rather a wonderful dinner at a very rich Russian's. He has 3 daughters—One is one of the greatest violin players in the world. And one is a singer of grand opera rank. A number of Russian and English officers were present, and some professional entertainers. But the conversation! You never heard such "bohemian" expressions. I wish Grant Fitch could have been present. One subject of merriment was the choice the women might [make] between being violated by Bolsheviks or Germans. I had to think up every "slimy ground" I had ever heard, but the English General outdistanced all of us at that game.

I enclose a photograph of a Woman's battalion. The Russians have a lot of them—and they are very useless and absurd.

I wonder what Clay is doing now? I suppose either acting as instructor in the second camp—or perhaps working for Crowder. I hope he'll do both, one after the other. . . .

We expect more or less to remove soon to Moscow but nothing is certain. I would hate to leave our good quarters and office here.

My office is haunted by poor Russian officers who wish to go to America. Their lot is an awful one. Their men kill them when they please—discipline is unknown. And now the Government is going to put them—or most of them—out—Suicide seems their favorite recourse.

September 25—I hear [?] a pouch going out tonight so I'm closing this. The temperature in my room is about 40 but I have lots of clothes on. We shall have a fire in a day or two, but fuel is so scarce we must count on being often uncomfortable.

Tonight I'm going to the opera (Butterfly) as guest of a Mr. Thompson, a copper king, who is here with Red Cross Mission. He has the royal box again. By the way, the ballets here are wonderful—far ahead of any we saw at Chicago—

My love to my love!

Yours,

SEPTEMBER 27, 1917. PARAPHRASE OF TELEGRAM SENT TO WARCOLSTAFF WASHINGTON. NO: -44-[22]

The operations recently give the enemy control of the left bank of the Dvina, in the district of Jacobstadt. The Russians have offered no proper resistance, lost 60 guns, and much supplies.

Many changes are occurring in commands throughout the Army. Marushevsky is succeeding Romanovsky as Chief of the General Staff. Volodchenko now commands the South West front and Cherimissov the North front. There is considerable evidence that the winter clothing supply for the Army is lacking. Incendiary outrages have caused great losses of war material. There is no improvement in the order or discipline of the Army. Public order exists principally by common consent. Labour troubles are increasing the disorganization of the National Industries.

The opening of the Democratic Convention is postponed until today. There is nothing certain as to the outcome, but it may be momentous.

The German activity in the Baltic Sea is increasing, but the objective is uncertain. It is probable that the descent will be upon Riga, Gulf of Finland, one or both.

SEPTEMBER 28, 1917. PARAPHRASE OF TELEGRAM SENT TO WARCOLSTAFF WASHINGTON. NO. 45.

That they have reliable information of intended air raids on Petrograd during and after October is believed by the Russians. The city at present is practically unprotected. If ordered can the U.S. quickly ship through a northern port twenty anti-air craft three-inch guns or larger with appropriate supply of ammunition? Query to England also being sent.

SEPTEMBER 28, 1917. PARAPHRASE OF TELEGRAM
SENT TO WARCOLSTAFF WASHINGTON. NO: -46-

The following transmitted at the request of the Head of the Red Cross Mission,[23] namely:—
"For Davison, National Red Cross Headquarters, Washington, D.C. 10000 - 26 -
September 27, 1917.
Inform Hutchins that his cable dated September 23 is indiscreet. The Breshkovsky Civic Committee[24] is the only agency through which negotiations should be made, and help furnished. Bearing in mind that we are living on a volcano, and that Russia is passing through such a crisis, that unexpected changes are always possible, we have arranged matters so that a fall of the Government will not prevent the continuance of the Breshkovsky Committees continuance of educational work. Although we have full confidence in the Committee, we know that our American friends wish us to be in a position at all times to control continuance of support. To this end it is necessary that all American money for this work be in my complete control, or that of my successor. All that we are doing is with the full knowledge and approval of the present Government, and we are in daily confidential conferences with them. We do not wish, nor can we expect to compete with the Germans in their corruption of the people, but we can assist through the medium of the Breshkovsky Committee to create enthusiasm and support for free Russia, which is only to be realized through winning the war, and the complete defeat of the German autocracy.
As the President of the U.S. and House do not know us intimately, consider it of the utmost importance that T. L. Chadbourne, and William Wallace Junior, be present at your conferences with them, and if our assurances cannot be accepted at 100%, and our policies and help recommended approved, someone, having implicit confidence to enable, and freedom of action effective, should replace us here. We know that this work must be done, and to ensure effective development of plans,

beginning with October, we should have one million dollars in the next ten days additional, and three million dollars monthly thereafter.

signed "Thompson".

This means of communication is desired by Thompson rather than through the Embassy for several reasons. His propaganda work is apparently sanctioned by, or known to, Colonel House. For other similar communications please wire instructions as to suitability of using my code.

SEPTEMBER 29, 1917. MEMO FOR EMBASSY.

The conditions on the Caucasian front are known to be bad as reported but they are practically equally bad everywhere on the Russian fronts, including that known as the Rumanian front. The broad strategic consequences of disaster are more to be feared elsewhere than on the Caucasian front.

The question of the segregation of nationals in special units is a political question, for the most part, and must be handled by the Russians. In so far as it is a question of adding to the strength of the Russian Army as a whole, through other considerations, it is also necessarily a Russian question at the present time.

There is some uncertainly whether a concentration of Armenians against the Turks would increase or diminish the chances of Armenian atrocities.

PETROGRAD. OCTOBER 1, 1917

Dearest,

I have your sweet letter from Washington, of Aug. 15. I am so glad you worked everything out so well and got such good news there. It is a great thing to feel at peace with the world—I was so glad to see you were feeling that.

I am giving a big dinner (only 8 but that is big here now on account of the food question)—Countess Nostitz—Countess Keller—Countess Frasso (an Italo-American variety) Gen. Niessel, Col. Blair, Count La Lonne—and a Belgian named Du Becker. Blair is the British Attaché. Gen. N. is a bully Frenchman—a great big man who has been doing things in France and who comes here full of enthusiasm plans and determination. I hope he will be able to work some things out (with our assistance) over the terrible inertia of our Embassies here. I am very glad he has come.

The weather here has become colder than November in Lexington— but today we start our furnace and expect to get comfortable at last.

There is a democratic (Socialist) convention in town which may have momentous consequences for Russia. It may put or try to put Kerensky out—or it may forbid or try to forbid his having any but socialists in the cabinet. Anything may result from a commune to a civil war—or then again things may go on as before. You never can tell—

Meantime we are beginning to expect German air raids, and are painting the street light glasses green etc. There is very little protection against air raids here and 85% of the Russian munitions plants are in Petrograd. We may have lots of fun.

I am trying to get over here Howard Elliott or another of our biggest R.R. men as advisor to the Russian Government. The Allies rather depend on us in R.R. matters and we haven't done our share.

I am writing to the Guaranty Trust Co. to send you check for my balance there you ought to get $150 or more.

I am enclosing a memorandum about our income tax which I hope will be self explanatory.

See that Clay has plenty of money and gets the best outfit money will buy. He should have a sheep skin lined coat with rain proof material on the outside. Big boots with room for the best and softest woolen socks that can be had—Fur cap and fur gloves—think the messenger in my old Balt.[imore] office can find some wonderful stocking (sleeping) in a trunk in the office.

OCTOBER 6, 1917. PARAPHRASE OF TELEGRAM
SENT TO WARCOLSTAFF, WASHINGTON: NO. -8- 52 11 A.M.

Copy through the National Red Cross to Davison.

The situation here is desperate, and desperate remedies are justifiable. The head of the Red Cross Commission here, Thompson, reports having contributed his own money to the extent of one million dollars for newspaper control and influence, hiring speakers, etc. This work similar to pre-election campaigns in the U.S. and similarly costly, say two million dollars or more per month. Thompson, assisted by Raymond

Robins acts through a special Russian Committee of Conservative Socialists.[25]. . . No U.S. Agency has the direction of the Thompson movement, and perhaps that is for the best. Thompson needs privately subscribed funds if no Government funds are available, or must discontinue the work before more than well started.

The French Military Mission, the British Military Attaché, and I, hope that the presentation by Thompson will meet immediate and favorable response. Ten million dollars, Thompson believes, of German money is used monthly in Russia, which seems to be a reasonable estimate. The American Ambassador prefers to remain in ignorance. . . .

OCTOBER 7, 1917. PARAPHRASE OF TELEGRAM
SENT TO WARCOLSTAFF, WASHINGTON: NO. -9-53. 1 P.M.[26]

A gradual disintegration of the power of the Government is taking place in all directions. Anarchy is nearer daily. Strikes and threats of strikes are everywhere, including railroads, where a general strike is imminent unless unreasonable demands are accepted. The revolt in Turkestan, the Don Cossacks refuse to quell, stating they have been long enough alternately police force and accused of treason. The Finnish Senate has prepared a project of practical independence of Finland, and Russian troops have recently refused to execute orders of Kerensky to oppose the alleged Finnish Diet.

The Democratic Convention has adjourned, having inaugurated a Parliament to which the Ministry is responsible until the Constitutional Assembly. The relations between such Parliament, which met yesterday, and the Ministry, are not determined. Kerensky appears to have submitted to the Convention, of which Tseritelli is the most influential member, and to the Preparliament. No Bourgeoisie are in the Convention, but a number will be admitted to the Preparliament. All elements in Russia but the Socialists are cowed. The Bolsheviks and anarchists are calling other Socialists counter revolutionary, and condemning the Convention of which they formed a large minority, are, through the Petrograd Soviet, calling conferences of the City Soviets [on 2 Nov.] which will be Bolshevik.

The Bolsheviks desire peace, separate or otherwise, distribution of land, and giving the factories to the workmen, all immediately. Other Socialists wish immediately a general peace, and a gradual realizing of a Socialistic economic program. The political conditions are overshadowing everything, but economical and financial disaster are hastening on. Paper money has been reduced in size to facilitate more rapid printing. Anti-American meetings have occurred, and the Bolsheviks regard American institutions as capitalistic and anti-democratic.

The German infantry divisions on the Riga front are reduced from 18 1/2 on September 20 to 15 1/2 now. The Germans appear to rely again mainly on propaganda, which is enormous. Lynching of officers continues. Bolshevik ideas are growing in the Army. In the Baltic Sea the German Fleet, with transports, is still reported at Sea.

PETROGRAD. OCTOBER 9, 1917.

Dearest:

I am ashamed to think how few moments I seem to be able to seize to set down the loving thoughts of my dear two which are always running through my mind. My writing place is cold—and full of people nearly all the time—and my own private writing seems almost impossible. . . .

I'm having lots of practice in my French—but today I started to have a daily conversation. I read two French papers every day and do lots of business in French. Soon I ought to be pretty good. My only trouble is when real Frenchmen will not parler lentement.

You are a wonder, with your journeys to Washington to straighten things out—& your nursing courses—If conditions were only a little different I'd have you come out at once. As it is I'm afraid it would be criminal. Not only is the journey long and difficult and sometimes dangerous but you can never tell when a regular commune will break out here with horrors like those of Tarnapol. Most of the American and English women have left and all the Russian women that could get away and had some place to go. Food also fuel may give out any time and there is generally the devil to pay. Americans and British—in fact foreigners in general—are not liked. The ignorant are beginning to recognize them as an influence keeping them in the war—and they want to quit.

Aug. 15 Since my last few lines I got off my "Monthly Summary"—political, financial & economic as well as military. It is a monthly volume with many enclosures and takes my own time for a week at least in each month.

Day after tomorrow I am going to Mogilev for a few days—Last time I was there Brusilov commanded. Since then he has been canned and

Kornilov has come and gone. . . . Now Kerensky is the commander-in-chief. He is there (Mogilev, sick now).

The Germans draw nearer to Petrograd. They have probably taken the islands enclosing Riga Gulf by now. We may have the big naval guns bearing on the city before long. In which case we would vamoose to Moscow I suppose. It all wouldn't occur if the Russian Army were disciplined and willing to fight.

Goodbye my angel. I am closing now, Oct. 16—well and as happy as one can be in such circumstance with his loved ones so far away.

The fire is in the furnace and we are relatively comfortable.

Your own

OCTOBER 10, 1917. TO: THE CHIEF, WAR COLLEGE DIVISION, GENERAL STAFF, WASHINGTON, D.C.
SUBJECT: MONTHLY RESUME (SEPTEMBER, 1917 TO OCTOBER 10). NO. 1225.

My last Monthly Resume carried the situation up to Sept. 3, 1917.[27] It included the fall of Riga as the principal military event and, on the political side, the Moscow Conference.

The spoils of Riga included 325 guns (1/3 of which heavy) and large quantities of railway, engineer and sanitary materials. The prisoners taken were about 9,000.

Soon after Riga fell the Germans extended their successes on the North Front to include Friederichstadt. Toward the end of September they attacked in the Jacobstadt region and succeeded in clearing the left bank of the Dvina . . . about 160 versts, as the crow flies, above the mouth of the river. Most of the Russian troops offered but little resistance. The losses included about 50 guns and 4,000 prisoners. . . .

In the last few days there have been signs (burning of villages, etc.) that the Germans intend withdrawing their lines east of Riga with a view to holding only a sort of enlarged bridge-head.

The German fleet . . . probably has immediate designs upon the defenses of the Gulf of Riga . . . and would place the Germans in a very threatening position as regards the Reval peninsula and Petrograd. . . . They might prefer to remain in a threatening position, able to bomb Petrograd at will, and exercising a great moral influence over the Russians if they can bring about a consideration of peace terms during the coming winter. Incidentally it may be said that Petrograd possesses practically no defenses against air raids and houses a large percentage of the munitions plants of Russia. . . .

Excited to that course by recent developments in Russia, it seems as though the Germans have again resorted mainly to propaganda work among the Russian soldiers and sailors and among the active political elements in Petrograd (workmen, radical socialists, anarchists, etc.). Under present conditions it is vastly cheaper and more efficacious to indulge in costly propaganda than it is to fight, from a German point of view.

There is no improvement in the morale of the troops or in their state of discipline. They heartily embrace the peace propaganda proceeding from German and idealistic sources. They lost what little confidence in their officers they formerly felt when Kornilov fell, and the lynching and dismissal of officers by soldiers is continuing on a large scale. . . .

. . . The new Minister of War, Verkhovsky . . . [is] young, energetic, intelligent, accomplished, ambitious. He seems to be a good politician. Some say he is unscrupulous. Many think he will be a large figure in the future of Russia. He has taken the foreign Military Missions into his confidence and he makes a very favorable impression upon me personally. . . .

. . . The situation is a desperate one and Verkhovsky's plans are probably the only ones open to him by reason of the political and anarchical conditions that exist. He certainly has a difficult task to make a fighting machine out of the Army, under present conditions, in a reasonable time, and no one need be surprised if he fails.

The overshadowing event in Russia during September was the Kornilov episode. As to the truth about this there will always remain many doubts. There was no proper organization and cooperation between the many elements which wished the movement to succeed. Many different motives actuated its supporters. Very many who were sympathetic with it were afraid to join it or did not know how or when to make themselves felt. It was badly planned and was sprung prematurely. Needless to say it failed utterly. The result was altogether bad, as it so disturbed the relations between officers and men and so aroused the radical political elements who saw their power threatened as to make the disciplining of the Army practically impossible. If all those favoring the movement had been as active as those opposing it it might have succeeded, but even this is uncertain by reason of the disposition of the soldiers generally.

The following is an account of the Kornilov episode as nearly as I can ascertain the facts.

For some time General Kornilov, the Commander-in-Chief, and Savinkov, the Adjoint Minister of War had been endeavoring to convince Kerensky (Minister of War and Marine, President of the Ministry and virtual dictator) that discipline could not be restored in the Army by words alone, nor by any methods then at the disposal of Kornilov. There were needed, they urged, certain laws and regulations which only Kerensky could establish. Kerensky agreed with them "in principle" but the laws and regulations were never forthcoming.

During the progress of this controversy, the Staff at Mogilev became almost frantic as it contemplated the continued disintegration of the Army . . . and was forced to observe the continued success of the enemy and such incidents as the horrors of Kaloutch and Tarnopol. . . . Even the foreign military representative at Stavka became so alarmed. . . .

. . . At the time the Kornilov movement began and for some time before we had no representative at Stavka. If there is suspicion anywhere that foreign Military Missions were involved in that movement, such suspicions could not attach to us.

On September 7th there arrived at Stavka one Lvov (not the former premier), a politician of some standing, who had previously had a general conversation on political subjects with Kerensky, to which it seems the latter attached but little importance. Lvov convinced Kornilov that he was an authorized messenger from Kerensky, bearing from the latter certain alternative propositions as follows:

(1) That Kerensky resign and allow Kornilov to form a Cabinet, of which Kerensky would be a member;

(2) That the Provisional Government resign, handing over complete authority to Kornilov who would act as dictator until the Constitutional Assembly should meet;

(3) That the Government resign and a Directory of five be formed, including Kerensky, Kornilov and Savinkov.

Kornilov chose the third proposition.

On September 8 Lvov presented himself to Kerensky with a document written by himself, purporting to convey an ultimatum from Kornilov demanding the handing over to the latter of all power, civil and military, in order that he might himself form a Ministry.

Kerensky just as Kornilov had done, accepted Lvov as a bona fide and reliable agent, and immediately ordered Kornilov to surrender his place as Commander-in-Chief and directed Klembovsky to supplant him.

Up to this point there had been only misunderstanding as between Kerensky and Kornilov. Lvov was later found to be insane.

Kornilov was of course well informed as to the desire of many elements that he or another assume a temporary dictatorship. A great movement was in progress to bring such a thing about, in which the intelligent bourgeois elements and many of the officers, including most of those at Stavka, took part. They believed that there was no other way to discipline the Army and save Russia. . . .

Kerensky was supported by the Executive Committee of the Council (Soviet) of Soldiers' and Workmen's Delegates and by the radical elements of Petrograd. Many thousands of armed workmen and large bodies of troops from the Petrograd Garrison moved southward to meet the Kornilov forces. . . . when any of these "hostile" forces met they refused to fight each other and as a military event the affair lost interest. The Soldiers' Committees, loyal to the Soviet, were with Kerensky, and this fact prevented the general use of the Army by Kornilov. The Committees seized the telegraph wires. Most of the elements that at heart were with Kornilov remained inert. Very soon it must have become evident to Kornilov that he could not put his program through. . . .

. . . On September 27 there met at Petrograd a so-called Democratic Convention, composed almost entirely of Socialists, and called together by the joint Executive Committees of Peasants', Workmen's and Soldiers' Delegates. More than one-third of the membership of this Convention was "Bolshevik" (pro-peace-on-any-terms, anti-Ally, almost frankly anarchistic). The more conservative Socialists, ably led by Tseretelli, controlled the Convention. The principal work of the Convention was the formation of a so-called Democratic Council.

Some 400 members of the existing Democratic Council, to be renamed the "Provisional Council of the Russian Republic," were members of the Convention, two-thirds of them Minimalists (or Mensheviks), i.e., Conservative Socialists, and the rest Bolsheviks. About 125 other members representing the "interests" ("bourgeois," "censitaires") are to be admitted. The Bolsheviks are raging at their defeat. They control the Petrograd Soviet which regards the formation of the Coalition Government as a coup d'etat and which has called a meeting of all the city Soviets, which are mostly Bolshevik, to be held here on November 2. This meeting, if it shall develop, is the next political incident promising trouble. The Bolsheviks plan an armed demonstration on November 2 that shall eclipse all previous efforts.

The various Soviets have great influence with the troops and if Bolshevik uprisings are arranged it is doubtful whether the government can find loyal troops enough to prevent them. . . .

. . . In behalf of the new Government Kerensky has issued a statement to the country, expressing conviction that a speedy general peace is required in the interest of Russia; promising to work along democratic lines in developing the fighting strength of the Army, including the provision of "a Commanding Staff of technical ability which will work in close harmony with the Army Committees"; and calling together . . . a "Council of the Republic of Russia" which will be the Democratic Council already in existence and described above. . . .

One John Reed, an American correspondent, parlor-socialist, pacifist and quasi-anarchist, who is in the confidence of the Reds here, states, as do many others, that on October 14, a holiday upon which peasants are accustomed to return to their villages, the soldiers, or many of them, will leave the trenches and start home. Many Reds desire to start a commune when the soldiers get back to the cities and it appears that the British Ambassador heads their list for extermination. The rest of us are high on the same list.

The workmen (who are nearly all Reds) have an excellent military organization. For example, from the Putilov Works can be started toward any point in Petrograd, in eight minutes time, an armed body of about 8,000 workmen. At least there is considerable evidence of the truth of this. . . .

There came to Petrograd with the American Red Cross Mission to Russia Lieut. Col. W. B. Thompson, who since the departure of Lieut. Col. Billings has been left in charge of the Mission. Thompson is a big man of the "magnate" type, who has large vision and large means. He has undertaken, as a personal matter, a large propaganda enterprise, in which he has sought to associate certain friends of his in America. While the Embassy prefers to remain in ignorance of Col. Thompson's operations (it is conversant with them in a general way) I have remained in close touch with them, in consultation with the French Military Mission and the British Military Attaché. The last two and I, in a cable from me, have expressed the hope that Col. Thompson's friends will support him financially, as it is quite apparent that the Governments concerned can not quickly furnish the large sums required. Propaganda is now trumps in Russia. The Germans are spending, it has been reasonably estimated, not less than $10,000,000 per month. To secure the necessary roubles they are collecting the many billions left in conquered territory, and retaining in Russia the proceeds from the sales of German goods, which are everywhere exposed in the stores, and which enter Russia by various channels. Colonel Thompson has in the last few weeks expended $650,000 of his own money, and will keep on for a time but if the work is to continue he naturally must secure contributions from his friends at home to whom he has appealed. . . .

Today there is no power in Russia strong enough to exercise the functions of government in any ordinary sense. No one knows whether the Army could be controlled in larger part by the Government or the Soviets (Bolsheviks).

In so far as the Allies can do anything in Russia, by opportunist policies, the situation must be nursed along to keep Russia in the war until its end, or if that be impracticable to keep her in the war as long as possible.

The chances are that if, at the Inter-Allied Conference in Paris in November, there be not a plan determined upon looking to an early peace, Russia will speedily go out of the war. . . .

With reference to the new Kerensky coalition Government the Petrograd Soviet, representing the active radical opposition, in a resolution adopted October 8 says: "We the workmen and soldiers of Petrograd will not give the bourgeois Government of autocracy and counter-revolutionary violence any support. The All Russian Convention of Soviets (called by the Petrograd Soviet) will create true revolutionary authority."

I am aware that in this summary I have handled many matters which should have been made the subjects of separate communications. I not only request the War College to condone this, but to assist by making excerpts from this summary for proper use and consideration. I can get neither enough typewriters nor stenographers here and my own time is occupied to the limit. . . .

The enemy yesterday (October 12) were landing troops in and near the Bay of Tavlagakhta. . . . It is reported that the coast batteries were demolished by fire from German dreadnoughts, but it does not yet appear that these batteries were the main ones defending the sea passages.

Under normal conditions, the Russians having had so long a warning, it might have been expected that the German operations would result in failure. In the present condition of the Russian Army anything may occur.

OCTOBER 10, 1917. PARAPHRASE OF TELEGRAM
SENT WARCOLSTAFF WASHINGTON NO. 17 -59- 3 P.M.[28]

Apparently the general railway strike which has been in progress in an imperfect fashion for the last few days has been called off. Kerensky has formed a new Ministry totalling 17, comprising, Independents 3, Kadets 4, and Socialists 10. An understanding between the Government and the Preparliament / known as the Democratic Council / exists, but it is of very uncertain character as to responsibility of Ministers, and with plenty of room for trouble. The Petrograd Soviet regard events as a counter-revolutionary coup d'etat, and will try to start trouble.

The Bolsheviks claim, that on October 14, when the Russian home-coming holidays occur, that the troops will leave the trenches and start for their homes. Many of them expect to start a Commune when the soldiers arrive back in the cities. It is said that the British Ambassador heads the list to be killed.

General Pershing has been informed as to the above.

OCTOBER 14, 1917. PARAPHRASE OF TELEGRAM
SENT WARCOLSTAFF WASHINGTON NO. 21 SIXTY 1 P.M.[29]

Not less than 400 tons ordinary civilian clothing and 500 tons shoes should be brought by each ship sailing from U.S. during this winter until May. Desperate Russian situation regarding these requirements must be met as proposed. I understand Russian Commission in U.S. is endeavoring to place orders for shoes and clothing for delivery at least as rapidly as above, but that owing to lack of credit some orders have been held up. Extension credit to cover these requirements and to secure delivery for shipment as above absolutely essential. Priority to articles in quantities mentioned has been suggested by Michelson Commission. . . .

What do you consider as proper channel for such recommendations as this? Do we have an American Board or Committee in U.S. having authority in matters of Russian orders? If we have not, by when is action taken on this recommendation? Should I not be in touch with it? If such a Board exists answer by cable explaining mechanism in detail at your end is earnestly requested.

OCTOBER 14, 1917. PARAPHRASE OF TELEGRAM
SENT WARCOLSTAFF WASHINGTON NO. 24 62 4 P.M.[30]

On October 12 the German fleet destroyed the batteries on the North shore of Esel Island, and on the South shore of Dago Island off the Riga Gulf. A landing party on Dago completed the destruction. On the same day one division landed on the North shore of Esel Island, since then being reinforced and moving South to take Czarel coast fortifications. Little hope of prolonged resistance. Probably 30,000 land troops of the Germans available. Fleet, including 6 Dreadnoughts, many cruisers, and about 35 torpedo boats. Russians on the two islands probably about 10,000. All the Coast defenses are Naval, with Naval gun crews. The largest guns are located at the inner island entrance and are 7" guns. 4 12" guns are located on Tserel Peninsula, but without parapets. Only a dredged channel leading due North from the Gulf between the islands and mainland. The principal defenses of Reval are 4 9.2" guns. There are some 5" and 6" guns located on a point West of Pernov.

General Pershing has been informed of the above.

OCTOBER 20, 1917. MILITARY NOTE. MOGILEV.

INTERVIEW WITH GENERAL VELITCHKO

Today I had a very interesting interview with General Velitchko, lasting several hours.

Gen. Velitchko is and has been for 20 years the leading Russian Military Engineer and one of the ablest engineers in Europe. He is now 64 years old. He took part in the Turko-Russian War and the Japanese War, and has been very active all through the present war. He is now a full general and is the Inspector "Du genie" at Stavka, supervising all engineer operations with the Army in the field.

Gen. Velitchko for many years was the chief antagonist of the school of Brialmont. Brialmont and Velitchko were personal friends but professional enemies.[31]

Gen. Velitchko said that Kuropatkin had been much abused for resorting as he did to trench warfare, and that he, Velitchko, had been characterized as Kuropatkin's evil genius. The General was much pleased that events had so completely demonstrated the wisdom of his theories.

The following information is from General Velitchko.

The next sheet contains information as to the division between Naval and Army responsibility for defense of Petrograd. (Coast defense in Russia is naval.) The same sheet indicates the 3 lines of defense for Petrograd (guns, mine fields, etc.).[32]

OCTOBER 25, 1917. PARAPHRASE OF TELEGRAM
SENT WARCOLSTAFF WASHINGTON NO. 38 66 7 P.M.[33]

I have been to Stavka for the past week.

The Germans are in full possession of the Riga Gulf and enclosing islands, and reconnoitering the mainland since October 17. A part of the Russian fleet fought well. The land troops fought poorly. Some escaped from the Islands. The Russians report that the Germans lost two dreadnoughts, one cruiser, 12 torpedo boats, one transport, and many trawlers. The Russians lost the battleship Slava, and one torpedo boat.

For the defense of Petrograd against naval attack, there are three lines, with coastworks and mine fields, across the Finnish Gulf, namely, a line from Helsingfors to Reval, a line near Viborg, and the Dronstadt line. The Navy is in charge of all. The General Staff expects the Germans to attempt to take the Reval Peninsula before the Winter.

Verkhovsky recently exhibited to the Military Missions a programme for reorganizing and redisciplining the Army by May 14, 1918. It provides for four million men at the front, 500,000 to replace losses, and three million for service in the rear, the total to be 7 1/2 millions including 165 infantry divisions, instead of nearly twelve millions less two million deserters as at present. Desertions continue in large numbers.

This programme includes tactical training of troops, educational and propaganda work, laws to restrict and define functions of Commissars and Committees, improvement in Military Courts, prompt punishment for offenses, increase of pay and authority for officers, organization of dependable troops, including volunteers, St. George and Attacking battalions, and Cossack units, partial restoration of salutes, continual improvement of fortified positions, and scouting and raiding to keep the soldiers busy. . . . The U.S. to be called upon for guns, aeroplanes and tractors, and for matériel and personnel to carry on cultural, educational, and recreational work. The death penalty may be abolished later.

The programme is in substance that formerly proposed by Kornilov, except as to the death penalty and other emasculations. The government agrees in principle, but must act promptly in practical details, or there will be no chances of success. Most Russian and foreign officers anticipate failure on account of the general demand of the soldiers to quit war, and through lack of practical measures by the Government.

Verkhovsky says there is urgent need of simple formulation of the aims of the war for soldiers consumption, in order to offset the German propaganda, which asserts that Germany is willing to stop, but the Allies refuse.

Preparliament, now known as the Council of the Russian Republic, met here October 20, with added Bourgeoisie members, apparently in harmony with the government. The Bolsheviks, in small minority, withdrew denouncing the majority as counter revolutionary, but later returned. The harmony which is existing between Kerensky and the Council is apparently largely promoted by the activities of Thompson. See my No. 52, October 6th.

General Pershing cabled as above, except last paragraph.

OCTOBER 28, 1917. PARAPHRASE MESSAGE
SENT WARCOLSTAFF WASHINGTON NO. 44
SIXTYNINE 3 P.M.[34]

Though changes in the high commands continue and such interference as is proposed by Yates would be fruitless and tactless. The government is perhaps politically stronger but lacks the bayonets with which to sustain itself. The opposition of the Bolsheviks, with 30,000 armed workmen and support promised from Kronstadt and Baltic Sea Fleet which apparently does not recognize the Government, is getting nasty. There may soon be an uprising. There are indications that most of Petrograd garrison will be neutral but some Bolshevik. When trouble begins a few divisions, relatively dependable, may be brought from the north front, but the government is afraid to bring them now as it is feared they may become corrupted; also probable that it is unable to get present rotten garrison out of Petrograd.

With reference to my telegram number 53 [7 Oct. 1917], great efforts are being made to prevent the meeting of the Soviets on November 2nd, Thompson propaganda assisting.

Conditions other than political are not improving, with the exception that the Trans-Siberian is functioning better due to efforts of Stevens and the arrivals of locomotives, etc. The Russian staff still anticipates enemy operations about Reval. The Germans have withdrawn their Riga front now to 20 versts east of Dvina, crossing latter 30 versts above Riga.

LT. COL. T. BENTLEY MOTT,
OFFICE OF THE CHIEF OF STAFF,
WASHINGTON D.C.

My dear Mott:

I have your very interesting letter of Sept. 15th[35] enclosing copy of a letter composed by you and addressed by the Secretary of War to the Secretary of State, dated Sept. 6, 1917. It was most heartening to receive both of these communications. I have read them both to Mr. Diamandi, the Rumanian Minister, and at the request of the latter I have made him a copy of a portion of your letter which he has forwarded to Rumania and which will certainly produce an excellent effect, much more so than any formal communication would. . . .

I have not been able to organize my Mission here on the same scale as is employed by either one of our principal Allies. It is still true that General Poole as a member of the Michelson Commission has about twice the force that I have for all the purposes of our Mission. It is also [true] that I am unable to cooperate as is urged by our Allies in counter-espionage on a proper scale or in many investigations which should be made to determine the exact and most urgent requirements of the Russians. . . .

I rather look now to see the Russians stay in the war indefinitely but without conducting offensives. If they can be kept far enough from a state of truce to detain 125 or more enemy divisions on this front, it will be the utmost that I expect. Nevertheless, any soldier must admit that in itself this would be an accomplishment which should be sought at all cost as the alternative, a separate Russian peace, would have an effect I dislike to contemplate. While I have thus attempted to prophesy a little I wish to put an anchor out to wind-ward. It is still true that almost anything may happen except, in my opinion, the creation of a first class Russian Army during the continuation of this war. There is always a possibility of the development of civil war and of the making of a peace as the almost inevitable result thereof. I do not now think that such a civil war, on a large scale and compelling a peace, will occur, but there is the deepest antagonism growing up between the Bourgeois and the radical socialistic element. The various forces are crystallizing into hostile camps although the great mass of course remains inert.

With kindest regards, I am,
Yours faithfully,

My Angels—

I'm just waiting for some people to come in to dinner with me—the Ambassador, and six or eight others. After dinner we'll dance, some others coming in.

We have in the house now a guard of soldiers which the Russians seem to think is necessary. The daily conversation is as to whether we'll have an event [?] before night or not. But we have gotten used to the thought and dwell little upon it.

Last night I dined with the French Mission as guests of the Mistress of the Minister of Foreign Affairs, Tereschenko. The latter is only 31 and looks like a moody Greek God. His M., Mademoiselle Noe, French, seems a very estimable and beautiful young woman. They say he may marry her if his mother ever consents. My work grows. I "sit in" on more things all the time although I can not say I (or any body else) am accomplishing much. If they don't have civil war I think Russia will stay in the war indefinitely—but without fighting much. The different elements are becoming more antagonistic—and whether they'll keep hands off each other or not cannot be foretold. While what I have said is true of the <u>active</u> elements, yet the masses remain more or less inert.

Nov. 7. Our civil war seems to have broken loose. For the past twenty-four hours the "Soviet" people (socialists anarchists etc.) have been gradually taking possession of the town. There has been considerable street shooting and I can hear it now, in the evening, while I am writing this letter. The Government showed no strength at all. Kerensky fled in an automobile, which he found trouble to secure, as he said to join troops en route to Petrograd. The rest of the Ministry, as nearly as we can ascertain is in jail. Most of the troops in town are neutral—some being "Soviet."

It is utterly impossible to say what will happen in the near future. I expect the socialists will form a government. I guess Kerensky is done for. It is hard to see how in such disorders the food supply, which was desperately short, can be kept up. In fact nothing looks possible that is good and reasonable—but the Russians have a way of emerging from such situations which is most astonishing.

I don't think they'll bother the embassy buildings—they may be seeking recognition for a new government in a day or two. Meantime I'm stocked up with food, have the bath tubs full of water and can stand a siege. I still have the soldiers—7 young fellows, fine chaps, from a military school—like West Pointers. Kerth and Haygood are here and we have 4 rifles besides those of our guard. Of course though we could only try to stand off marauders—not the forces of the new "government." We may have some nice fighting when (and if) Kerensky comes back with troops. Of course you will have read all about it in the papers when you receive this and it may prove to have been a flash in the pan.

The socialists want peace at once. It may (if they succeed) result in a general peace or a separate peace and a long war. In any event it may lead to my return home. It is awfully interesting here—but wouldn't it be fine to see home again and my angel and my other angel.

A lot of pouches came in tonight and I expect letters tomorrow—wouldn't I love to have them now when it is raining bullets too thick even to walk out a bit. . . .

With all my love to you both I am

Your own,

NOVEMBER 4, 1917. PARAPHRASE OF TELEGRAM
SENT WARCOLSTAFF WASHINGTON SERVICE NO. 55,
NO. 74, 3 P.M.[36]

By request, Verkhovsky has resigned or has been given indefinite leave of absence. Apparently too far to left politically for Tereschenko and Kerensky. Held that unless told definitely why, soldiers could not be made to fight. Manikovski will act probably—old professional general not in politics, conservative, able, plodding.

On the Baltic Sea-Black Sea front . . . many divisions weak and best men being withdrawn to other units. Since October 1st about 12% of total strength of enemy has been withdrawn.

It seems probable that unless anarchy results Russia will remain in the war, without power to make great offensives against determined resistance. That she may be able to organize dependable troops, including several Polish corps, volunteers, Cossacks, artillery, battalions of death, etc. is best hope, and thus with other measures stiffen army generally, to maintain active defense with local offensives.[37]

Russians say chance of German combined operations against Finland or Reval peninsula still exists, but ice will form in two or three weeks.

On German initiative, fraternizing is being resumed on a large scale. *Discipline of Army grows worse* and shortage of food is increasing.

Ability of Russians to detain enemy forces in spring and number thus detained *will depend* within very wide limits *on* helpful and sympathetic *attitude of Allies. Relatively small expenditures on Russia will probably produce ten times result on course of war as would be obtainable at the same cost anywhere else.*

Propaganda should be facilitated *on enormous scale*, if possible along lines begun by Thompson, which *might cost $25,000,000 for one year.*

Russian credit should be kept at a point so as to permit utilization of all available tonnage from United States to Russian ports. . . . It may be assumed that accumulations awaiting shipment at American ports and accumulation at Vladivostok will continue large but be reduced gradually.

The differences become accentuated between Soviets and other active political elements. On November 7th Soviets meet in convention here with slogan all power to soviets. They claim they represent the majority Russian people—workmen, soldiers and peasants—and fear other elements will govern in interest of minority-bourgeois class. Propaganda, especially Thompson's, has reduced importance of Soviet convention but latter may possibly have enough vitality to attempt to forcibly seize state. Such a seizure or civil war might upset all hopes. Elections, Nov. 27th for constitutional convention, and meeting of same December 13th may act as sedative.

Cabled above to Pershing

Judson, the Bolshevik Revolution, and the Bolsheviks

Mapping a Plan of Action

I have greatly enjoyed reading your telegrams and they constitute the best information on Russia we get. I sometimes wonder how closely you work with the Ambassador. It may be at times trying to you; but I take the liberty of pointing out that it is very difficult to get anything done for Russia or Rumania unless he [Ambassador Francis] approves.

T. Bentley Mott, Office of the Chief of Staff, War Department, Washington, in a letter to Judson at Petrograd, 25 September 1917.[1]

The Bolshevik seizure of power on 7 November 1917 was a great disappointment and source of alarm for the entire Allied community in Russia. Only a handful of leftwing socialists like journalists John Reed and Albert Rhys Williams welcomed—and even served—the Lenin-Trotsky government. The Bolshevik propaganda slogans were immediately implemented in Lenin's Decree on Peace, issued the day after their seizure of power. Before the Second All-Russian Congress of Soviets of Workers' and Soldiers' Deputies, Lenin called for all belligerents to convene armistice negotiations and a peace conference to end the war. This was the unilateral Bolshevik initiative that had been promised in party policy statements even before the abdication of the czar.

However, the British, French, and U.S. leadership were in no way disposed to such a resolution of the issues. The "war to end all wars," "to make the world safe for democracy," and to ensure the principle of "the self-determination of peoples," was to be prosecuted. No Allied reply was made to Lenin's proclamation, and, as expected, the German foreign office immediately communicated its willingness to begin armistice talks. The feared bogey of a separate peace between Russia and the Central Powers was in process. Judson and his colleagues had to reconsider completely what their task in Russia was. Would the Kerensky forces manage a return? Would the army under old-guard officers manage to overwhelm the Bolshevik forces and reestablish their order? Should the Allied representatives in Russia commence negotiations with the Bolshevik leadership in the hope that such discussions would provide the Russians a strong negotiating position in their talks with Germany? What were the chances of sabotaging those negotiations for a separate peace?

As chief of the American Military Mission and military attaché, Judson had to redefine how he would fulfill his responsibilities in Bolshevik Russia. Given the antiwar, anti-imperialist extremes of Bolshevik rhetoric, he had to consider whether or not the Allied personnel in Russia would be safe from harm at the hands of the new government. He wondered if it would be prudent for the men under his command to leave Bolshevik Russia as soon as possible. Within days of the Bolshevik Revolution, the Wilson administration wired its directives to the American ambassador in Petrograd. There were to be no official communications between representatives of the U.S. government and those of the Bolshevik government. Judson's subsequent reports, observations, and recommendations should be considered in this light.

Beginning on 14 November 1918 and nearly daily until his return to Washington on 20 February 1918, Judson kept a formal diary to supplement all other communications. For the period from 14 November 1917 through 21 January 1918, the diary was kept in typewritten form and totaled 68 pages. Periodically, he dispatched portions of this diary to the War College Staff. After 21 January, when he was en route from Petrograd to Washington, the diary was kept in handwritten form on loose pages, and apparently was not submitted to the War College Staff.[2]

NOVEMBER 7, 1917. PARAPHRASE OF TELEGRAM
SENT WARCOLSTAFF WASHINGTON. NO. 60
SEVENTYSEVEN. 2 P.M.[3]

During the past twenty-four hours the Soviet element has been gradually taking over Petrograd. The Government now finds itself with scarcely any power locally. Part of the troops here and 30,000 armed workmen are controlled by the Soviet element, most of the remaining troops being neutral expecting to regain power after a few days with one or two divisions [Kerensky] thinks are approaching to aid him. Kerensky is leaving Petrograd in an automobile, which he had difficulty finding, to join them. Fearing that the balance of the Ministry will be arrested, Kerensky requested a Russian officer attached to me to advise our Ambassador to refuse recognition to Soviet government temporarily. Orators of the Soviet urge making peace, putting the bourgeois to work seizing private property, etc.

It seems that Savinkov in the background in behalf of a third stronger government has some arrangement with the Cossacks. Accuracy may be somewhat sacrificed to promptness in above.

The above is being cabled to Pershing.

NOVEMBER 8, 1917. PARAPHRASE OF TELEGRAM
SENT WARCOLSTAFF WASHINGTON. NO. 63
SEVENTY-NINE 1 P.M.[4]

The city of Petrograd including the State Bank, telegraph and all other local governmental agencies is now in the hands of the Bolsheviks. The Winter Palace was bombarded last night and the entire Ministry excepting Kerensky surrendered. The Council of the Republic has been forcibly dissolved. As the old government was relatively powerless there was not much bloodshed.

Last night the Soviet Congress met and all but the Bolsheviks, constituting about one-half, withdrew protesting against occurrences. It is proposed by Lenin, Trotsky and others in charge to form a government responsible to the Soviet Congress, appealing for the support of the army and the rest of the country. Evidently there is a desire on their part to maintain order. A prompt meeting of a democratic constituent assembly, control by the people of the means of production and distribution, immediate peace and the giving of the land to the peasants is included in their program.

It is believed that Kerensky has joined troops between Petrograd and the north front.

It seems probable that anti-Bolshevik forces may regain control, notwithstanding the state of the Army and the popularity of peace therewith. Due to ignorance and lack of communication, some forces which might otherwise support the Bolsheviks will probably be inert. As possibly leading to future opportunities, some of the conservative elements seem gratified by occurrences. Reliable prophecy is impossible owing to the confusion of the situation.

The above has been communicated to Pershing by cable.

Kindly inform Davison of the Red Cross that all are well here.

NOVEMBER 8, 1917. NO. 1238 TO: SECRETARY,
WAR COLLEGE DIVISION, GENERAL STAFF, WASHINGTON D.C.
MONTHLY RESUMÉ (OCTOBER 10TH TO NOVEMBER 13, 1917)[5]

<u>DISCIPLINE OF ARMY</u>

The program for the reorganization of the army and the restoration of discipline, which I described in my cable of October 25 (No. 66) has been hanging fire. General Velitchko came to Petrograd from Stavka to find out why and he told me the Provisional Government and the War Minister, Verkhovsky, were to blame through not being able to agree on details. It seems to be the old Kornilov story over again. They wish the army disciplined "in principle" but will not adopt the necessary measures or give approval to them.

<u>VERKHOVSKY'S RESIGNATION</u>

On November 4 it leaked out that Verkhovsky had broken with the rest of the Government and had resigned (by request) or been given indefinite leave of absence. It appears that Verkhovsky has become more popular with the radicals than are the other Ministers; and his demand that there be adopted an explanation to the soldiers as to why they are fighting, has probably been misconstrued into a demand for a separate peace. Verkhovsky will be succeeded temporarily by Gen. Manikovski, now Assistant War Minister, an able old general, industrious, a good administrator and with no interest in politics. Nov. 8. <u>Later</u>: General M. is now in jail as a result of Bolshevik Revolution of Nov. 7–8, 1917.[6]

<u>POLITICAL</u>

The first regular session of the Council of the Republic occurred on October 20. While the membership is much mixed as to political complexion it may be said that there are approximately 388 Socialists including some 60 Bolsheviks, and about 167 "Bourgeois." Generally speaking the Council meets 3 times a week, gives moral support to the Kerensky Government, does not attempt to legislate and affords great opportunity for debate and criticism. The principal Ministers including Kerensky and Tereschenko, frequently address the Council.

The Soviets (Workmen's and Soldiers') which were called to meet here in convention on November 2 have encountered some opposition from the Army Committees, the Peasants' Soviet, the Provisional Government, the Council of the Republic, and from the propaganda carried on by the Breshkovsky Committee, the latter largely financed by Col. Thompson as described in my last resumé. The meeting of the Soviets has been postponed to November 7. It will not be as large as its proposers wished. Whether it will be Bolshevik or Menshevik is a little uncertain but it will probably be the former. Some of the principal leaders behind this Soviet movement, including Trotsky, the President of the Petrograd Soviet, hold that the Soviet Convention should at once effect a coup d'etat "in behalf of the majority, —soldiers, workmen and peasants." They hold that the elements now in control of government represent only a minority and that from a democratic standpoint it is "immoral" to permit the minority to continue to rule. Trotsky is a Jew recently returned from America whose real name is Bronstein. It is understood that in America Trotsky was an anarchist.[7]

If the majority of the Soviet Convention is Bolshevik it will doubtless start trouble and it may start the same in any event. They have many armed workmen ready and have great influence with the troops. It is not certain that they could be subdued. If the majority is Menshevik, the argument may prevail that the Constitutional Convention is approaching; that civil war might ensue in event of an attempted coup d'etat, making elections to the Constitutional Convention impossible; and that it would be better to endure a usurping government a little longer since the Constitutional Convention will so soon set an end to it. No one can tell what the next few days may bring forth.

Disorganization for the moment grows. The present state of affairs may be described as one of benevolent anarchy. And yet as time goes on doubtless there are gathering together by a sort of political crystallization the elements which may later be competent to govern Russia. The enormous area and population of Russia; the lack of education, and the absence of previous political experience make the problem of the inauguration of proper democratic government an experiment unique in the world's history. While it is hard to believe that the problem can be solved in less than many years time, and while episodes of mild civil war may be expected, yet the philosophical character and gentle nature of the Russian people may keep these episodes within less destructive limits than some pessimists may anticipate. In the mean time any political sedative which might tend to keep things momentarily quiet seems to be so much gain.

The situation here is so kaleidoscopic that before a report as long as this can be completed there often occurs a great change in the complexion of affairs. I am writing this as an insert after substantially completing this communication. Within the last 24 hours the Soviet element has evidently decided to seize the State. With a considerable show of force (30,000 armed workmen, armed sailors from Kronstadt, and a part of the Petrograd garrison, the rest being nearly all neutral) they are gradually taking possession of post-offices, telephone exchanges, telegraph offices, the Fortress of St. Peter and St. Paul, etc., and there has as yet been but little bloodshed. Kerensky has fled in an automobile he "borrowed" from one of our Secretaries of Embassy and is proposing to join 1 bicycle company, 1 division of Cavalry and 1 division of Infantry which he understands are en route to Petrograd to restore the situation. He left word with a Russian officer, officially attached to me, that the rest of the Ministry might be arrested today and that he hoped our Ambassador would not recognize a Soviet Government, inasmuch as he hoped to restore the power of his own Government in 4 or 5 days.

The paragraph last preceding being written on November 7. What precedes and what follows were written a day or two before. I still believe that the general situation is much as I have described it before November 7, or will be restored sooner or later to that.

RUSSIA AS AN ALLY

Unless we have civil war or a Bolshevik government of some duration (which is less probably than a flash in the pan) it seems to me likely that Russia will in some fashion remain in the war but without the capacity to conduct great offensives. On the other hand she may through organization of certain dependable troops be able to oppose a sufficiently active defense, with punitive local offensives if the enemy grows negligent, to detain during the course of the war a very large enemy force—say 120 or more divisions (infantry and cavalry).

It seems to me vital that the Russians should perform this function if the war is to go on to a favorable conclusion. The result of the war seems largely to depend upon the course of Russia. It must not be forgotten that on October 1 the Russians were detaining on the Black Sea-Baltic front (i.e. not counting the Caucasian front) 156 divisions (131 1/2 infantry and 24 1/2 cavalry). What happens when some 12% of this force is even temporarily released is now being experienced in Italy. What would happen if all were released; if nearly 2,000,000 prisoners were released from Russian hands; and if certain supplies could be obtained from Russian territory are consequences that must be honestly contemplated. . . .

The delegates from Russia to the Paris Conference are to leave Petrograd in a few days. There is a great confusion of ideas among them as to the views they are to present and inasmuch as today, November 7, we are in the midst of a most serious crisis it is impossible to say what will be determined upon. It has been planned that the Foreign Minister, Tereshchenko, be the principal representative of the Government. He is but 31 years of age, independent in politics, very rich by inheritance from a father who made a fortune in the sugar business, was allied to the Terrorists before the Revolution (having once plotted to assassinate the czar) and is now classed by the Radicals as a Bourgeois, reactionary capitalist out of line with the majority and its peace aspirations. It is also planned that the Socialist Skobelev accompany the delegation representing "Democracy." Skobelev is also a rich man, has been in the Ministry, has the confidence of a large number of the Radicals and has received some instruction, not entirely in harmony with each other, from the Central Executive Committee of the Council of Workmen's and Soldiers' Delegates and from the Peasants' Soviet. In general these instructions relate to conditions of peace. It is certainly the opinion of those active in Russian politics that there should be an endeavor to arrive at Paris at a formulation of peace terms. The Bolsheviks are for a separate peace if necessary. The other Socialistic elements dwell only on the necessity of a general peace. Later: Tereshchenko went to jail on Nov. 8, 1917 (Bolshevik Revolution).[9]

FINANCE

As indicative of the rate at which the finances of Russia are approaching the precipice, there may be mentioned the present value of the rouble, which is ten cents and the circumstance that roubles which were printed to the extent of 1,800,000,000 in September, are now being printed at the rate of more than 500,000,000 per week. The outstanding issue of roubles is now 17,858,000,000 against which there is an equal issue of short term notes deposited with the State Bank.

Subscription to the Liberty Loan now are at the rate of but about 5,000,000 roubles per day as against 50,000,000 to 60,000,000 roubles per day two months ago. And yet a new guaranteed railway loan for 750,000,000 roubles was very recently greatly oversubscribed.

Nov. 7: Last night in anticipation of the meeting of the Soviet Congress today, the Red Guard (armed workmen, etc., of which there are nearly 30,000) together with a part of the Petrograd garrison, began taking over government institutions in Petrograd in behalf of the Bolsheviks. The Provisional Government was without power to make any material resistance.

At about 10 A.M., in an automobile borrowed from a secretary of our Embassy and with the American flag still flying on it, Kerensky escaped from the city to join the troops of the Northern Front. Kerensky told Baron Ramsay, a Russian Officer attached to my mission, that he would be back in a few days at the head of troops to restore the Provisional Government, and asked that our Ambassador be advised not to recognize the Bolshevik government.

Nov. 8: Last night the Winter Palace was bombarded and stormed by the Bolsheviks. The Ministry (except Kerensky) was arrested and confined in St. Peter and St. Paul. A few Military School cadets and a few companies of women offered futile resistance. After their capture many of the women were distributed among the barracks and outraged.

The Soviet Congress met last night at 10. About one-half (all but Bolsheviks) withdrew protesting at the violence that had been employed. The Congress adopted a program looking to immediate peace, the distribution of the land among the peasants and the seizure by the people of the means of production and distribution.

The Council of the Republic was forcibly dissolved.

There has been some bloodshed.

Nov. 9: The Soviet Congress adopted a resolution proposing to the people of the warring nations and to the present governments thereof a three months' armistice and an immediate peace without annexations or indemnities.

Another resolution it adopted distributing the lands leaving the details for further action.

It formed a government called the Commission of People's Commissars, Lenin being Chairman and Trotsky Commissar of Foreign Affairs. Then the Congress adjourned at 4 A.M. this day

During the day there has been no general disorder but many street assassinations have occurred and there have been small street fights in various localities.

We have heard of no movements from outside to repress the Bolsheviks. All news is censored by the latter, many journals having been suppressed.

We hear that Moscow has gone over to the Bolsheviks and a large part of the troops of the North Front.

Nov. 10: Many elements within Petrograd have united to form an "All-Russian Committee for the Salvation of the Fatherland and Revolution," including the Petrograd Duma, the former Central Executive Committee of the Workmen's and Soldiers' Delegates, the Executive Committee of the Peasants' Council, the Front group of the Soviet Congress (from the army), the Social Revolutionists, including the Minimalists [Mensheviks], the Council of the Russian Republic, etc. It is remarkable that these elements can be so active when the Bolsheviks have the town. It shows that they have not yet digested what they have bitten off.

For some time we have heard that Savinkov (formerly War Minister and friend of Kornilov) was organizing some forces, including Cossacks, to restore order when the times might demand, or perhaps to effect a coup d'etat. This morning we hear Savinkov heads certain troops (perhaps a division of Cossacks, with artillery) which fought a successful engagement with Bolshevik forces 30 versts south of town last night. We hear that now (2 P.M.) Savinkov is but 8 versts out; that Bolshevik troops surrender to him rather freely; that Kerensky is with Savinkov, practically a prisoner of the latter; that Moscow is driving the Bolsheviks into the Kremlin and besieging them there; that certain troops in Petrograd are ready to switch from the Bolsheviks.

There is occasional indiscriminate firing on the Nevsky in the neighborhood of the Municipal Duma. The Bolsheviks are probably trying to suppress the All-Russian Committee and to prevent the publication and the distribution of journals which have not submitted to the repressive edicts of the Bolsheviks.

Trotsky yesterday visited the Department of Foreign Affairs and was received "superciliously" by the employees, who later quit in a body, there being none on duty there now. The General Staff building is practically closed.

The Railway Employees Union is operating trains, mostly as usual. Whom they recognize, if any one, is uncertain.

Military news of a reliable character is absent. There are rumors that the Germans have equipped the Aland Islands, off the Finnish coast. Later this was denied.

Nov. 11:   Disorder grows. There has been fighting all day about the Telephone Exchange which was seized from the Bolsheviks this morning by student officers acting presumably for the All-Russian Committee, Several of the military school buildings have been besieged (the student officers having opposed the Bolsheviks) and one of them is on fire. The Telephone Exchange was retaken, the cadets suffering great losses as they did at the schools, all of which were taken.

. . . Not so many soldiers are visible as ordinarily. Some have been sent south with Red Guards to oppose the troops with Savinkov and Kerensky. They seem to be entrenched 12 to 15 versts south of town. It begins to look as though there were not enough troops loyal to their undertaking, certainly within easy reach of Petrograd, to subdue the Bolsheviks. At any rate we cannot understand otherwise why the delay occurs in the advance upon Petrograd.

Nov. 12:   This morning 4 regiments of Cossacks, quartered in the town, started out bent upon certain anti-Bolshevik activities, but changed their minds and resumed neutrality.

The Chairman of the All-Russian Committee has been arrested and will be tried at once, it is said by the Tribunal of the Revolution.

Local resistance to the Bolsheviks is becoming less, in fact it persists only in isolated spots.

We have heard that in Moscow the Bolsheviks are again in the saddle; that among those opposing them were several hundred French soldiers . . . and that these Frenchmen are among others who surrendered. The presence of these Frenchmen is an unfortunate circumstance. The killed and wounded at Moscow are reported at 2,600.

It is said that Kerensky troops south of town have been defeated and that a part of them have come under Bolshevik influence; that other troops however are coming from more or less distant places, in small bodies for the most part, although Kaledin is reported coming with large numbers of Don Cossacks. He is a long way off, however, and is reported today to have been seizing the Donetz coal field and engaging in disputes there with the miners which have induced the latter to stop work.

The Railway Union is still operating the railways. They sent an ultimatum today to the warring elements to cease their fighting and get together or they would soon strike. They really hold the whip hand.

The active army through the Chief of Staff, Dukhonin; "the Assistant Chief of Staff on matters of citizenship," Vyrubov; and the Chairman of the Army Committee has published a demand that Bolshevik violence cease, and that there be complete subordination to the Provisional

Government, "The only body capable of guiding the nation to the Constituent Assembly, the Master of the Russian Land."

This afternoon I sent Captains Riggs and Prince to the Smolny Institute to interview Trotsky on the subject of a guard of student officers we have had at the Military Mission since before the Bolshevik revolution. All of the student officers in town, except these, have been shot, drowned, beaten up and imprisoned or driven into hiding. Riggs was instructed to ask that we be allowed to keep the guard as against hooligans, on my agreement that they would not be used against the Bolshevik government forces. Trotsky agreed to this and said he would send us a paper to that effect. He would also let us know a reliable regiment to which we could appeal for assistance if it ever became necessary.

Trotsky expressed a very friendly feeling for American citizens as distinct from their government and said that as long as he was in power they should be safe in body and spirit, but that these were troublous times, with civil war in progress. . . .

The opposition to the Bolsheviks, in its complete disorganization, represents political anarchy.

It is hard to see how there can be a coming together. All the time in the background is the great inert 99 per cent, the active elements being but the froth on the surface, which when it settles down for a moment is disturbed by the slightest heave of the great mass beneath.

It may be that a tragedy is approaching which will dwarf that of the Great War. With anarchy in a country of 180,000,000 ignorant people, occupying one-sixth of the land surface of the earth, existing under conditions which make necessary for life itself a certain orderliness of production, transportation and distribution, it is possible that any imaginable evils may accompany the introduction of a more complete anarchy than has already prevailed here. And today it is complete anarchy that faces Russia, although there may be stages between here and that which may offer opportunity for recovery. It is time for the whole [world to] offer opportunity for recovery. It is time for the whole world to give consideration to the plight of Russia, some day destined perhaps to be the greatest of the nations.

Perhaps the collapse of Russia may be even a greater blow at democracy than would the continued political existence of the Kaiser. In fact the one might necessarily involve the other.

Nov. 13: The Bolsheviks are still in complete charge of Petrograd.

I visited the British Embassy this morning and found them disturbed as to the safety of the Embassies. I saw Sir George Buchanan (the Ambassador) and General Knox, (the Military Attaché) and the former told us he had had advice from Stockholm indicating probable attacks upon his Embassy and person. With Sir George and Knox I visited the French Embassy where we saw the Ambassador and General Lavergne (the Military Attaché). The Ambassador read us several telegrams from Moscow. They were very conflicting as to whether the Bolsheviks or their opponents were gaining the upper hand. The Ambassador said . . . French troops had taken no part in the fighting at Moscow.

Knox, Lavergne and I then visited the office of the Petrograd Staff. There were many "tavarischi" ("comrades") on duty,—armed workmen, etc.,—but no Staff in the ordinary sense. Finally Colonel Muraviev came in looking very tired and nervous. He commands the Bolshevik troops and had just returned from south of town where he said Kerensky had been defeated and driven out of Czarskoe Selo, the armored cars having shot up the Cossacks badly. Colonel Muraviev said he would establish pickets to look out for the Embassies and arrange for their protection in case of need by regiments already domiciled conveniently near them.

There is no news indicating at what rate, if at all, the anti-Bolshevik forces will be able to build up their forces south of town. For the present it appears that the Bolsheviks locally are more than a match for those facing them. Nor is there news of any character from out of town which is more than wild rumor. We do not know whether Moscow is in a state of truce or civil war. But various socialistic elements appear to be discussing compromise there.

Here they talk also of a compromise between the Bolsheviks, Minimalists and Social-Revolutionists. The last two will not agree to let the Bolsheviks in a new government. . . . No one speaks much any more of participation in a new government by the Kadets (bourgeois).

It is readily to be seen from what precedes that Russia faces more or less complete anarchy and civil war.

NOVEMBER 10, 1917. PETROGRAD
MEMORANDUM FOR AMBASSADOR:

Ever since the Russian Revolution occurred and our country entered the war I have been sure that for purposes too numerous to mention, including example, propaganda, protection etc. I have been an advocate of sending American troops to Russia.[10] My opinions as expressed months ago were not endorsed by Mr. Root or General Scott and of course they have remained in abeyance, although they have remained with me and been reinforced by the expressions of many Russian officers of rank, experience and judgment. When I was at Stavka recently I submitted informally a proposition to the Chief of the British Military Mission to send allied troops to Russia, but found him then opposed to such an understanding and I pursued the subject no further although I had mentioned it to you.

Now I am informed by General Knox that he will place before the British Ambassador a proposition that there be sent to Petrograd 1,000 each (or 500 at any rate) of French, English, American and Japanese troops, to form guards for Embassies, to constitute strong points in Petrograd, the presence of which might discourage disorders etc. I am informed that the French Military Mission endorses this proposition.

I take advantage of this opportunity to give renewed expression to my belief that allied troops should be sent here. I wish I could join my colleagues, or rather that they would join me, in suggesting that more be sent than are above proposed.

It is believed that any new government, under the spur of recent occurrences, will readily assent to the proposition, and that the early days of the existence of any new government will offer favorable opportunity to place the matter before them.

If you see fit to regard this matter favorably I will also take up the matter with the War Department.

NOVEMBER 10, 1917. PARAPHRASE OF TELEGRAM SENT TO WARCOLSTAFF WASHINGTON. NO: -67- 81 4 P.M.[11]

Today the Bolsheviks are in undisputed control of all Governmental agencies with which we are in touch, and we hear that Moscow and many troops on the North Front have joined the movement of the Bolsheviks. There are many journals suppressed, and all news is censored by the Bolsheviks.

The Soviet Congress has chosen a Ministry with Lenin as President, and with Trotsky as Minister of Foreign Affairs.

There is no general disorder yet, but many murders have occurred, and the situation is ominous.

No signs are visible to us that the Bolsheviks will be overcome in a few days. The food supply is the vital and perhaps determining question. Railroads are still functioning, although precariously.

10 A.M. November 10, 1917. We hear that troops are approaching under different leaders, including Savinkov and Kerensky, and with Guchkov in the background, with the common end to suppress the Bolsheviks. There are many elements in Petrograd planning against the Bolsheviks.

A fight which has occurred last night 30 versts South of Petrograd, has gone apparently against the Bolsheviks, and overcoming the latter is growing more probable. However, news from the outside is very uncertain and conflicting.

General Pershing has been informed of the above.

NOVEMBER 11, 1917. PARAPHRASE OF TELEGRAM SENT TO WARCOLSTAFF WASHINGTON. NO: -69- 82 4 P.M.[12]

The Bolshevik Congress has adjourned sine die on November 9, at 5:15 A.M. having passed decrees abolishing private ownership of land, and proposing to belligerent nations and governments, a three months armistice and democratic peace, without any annexations or contributions, having appointed a Government entitled Commission of Peoples Commissars, with Lenin as Chairman, with Trotsky as Commissar of Foreign Affairs, and with eleven others; and having also provided for a Central Executive Committee of 100.

According to the Bolshevik reports, troops are approaching, but not in sufficient number, or possessed of spirit enough to overcome them. The advancing troops are apparently not making much progress against the entrenched Red Guard and Bolshevik troops.

Street shooting is increasing all over the town. Kerensky is apparently in a form of duress in the hands of the Cossacks.

Not much stomach for fighting or certainly as to preferences among the troops anywhere. The Red Guard is undisciplined, but knows its own mind, and has determination.

There are some small naval vessels in the River, and reported off Peterhoff assisting the Bolsheviks. The position of the Navy is divided, but probably has a tendency to the Bolsheviks. Active elements are relatively small, and each side claims everything. The side will win that is believed. If the Bolsheviks are subdued, the other elements will find difficulty in agreeing. The outlook is for more complete and less benevolent anarchy than has prevailed formerly. The news is still conflicting and uncertain.

General Pershing has been informed of the above.

NOVEMBER 12, 1917. PARAPHRASE OF TELEGRAM SENT TO WARCOLSTAFF WASHINGTON. NO: -72- 84 4 P.M.[13]

I have just learned from the Ambassador as to his query of what attitude the United States would assume towards a request from the Russian Government for several divisions. During the present crisis advise suspension of judgement. I have believed from the beginning of the War that it is advisable to send a division here for purposes of example, propaganda, guard, etc. Root, Scott, and I understand, Francis all opposed. Many Russians opinions of value have lately urged sending. I recently made proposal to the British Mission regarding composite Allied Corps but obtained no concurrence of opinions. Military Missions now propose urging Ambassadors, after formation of stable Government, to secure consent towards bringing in 500 or 1000 each of British, French, American, and Japanese respectively, as Embassy guards etc. Although I concur, I personally still believe in more.

General Pershing has been informed of the above.

NOVEMBER 13, 1917. PARAPHRASE OF TELEGRAM SENT TO WARCOLSTAFF WASHINGTON. SERVICE NO. 75. NO. 85. 11 A.M.[14]

Fighting taking place South of the town is indecisive. Barely possible that attacking forces will build up by gradual accretions from scattering localities, but additional troops in town are joining the Bolsheviks. Four Cossack regiments are waiting here to join the victors. The Bolsheviks are keeping fair order in Petrograd today.

Trotsky has assured two of my officers that they would protect foreigners. Civil war seems to be extending geographically. We are cut off largely from reliable news. The only way to tide over until the Constitutional Congress, appears to be through a Socialist Coalition Ministry, but influential elements still hope to omit the Bolsheviks. Immediate peace by such a Government would be impracticable. It might prove that Russia would stay in the War until a fair conclusion.

General Pershing has been informed of the above. Request Pershing and myself be advised by cable as to assignment of code word for Bolshevik, and myself one for Michelson.

NOVEMBER 14, 1917. PARAPHRASE OF TELEGRAM SENT TO WARCOLSTAFF WASHINGTON. NO. 78. 4 P.M.

A copy of this telegram immediately to Postmaster General Burleson in order that he may show to the President should he see fit.

Russia may be put into anarchy and out of the war as a result of the shock of the present crisis on top of her past experiences. Under conditions requiring for life itself some order and system in production, transportation and distribution, there exist in Russia 180,000,000 people mostly ignorant as plantation negroes [sic], scattered over one sixth of the land surface of the earth. All order and system are departing. Conditions make possible a cataclysm which may dwarf the great war and be a tremendous blow to democracy. The resulting world-shock is apt to lead everywhere to an accentuated struggle between extreme socialism and severe reaction with a general setback to civilization and democratic system.

The blow to democracy due to cataclysm in Russia would immensely increase the chance of a second blow due to the increased political security of autocracy in Germany.

A conviction is held by the German soldiers that the Allies seek to crush Germany. This thrice arms Germany, in degree protecting her army from democratic or socialistic propaganda until too late.

A similar conviction has been impressed by Germany on the Russian army and on strong groups now seeking political control here. Such conviction makes Russian army impotent, fosters Russian anarchy and helps defeat Kerensky.

This problem could perhaps be solved by our President.

Such solution apparently must include effort to state practical terms of peace which neither side could refuse without an appearance of unfairness to simple but honest minds, German perhaps as well as Russian.

The peace program of the Russian socialists is not so far from that advanced in December 1916 by our President. The Russians think the French simply war-crazy but distrust the British. The lead must apparently be taken by the United States and our President.

The action suggested is dictated in my opinion by military necessity and need not lead to a peace that is not desirable.

In the near future any Russian Government formed must have peace program but unless complete anarchy prevents, will remain at war if Germany does not meet fair terms.

NOVEMBER 14, 1917. PARAPHRASE TELEGRAM SENT WARCOLSTAFF WASHINGTON. NO: -75-5 P.M.

The Telephone Exchange was seized from the Bolsheviks yesterday by the student forces. Some 600 of these cadets were defeated at the Telephone Exchange, and also at their schools, with great slaughter. Armed resistance to the Bolsheviks within Petrograd, has been practically suppressed. A famine is impending. The Railway Union, operating trains, may hold the whip hand, and threatens to strike unless all varieties of Socialists form a Coalition Government. The Moderates refuse to join the Bolsheviks, and all reject non-Socialists. The active Army Staff has published statement supporting the Provisional Government, but the Army appears not to follow the Staff. The General Staff in Petrograd is entirely out of business.

Kaledin appears to have seized the Donetz coal fields, occupied certain Railway lines, and organized the Don Cossacks against the Bolsheviks. Moscow experiences appear to be parallel to those of Petrograd, but the Bolsheviks are having greater difficulty. The Bolsheviks seem strong in many places, including large parts of the Army. Kerensky is still skirmishing a few versts South of the town, but is not apparently strong enough to win.

NOVEMBER 14, 1917. DIARY[15]

Today has been quiet in town, but there is an immense amount of plotting going on. There are two committees, on "Salvation of Russian Republic and Revolution," belligerently Anti-Bolshevik, and one on "Public Safety," which is neutral. Many men are at once members of both. . . . The Salvation Committee is plotting and directing various movements against the Bolsheviks. It is made up of Conservative Socialists.

Negotiations go on as to a new government. There are two ideas among the Conservative Socialists; one to form a non-Bolshevik Socialist government with such men on it as Tseretelli, Chernov, Verkhovsky, Avksentiev, and the other to permit Bolshevik (but no Bourgeois) participation. The "no Bolshevik" adherents are quite uncompromising. Their plans are either (1) to let the Bolsheviks form a government and then practice sabotage against it if necessary so that it would fail almost at once, or (2) to form an opposing government outside Petrograd, consisting of all Socialist elements except Bolsheviks and proceed to civil war. . . .

The Salvation Committee appears rather to favor the non-Bolshevik civil war horn of the dilemma. They would probably fight Kaledin and his Cossacks (on the theory that they are counter-revolutionary) as well as the Bolsheviks. . . .

General Verkhovsky visited me today. He said he had been at a monastery from the date of his enforced departure until yesterday. . . . He is going to Mogilev to handle the army as against the Bolsheviks. He is opposed to coalition with the latter. He wishes Allies to help formulate terms of peace which will appeal to the simple Russian soldiers. If this is not done they will not fight.

NOVEMBER 15, 1917. PARAPHRASE OF TELEGRAM SENT
TO WARCOLSTAFF WASHINGTON. NO: -79-
EIGHTYEIGHT 11 A.M.[16]

The troops in the south of the town having made a truce Kerensky with a few supporters is a fugitive.

Division into three classes of the Anti-Bolshevik Socialists. First class favors a coalition with the Bolsheviks. The second class favors letting the Bolsheviks govern but in the meantime practicing sabotage against them. The Third class favors conducting a civil war after establishing a government outside of Petrograd. Complete control here now in the hands of the Bolsheviks. Allegiance of army all split up and in various parts of Russia there is fighting. There is a strike on here of the bank, telegraph and government employees and there is a suspension of the administrative functions of the government. Famine is approaching. Railways operating feebly.

Pershing cabled the above message.

Kerensky a fugitive with few supporters, troops south of town having made truce.

. . . Bolsheviks in complete control here. Army allegiance all split up and fighting going on in various parts of Russia. Bank, Telegraph and Government office employees here on strike and administrative functions of government suspended. Railways operating feebly. Famine impending.

Yesterday Kerensky's Cossacks compromised with the Bolsheviks and Kerensky was advised by the former to surrender. He is reported however to have escaped. Today the Bolsheviks marched triumphantly back through town with bands playing. The Military Revolutionary Committee is trying to send Red Guards to assist the Bolsheviks of Moscow but the Railway Union has refused to haul them. Excellent order in town today. We hear they were still fighting in Moscow yesterday, where there has been some damage to the Kremlin and to many buildings by artillery fire and much loss of life. Apparently the Bolsheviks in Moscow have much the best of it.

NOVEMBER 15, 1917. PETROGRAD

Dearest—

For nearly 10 days we have been watching the Bolsheviks gradually take possession of the town. With much street fighting—lots of deaths and many pathetic incidents. Kerensky is down and out. Nobody loved him. The anti-Bolsheviks are all at sixes and sevens. The army is split into factions fighting each other. If there is no issue from this, we'll probably be on the way home in a week or two. There will be famine in the town soon. We have lots to eat.

I have a Red Cross Commission living with me and that makes company.

The telegraph is closed and all the government buildings—the old employees being on strike. Thus the Bolsheviks have no administration machinery. Anarchy is with us.

Have just heard of a pouch going off today from the British Embassy. I'll have to write dispatches—most important ones—to be cabled from Stockholm. So I'll close, with a heart full of love and good wishes for you and Clay.

Faithfully

NOVEMBER 16, 1917. MEMORANDUM FOR AMBASSADOR:

One purpose in the maintenance here by our Government of a Military Mission and Military Attaché is of course in order that the Ambassador may be furnished promptly with advice of a military character from a Professional source. In these days with our principal interest in Russia a military interest, many more matters have a military side than is always apparent at first thought. By reason of the facts above recited, I may seem, in loyalty to you as Ambassador, to my own duties and to my Government, to offer opinions and advice more frequently than would otherwise appear reasonable.

The military situation among other things is such that it is not probable that any terms of peace proposed by the Bolsheviks would be immediately if at all acceptable to Germany. Therefore I do not believe that there is any immediate danger of Russia formally withdrawing from the war.

The Bolshevik government appears locally to possess control of military forces sufficient to ensure it a certain duration of power, certainly in Petrograd.

In other parts of Russia too the Bolsheviks appear to possess control of very considerable military forces when compared with other such forces as are willing to engage in any present activities.

The Kerensky element and the Bourgeois element appear to have no present importance in the situation.

The non-Bolshevik left and centre of the Social-Revolutionists and the Minimalist group of the Social Democrats appear to possess all present importance (aside from the Bolsheviks). These two elements are working together but seem among themselves to possess 3 opinions as to the proper immediate course of action. The first opinion is that there should be a coalition of all Socialist elements including the Bolsheviks. The second is that the Bolsheviks should be unopposed by force and unassisted, the Bolshevik government being assailed by methods of sabotage so that it could not successfully administer government, thus causing its speedy collapse. The third opinion, held by Verkhovsky among others, is that the non-Bolshevik Socialists should set up a government in some convenient place away from Petrograd and engage in civil war with the Bolsheviks with a view to overcoming them by force.

The second opinion has the weakness that it would result at least temporarily in anarchy and no one can be sure how long such a condition would endure.

The weakness of the third option is that it frankly contemplates civil war.

In my opinion prolonged anarchy or civil war would probably endanger allied interests of a military character in Russia to a greater degree than would any other course of events. Either might result more effectively than any other course in a practical loss of Russia as a partner in the war.

With Russia out of the war, after what has happened to Italy (and admitting that Rumania must follow Russia) it appears that Germany can be decisively defeated with the greatest difficulty if at all. Certainly it will be safe for us to act here on that hypothesis and spare no effort to keep Russia in the war if only formally and with but a certain detaining function, and for as long as we can, if not until the war's conclusion.

Please regard military secrets thus communicated to you as confidential. A discovery by the enemy or by disaffected Americans or even by Russians that the facts are as stated in preceding paragraph for example, would do incalculable harm.

Read to Ambassador Nov. 16, 1917, W. V. J.[17]

NOVEMBER 16, 1917. PARAPHRASE OF MESSAGE SENT
TO WARCOLSTAFF WASHINGTON. NO: -82 NINETY 6 P.M.[18]

At the request of the Bolsheviks under Manikovsky, Assistant Minister, released from jail the War Department is beginning to function. Endeavoring to administer without politics for the good of the country against enemy but fractions take part in civil war. Command of the army has been assumed by Dukhonin vice Kerensky whose whereabouts are unknown. Bolsheviks maintain order here. They are sending troops from here to Moscow where they are apparently gaining. Most of the troops inert; everywhere the numbers engaged relatively small.

There will be a revolution in Finland shortly Bolsheviks against the Bourgeois according to information from Trotsky.

Any intention of separate peace is denied by many of the Bolsheviks. They say that they simply wish to arrange a speedy general peace and if Germany will not grant fair terms they will fight to the death.

At present the principal element opposing the Bolsheviks are the three divisions of the Anti-Bolshevik Socialists: . . . [see 16 November 1917 memorandum for ambassador, above]. Impossible for anyone to guess the requisite duration of either method proposed to end the Bolsheviks. While he might be on the winning side later at present the Socialists' strength in and out of the army is probably too strong for Kaledin's movement.

Nov. 17th Morning. Nothing new except that body of troops advancing 100 versts south of this city are hostile to the Bolsheviks perhaps under Verkhovsky.

Pershing cabled the above message.

NOVEMBER 16, 1917. DIARY

Col. Golievsky called us to the General Staff today (all Allied Attachés) and read to us an order by General Manikovsky, Assistant Minister of War, assuming administrative control of the War Department in the interest of the Army and the Nation. He had accepted this duty on the condition that he would have no political functions whatever and enjoined upon officers to resume their military duties, taking no part in politics.

Col. Golievsky complained of alarming reports that Foreign Missions were about to leave Petrograd, the Aaland Islands were captured, etc. He said the Russian Daily News was the chief offender. Golievsky said there had been a slight German demonstration on Minsk front but that it had been repulsed; that there had been no landing on the Aaland Islands; that the Republic (Petropovlovsk) had been seriously damaged by a mine; that liaison between War Department (and General Staff) and Stavka was being reestablished.

Col. G. said arrangements would be made to protect the Foreign Missions (by the Bolsheviks) that Trachtenberg had been indicated to have this in hand. . . .

Lieut. Bukowski[19] had an interview with Trotsky today. He said we might keep our Polish guard until all such were withdrawn; that Finland was on eve of civil war (between Bourgeoisie and Bolsheviks); that no enemy had landed on Aaland Islands or advanced near Minsk; that the Germans would not be such fools as to attack Russia in view of her peace declarations, but that if they did, the Russian soldiers would resist to the last; that Russia's peace negotiations with Germany had not yet begun but would begin today; that Kerensky is in all probability in hiding at Gatchina.

NOVEMBER 17. DIARY

. . . "Truces" are being effected in a number of localities, there being a rising feeling against civil war, per se. These truces generally inure to the immediate advantage of the Bolsheviks, as at Moscow for example, where apparently the truce took the form of a surrender of the forces opposing the Bolsheviks, with the condition that such opposing forces should be allowed to lay down their arms and depart in peace.

NOVEMBER 18, 1917. PARAPHRASE OF MESSAGE SENT
TO WARCOLSTAFF WASHINGTON. NO: -85 NINETYONE 11 A.M.[20]

As a result of the surrender of opposing forces, Moscow is now Bolshevik.

The Ministry of the Bolsheviks is split up and about one-half have resigned holding that the government should broaden out and include all socialistic elements while Lenin says that he and Trotsky can, if necessary, run the government. Apparently the Bolsheviks are having trouble in getting the Petrograd garrison troops to go south and oppose the troops, now less than 100 versts away, advancing from the front. As yet no great importance is attached to the movement.

It is reported that the Ukraine has declared independence and are opposing Kaledin.

Against the development of civil war there is a strong and widespread feeling. Trend of events cannot be foretold as yet.

Against the Baltic Sea-Black Sea front or Finland or the Aaland Islands there are no important movements on the part of the enemy. The Germans intend Finnish operations to cut the Torneo railway line, according to reports from agents, but recent events may change their plans.

Above message was cabled to Pershing.

NOVEMBER 18. DIARY

We hear that the Bolsheviks have ordered troops from the Petrograd garrison south to oppose the troops advancing from the front, who are supposed to be about 100 versts away. It is said that but few of the Petrograd troops are obeying this order.

It is reported that Col. Muraviev, Commanding the Bolshevik forces, has submitted his resignation.

There seems to be a serious split in the Bolshevik "Ministry." About half of the "Commissars" have resigned, demanding an all Socialist Coalition Ministry.

NOVEMBER 19, 1917. MEMORANDUM FOR THE AMBASSADOR:

The source of military authority in Petrograd today is at the Smolny Institute.[21] As I have to secure military information for our government which is of enormous importance at this time, I shall assume that in warning me not to recognize the Soviet Government you do not wish me to refrain from such trivial intercourse with Smolny—on matters of telephones, guards and the like—as will enable me to secure such information. Such trivial intercourse is had by the other Military Missions.

NOVEMBER 19, 1917. PARAPHRASE OF MESSAGE SENT TO WARCOLSTAFF WASHINGTON. NO: -88 NINETYTHREE 1 P.M.[22]

From the standpoint of American interest I believe that the situation is not necessarily hopeless and that Russia may continue detaining the troops of the enemy indefinitely. No attacks on any Russian political elements or desires and a continued display of sympathy is advisable.

The Staff has issued no reports since Nov. 7th giving the movements of the units of the enemy. On that date the last estimates were that there were on this front 112 enemy divisions plus 20 divisions of cavalry. Since then important number have probably left for other fronts. The remaining divisions of the enemy on this front are also probably still further weakened in artillery and effectives.

All men under 35 are being withdrawn from certain of the units of the enemy. Two Land-wher Brigades have been raised to Divisions. More will probably follow these.

Above was cabled to Pershing.

NOVEMBER 19. DIARY.

Today we hear that last night the committee of 100 of the Soviet (of whom about 2/3 have not resigned), by a vote of 55 to 5 gave Lenin dictatorial powers.

Trotsky today announced that he would visit the foreign office at 1 P.M. and that all employees not then present would be considered dismissed.

The Bolsheviks today demanded 15,000,000 roubles from the State Bank. They said they would take possession of the funds and books of the bank if the money was not promptly delivered.

It is said that the troops near Luga are the 49th corps from the S.W. front and that in the interest of Kerensky the Wild Division is in the same neighborhood. . . .

Query. Is it not possible that Russia will temporarily break up into a number of more or less independent states, each endeavoring to preserve itself from the universal anarchy? The Ukraine, Finland, S.E. Russia under Kaledin, and Siberia readily suggest themselves as possible independencies of this character.

NOVEMBER 19, 1917
MEMORANDUM FOR THE AMBASSADOR:

It is quite certain that in Petrograd and vicinity (as well as in many other parts of Russia) the Soviet or Bolshevik Government at present has complete military control. The responsibility is thus thrown upon that government to guard the lives and property of foreigners, including foreign Missions. This responsibility it seems to recognize and has accordingly made or proposes to make, certain arrangements of a military character which appear to be reasonable and adequate to meet existing conditions or those to be soon apprehended if looting shall break out as the result of hunger.

I have been giving a great deal of thought to your intention to defend the Embassy, under certain circumstances with armed civilians and servants and I must respectfully place before you what seem the dangers of such a course.

The lives of the few Americans and their property and the property of our Government are per se of the very slightest importance. But of the very greatest importance is the possible effect that the loss of any such lives or the loss of Russian lives at the hands of any Americans may have upon our international relations. A single shot by a nervous or overwrought clerk or servant unaccustomed to the use of arms might precipitate an affair. . . . On the other hand any active steps, involving loss of lives perhaps, which are taken by Russians against Russians, would leave us relatively unaffected and unconcerned and free to pursue a course designed to keep Russia in the war . . . as long as possible. That Russia should be thus kept in the war is of primary importance.

To sum the matter up, I do not think that we should assume the responsibility of a civil guard when such a course might, by a reasonable sequence of events, hinted at above, even threaten adversely to affect the result of the war itself.

NOVEMBER 20, 1917

DRAFT OF PROPOSED APPEAL (CABLE TO WAR DEPT) IN MATTER OF INJUNCTION BY AMBASSADOR AGAINST INTERCOURSE WITH THOSE IN MILITARY CONTROL HEREABOUTS.

Probably German Staff Officers operating here.

Other Allied Military Missions freely communicating on details such as passports, protection information etc. with Bolshevik Government, which exercises all military control here and at certain frontiers, and which also controls to certain extent general staff operations here. Fearing lest recognize Bolshevik Government Ambassador has forbidden me or my subordinates to communicate with Bolshevik authorities including general staff on any matters. This cuts me off from sources of military and related information enjoyed by other Military Missions including German and from other minor useful functions performed by English and French.

Request Ambassador be advised that such minor communications, acceptance of guard at Embassy, arrangements for protection foreigners, acceptance of permission by Americans to cross frontier at Torneo, etc. do not constitute recognition, and that Military Mission should be allowed some discretion in public interest. My office handles passport control and has a small intelligence section.

(Above read by me to Ambassador Nov. 20 '17. To be filed with my letter of Nov. 21 to Ambassador [below] which made proposed appeal ((above draft)) unnecessary.) W. V. J.

EMBASSY OF THE UNITED STATES OF AMERICA
PETROGRAD, NOVEMBER, 20, 1917.

TO THE MILITARY ATTACHÉ,
OF THE AMERICAN EMBASSY.
PETROGRAD.

Sir:

I write you for the purpose of making a record of a conversation we had yesterday concerning the relations of the Embassy and yourself as Military Attaché to the Bolshevik officials who are attempting to administer affairs from Smolny Institute and also from staff headquarters.

You will remember that I told you it was my policy to do nothing or permit no act to be performed by anyone connected with the Embassy or under my control that could be construed as a direct or indirect recognition of what is generally known as the "Bolshevik" government. I desire herewith to repeat that instruction.

I note your memorandum states "You do not wish me to refrain from such trivial intercourse with Smolny—on matters of telephones, guards and the like". When I asked you to confer with me before having such intercourse you said that emergencies might arise which would not give you time to confer with me. My reply was that I was in the Embassy and accessible at all hours.

(Signed) DAVID R. FRANCIS
American Ambassador.

NOVEMBER 20, 1917. PARAPHRASE OF MESSAGE SENT TO WARCOLSTAFF WASHINGTON. NO: -91 NINETYFOUR.[23]

In the army hunger is commencing. Ten thousand cars of provisions are said to be in Moscow and on many roads the trains are tied up with little moving. There is only a little food arriving in this city and only enough here for a few days.

Lenin is claiming authority throughout Russia and is the practical dictator hereabouts. At Moscow he controls [?] and as far as Torneo and Archangel on passport matters.

A strike is still on among the administrative personnel of government departments, banks, etc. Lenin has need of money and is having difficulties with the personnel of the State Bank. There are no funds for the army paymasters. Lenin claims that the opposing elements are practicing sabotage and threatens severe measures. Many journals are still suspended. Many arrests occur daily.

To escape anarchy many sections may attempt to organize separate governments, as the Ukraine, South East Russia under Kaledin, etc.

General dissention and breakdown of administrative functions, with famine are the only things that immediately threaten Lenin.

Pershing cabled the foregoing.

NOVEMBER 20, 1917. DIARY

A decree has been published over Lenin's signature announcing "the success of the revolution of the peasants and workmen" and the overcoming of the capitalists and bourgeois. This decree states that the opposition is trying to sabotage the government and offset the power of the people, but that the power of the opposition is broken. It enjoins the common people to group themselves around their soviets and to preserve the resources of the country. . . .

At a meeting of the Central Executive Committee of Soviets on Nov. 17 after a long debate Lenin was sustained by a vote of 29 to 23 in issuing decrees without consulting the committee. This virtually makes Lenin dictator.

Trotsky took physical charge of the Foreign Affairs Ministry yesterday. But few of the chiefs of bureaus, etc. were present. T. was handed the keys by an assistant minister, who, with most of the other officers, soon departed, leaving Trotsky alone with his private secretary, Zalkind. The latter submitted to an interview in which he said that "on that very day" the foreign missions would be notified of the change of government. He said further that there would be a change in the diplomatic representation of Russia abroad.

NOVEMBER 21, 1917

THE HONORABLE DAVID R. FRANCIS
AMERICAN AMBASSADOR, PETROGRAD:

My dear Mr. Ambassador:

Referring to your two letters [short letter on communication, long on civilian guard; latter not included here] of November 20 addressed to me as Military attaché, and to our conversation of same date in which we came to a satisfactory understanding as to certain of my duties, I write the following simply for record.

Your longer letter, relating to a proposed civil guard at the Embassy, was written under the misapprehension that that matter was the one I had said I would feel obliged to take up with the War Department. In fact it was as to the other matter, concerning the relations of the Military Mission with the actual military authorities here, that I felt an appeal from your previous injunction of non-intercourse was a matter of duty (as to which reference is made to my memorandum on that subject of November 19; and to draft of the cable I proposed to send, which I read you yesterday).

The whole misunderstanding is now "liquidated", as the Russians say, and as a result of our conversation of yesterday it is understood that I am to be careful not to "recognize" the Bolshevik government in a diplomatic sense, but after any necessary intercourse, for convenience, with those in actual possession of the military power hereabouts I am to inform you of it.

Thanking you for this satisfactory solution of my difficulties, I am,

Yours very respectfully,

NOVEMBER 22, 1917. PARAPHRASE OF TELEGRAM SENT WARCOLSTAFF WASHINGTON. NO. 97 NINETYSIX 5 P.M.[24]

Finland is in the control of Socialists akin to the Bolsheviks. Besides one declaring independence various other socialistic laws have been passed and a Socialist ministry is forming. For several days there has been a mild reign of terror in Helsingfors and elsewhere apparently subsiding now. To avoid civil war the Bourgeois have yielded. All Finns seemed to desire independence. Russian sailors and soldiers supported the Socialists. The Red Guards have the police power in Helsingfors and many towns.

That the Germans expected assistance from some Finnish Bourgeois elements in return for independence, general good will and preservation from the Bolsheviks is somewhat evidenced. At present such a course might embarrass German interests here and it seems reasonable that there will be no German intervention in Finland at the present. It is reported that the enemy have largely cleared the Gulfs of Finland and Bothnia from mines.

NOVEMBER 22, 1917, 10 A.M.

For the time being opposition to the Bolsheviks in Russia is apparently paralysed by the popularity with the Army of the Peace and land programs of the Bolsheviks. Anti-Bolshevik sentiment in the directing forces of the army including some of the committees but not among the soldiers.

The movement of Kaledin is local to the Don district.

The two corps of soldiers that are 100 versts south of Petrograd have not made up their minds what to do as yet.

If backed by even one reliable army corps there are elements available that could organize a workable socialistic government. The situation is thus in an unstable equilibrium. The latter may be disturbed by hunger and propaganda. For the Bolsheviks the economic conditions are growing worse. Another and more serious reign of terror will probably take place in Petrograd soon. Now contemplating requisitions upon the inhabitants. At the front and in Petrograd the food supply is dwindling. As yet actual suffering has not begun.

Dukhonin has been directed by Lenin to propose an immediate armistice to the Commander-in-Chief of the enemy and has notified at least one Allied Embassy of this action. It is unknown what course Dukhonin proposes to follow.

Above to Pershing.

NOVEMBER 22, 1917. PARAPHRASE OF TELEGRAM SENT WARCOLSTAFF WASHINGTON. NO. 99 NINETYSEVEN 10 P.M.[25]

The Allied Military Representatives at Headquarters of the Supreme Commander have presented a protest against armistice mentioned in my cable number 96 dated November 22nd. Failing to obey orders of Bolshevik Government to negotiate truce, Dukhonin has been relieved of his post as Commander in Chief.

General Pershing informed of the above.

NOVEMBER 22, 1917. DIARY

Six Allied Missions received notes from Trotsky informing them of the existence of the new "Government" and of the instructions to Dukhonin of yesterday to arrange a truce with the enemy commander.

There was a meeting of the Allied Missions today, at which it was decided that no joint action on the note would be taken, each representative handling it as he might see fit. Our Ambassador announced that if called upon to make reply he would say that he had informed his government of the contents of the note as was his custom in connection with important happenings in Russia.

At Stavka the Allied Military representatives were called together by Gen. Dietrichs the quartier-general, and informed of the character of Gen. Dukhonin's instructions, protested against the truce. Gen. Dukhonin, when called to the telephone by a representative of the Bolshevik government here, pointed out the difficulties in the way of an arrangement of a truce by him, asking as to the Rumanians who are under his orders, expressing doubt as to whom they wished him to negotiate a truce with, and saying that this was a matter for the government and not for him. When he seemed indisposed to start arranging a truce at once, he was relieved from duty peremptorily by telephone and the "Peoples' Commissar for War" Krylenko,[26] was named as his successor. . . .

. . . A telegram from the North Front today said that famine had set in among the troops there, and demanded an immediate reply to a request for food.

Soon, probably, induced by individual fears of starvation, the front will begin to break up, some surrendering and others struggling to the rear.[27]

NOVEMBER 23, 1917. PARAPHRASE OF TELEGRAM SENT WARCOLSTAFF WASHINGTON. NO. 102 98 11 A.M.[28]

Krylenko replaces Dukhonin as Commander-in-Chief. Krylenko is the Bolshevik War Minister and is now called the Peoples Commissar for War.

Kerth is at Stavka. It is reported that Stavka will move from Mogilev to Novocherkask, which indicates that Dukhonin may not surrender command as ordered.

Petrograd wired by the Northern Front that food urgently needed or the troops will starve and a quick answer is demanded.

Famine may probably cause the surrender of many troops and the rest to proceed to rear in great disorder. Troops to the south including the Rumanians are better supplied at the present moment.

The regiments at the front directed by Lenin to arrest their generals and to negotiate through committees truces with opposing enemy troops.

If various socialistic elements could be induced to form a coalition government and conduct orderly administration even including peace negotiations, time might be gained. General Pershing informed as above.

NOVEMBER 23, 1917. DIARY

I visited Gen. Manikovsky today. He said he was having a hard time administering the War Department on the technical and supply side. He described a "knot" at Moscow, where 276 trains (11,000 cars) produced a congestion that forbade train movement through Moscow. He said that the removal of this congestion was apparently hindered by the lack of confidence and cooperation between the Railway Men's Union and the officials of the Department of Ways and Communications. He said he thought that the situation could be cured by quick action by the American Railway Commission or other "neutral" railway agencies. He did not know that the only railway man we have in European Russia is Mr. Horne, who acts apparently under the immediate orders of the Ambassador and who has done nothing yet but get reservations on trains for Americans.

I visited Horne immediately, who said he could do nothing without orders from the Ambassador whom he would see at luncheon. Horne said in effect that he had no office, no assistant, no interpreter and no duties, — in fact that all he had was a toothache. He blamed the American Red Cross, with which he was formerly affiliated, that he was without interpreter.

I immediately saw Thacher of the Red Cross and made arrangement to provide Horne with an interpreter at once, at my expense or Thacher's or that of the Red Cross.

Then I saw Gen. Niessel. He immediately said he would send his transportation man, De Castel, to Moscow on the evening train. I suggested that De Castel see Horne and Gen. Poole (British) with a view to having Horne and possibly De Candolle (English R'way General) accompany him, and that he make preliminary arrangements with the Ministry of Ways and Communications and the Railway Union. . . . At 2 I went to our Embassy. Horne was there and the Ambassador took charge but did not change any of the arrangements I had made. Horne, De Castel and perhaps De Candolle go to Moscow tonight.

The Bolshevik Government has ordered regiments at the front to arrest generals not favorable to the Bolsheviks' plans and through committees to negotiate truces with enemy troops on their fronts. . . .

. . . The Council of People's Commissars (Bolshevik Government) has sent an emissary to Stockholm to conduct peace negotiations with enemy countries.

A decree is being prepared to nationalize banks.

The Central Army Committee at Stavka has issued an appeal to all the Army Committees to save the Country.
They demand:

(1) A cessation of terrorism and a reconstitution of personal liberty.

(2) The convening of the Constitutional Assembly and a guarantee of fair elections therefore.

(3) The transfer of land to the land Committees.

(4) The immediate commencement of peace negotiations.

This Committee recommends the formation of a government by Chernov which shall be all socialistic but without Bolsheviks.

On the North Front where conditions as to hunger and discipline are worst, soldiers are burning munitions and are much wrought up by tales that they are missing opportunities which are being availed of by others to loot the property of the rich in the cities.

Many officers, cadets, etc., are going south to join Kaledin, mainly for protection, I think, Kerth in his telegram quotes the Chief of Staff as saying that it may be necessary to remove Allied Attachés from Mogilev. . . .

Trotsky day before yesterday made rather a remarkable speech in which he attempted to analyze the motives of the contending nations. He says our capitalists demanded war to enable them to keep up their profits, etc.; and that we will be quite satisfied with the present exhaustion of all the contending nations as contributing to our future financial supremacy. I have sent to the War College a copy of this speech.

NOVEMBER 24, 1917. PARAPHRASE OF TELEGRAM SENT WARCOLSTAFF WASHINGTON. NO. 105 99 1 P.M.[29]

IN GENERAL THE SITUATION IS UNCHANGED.

A good many officers and political leaders are going to Kaledin principally for protection.

Chief of Staff at Stavka quoted by Kerth as saying that agents of Bolshevik government are planning a civil war to force Russia to request Germany to come in and restore order, but that Germany will not consent except on condition of political and economic alliance. Personally I do not believe this to be the intention of the Bolsheviks though their actions may lead in that direction. The Bolsheviks are more internationalist than patriotic, though not wholly even that; they are fanatics seeking peace and a social and economic revolution in the interest of the proletariat.

An appeal for new socialist government with Chernov as premier has been made by the Central Army Committee at Stavka which probably without much remaining influence. Peace, land distribution programme and fair elections to the Constituent Assembly are planks endorsed. These elections mentioned begin tomorrow and will last three days, the Assembly itself meeting in Petrograd on December 13, but conditions for elections are very bad and in some places there is talk of postponement of Assembly meeting.

Fearing cables may not be getting thorough request you cable acknowledgement of this and preceding cables. Copy of above to Gen. Pershing.

NOVEMBER 24, 1917. DIARY

. . . Lenin has announced that "The People's Commissars did not authorize Dukhonin to <u>conclude</u> an armistice, nor does the Soviet propose concluding a separate armistice; it is proposed to have an armistice of all belligerent nations. Our party never stated it will give an immediate peace. We announced that we will make an immediate peace proposal and will publish the secret treaties, which we have done."

NOVEMBER 25, 1917. PARAPHRASE OF TELEGRAM SENT WARCOLSTAFF WASHINGTON. 11 A.M., NO. 109-100[30]

Announcement made by Lenin that Dukhonin was never directed to conclude an armistice, he only had instructions to begin negotiations for one; says his government never contemplated a separate armistice but one affecting all belligerents; he states that he never promised immediate peace but only would make immediate peace proposal.

In my opinion situation is such that some government and order with promise of benefits to allies could be brought about now through diplomatic intervention. Ambassador has been urged this by me. Each element probably ready to abandon irreconcilable stand if it could save face. In my own work I am impeded by Ambassador's attitude towards communication of this Mission with actual military authority here which is Bolshevik. Other Military Missions have greater independence in their actions with correspondingly better results, and they are able to keep in touch.

It is with great difficulty that I arranged for American, British and French railway mission at Gen. Manikovski's request to assist handle Moscow situation where congestion of 11,000 cars blocks traffic.

Troubles of Bolsheviks increase on account of internal dissensions and administrative failures.

That an enemy offensive is contemplated on the Macedonian and Mesopotamian fronts is persistently rumored. Enemy gain in Mesopotamia in past two weeks, is 3 divisions of troops. Pershing advised of the above.

[NOVEMBER 25, 1917] 12/25TH, NOVEMBER, 1917.

TO THE CHIEF OF THE RUSSIAN GENERAL STAFF, PETROGRAD.[31]

There has been brought to my attention the following press communication from the United States:[32]

"The American Government has announced that no shipments of military supplies and provisions to Russia will be effected until the situation of this country will be established. The government before permitting the export of American products wants to know into whose hands they will get in Russia. The exports to Russia will be resumed only after the formation of a steady government which can be recognized by the United States, but if the Bolsheviks will remain in power and will put through their program of making peace with Germany, the present embargo on exports to Russia will remain in force. The credits to the Provisional Russian Government reach to the present day 325 million dollars, of which 191 millions have already been appropriated, the larger part of this money has already been spent for the purchase of supplies, which are ready for loading. The ships allotted by America for the carrying of this freight are ready for sailing but do not receive permission to leave the ports and they will be refused coal."

It occurs to me that it is but fair to convey to your Excellency the circumstance that neither I nor the American Ambassador has as yet received from the United States of America instructions or information similar to that contained in the press report above quoted. Nevertheless, it seems but fair to express to your Excellency the opinion that the press report correctly states the attitude of the Government of the United States. We are in daily expectation of receiving information similar to that conveyed by the above-mentioned press report.

Before sending you this communication I have submitted it to the American Ambassador who concurs in the expressions contained in it.

I shall avail myself of this opportunity to renew to your Excellency the assurance of my high consideration.[33]

NOVEMBER 25, 1917. DIARY

This is Sunday, the first day here of the elections to the Constituent Assembly. Although there are understood to be two sets of election officials (those appointed long ago by Kerensky and the more recently appointed Bolshevik ones) there does not appear to be any disorder. . . .

In the evening I sent a letter addressed to the Chief of Staff in which I quoted Associated Press reports to the effect that U.S. would send no more ships with supplies to Russia until it was satisfied a steady government exists in Russia, etc. . . .[34]

. . . The Bolsheviks are said to have located some flour on shipping near this port which may postpone the beginning of famine in Petrograd.

It is said that Lenin has abolished all titles and indications of classes; also all civilian ranks. . . .

. . . At the Zemstvo and Town Conference recently assembled in Petrograd there was a discussion between Vinaver (Kadet) and Tseretelli (Social Revolutionist). . . . Both were agreed to fight against the Bolsheviks but could not agree as to what to fight for; the Kadets insisting that only the Constituent Assembly can decide the question of land and peace but not a government which may be formed now. The Socialists contend that it is impossible to delay these questions for another month. The Tseretelli resolutions were carried by a large majority. These resolutions are briefly as follows:

1: A guarantee for the convening of the Constituent Assembly and its recognition as the only government in the country from the day it meets.

2: The reestablishment of all violated privileges and of the independence of local self-government.

3: The beginning of peace negotiations with a view to an immediate peace.

4: The transfer of all land to the land committees.

These resolutions were carried by a vote of 22 to 6.

There was a conference of the Petrograd Garrison yesterday at which were present 4 delegates from each of the 31 army detachments. The speakers represented all parties from Peoples Socialists to Bolsheviks. The resolution passed was a combination of the Bolshevik and Left Social Revolution resolutions and promised support and confidence to the Council of Peoples Commissars and demanded that the Left Social Revolutionists should join the Soviet Government. It also offered the representatives of all socialistic parties posts in the Central Executive Committee. Until the convening of the Constituent Assembly the Council of Peoples Commissars to be given all support. This resolution was carried by a vote of 61 to 1, 12 not voting.

NOVEMBER 26, 1917. MEMORANDUM FOR THE AMBASSADOR:

Referring to representations of recent dates submitted to you by me, I now for record repeat same in the form of this memorandum.

It seems to me that in the state of anarchy which now exists in Russia may be seen the interaction of many political elements which are prevented from working in cooperation for the administration of government in Russia by irreconcilable attitudes previously taken and by pride of opinions.

The evils of the present situation certainly by now have impressed themselves upon all. The failure of administration will soon lead to the physical results of starvation in the cities and at the fronts and to a dispersal of the troops upon the fronts by surrender and by straggling when the situation becomes such that each will try to save himself.

In the political turmoil that exists it has come to seem to me that it might be easy for some outside element in interjecting itself to clarify the situation in much the same way as eggshells dropped into a pot of boiling coffee precipitate the grounds.

If in a patient and understanding way the Allied Missions could offer suggestions at this time it seems to me that the opportunity which would be afforded to many contending elements to save their faces might be availed of and some government might be formed as a result of such suggestions.

It will soon be too late to do anything. The army will soon have disintegrated and Russia will soon cease to be of the least military assistance unless action is taken quickly. Perhaps it is too late to save the situation but unless something is done it is certainly and forever lost.

Even the Bolsheviks in my opinion might now be brought to some state of reason. They fully appreciate the difficulties of their position and may soon seek some exit from it.

NOVEMBER 26, 1917. PARAPHRASE OF TELEGRAM SENT WARCOLSTAFF WASHINGTON. NO. 112-101. 2 P.M.[35]

The general situation is unchanged.

Under instructions from their governments, the military representatives at Stavka, of Rumania, France, Italy, Japan and England have presented a formal protest to Dukhonin against violation of treaty between the Allies, dated Sept. 5th 1914 which forbids separate armistice. I have instructed Kerth to protest against separate armistice on ground that U.S. and Russia are virtual allies in present war for democracy against autocracy.

There are now between 101 1/2 and 105 1/2 enemy infantry divisions, and 17 1/2 cavalry on Black Sea-Baltic Sea front. On Caucasus and the Mesopotamian front there are between 23 and 25 infantry and 1 cavalry divisions.

Kerth may cable you direct in which event he will employ the previous cipher table and key number.

Pershing cabled above information.

NOVEMBER 26, 1917. DIARY

Trotsky has complained bitterly of the united protest to Dukhonin at Stavka. He alleged that the following words constituted a threat against Russia: "any violation of this treaty by Russia will produce the gravest consequences." The British Ambassador, Knox tells me, and Knox himself are very much displeased with this expression, which was very unfortunate, being susceptible of either of two interpretations, Trotsky's (and that of all the press) and a second wherein consequences might refer to general consequences upon the course of the war. Knox said General Barter, at Stavka, might be requested to deny the menace.

The railroads are functioning better and food is moving more satisfactorily.

NOVEMBER 27, 1917.
MEMORANDUM FOR THE AMBASSADOR.

The Chiefs of the Allied Military Missions and Military Attachés were . . . given typewritten copies, in French and Russian, of a memorandum written by Mr. Trotsky. We received the papers and told the Chief of the General Staff, General Marushevski, that we would hand them to our respective Ambassadors.

Enclosed herewith are the two papers mentioned and a third, an English translation made in this office.

Respectfully yours,

TRANSLATION OF COPY.

MEMORANDUM WRITTEN IN LONGHAND BY

L. TROTSKY, RECEIVED BY THE CHIEF OF GENERAL STAFF,

NOV. 13/26, 1917, 8 P.M.

1. As evidenced by all our steps, we are striving for a <u>general,</u> and not a separate armistice.
To a separate armistice, we may be forced by our <u>ALLIES</u> if they will close their eyes before the facts.
2. We are ready, at any moment, with any representatives of the Allies (of any of the Allies, is the true meaning though literally translated as above—sic) to conduct negotiations for immediate accomplishing of an armistice.
We do not demand a preliminary "recognition," we are recognized by the people.
We want business (serious) negotiations. We reserve the right to publish protocols (proceedings) for the information of all.
3. That negative attitude with which our peace initiative is being met, from the side of several of the Allied Governments, cannot in the slightest change the course of our policies.
The Allies should answer: are they willing to begin negotiations for immediate armistice aiming at the conclusion of peace on democratic principles?
Are they agreeable to support our initiative in this direction?

Do they demand other measures? What kind?

4. As long as Allied Governments answer with bare "no-recognition," of us and our initiative, we will follow our own course, appealing to the people against the governments.

Should the results of this policy bring separate peace, which we do not want, the responsibility will fall completely on the Allied Governments.

(signed) Trotsky.

November 13/26, 1917. Smolny.

(TRANSLATION FROM ORIGINAL FRENCH)
NOVEMBER 27, 1917.
RUSSIAN GENERAL HEADQUARTERS [MOGILEV]
HIS EXCELLENCY GENERAL DUKHONIN,
COMMANDER-IN-CHIEF OF THE RUSSIAN ARMIES.

Excellency:

In compliance with very formal instructions from my Government, sent to me by the Ambassador of the United States of America at Petrograd, I have the honor to bring to your attention that, the Republic of the United States and Russia being united in a war which is essentially a conflict between democracy and autocracy, my Government formally and energetically protests against any separate armistice that may be concluded by Russia.

I request the goodness of your Excellency to acknowledge receipt of this communication in writing and to accept the assurance of my high consideration.

(signed) M. C. Kerth.[36]

[NOVEMBER 27, 1917.] 12/27TH, NOVEMBER, 1917.
TO THE CHIEF OF THE RUSSIAN GENERAL STAFF, PETROGRAD.[37]

Excellency:

Referring to my letter of 12/25th November, 1917, relating to a quotation from American press reports, I desire to say that nothing therein should be construed as indicating that my government has or may be expected to express preference for the success in Russia of any one political party or element over another. Americans have the greatest sympathy for the whole Russian people in the complex situation in which they find themselves, and do not wish to interfere except helpfully in the solution of any Russian problem. Their sympathy extends to all sections of the Russian people. Their representatives here are now informed that no important fraction of the Russian people desires an immediate separate peace or armistice. And it is certainly within the rights of Russia, in the position in which she now finds herself, to bring up the question of a general peace.

There is no reason why the attitude of her Allies toward Russia or toward any important elements in Russia should be upon anything but a most friendly foundation.

I desire to avail myself of this occasion to renew to Your Excellency the assurance of my high consideration.[38]

NOVEMBER 27, 1917. DIARY[39]

Referring to my letter to the Chief of Staff (see diary of Nov. 25th) I find that it is being construed as a menace, as was certain language in the Stavka protest (see my diary of Nov. 26). . . . Under the circumstances it seemed best to write a second letter to the Chief of Staff of a friendly character denying American intention to interfere in Russian politics, noting that no Russian elements now desire a separate peace, recognizing the right of Russia to bring up the subject of a general peace and expressing sympathy for the Russian people in their present difficult and complex situation. The Ambassador said he had no objection to this letter.

Today at 3 P.M. all Chiefs of Missions were called to the General Staff and presented with a communication from Trotsky which denied intention to negotiate a separate peace; asked any or all Allies to join in negotiations for a general peace; expressed indifference as to formal recognition in the face of the fact that the Bolshevik Government had been recognized by the people; promised to appeal to the people of the Allied countries if their governments did not respond; and cast upon the Allied countries the responsibility if their neglect should lead to a separate peace. . . .

I saw Mr. Raymond Robins, connected with the Red Cross, who was an important agent in Mr. Thompson's recent propaganda and who has money from Thompson with which he employs a number of agents and keeps touch with the Bolsheviks. Mr. Robins has close touch with

Trotsky and believes the Bolsheviks must be counted with and that they will be in power for some time (i.e. at least for weeks). When Mr. Robins asked Trotsky why he had directed units at the front to effect truces and fraternize with German units opposite if he did not favor a separate peace, Mr. Trotsky, acknowledging that he had issued such an order, said that his purpose was to demoralize the German units as fighting bodies and to instil into them the principles of revolution, socialism (including land distribution) and peace. He said that the Russian troops had already lost their fighting power and that everything was to be gained and nothing lost by this proceeding.

There is certainly some truth in the theory advanced by Mr. Trotsky.

Mr. Robins has also seen a pamphlet, of which he says 1,500,000 copies have been passed over into the German lines, which is admirably calculated to demoralize the German soldiers.

The propaganda being indulged in among the German soldiers is strong evidence that the Bolsheviks are not working under German direction.

The Bolsheviks are beginning to exhibit the only "guts" visible among all the different contending political elements in Russia. They are the only ones apparently who can do anything with the soldiers and if the latter are to stay in position and ever do any fighting (even defensively) it may be that it must be under the Bolsheviks.

As the Bolsheviks remain longer in power there is evidence that they become more conservative.

NOVEMBER 28, 1917. PARAPHRASE OF TELEGRAM SENT WARCOLSTAFF WASHINGTON. 11 A.M., NO. 118-103.[40]

All military representatives were called to Chief of Staff yesterday and handed copies of manuscript signed by Trotsky, which we in turn handed to our respective Ambassadors. In this communication it is stated that effort [is] being made for general and not separate armistice and offer is made to join any allies' representatives in negotiations for armistice; no preliminary recognition demanded since people themselves recognize them (Soviet Government); right reserved to publish protocols, answer requested from Allies to the question whether they are willing to begin negotiations for immediate armistice looking to peace or democratic principles; asked whether Allies demand other measures and if so what they are; if no answer is received own course will be followed appealing to people against governments; if separate peace results responsibility placed on Allied Governments.

Raymond Robins of American Red Cross here who is keeping in close touch with the Bolsheviks, *informs me that local truces have been directed by Trotsky, to be made by units at front for purpose of propaganda among German soldiers, holding that Russians already demoralized for fighting and all fraternizing would be clear gain. One and Half million pamphlets furnished by Trotsky to teach Germans social democracy and advantages of democratic peace. This does not look like German direction.*

Doubtless the Germans would now be glad to see more conservative government replace the Bolsheviks. Any such government would in response to practically universal Russian demand attempt to make peace. There is a great chance that negotiations by any Russians will fail. In that event, perhaps Bolsheviks could best hold army on the front. If we must lose Russia it might be better to leave the Bolsheviks in control, to the greater annoyance of Germans, rather than anyone else. Above considerations are not controlling but they do deserve consideration and attention.

Emissaries from the North front, under direction of Krylenko, who is now Commissar for War, entered the German lines yesterday afternoon and secured an agreement with German local high command to conduct negotiations for armistice on all fronts. The proposed date of negotiation is fixed for December 2nd and Trotsky in a so-called decree calls on Allied Governments to join in these negotiations for armistice and peace and appeals for support to laboring masses of all Allied and enemy countries. Should Allies fail to send representatives Trotsky says separate negotiations will be conducted, though he desires general peace, and responsibility shifted to Bourgeois of allied nations if forced to make separate peace.

Appeal issued by Dukhonin to Russian people to unite and save the army and country from anarchy especially addressed to representatives of municipalities, zemstvos and peasants.

Stavka and Commissar Govt. relations approaching breaking point. Stavka expects support from Rumanian, Southwestern and Caucasian fronts. North front thoroughly Bolshevik. Command machinery of west front destroyed. Bolsheviks probably also strong on other fronts but without administrative machinery.

Recommend manufacture of munitions for Russia be suspended, that Russian munitions shipments and metals except RR materials to Vladivostok be held up. Red Cross shipments, Rumanian supplies etc., should not now be stopped. Pershing cabled.

NOVEMBER 28, 1917. DIARY

This morning we learn that yesterday under Krylenko's direction par-
liamentaires from the North Front entered the German lines and secured an arrangement with Germans (signed by a Division Commander
but approved by the German Supreme Commander) looking to negotiations on December 2nd for an armistice (presumably on any or all
fronts).

Trotsky in a so-called decree dated Nov. 27 calls on the Allied governments to join in the negotiations of Dec. 2nd for an armistice and peace
and appeals for support to the laboring masses of Allied and enemy
countries. If the Allies will not send representatives Trotsky says his
emissaries will negotiate alone, desiring a general peace. If a separate
peace results Trotsky says the blame will rest upon the Bourgeois of the
Allied nations.

NOVEMBER 29, 1917. PARAPHRASE OF TELEGRAM SENT
WARCOLSTAFF WASHINGTON. NO. 124-105. 2 P.M.[41]

A letter in German signed by a commander of a German division states
that the Commander in Chief of Eastern front, by virtue of authority of
German Supreme Commander will enter into armistice negotiations
presumably on any or all fronts, with a commission named by the Russian Supreme Commander, presumably Krylenko, on a day and place
which the Russians may select.

The formerly anti-Bolshevik Peasant's Soviet passed last night, by a
small majority a Bolshevik resolution and its executive committee has
joined that of the Bolshevik's Soviet, as will representatives from the
army and fleet, and professional, railway and post and telegraph unions.
This forming broader body to which Council of Commissars will be
more or less responsible. On the grounds that existing Peasant's Soviet
not representative, Chernov has summoned a new one.

Manikovsky said to be about to resign his post; Marushevsky has resigned his post of Chief of the General Staff.

The Constitutional Assembly election results in Petrograd are as follows: Bolshevik 415,000, Kadets, 245,000, Radical Social Revolutionists,
149,000, scattering vote 80,000. Results of other localities are not yet certain but Bolsheviks polled heavy vote everywhere. Nearly one half of
members not yet elected, postponement due to disturbances.

Ambassador being asked by me to consent that I urge Bolsheviks to provide for immobility of the troops of the enemy during armistice, if armistice is negotiated.

Pershing advised.

NOVEMBER 29, 1917. DIARY

It is reported this morning that Gen. Marushevski, Chief of the General Staff has resigned, and the Gen. Manikovsky will resign as head of the War Dept. for Technical Affairs.

It is also reported today that the Peasants Soviet, which has been against the Bolsheviks, has by a small majority gone over to the latter due to the progress made in the peace program, etc. There is talk of a broader foundation for government consisting of a larger Soviet composed of representative from the Bolshevik and Peasants Soviets, Railway Union, etc.

NOVEMBER 30, 1917. DIARY

. . . On the same day, [as Kerth's protest of a separate armistice to General Dukhonin] November 27, Gen. Lavergne, the French representative at Stavka addressed a communication to Dukhonin in which he stated that the French Government does not recognize the Government of Peoples' Commissars, and that "having complete confidence in the patriotism of the Russian High [Command], it counts upon its firm intention to put aside all criminal negotiations," etc.

. . . Mr. Trotsky made a statement that the Soviet Government cannot permit such interferences with the internal life of the country, "which tend to kindle civil war." Further, such steps, says Trotsky, will bring severe consequences in their train for which he says his government refuses to accept responsibility.

Whitehouse[42] has been informed confidentially, and conversations I have had with Knox and the British Ambassador tend to confirm the truth of Whitehouse's information, that the British Ambassador has asked his Government to adopt a modus vivendi here which would result in better relations, and even to release Russia from any engagement to make no separate peace. Last night, at dinner with the British

Ambassador, I was informed by him that he thought the time for peace (presumably general) had arrived.

All day I have been talking with our Ambassador and other of our Embassy people, and . . . with the British Ambassador, Gen. Niessel and Gen. Knox, on the subject of the desirability of talking to Trotsky on the armistice question.

Day after tomorrow the Russians enter into negotiations with the Germans (and Austrians?) for an armistice (general if possible, which it apparently isn't, and otherwise separate as to Russia).[43] *The enemy will be represented at these negotiations by very able men who will know what they want and will of course try to get the best of Russia and her Allies. Under the disturbed conditions in Russia the latter probable cannot be so well represented as the enemy. It is my idea that the interests of Russia and her Allies to a certain extent run parallel in this matter and that we (some subordinates, without raising the question of recognition) should have communication with Trotsky on this subject.*

There is a wide margin among the possibilities. Something may yet be saved of favorable Russian influence upon the interests of the Allies.

Sir George Buchanan was at first upon the fence on this proposition and Gen. Knox rather favorable to it, wondering whether Sir George would let him accompany me to Trotsky. Finally Sir George expressed himself as rather against the proposition, while Knox assumed a position of doubt, thinking it best perhaps to await advices from England.

Niessel was frankly against the idea. The French are implacable and appear to be more bent upon expressing their opinions than upon substantial accomplishments.

I reported to our Ambassador what had occurred at the British Embassy and asked him what to do. Wright (Counsellor of the Embassy) and Sisson (recently arrived from America in charge of publicity and propaganda) had advised the Ambassador to let me go ahead. And it was so decided.[44]

DECEMBER 1, 1917. PARAPHRASE OF TELEGRAM SENT
WARCOLSTAFF WASHINGTON. NO. 131
HUNDRED EIGHT 11 A.M.[45]

In regard to the importance of cooperation between home authorities and U.S. military representatives in the matter of supplies purchased in the U.S. for Russia (see my various communications by mail and cable, in this connection) I beg to call your attention to the following facts: According to information just received from my British fellow member of the Michelson Commission the S.S. <u>Oconee</u> left New York on November 15th for Murmansk with 1,791,000 lbs. of copper. It was well known to all of us here including the Russians that at about the time of this sailing, there was no need of imports of copper. I assumed that under your instructions you would be advised by the Russian Commission in the U.S. This problem could have been avoided if according to my suggested program efficient exchange of information had been established, the said copper could have been sent to a place where it was needed and 800 tons of shipping space saved for actually needed supplies, boots for example.

DECEMBER 1, 1917. PARAPHRASE OF TELEGRAM SENT WARCOLSTAFF WASHINGTON. 6 P.M., 133-110.[46]

I had long interview with Trotsky this morning on military features of Lenin-Trotsky program especially relating to armistice negotiations beginning tomorrow. I emphasized unofficial character and had Ambassador's consent. I pointed out the parallel features, in many ways, of Russia's and Allies' interests and argued that if any armistice is made it should be of long duration, with enemy troops remaining in position and no exchange of prisoners or products. Trotsky was very responsive. He implied that his principles and desire for peace left him wide latitude in armistice negotiations and stated that he would be glad to have me cable to the United States that in the negotiations he would observe and endeavor to protect the interests of Russia's Allies; he further stated that the points I raised appealed to him or had already been in his mind and that armistice commission would be given instructions in accordance therewith. A week would elapse before armistice protocol is signed, he said, for purpose of debating matter after preliminary negotiations and to give Allies further opportunity to protect their interests.

Stavka may soon be entirely in control of Bolsheviks like war department and General Staff. General Dukhonin arrested. Bolsheviks are being strengthened by peace program. No opposition to peace by any important element here except to annoy Bolsheviks.

Marushevski and Manikovski resignations are denied.

Austrians have agreed to join in negotiations tomorrow regarding armistice and general peace. Internment threatened for some British subjects, all of whom are prohibited from leaving Russia, unless two Russian Socialists are released in England.[47]

DECEMBER 1, 1917. DIARY

. . . Trotsky says the Soviet Government will have Stavka in 48 hours. It is not probable that any forces in Russia can be found successfully to oppose the Bolsheviks in any large way at this time.

This morning I had an interview of about 40 minutes with Trotsky, the "Commissar for Foreign Affairs" who appears to be the practical man of the Bolshevik administration. I represented to him that I came as an individual; pointed out certain directions in which the interests of Russia and her Allies still run parallel; and secured voluntary recognition that Russia has certain obligations to her Allies. I represented that a long armistice rather than a short one would be of advantage to all interests except of our enemies. As to the Russians, it would give them time and opportunity to indulge in propaganda with a large number of German and Austrian soldiers and if any peace negotiations were begun would strengthen their hands as against the enemy, as the latter would not be able to take advantage of the haste with which the Russians would be obliged to act, for political reasons, if the armistice were a short one.

I also pointed out why provision should be made in any armistice protocol to retain the enemy troops in position (so that there would be opportunity for propaganda; so that the last shreds of Russia's reputation [I didn't put it that way][48] *might be preserved; so that the war would be shortened; so that Russia would have a greater leverage in any further negotiations looking to peace, etc.).*

Then I made appropriate arguments against exchange of prisoners, and products. I showed that an exchange of prisoners could but lengthen the war and increase the chance of Russia having a victorious and autocratic neighbor upon her borders, while at the same time it would take away something that would make Russia stronger, in any subsequent negotiations for peace. I pointed out the skill the Germans would summon to the council table and the need of skill on the part of the Russians.

Trotsky was very amiable and very responsive. He said the matters I brought up appealed to him or were already in his mind. He said he would be glad to have me cable America that in so far as was consistent with his principles and the peace aspirations of Russia he would observe and protect the interests of Russia's Allies.

Trotsky said that the terms arrived at as a result of the preliminary negotiations beginning tomorrow would be debated for at least a week before final approval, during which time the Allies of Russia would have further opportunity to examine into and offer suggestions as to said terms; but that if the Allied governments failed to do this there would be appeal to the peoples of the Allied nations.

My interview was very satisfactory but I recognize there may be an aftermath of great personal embarrassment if Trotsky makes a speech and misquotes or misrepresents me. I know however that I cannot have harmed our cause and may greatly have advanced it.

. . . The British are getting into difficulties. Trotsky promises to intern "counter-revolutionary" Britishers if 2 comrades in England are not at once released and meantime has forbidden Britishers to leave Russia.

DECEMBER 2, 1917. PARAPHRASE OF TELEGRAM SENT WARCOLSTAFF WASHINGTON. NO. 136-111. 2 P.M.[49]

Semi-official statement of conciliatory nature by British, in press today. Report of my interview with Trotsky less inaccurate than might have been expected.

Unanimous opinion in Stavka, according to report from Kerth, is that armistice is a certainty; discussion now with Russia of concrete peace terms advocated by him since the United States wish nothing Russia will not agree to, even including acceptance of terms of peace by the German people; he states that majority of other allies could also be reasonably satisfied at present; that Russia would continue to fight if fair peace terms are rejected by the enemy; that this is no time to sacrifice all by stand on dignity; that such an attitude of dignity will result in the following successive steps: separate Russian armistice; separate Russian peace; reorganization of Russian Government and administration aided by Germany; neutral Russia assisting Germany; Russia German's ally.

Kerth states matters correctly, in my opinion. Pershing cabled as above.

DECEMBER 2, 1917. PARAPHRASE OF TELEGRAM SENT WARCOLSTAFF WASHINGTON. NO. 138-112. 4 P.M.[50]

Owing to lack of proper reconnaissance except during fraternizing, identification of enemy units increasingly difficult on this front. Enemy strength believed to be between 101 and 115 infantry divisions and between 18 1/2 and 23 cavalry divisions on front from Baltic Sea to Black Sea. In certain sectors, the enemy is reported as being very weak with withdrawal of young men and artillery and officers. Preparation for an offensive region Kovel, persistently rumored last week, for which purpose enemy strength this region reinforced by two German divisions. Important activities in German rear along the railways in Kovel sector. It is also rumored that the Germans propose straightening line at Chernovitz by means of local advances; a raid on Ireshti, Tekuci is being prepared by 9th German Army in region of Focshani, but there is a general agreement between Russians and Germans to cease firing until termination of armistice negotiations and no offensives are expected by me in the near future. No change in the Caucasus.

It is reported by Kerth that the attachés are about to leave Mogilev for an unknown destination. He is being summoned here by me lest he become a wanderer with fugitives. Pershing has been advised as above.

DECEMBER 2, 1917. DIARY

In the News Resume there appears Mr. Trotsky's account of my interview of yesterday. . . . Before the interview I well knew that Mr. Trotsky might be tempted in the manner common among politicians to distort the circumstances and substance of it, and I had determined that whatever the result I would engage in no debate as to what happened. His account was less inaccurate than I apprehended it might be. It excited the Ambassador, as I knew it would, but I have urged him as insistently as I know how to make no comment to anyone on any discrepancy. . . .[51]

. . . Captain Proctor of the British Military Mission, stationed at Archangel, came in today and after hearing his story I took him to the Ambassador where he repeated it. He said he came from Admiral Kemp, Commanding at Archangel the British flotilla, etc.: that the Admiral was much concerned over the responsibility he felt for the safety of Allied foreigners who could only escape via Archangel: that he was convinced Petrograd would be cut off, within 3 weeks, from all communication with the outside world: that when hunger came the city would be sacked by some of its occupants and by soldiers coming back from the North front and that the Embassy people would be murdered: that the Allies ought at once to adopt a conciliatory policy, including a release of Russia from any obligation to keep on with the war and a release of certain Russians whose internment in England has caused the Bolsheviks to refuse exit from Russia to all British subjects: that then all foreign troops (400 Belgian, 500 French, several hundred British soldiers, the crews of the British submarines in the Gulf of Finland and 4500 Serbs now at Vologda) should be gotten to Archangel as soon as possible: that 2 powerful ice breakers and appropriate transports and relief ships should be sent at once to Archangel. Captain P. thought the inhabitants of Archangel, if fed by relief ships, would be friendly, and that in any event, with the troops and with the munitions at Archangel (about 100,000 tons) a siege could be endured if necessary. Following the troops, Captain P. thought all Allied citizens and subjects, including Embassy people, should be gotten to Archangel as quickly as possible. . . .

DECEMBER 3, 1917
MEMORANDUM FOR THE AMBASSADOR:

I respectfully ask that directions be given which will enable me to see important cables passing between Washington and the Embassy,—such cables at least as it would not be improper for me to see.

Under directions from Washington and in pursuance of my duties I am cabling to Washington once or several times a day on all manner of subjects relating to the present vastly critical situation, which is so largely of a military character and so critical in all respects by reason of the military consequences involved.

If I can conveniently see the Embassy cables to which I refer above I can certainly better advise the Department of our Government with which I correspond—and in some respects I might be able to make my communications more harmonious with yours, which would be of obvious advantage to our Government.

above request refused[52]

DECEMBER 3, 1917
MEMORANDUM FOR THE AMBASSADOR:

I respectfully bring to your attention that Petrograd is now an armed camp occupied largely by an untrained and undisciplined soldiery. Under these circumstances it is especially necessary to observe all reasonable policy regulation which those make who are in control of the city. The requirement of a permit for an automobile is one of these police regulations which is reasonable under existing circumstances. If you desire a permit I will be glad to try to procure one for you. Unless you have such a permit I have the honor to advise you that if you take out your automobile something may happen which would seriously threaten the military interests of the United States. Under the existing military government it would be proper for you to ask for a permit.

DECEMBER 3, 1917. PARAPHRASE OF TELEGRAM SENT WARCOLSTAFF WASHINGTON. NO. 140-114. NINE P.M.[53]

According to a telegram from Kerth at Stavka, Dukhonin about to depart with staff and presumably Allied officers was stopped on December 1st. His own few troops stopped him and demanded that he fight with them or surrender with them. In the opinion of Kerth Dukhonin will not fight. As a result of this incident reports were current here of Dukhonin's arrest, though there is no further news on this subject. Prior to the receipt of the above message from Kerth, I ordered him to return to Petrograd if he found no reason against his return, as I do not wish him to become fugitive.

The Government Commissar at the Headquarters, Stankevitch, who is working with Dukhonin and until the present moment a tower of anti-Bolshevik strength, submitted to the Allied representatives at Stavka, a communication saying that masses of Russian people demand peace, believing that Germans equally wish peace and will stop on fair terms, and that no persuasion, in the opinion of Stankevitch, has been able to alter this demand. He proposes that the Allies and proper representatives of Russia (presumably not Bolsheviks) arrange at once peace conditions. Nearly all anti-Bolsheviks at present assume this position.

Anyone advocating course other than serious and immediate effort for peace becomes fugitive without any followers; there are no elements which do not demand peace or serious and immediate effort for same. Propaganda against same would not be permitted.

To oppose Bolsheviks or similar elements, there are no volunteers, death battalions, Cossacks or others available in considerable number, except locally.

Conditions in Caucasus, Ukraine and Don Basin not accurately known here yet movements there are only local and not strong, not pro-war and devoid of great immediate importance.

Bolsheviks helped by opposition of Allies since masses think peace is opposed by Allies.

Policy which does not recognize facts as above is not possible.

Above has been cabled to General Pershing.

DECEMBER 3, 1917. DIARY

. . . Yesterday the peace negotiations began. The Russians were represented by 5 politicians, a workman, a soldier, a sailor, a peasant and a secretary. Two naval officers and 6 general staff officers accompanied as technical advisers. . . .

I look forward with great apprehension to the arrival of instructions at the Allied Missions here. I am afraid that the conditions may not be understood elsewhere and that France, guided by Clemenceau, the tiger, may guide us into an impossible policy which will lead by successive steps to the active support of Germany by Russia. There are no elements in Russia which are willing to go on with the war or which could win politically without a peace program. This is clearly indicated in every direction—by the statement to me of Verkhovsky, anti-Bolshevik: by the tacit assent of Guchkov, Kadet: by a statement to the military representatives of Stankevitch, supporter of Dukhonin, brave old Commissar at Stavka of the former Provisional Government, anti-Bolshevik: by the statement to me this morning of the Commissar of the 12th Army, acting under commission of the former government, anti-Bolshevik: by Soldatenko today, formerly close to Tereschenko in the Foreign Office: by the testimony, practically universal, of all witnesses, either individual or journalistic. These are no pro-peace forces. As far as anyone goes is to demand that peace be made in an orderly fashion with Allies participating unless the enemy refuses obviously fair terms; and the most conservative friends of the Allies demand now a statement of plain, simple and fair peace terms by the Allies.

DECEMBER 4, 1917. PARAPHRASE OF TELEGRAM
SENT WARCOLSTAFF WASHINGTON. NO. 143-115. SIX P.M.[54]

Yesterday, both Marushevski and Manikovski were arrested here.

The Soviet Commissar for War and Supreme Commander, Krylenko took possession of Stavka without resistance yesterday. Some Allied officers including Kerth still at Mogilev but Chief of Allied Military Missions left for south.

Because he facilitated Kornilov's escape, Dukhonin was killed yesterday by sailors, despite efforts of Krylenko to prevent lynching.

Forming a front with Rumanians, Ukrainians, Kaledin etc., according to any plan, appears most chimerical, and might result in ineffectual civil strife possibly finishing with reestablishment of monarchy and without any conceivable benefit to the Allies. No Russians have or can sustain a policy of war; Russia is past carrying on war although if Bolsheviks do not succeed in armistice negotiations or peace negotiations, it may be possible for them to hold troops for a while. Of the many Russians, the landed class especially would like to see Allies used for strictly internal political purposes in the country. Russia would probably be soon thrown into arms of Germany, should any Allied policy involving civil war, be adopted in hopeless effort to keep part of Russia in war.

Shcherbachev appointed Supreme Commander by Dukhonin to follow him; Shcherbachev formerly commander of Rumanian front.

In opposition to Naval Attachés' recent request, no foreign marines should attempt to come in under present conditions. This is important. Gen. Pershing is informed of the above.[55]

DECEMBER 4, 1917. DIARY

This morning came news of the killing of Dukhonin at Mogilev at 5 P.M., Dec. 3rd. At 11 A.M. on that day a small number of Soviet Government troops began to arrive there and at the same hour the Senior Allied Military Representatives left by train for Kiev. Kerth stayed at Mogilev with other Allied officers. At 5 Krylenko arrived and was unopposed. At the time of Krylenko's arrival sailors, despite Krylenko's efforts to prevent, lynched Dukhonin at the railway station, alleging as a reason that he had facilitated the escape of Kornilov.

Kornilov, released or escaped, is en route south with some 400 of the wild division.

I visited Gen. Knox today and Gen. Poole visited me. Poole and Banting, his assistant, expressed themselves as in accord with what I may call "my policy" of conciliating the Soviet Government to a certain extent with the object of saving what is possible from the wreck. I am confident that Knox feels the same way about it, although the British are still awaiting instructions from home, most impatiently. Knox said he expected personal trouble as he had wired home that Dukhonin's death was due to delay in the receipt here of instructions from home. . . .

I note below my impressions of Trotsky gathered on the occasion of my interview of Dec. 1:

Of medium stature and build; dark complexion, with a black mustache and small beard or goatee; wears glasses; nose slightly aquiline; complexion pale; eyes dark and penetrating; forehead high; of very intelligent appearance; manners quiet and pleasing; in perfect control of himself; might be taken for a New York East Side doctor or prosperous druggist, or even after intercourse for a small-college professor. Trotsky produces the impression of being a practical man able to do work without fuss or nervousness and without wasting words or energy.

Lenin I have not seen. He is said to be the philosopher and accomplished theorist of the pair who constitute perhaps the principal figures in Russia today. Brown of the Chicago Daily News says Lenin's is the finest intellect he has ever come in contact with and that Trotsky is almost equally able. All of our newspaper people (Brown, Fleurot, Bessy Beatty, etc.) are much impressed with Lenin and Trotsky.[56]

DECEMBER 5, 1917. PARAPHRASE OF TELEGRAM SENT WARCOLSTAFF WASHINGTON. NO. 145-116. SIX P.M.[57]

Chiefs of Allied Missions at Stavka left for Kiev. Stavka now in charge of Krylenko as Supreme Commander who, apparently, has former staff there continuing its duties for him. Bonch-Bruyevich,[58] partisan of new regime and peace programme, has been appointed by Krylenko as Chief of Staff.

Press announces today that with the consent of Rumania, Shcherbachev commenced negotiations for armistice on Rumanian front. This not confirmed.

Most recent election returns, according to press reports show following votes cast for Constituent Assembly members: Bolshevik 2,700,000; Kadets 2,350,000; Social Revolutionsits 2,200,000. It is said that many of the conservative Social Revolutionaries have voted with the Kadets. Present probability is that union between Bolsheviks and Social Revolutionists will control. The Bolsheviks and Social Revolutionists differ mainly in land programme; former would permit each individual to use as much as he can till, while latter would not disturb very small proprietors.

Better functioning of railroads and, at least temporarily, more food moving. More harmony in relations between Railway Union and Soviet (Bolshevik) Government.

Negotiations for armistice presumably under way since December 2nd, the Russian Armistice Commission being attended by two old staff officers in the role of technical assistants.

General Pershing informed of above. . . .

Owing to Riggs great assistance to me his promotion in National Army per my recommendation of Nov. 1st would be of public benefit and fully deserved.

DECEMBER 5, 1917. DIARY

. . . I saw General Niessel today and asked him and General Knox (British Attaché) to luncheon day after tomorrow. Niessel is sore because I visited Trotsky but he has pulled in his horns and no longer advocates threats and protests and incitements to civil war and chimerical policies to form a new front with Kaledin, Ukrainians, etc. Niessel is a fine soldier and man of action but deficient in statesmanship or political wisdom or whatever else it is we now require. During these last trying days Niessel really never took the time or trouble to propose any plan of action to me and gave scant attention to my own proposed plan which I sought to discuss with him at our Ambassador's on Thanksgiving Day and at the British Ambassador's at dinner on the day thereafter.

Mr. Francis, our Ambassador, seems to me completely exhausted and overwrought by the strain he has recently been under. This circumstance is most distressing. The American Ambassador never required more than now to be able to act with cool wisdom and vision.

Some of the Ambassadors have received instructions, following the Paris Conference, but ours had not up to 2 o'clock today. At 3 the Allied Diplomatic Missions will meet at the call of Sir George Buchanan . . . [and are] involved [in] a policy of careful waiting, avoiding offensive actions, and letting it be known that the Allies are willing to revise the aims of war when Russia should have a government which could be recognized.

DECEMBER 6, 1917. PARAPHRASE OF TELEGRAM SENT
WARCOLSTAFF WASHINGTON. NO. 147,
HUNDRED SEVENTEEN, 5 P.M.[60]

I propose the following plan for immediate adoption for the purpose of covering the contingency of a possible failure of Russian armistice or peace negotiations at the present time.

Authorize me, in the event the above contingency should arise, to express to the Soviet government the friendly appreciation on the part of the United States of the desperate situation in which Russia finds herself, denouncing wickedness of Autocratic Germany in refusing an armistice or peace except on unfair terms which would dishonor Russia and promising instant action by America sister democracy. In order to avoid recognition of the Soviet government I suggest myself.

Also authorize me to offer the following: all American troops the Trans-Siberian Railway can transport; a real American railway adviser with a great staff or a railway administrator with same; American operation of the Trans-Siberian system and in so far as may be practicable of the trunk lines thence to Odessa, Moscow, Petrograd and the front; utmost efforts largely to increase shipments of railway material to the port of Vladivostok; assistance on a larger scale of every other character; the creation in Russia of plenipotentiary American commission of three empowered within wide limits to direct not request action in or material from the United States for Russia.

The plan above outlined might shift the energies of America partly from France to Russia as our force in France could not be greatly augmented because of tonnage requirements for movement to Russia.

Exact a broadening of its foundations from the Soviet government that will include perhaps the Social Revolutionists, thus basing the government on a natural majority. Exact also the speedy convening of the Constituent Assembly. Promise a recognition of the following facts: that those nations which have been long in war, especially including Russia and certain of the enemy nations, require peace to avoid permanent setback; that peace without gain to any nation as a result of the war, more than any other result, will discourage wars in the future; that the United States will lead movement to define concrete peace terms now on principles laid down already in the United States in December 1916 and later in Russia and to seek the quick adoption of such terms that demand will be made for action on peace terms by the German people.

At the psychological moment such a stroke might partially restore the morale and fighting ability of Russia. This is the only conceivable chance to keep her in the war for a reasonable time and avoid the chance she may drift into Germany's arms. In addition to Americans, many volunteers, Polish troops, and Rumanians would reinforce units of the Russian Army. No anti-war party would have extensive ground to stand on. Much enthusiasm for plan might arise. Some risks involved perhaps but the war is full of risks and desperate remedies are required.

The only Allied nation possessing the confidence of Russia sufficiently to act is the United States which should therefore act alone but in the interest of all of the allied powers.

Troops moved in would not exceed 10 to 12 divisions in a long time.

We have seemed to the simple Russians too much like purchasers here of cannon fodder.

For many weeks we have had no American railway man in European Russia except Horne and he sometimes not even with interpreter or office.

This omitted in copy to Amb. As above plan is a matter of military vision there is no use my suggesting it to the Ambassador.[61]

DECEMBER 6, 1917. PARAPHRASE OF TELEGRAM SENT WARCOLSTAFF WASHINGTON. NO. 148-118. SIX P.M.[62]

A confirmation comes from Kerth who is now in Mogilev, that Shcherbachev at Jassy is now conducting truce negotiations; he is more or less in control of administrative machinery of the Rumanian and Southwestern fronts. An announcement is made by the Soviet Government concerning the progress of the armistice negotiations. A demand was made by the Russians that there be no movement of enemy troops; also the surrender of Moonsund Islands and the extension of period proposed by Germans for armistice namely 14 days, to 28 days and a period of one week's time for adjournment before conclusion of terms of armistice. A declaration has been made by enemy representatives pointing out that Russian terms were not acceptable and that counter proposals would be made. An immediate appeal to the nations not represented at the conference is proposed by the Russians, asking them to join in formulating the terms of a truce. The enemy Governments have been asked by the enemy representatives, to give necessary authority.

The announcement of the Soviet refers to efforts or intentions to protect interests of Allies.

The West front in Russia is apparently getting ready to propose a truce involving only the West Front. The proposed terms include the holding of enemy troops.

General Pershing cabled as above.

DECEMBER 6, 1917. DIARY

. . . There has been no mention of an exchange of prisoners in connection with the armistice. In the communication to the Embassies (signed by Trotsky) it is stated that the enemy representatives, on demand of the Russians, have asked authority to consider the subject of a general armistice. Trotsky appeals to the Allies for recognition and that they join in the negotiations.

The press distort much my interview with Trotsky, saying that I represented America, etc. It would be folly to debate what occurred, of course. Fortunately Reuter has a telegram which will doubtless be published tomorrow saying that Kerth and I have acted without instructions from our Government. The only embarrassment in this is that Kerth in his protest, quite properly doubtless, but without authority, stated that he protested by order of his government. etc. My wire to Kerth simply directed him to protest on the ground of virtual alliance between Russia and the United States in the contest between democracy and autocracy. Incidentally, after I wrote this cable but before it was sent I went to the Embassy where the Ambassador directed me to order Kerth to protest, and where I showed him and received his approval of the wire prepared for Kerth.

DECEMBER 7, 1917. PARAPHRASE OF TELEGRAM
SENT WARCOLSTAFF WASHINGTON. NO. 151-119, 9 P.M.[63]

On December 5th, the Soviet negotiations for an armistice have been adjourned for one week's period.

All enemy nations were represented. The place of the future as well as of the past meetings is Brest-Litovsk. . . .

. . . Trotsky informed Allied Missions of proceedings and he says that time is sufficient for Allies to determine whether they will join in negotiations. Should Allies refuse to participate he calls upon them to "announce before all humanity, in the name of what ambitions should the peoples of Europe shed blood during the fourth year of the war."

General Knox, British Military Attaché, and Chief of French Military Mission agree substantially with My No. 117 [6 Dec. 1917, above]. It was concluded by all of us that after the outlined plan was well started, the Japanese could be added and sending of American later reduced.

Yesterday, there was published a draft of the proposed decree cancelling all Russian foreign obligations held abroad.

In a decree signed by Lenin religious toleration is promised to Mohammedans: he also calls on the Mohammedans in India to revolt in same decree.

DECEMBER 7, 1917 [CIRCA]
MEMORANDUM FOR THE EMBASSY: THE EXCHANGE OF
PRISONERS THROUGH THE RED CROSS

In an interview on December 7th with Captain Riggs, Mr. Chamansky, Head of the Chancery of the [Russian] Red Cross, made the following statements:

(1) The proposition to exchange prisoners across the Danube and by the Black Sea and the Baltic Sea, in addition to the existing arrangements through Sweden, was proposed by the Austro-Hungarian Government some six months ago. The safety of transport on the Baltic Sea could not be guaranteed by the German Government and the exchange of prisoners by the Danube and the Black Sea was not agreed to by the Russians.

(2) At a Red Cross and Prisoners of War Committee conference at Copenhagen which adjourned about ten days ago the question was again brought up and was categorically refused by the Russian Red Cross representative.

(3) About ten days ago Prince Charles of Sweden addressed a letter to Mr. Trotsky asking that the question be again raised.

(4) What decision will be taken by Mr. Trotsky is not known at this time but the Red Cross will protest against any method of liberating or exchanging prisoners except through Sweden.

(5) The Red Cross cannot guarantee the safety of enemy prisoners who leave prison camps except under its auspices.

(6) The officer in charge of War Prisoner Section in the General Staff, Colonel Mascalov, knew nothing of any new arrangement day before yesterday.

(7) It is thought that the Danish Minister may also protest against an exchange of prisoners except through Scandinavia.

I gather that unofficially many prisoners, particularly those near the front, have already been informally liberated perhaps without action from the central authorities.

DECEMBER 7, 1917. DIARY

Today Gen. Niessel and Gen. Knox lunched with me. I read them my long cable No. 117 [6 December 1917, above] (plan for action if armistice or peace negotiations fail). They agreed with me substantially as to the soundness of the plan proposed. . . .

. . . I saw Niessel today, at his request, and he told me the French were about to put out a pro-revolutionary pronunciamento. He also said he had received a large sum (1,000,000 francs) for propaganda, with more to follow. I made an appointment with him to see our propaganda people (Sisson et al) Monday at 11.

I saw Sisson and Bullard[64] (who has been taken on by Sisson to run the newspaper side of our propaganda), made an appointment to bring in Niessel and Knox Monday, and put before them the item of news as to supplies to Russia. They thought it excellent propaganda material and will doubtless put it out.

DECEMBER 8, 1917. PARAPHRASE OF TELEGRAM SENT
WARCOLSTAFF WASHINGTON. NO. 154-120, 4 P.M.[65]

Negotiations, according to reports, have begun on the Caucasian front for an armistice there. One lasting three months with no movement of troops, will be asked by the Russians.

A so-called confession covering two columns in the papers, alleging that American Red Cross was supporting pro-war parties and propaganda, is published as emanating from private secretary of Breshkovsky, Chairman of Committee which Thompson assisted. The report goes on to state that great sums of money were furnished by American capitalists for this purpose. The only American name mentioned is that of Robins.

Gen. Pershing has been cabled the above also.

DECEMBER 9, 1917. PARAPHRASE OF TELEGRAM SENT
WARCOLSTAFF WASHINGTON. NO. 157-121. 5 P.M.[66]

Additional information pertaining to principal armistice negotiations shows that the Russians proposed one of half years duration, included the immobility of confronting troops, called for evacuation of islands in Riga Gulf by Germans, annulment of partial or local agreements for armistice, and included in same naval forces.

General [Max] Hoffmann who was the spokesman for the enemy said that such terms were fit for proposal to a conquered nation. Objections were made by Hoffmann to each Russian condition and he proposed substitutes therefore, the significant ones being: term of truce 28 days; there is to be no grouping of enemy troops for advance on Russian front; commercial communications along special routes and by special arrangements may be resumed; both Russian and Turkish troops are to evacuate Persia which is neutral; immediate beginning of peace negotiations.

Remaining conditions of both proposals were purely technical and unimportant.

Russians and enemy apparently far from actual agreement.

Allied Military Representatives listened to account of proceedings at General Staff here, as related by one of Russian Technical Advisers, an officer of the General Staff.

Former Quartermaster General Potapov accepts appointment as Chief of General Staff including taking charge of certain War Department technical work.

Potapov and Sisson informed by me that no embargo has been placed on supplies from America to Russia.

Present estimate of enemy divisions on the front from the Baltic to the Black Sea is about or between 105 and 117 infantry and 22 and 25 cavalry divisions.

Reports from various sources state German concentration on West front, in Verdun-Nancy sector and in Flanders.

The above has been cabled to Gen. Pershing.

DECEMBER 9, 1917. DIARY

. . . A most important event is the meeting of the Constituent Assembly Tuesday. But little more than half of the members have as yet been elected, or being elected will have time to reach Petrograd by Tuesday. The question is what will the Bolsheviks do about the Constituent Assembly.

Several days ago the Winter Palace wine cellars were looted. For several nights there has been great disorder in the city resulting from the actions of drunken soldiers. The Red Guard and the sailors have tried to suppress the disorder and there has been much street firing. I was held up by armed drunken soldiers night before last, apparently for purposes of robbery. Although one soldier drew his revolver, they finally but reluctantly yielded to my representations that I was an American and let me pass on.

DECEMBER 10, 1917. DIARY

Tomorrow meets the Constituent Assembly. There is every sign of trouble brewing. Soldiers on the street are surly. Red Guards have their pickets everywhere. Every night there is much street firing. Irving reports that parts of the Litovsky, Izmailovsky and Semenovsky regiments have declared for the Constituent Assembly and will come out tomorrow armed, to protect the members thereof; that "Death Battalions" are arriving piece-meal for the same purpose; that some 300 Cossacks have come to town to fight the Bolsheviks; that a Jewish pogrom is on the carpet for tomorrow; and that the streets will be dangerous tomorrow for foreigners, especially in uniform. . . .

. . . This morning Generals Niessel, Rampon and Knox, Major Thornhill, Bullard . . . and I had a meeting at Sisson's rooms on propaganda but it developed that we discussed more basic matters and plans of action.

Niessel was practically alone in thinking we could do something by propaganda or otherwise along the separate nationality line (Ukraine, Cossacks, etc.). Knox agreed with me that we ought to work to have the armistice, if made, along as favorable lines as possible for the Russians and ourselves and we agreed it would be well to strengthen the hands of the Russians in the negotiations (which will be renewed Wednesday, Dec. 12) by letting them know that if they fail to come to terms we will jump in and help them with redoubled energy, along the lines of my No. 117 [Dec. 6 1917, above] cable.

Obviously, if the Russians think they may still count upon their allies if they have to go on with the war, they will be more apt to hold out for reasonable terms. If they think they have lost the support and friendship of their allies irretrievably they may finally accept any terms offered and fall into the lap of Germany.

Knox thought this information could be given in a newspaper interview. I was of the opinion it should be given to Trotsky or the Chief of Staff—but a cable from Washington today states the President desires American representatives to withhold all direct communication with the Bolshevik Government. This cable is probably based on American press reports originating with Brown of the Chicago Daily News, who is very unfriendly to our Embassy. . . .

. . . In my opinion, the best thing we could do today would be to assure Trotsky that if the negotiations fail, far from finding only peevish and angry Allies to deal with, Russia may count upon their redoubled efforts to assist with troops and in every other practical way. . . .

Unfortunately for this plan, we are now forbidden to have direct communication with the Bolshevik Government, as a result, I suspect of Brown's ignorant or malicious journalistic activities.

DECEMBER 11, 1917. PARAPHRASE OF TELEGRAM
SENT WARCOLSTAFF WASHINGTON. NO. 164-125 3 P.M.[67]

Meeting of Constituent Assembly scheduled for today. Not all members yet chosen and only few here. Decree by Lenin states meeting will take place when 400 members arrive; total membership of Constituent Assembly about 760.

For several days city has been increasingly disorderly. Looting of wine cellars by soldiers going on. It is reported that some soldiers of the Petrograd garrison organized and others of death battalion are arriving surreptitiously to support Constituent Assembly which is due to meet in several days.

Resumption of truce negotiations tomorrow. Desirable if Russians could know that if they should fail in securing armistice Allies will support them and not desert them. This action would naturally reinforce Russian contentions in negotiations to our advantage. It may be possible to convey this idea without violation of injunction against direct dealings and relations. *The Chief German Parliamentaire Hoffman protests against proclamations printed in German, signed by Lenin and Trotsky being spread in German trenches. This too, does not look like German direction of Bolsheviks. Their interests ran parallel until recently but now we should recognize that they are clearly opposed.*

My dear Yates:

I have your letter of Dec. 3 and your wire of a few days later date asking me to cable concurrence in your plan for future Rumanian operations. The trouble is that I agree with your letter (and not your telegram)— that the Ukraine will not fight and the Cossacks only if invaded. I also think that the Rumanians will have to make peace willy-nilly—the Poles will do nothing without more support than it is possible to find and certainly not under civil war conditions.

Kaledin only wishes local order in his own country. Many people with him wish the monarchy restored and perhaps he does too. Perhaps he could be induced to support or to become Military Dictator. Perhaps a civil war may result. But no Russians wish to go on with the war and none will. They are interested in their own affairs now, and God knows it is enough to engage their serious attention. If civil war comes I look to see a restoration of monarchy and then the following successive steps—

1: Pacification and reorganization under German auspices.

2: Russia benevolently neutral toward Germany.

3: Russia ally of Germany.

Our only hope is that we can get the most possible out of the armistice and peace negotiations, or a failure of either or terms somewhat to our advantage. I have been urging Trotsky along these lines (to have expert advisers; to demand a long rather than a short armistice; to require enemy troops to remain in position; to have no interchange of prisoners or commodities, etc., etc.). There is still a big margin between the extreme possibilities. And I have some time ago proposed to Washington that I be authorized, in case negotiations fail, to offer troops and the utmost assistance.

I hope northern Russia is not as bad as you suggest although I fully recognize the possibilities. We will have to take a chance.

I may say I have foreseen present conditions for many months—they were approaching like an avalanche and that was why I may have seemed so unsympathetic to some of your propositions, which would not have averted the inevitable. I told them at home in July or early August that larger war plans would be based on Russia going out of war in a few months.

There is one chance in a thousand that if armistice or peace terms fail a reasonably united Russia will stay in a state of war for a time longer, during which new elements can build up a new front. Only failure of <u>Bolshevik</u> attempt to negotiate can thus eventuate—and only Bolsheviks if any can make any Russians stay in the trenches for any time at all.

With kind regards and thanks for your letters and offers, I am,

Faithfully yours,

DECEMBER 12, 1917. PARAPHRASE OF TELEGRAM SENT WARCOLSTAFF WASHINGTON. NO. 116-127 6 P.M.[68]

There gathered yesterday, in a private meeting at the Tauride Palace, about 30 members of the Constituent Assembly, all social revolutionaries or Kadets, who declared the Constituent Assembly open and postponed first regular meeting until sufficient number of members arrives to constitute a quorum.

There is some talk of the formation of a "Union for Protecting the Constituent Assembly," which it is reported the Railway Union is about to join and Post and Telegraph Unions have joined. If the Assembly is dissolved here, there is also talk of it going to Kiev. Indications tend to show that the Soviet Government will not dissolve it however.

Lenin and others have issued a decree enjoining watchfulness over Kadet party by reason of its connection with Kornilov-Kaledin civil war against revolution and declaring certain unnamed members of the Kadet party subject to arrest.

The armistice made by Shcherbachev is to last until the question of war or peace is settled by the Constituent Assembly or until an armistice is concluded for the entire Baltic-Black Sea front; his armistice provided against movement of troops and Rumanians have joined him.

Proclamations of Lenin-Trotsky advising German soldiers, among whom these proclamations are being spread, that if they turn bayonets inland they need not fear Russian bullets in the back. Inspired Bolshevik statements say that it is necessary to prevent shifting of troops by Germans to fronts of Russia's Allies; that Russia's negotiations are not those of a capitulating side but "as empowered representatives of a risen people to which are directed the hopes of millions of workmen and peasants of the entire world."

Trotsky quoted in press as saying that Chief of American Red Cross here, Robins, said at Smolny that Russia never had such a strong government as at the present time. This statement is denied by Robins.[69]

Gen. Pershing cabled as above.

DECEMBER 12, 1917. PARAPHRASE OF TELEGRAM SENT WARCOLSTAFF WASHINGTON. NO. 169-128 10 P.M.[70]

. . . At present, following independent governments are struggling more or less successfully to exist. Siberia, Finland, Ukraine, Trans-Caucasia, and various Cossack districts with some unity among some of them. Dutov is elective chief or ataman of Orenburg Cossacks and Chairman Cossack Central Committee. Kaledin, Dutov, Kornilov and Miliukov have been reported as leaders in Anti-Bolshevik Cossack-Kadet movement but Rodzianko and Alekseev are also in Cossack Country to which many officers and old regime persons are fleeing. Current rumors and alleged messengers from Cossacks arriving point to approach of civil war. Financial support of Allies sought by many, but I can see no gain in fostering civil war. Doubt if success of either side would prolong war to any extent and very likely civil war is of most interest to Germans.

Gen. Pershing informed of above.

DECEMBER 12, 1917. DIARY

Civil War has begun apparently in earnest.

The Bolsheviks have published a Lenin (et al) decree outlawing the principal and active Kadets and providing for their arrest. The announcement accompanying the decree stated that the Kadet Central Committee at Petrograd was the political general staff of the "revolt" in southern Russia, which they say constitutes an enormous menace. Either, the Bolsheviks are greatly alarmed or are creating camouflage behind which to arrest Kadets, perhaps with the object of keeping them out of the Constituent Assembly.

There are now independent republics struggling more or less successfully to resist in Siberia, Finland, the Ukraine, Trans-Caucasia and in various Cossack regions (Don, Kuban, Terek, Ural, Orenburg), with more or less union among some of the latter. . . .

. . . It remains to be seen whether the Bolsheviks will be able to employ as an effective military force much of the old, demoralized army which in such large degree is a Bolshevik mob. . . .

Another question is the following: What will the non-Bolshevik Socialists do? In my opinion they will divide into 3 parts, pro-Kaledin, pro-Bolshevik and neutral. Perhaps most of them will be <u>neutral</u> but no one can tell. . . .

Kaledin and his adherents desire Allied moral and financial support. Alleged messengers from him report variously that by Jan. 2 he will be besieging Petrograd and Moscow; that he will become active and put out the Bolsheviks if he receives financial support from and is promised recognition by the Allies, etc. . . .

The disorganization of traffic, etc., due to civil war would probably soon cause hunger and cold to settle down upon the fronts and upon northern Russia. This may force the Bolsheviks to give up, but probably not before many things have happened which it is not pleasant to contemplate. . . .

. . . A "union for the protection of the Constituent Assembly" has been formed. The union of Post & Telegraph employees has joined it and it is reported that the railway union is favorably inclined toward it.

DECEMBER 14, 1917. PARAPHRASE OF TELEGRAM SENT WARCOLSTAFF WASHINGTON NO. 175-131 1 P.M.[71]

Armistice negotiations resumed yesterday with the principal discussions centered on troop shifting, questions of naval importance and fraternizing. . . .

Since Allies are not represented Trotsky states that separate truce will be made for Rumania and Russia; that Russian emissaries are authorized to proceed at once with negotiations for peace on the principle of no annexations or contributions and the fate of people to be determined by referenda; districts which suffered severely to be compensated from international fund raised by taxation of capitalist classes responsible for the war; that old treaties "which represented acquisitive instincts of capitalistic classes" are not binding upon Russia. To assist in formulation of democratic peace on above-mentioned terms, Trotsky calls upon the working classes of all belligerents.

The Bolshevik organ "Pravda" publishes column of the President's message making no comment except the headlines, "The basis of a just peace," and "America friend of the German people."

... *That neither Ukraine nor Cossacks will fight Central Powers and that Rumania will make peace through compulsion is growing certainty.*

Services offered to U.S. by some soldiers and many officers. I tell them it is impracticable. Gen. Pershing informed of above.

DECEMBER 14, 1917. DIARY[72]

... In the Don country the Bolsheviks this morning claimed successes over the Cossacks at Rostov ... and at several other points as well. At Kaluga they claimed to have taken several death battalions without fighting. They said Ukrainian troops had been ordered to intercept Kornilov who was moving on Poltava. They admitted 50,000 Cossacks were under arms and more assembling but said they were concentrating troops against them from many directions. They claim the support of the Black Sea Fleet.

By evening the Cossacks had denied the reported Bolshevik successes, claiming to hold Rostov and alleging that most of the Black Sea Fleet was neutral. Ukrainians form a large part of the personnel of the fleet and the Ukrainians appear to be neutral, although it is stated that at Kiev the Ukrainian troops have ejected the Bolsheviks. ...

The British are reported to have released 2 Bolsheviks whose internment in England caused the Bolsheviks to refuse to permit British subjects to leave the country.[73]

DECEMBER 15, 1917. PARAPHRASE OF TELEGRAM SENT WARCOLSTAFF WASHINGTON NO. 182-135 4 P.M.

... There has been smuggling going on in Finnish ports since 1914 to Germany and same has latterly increased but ice will stop it soon. The Russian and de facto Finnish Governments should be asked to prevent. Neither has authorized shipments but neither very potent. *To protect most important Allies interests ... I, as Chief of Military Mission, should be authorized immediately to have free unofficial intercourse with these Governments.* The present negotiations for purchase of field guns and materials are not important but later these will fall into German hands unless large funds are here quickly and we have a free hand. There is some evidence to the effect that 400 cars of copper, lead and lubricating oil have been purchased by Finnish agents and are seeking exit to Germany via Riga and other routes. It is understood that Trotsky is stopping this but I should have authority to interview him immediately.

DECEMBER 15, 1917. PARAPHRASE OF TELEGRAM SENT WARCOLSTAFF WASHINGTON NO. 180-134 6 P.M.[74]

The Russians report that in the armistice negotiations the condition providing for no operative transfers from the Russian front until January 12th except such as have been inaugurated before the conclusion of the agreement, have been accepted by the enemy.

According to reports in the press the following are results of elections to the Constituent Assembly: 148 Socialist Revolutionaries, 88 Bolsheviks, 14 Kadets, 13 Minimalists [Mensheviks], 13 Ukrainian Socialists, 7 others.

Passage to troops bent on civil war has been forbidden by Ukraine.

DECEMBER 16, 1917. PARAPHRASE OF TELEGRAM SENT WARCOLSTAFF WASHINGTON. NO. 185-137 4 P.M.[75]

The enemy forces on the Baltic Sea-Black Sea front are now estimated between 106 and 113 Infantry and between 22 and 25 Cavalry Divisions. The indications are that [al?]etape and landsturm battalions on this front are being formed into regiments and divisions.[76] It is reported that the Vilna recruiting stations are being emptied: also several statements have been made that much artillery and ammunition is leaving this front.

Yesterday, an armistice has been concluded, according to reports, lasting until January 12th; the terms are not yet fully known. The provision against operative transfers of troops was opposed by the Germans and fought by them. However Trotsky, the Commissar for Foreign Affairs made it sine qua non and this provision was finally accepted. See my telegram number 110. [1 Dec. 1917, above.] Trotsky's commitment, in my interview with him, by virtual promise to the United States had some effect.

Without rest of Russia, neither Kaledin nor Ukrainians will fight the enemy and it is believed that the same is true of Trans-Caucasia. Troops from Finland and Lettish troops are being brought to Petrograd. Disorders are increasing and frequent street firing takes place.

All banks are practically closed and currency almost impossible to obtain.

The publication of a decree cancelling officers' commissions, civil rank, decorations and so forth and providing for elections of army unit leaders is expected.

Fighting between Ukrainian and Bolshevik troops in progress in Odessa, with Black Sea sailors on both sides. The Ukrainians oppose sending of Odessa troops by Bolsheviks against Kaledin, which Bolsheviks desire to do.

DECEMBER 16, 1917. DIARY

. . . I am informed today by General Danilov, who is very intelligent, formerly commanding the 5th Army and a Ukraine proprietor, that the Cossacks and Ukraine are opposed to the Bolshevik land policies, they already owning more than the Bolsheviks would give them (the Ukrainians embracing many small proprietors) but that absolutely neither would go on with the war. All of Russia is for peace. These views are samples of those held universally by well-informed Russians and others. . . .

DECEMBER 17, 1917. PARAPHRASE OF TELEGRAM SENT WARCOLSTAFF WASHINGTON. NO. 187-138 TEN A.M.[77]

Most severe penalties are threatened by Trotsky to Military Missions of Allies, if intercourse is continued with Kaledin etc. . . . Such intercourse would be absolutely futile and ill-advised and this Mission has none.

Friendly, if unofficial relations must be maintained with Soviet personnel if any war materials in Russia are to be kept from German hands and any but German relations with Russia after separate peace are to be encouraged. Please look at my number 135 [15 Dec. 1917, above]. Recognizing the Bolshevik Government, the Central Powers will probably have representatives with immense staffs here in two or three weeks, prepared to cement relations and make purchases. Repairing of the German Embassy is under way. *We cannot hope to compete with Germans in any direction if we remain aloof and somewhat antagonistic as at present;* in fact we may have to abandon hope of it. Departure of Allied Missions from Russia, including American may be necessitated by conditions; departure for South Russia would doubtless not be allowed by the Soviet Government. *Authority is requested now unofficially to promise support if peace negotiations fail which can only occur through excessive German demands.* Note my No 117 [6 Dec. 1917, above].

The Germans may prefer indefinite armistice with option to exact considerable from Russia at time of general peace.

Briefly, the armistice terms are as follows: Expiration on January 14th, noon, or 21 days from date of signature. . . . It covers all the aerial and land forces of Russia and enemy on the front from the Baltic to the Black Sea as well as the Russo-Turkish fronts; it also contains the usual provisions against reinforcing and regrouping; for preparing an offensive no strategic troop transfers; . . . demarcation lines in the Baltic and Black Seas; . . . authorization of commercial navigation of Black Sea and Baltic Sea; . . . provides for withdrawal of troops from Persia; provides for immediate opening of peace negotiations. . . . Furthermore Russians proposed in principle, the exchange of civilian and invalid prisoners across the front; improvement of conditions of war prisoners; facilitation of cultural, postal and commercial relations. Mixed commission to meet in Petrograd with a view to perfecting arrangements. Enemy accepted above.

. . . Bolshevik victories reported in Rostov and between Rostov and Novocherkask.

Russian west front committee elected 18 Bolsheviks and 2 social revolutionaries. . . .

. . . Analysis of the armistice terms is based on Russian telegraphic report and any error discovered later will be corrected.

Gen. Pershing informed of above.

DECEMBER 17, 1917. DIARY

I saw Robins today; he told me that he had conversed with Trotsky last night and been assured, with reference to several points in the armistice terms, as follows: that if the armistice is extended automatically, then also automatically is extended the provision for prohibiting strategic

transfers of troops; that commercial intercourse is as yet practically prohibited, whether by land or sea, and that the joint commission to meet
at Petrograd will not authorize intercourse in war materials.

Robins promised to look further into these matters. He said his position with Trotsky might grow weaker if he continued able only to talk,
without authority to promise or deliver anything.

. . . Trotsky has appealed directly to the Ministers of Foreign Affairs of the Allied governments to delegate representatives to a general
peace conference. Trotsky announces if the Allied governments continue to practice "sabotage" in this matter Russia will make a separate
peace.[78]

DECEMBER 18, 1917. PARAPHRASE OF TELEGRAM SENT WARCOLSTAFF WASHINGTON. NO. 191-140 5 P.M.[79]

It is stated by Trotsky that automatic extension of armistice also provides for the non-transfer of troops; he also states that he will demand
such interpretation and that no commerce will be permitted with the
enemy in war materials certainly prior to conclusion of peace. After
peace, it may be possible to induce him to prohibit all exports of war
materials.

The German Minister of Foreign Affairs and the Austrian Premier are
now at Brest requesting Trotsky's presence in connection with peace negotiations. A demand will be made by the Russians for concrete terms
by the enemy on the basis of no annexations nor contributions and allowing self-definition of nationalities provided the enemy will agree to
such a basis. For proposes of a discussion, a week or more will follow
the first pour parles.

Have written Robins, who is now the head of the American Red
Cross Mission to Russia, denying in my letter that the Military Mission
has any emissaries with Kaledin. Such a letter was needed by him and
he is an excellent intermediary.

General Pershing has been informed of the above.

DECEMBER 18, 1917. DIARY

It appears quite certain now that Kaledin in the Don country, and especially at Rostov is getting the best of the Bolsheviks—at least for the
present. . . .

In the Peasants' Soviet yesterday a resolution was passed demanding the convening of the Constituent Assembly, the ending of civil war, etc. Thus the Bolsheviks appear to be losing ground in certain directions; whether this is simply a crystallization of the forces opposing them can not yet be seen.

I am told the Bolsheviks are perfecting administrative machinery very rapidly. On the other hand I am told that Trotsky has sent his wife out of the country and is arranging for his own speedy departure in case of need. It is impossible as yet to integrate properly the great quantities of conflicting information which comes to hand. . . .

Robins came to see me today. He had received assurances from Trotsky that the provision in the armistice protocol for non-transfer of troops would be co-extensive in time with the armistice itself. . . . I am sure Robins is doing good work in presenting these matters so ably to Trotsky. He asked me to inform him in writing that I had no Military Mission representatives or agents with Kaledin, if such were the case, and I addressed him such a letter. I dislike extremely the personal embarrassment that such a letter may cause me, as for example if it be published. But if it will help Robins in his most important and useful work, it is no time for me to seek to save myself.

DECEMBER 19, 1917. DIARY[80]

Yesterday occurred an interview between Trotsky and the French Ambassador Noulens. The latter said afterward that Trotsky made a favorable impression upon him. They discussed the question of the presence of French officers with the Rada, etc. with whom the Petrograd government is at war. Noulens explained that they would not interfere with the internal affairs of Russia. There did not appear to be a final understanding on this subject. At Noulens' request Trotsky explained the basis of the peace contemplated and said that no peace would result if the enemy did not accept this basis ("no annexations" etc.).

. . . The Central Powers said they desired to negotiate a peace with . . . all the warring countries. The Central Powers also stated that they considered the armistice already entered into as preliminary to a general armistice. If no such general peace congress could be secured, the Central Powers do not exclude the possibility of negotiating a peace with the powers that entered into the existing armistice.

Generals Manikovski and Marushevski have been released.

Today was published a secret treaty, news of which will probably create a sensation in America. It is dated July 3, 1916 and in it Russia and Japan agree to come one to the assistance of the other if their mutual efforts do not succeed in preserving China from the political mastery of a third power, and if the consequence either is attacked by such third power. They agree to terminate such a war only when both agree. There is a provision releasing either party from its engagement if its allies will not assist it in proportion to the seriousness of the impending conflict. The treaty is to last 5 years or longer and may only be terminated on a year's notice by either contracting party.

I cabled home the substance of this treaty and certain other probable facts as follows from recently published secret documents: that Japan apparently believes the great war can not be won with Russia out of it; that Japan has decided irrevocably to send no troops to any present theatre of war; that Japan does not interpret as we do the recent entente with us, attaching much more importance than we do to the phrases relating to the "special situation" and "special interests" of Japan in China. The Japanese Minister of Foreign Affairs gave the Russian Ambassador at Tokyo to understand that Japan would be able to enforce its own interpretation in case of any differences of opinion.

DECEMBER 20, 1917. DIARY

There are published threats against Americans if "Russian Comrades" in America, (Berkman, for example) are persecuted.

The Japanese Embassy announced today that the Secret treaty between Japan and Russia published yesterday did not at all betray ("double-cross") England. This announcement referred to the headlines placed by the Soviet News over the treaty in question, which referred to the treaty as a threat against America and England.

Today appeared the first issue of "The Torch" published in Russian and German under the auspices of Trotsky, the "Organ of the Russian Revolutionary Workmen's; Soldiers'; and Peasants' Government." It is for free distribution among the German brothers and is for propaganda purposes. Two articles are by Trotsky, one being his "Appeal to the labouring oppressed and bleeding nations of Europe." Others are designed to prove, by hitherto secret documents, that Germany started the war, in part to support monarchy by attaining victory in the war.

DECEMBER 21, 1917. PARAPHRASE OF TELEGRAM SENT WARCOLSTAFF WASHINGTON. NO. 198-142 1 P.M.[81]

A hitch in the preliminary peace negotiations is reported in the press. That the enemy agrees to no annexations or contributions but finds impracticable the self-definition of nationalities is being alleged. *Apparently the difficulties are increasing in the way of a separate peace.* Failure to make peace would greatly impair for the Bolsheviks their principal political capital and a great change might come in the situation. A speedy meeting of the Constituent Assembly is now desired by the Bolsheviks according to some indications. From a press report the elected members are as follows: Social Revolutionists 197; Bolsheviks 110; Kadets 11; others 20.

For a short period civil war in Russia might incommode the enemy but in the long run it might prove a benefit to them. The best attitude for us, practically announced or adopted by the French Ambassador and the British Embassy, seems to be a patient policy of non-interference in internal affairs and friendly unofficial relations with all elements. . . .

DECEMBER 21, 1917. DIARY

. . . Today a most unfortunate incident occurred. The American Red Cross Commission to Rumania (through its chief, Col. Anderson), wired its agent, the Russian Col. Kalpashnikov (the telegram being addressed by Minister Vopicka to our Ambassador) to send automobiles to Rostov, apparently having in view a retreat of the Rumanian Army. Later this request was cancelled. Yesterday Kalpashnikov tried to ship ten machines to Jassy, and it seems that the Soviet Government had forbidden this, which I at any rate knew nothing about. Kalpashnikov called at the Embassy yesterday, and was told by the Ambassador and myself, who happened to be present, that he should not ship the automobiles under any circumstances without the consent of Smolny. At 2:00 this morning Kalpashnikov was arrested and there were seized certain of his papers, among them the telegram from Vopicka to Francis. On the face of the thing it certainly appeared that our Embassy and Red Cross were concerned in attempted shipments to the Don, which is enemy country from the Soviet point of view and which we would never have had anything to do with.

One of the papers taken with Kalpashnikov was a letter from the latter rather abusive of Robins, indicating clearly that the latter was innocent of any intention to act in bad faith with the Soviet Government.[82]

DECEMBER 22, 1917. DIARY

The daily papers spring the sensation as to the arrest of Kalpashnikov. Trotsky in a speech last night was quite severe on the Ambassador. Said that one who would do such counter-revolutionary things was no Ambassador but an adventurer and that the Revolution would know how to deal with him with a heavy hand. He said that the Ambassador would now have to break his golden silence.

. . . I had a long talk with certain Poles as to the relief of refugees, etc. I asked Major Thacher of the Red Cross to be present. It was agreed I should telegraph the circumstances home and suggest relief through a loan to the Polish National Committee in Paris . . . but . . . would require the sanction of the Soviet Government.

DECEMBER 23, 1917. PARAPHRASE OF TELEGRAM SENT WARCOLSTAFF WASHINGTON. NO. 202-144 1 P.M.[83]

The loss of our facilities for written and telegraphic communication or for doing any business here may soon result from the troubles arising from our studied non-intercourse with the Soviet Government on minor matters as to which they have power.

. . . We are becoming isolated in our position of apparent repulsion of the Soviet Government. It would involve direct intercourse, but I am sure I should send representative to Stavka where the Commissar for War is the supreme commander.

On good authority I am informed that a side issue of the Cossack movement is the reestablishment of a monarchy. They are asking for $250,000,000 in American bank on which to base paper currency here. They say they will be compelled to seek German assistance unless they have immediate support. This I cannot recommend and if I did I would expect action unfavorable.

In an eloquent speech Trotsky expresses the opinion that war can go on if "imperialistic stranglers" refuse democratic peace terms; he says peace will be impossible if German masses do not awaken. *The psychological moment is now here . . . in which to offer whole-hearted support if peace fails. On this subject see my recent cables* [e.g., 6 Dec. 1917; 147, 117, above] *to which no replies have as yet been received.*

The first meeting of the peace commission at Brest took place yesterday. . . .

. . . Strenuous efforts are being made by Trotsky for propaganda in Germany. Germans opposing and protestations are being made by Trotsky.

[The following memorandum was composed by Lieutenant Colonel Monroe C. Kerth and then endorsed by Judson and sent on to Ambassador Francis. As an afterthought, on 26 December, Judson decided to formulate a new draft, addressed directly to the ambassador, and jointly written, to replace this 23 December draft. Judson's handwritten notation on this draft reads: "See communication of Dec. 26 which we asked be substituted for this. The Ambassador said he would return this but neglected to do so." It is instructive to compare the two documents, especially since the 26 December memorandum has been widely cited (by Kennan, William A. Williams, Salzman) as a statement of an alternative to U.S.-Bolshevik policy at that time. Kerth's earlier draft is written with more specific evidence, and even greater urgency and passion, which perhaps explains Judson's desire for a more measured approach in so conflictual and inflamed an atmosphere of the first weeks following the Bolshevik seizure of power. On 18 January 1918, Judson requested that Kerth write another memorandum expressing his "views as to the situation in Russia and what can be done to improve it." The resultant report, dated 22 January 1918, is an excellent statement of the "recognitionist" position, shared by Judson, and William B. Thompson and Robins, both of whom served in succession as head of the American Red Cross Commission to Russia.]

DECEMBER 23, 1917
MEMORANDUM FOR GENERAL JUDSON
FROM COLONEL M. C. KERTH

The internal affairs of Russia are now in a sadly disrupted condition.

The Bolsheviks are in control of all of Great Russia, Finland has declared herself an independent government, Ukraine has an independent government, as have the Cossacks, Siberia has established a separate government, the Polish troops apparently recognize no authority other than Polish organizations, etc.

The Allied Governments, refusing to recognize the Bolshevik government, have their Ambassadors here in Petrograd and have *no* communication with any of the above mentioned de facto governments. As a result, all Allied aid to the Russian people is at standstill while the German emissaries are everywhere, working day and night in the interests of autocracy. The terrible responsibility for this deplorable condition, fraught with untold dangers not only to the Russian Democracy but to the Democracy of the world, rests entirely upon the Allied Representatives, Diplomatic and Military, in Petrograd, until they in a joint meeting take united and concerted action to remedy it.

I use the terms "united and concerted action" of "Diplomatic and Military Representatives," advisedly. Inasmuch as the Military Representatives cable direct to their respective War Departments and the Ambassadors to their respective Foreign Departments, conflicting recommendations tend to destroy team-work which has already cost the Allies thousands of lives and millions of dollars and untold suffering. I deem it a reflection on the intelligence and loyalty of the Allied Representatives here and a crime against humanity to assume [that] the above "united and concerted action" is either impossible or undesirable, and if an attempt was made to secure such "united and concerted action" and it failed [that] the person or persons responsible therefore could be determined and made to shoulder the condemnation of the people of the Allied countries after the war.

It is therefore proposed that such a joint meeting take place . . . as is necessary or desirable to insure concerted action at all times.

To secure concerted action by the representatives of the Allies here it is necessary that the Allied Governments—France, England and the U.S. adopt in common and at once a broad Russian policy.[84]

DECEMBER 23, 1917. DIARY

. . . Last night the Ambassador was here. I presented to him a communication signed by Kerth and forwarded to the Ambassador by my endorsement which was jointly composed by myself and Kerth who find ourselves in agreement in the matter. This communication is in the nature of an urgent appeal to the Allied Missions (diplomatic and military) to get together on a policy, and the latter is outlined as we think it ought to be adopted.[85]

DECEMBER 24, 1917. DIARY

Today we had a meeting at the British Embassy on the subject of purchases in Russia, to deprive the Germans of war material.

"Stoppage of Supplies to Germany from Russia.

"The supplies which Germany can obtain from Russia at the present time can be divided into 3 categories:—

"(1) Supplies shipped by the Allies to the Ports of Archangel and Vladivostock.

"(2) Supplies of raw materials and finished articles at the mills, works and mines.

"(3) Supplies on the open market. . . .

". . . A Central Committee, consisting of the same three heads of the present Missions as for item (1) will be formed to control the financial operations and to coordinate the work of various small committees consisting of the best business men of the Allied nations in their particular lines of trade.

"It is proposed that a small committee should be formed for each of the following items:—

Metals	Chemical Products	Timber
Rubber	Fats and oils	Coal
Machinery	Food stuffs	Clothing

Leather and raw hides . . .

". . . All matters which require ventilation in the Press or investigation or the Railways will be referred for action to these sections. In both these cases it will probably be necessary to have definite agents in various parts of Russia."

———

Robins received his non-intercourse instructions today. Only this morning he was able by personal representation and in no other way to get off a train load of supplies for Rumania. Certain, frank and friendly intercourse is essential if we are to do business here.

DECEMBER 25, 1917. PARAPHRASE OF TELEGRAM SENT
WARCOLSTAFF WASHINGTON. NO. 206-
HUNDRED FORTYSIX 5 P.M.[86]

A conference composed of British, French and American Military Missions was held yesterday at the British Embassy to consider what measures were necessary to prevent the falling into enemy hands of Russian war materials. It was unanimously agreed that it is necessary that prompt and joint action be taken by the Allies. For direction and financial control a Joint Committee has been formed consisting of the heads of the British, French and American Military Missions, this Committee to have power to appoint subcommittees from trustworthy business firms, regardless of whether they be British, French or American or Belgian. Purchases should probably be begun by these subcommittees as soon as the home governments give the necessary authority and provide for financial advances.

This is in accordance with my telegram number 135. The $10,000,000 requested therein as a preliminary should be made utilizable under direction of joint committee, if favorable action is taken on this.

If we can offer commodities for civilian use in exchange for war materials our position in competition will be strengthened greatly. The Russians are not confident that America is able or willing to assist in this way to supply the people with urgent necessities, and for this reason they are turning to the enemy neighbor with hope. It is possible, by prompt action, to compete with this enemy if we can offer the commodities which are needed. More can be bought by Boots and Shoes than by Dollars or Marks. Is it possible for such commodities to be procured for Russia in the U.S. and will you authorize me to make this kind of proposition here?

We cannot do business here without a free hand in a friendly intercourse, in my opinion. . . .

There is an increasing probability in the failure of the negotiations for peace and now is the time for the adoption of a policy which, for this contingency, has been previously recommended by me. . . . In presenting this matter a free hand should be given to me so it shall not seem simply like propaganda.

7 members of the left wing of the Social Revolutionary Party have entered the cabinet of the Soviet.

DECEMBER 25, 1917. DIARY

. . . I believe in the necessity of frank and friendly intercourse with all, discouraging strife, honest non-interference in internal affairs and the offer of assistance to all when such offers are opportune. I feel sure that this policy[87] would prove a boomerang in the not distant future. The peace negotiations seem to be approaching failure. If the Bolsheviks cannot make peace they cannot longer demand an immediate peace from any other Russian party. They, the real pacifists, will become pro-war and anti-German. Then all elements can perhaps do something, with the assistance of the Allies, to hold some kind of a line, for the honor of Russia and the effective support of her Allies. . . .

The left social-revolutionists have accepted seven places in the Council of People's Commissars.

DECEMBER 26, 1917.

HON. DAVID R. FRANCIS,
AMERICAN AMBASSADOR, PETROGRAD.

Sir:—

The Bolsheviks are in control of Great Russia.

The American Government has its Embassy here in Petrograd and has no communication with the <u>de facto</u> Bolshevik Government. As a result all American aid to the Russian people is at a standstill while the German emissaries are everywhere, working day and night in the interests of the enemy. The terrible responsibility for this deplorable condition, fraught with untold dangers not only to the Russian Democracy but to the Democracies of the world, rests primarily upon the Ambassador and the Chief of the Military Mission, upon each of whom is imposed the duty of informing the American Government as to conditions here and of suggesting appropriate action.

It is necessary that the United States adopt at once a broad Russian policy.

In our opinion this policy should be based upon the following general principles:—

1: In view of the fact that the Bolshevik Government is the most important and extensive in Russia today, enter into helpful, sympathetic and friendly relations with it.

2: Pour oil on troubled waters. Try to discourage civil war by all possible friendly intercessions, representations and advice. Seek to convince all elements that a fair constitutional convention is necessary.

3: Recognize the almost insuperable difficulties confronting Russia today, which well might incline even the most conscientious and patriotic Russian to believe that his country is not justified in seeking further to conduct war if reasonable and honorable peace terms can be secured. Self-preservation knows no law. If Russia feels thus constrained to seek peace and can secure reasonable terms, let us assist her to make them as favorable to herself (and as disadvantageous to her enemies and ours) as is possible. If on the other hand Russia finds her enemies refuse to consider terms which are acceptable to the Russian people and consistent with their honor, then offer her the material assistance of her Allies on a far larger scale and of a more practical character than has heretofore been considered necessary or advisable; offer also to immediately assist her in the reorganization of all the elements of military strength still present in Russia, in order that she may be better prepared to continue her defense in case the present peace negotiations fail.

4: Do not stand on dignity. Such conduct might be in order if we were dealing with an established power experienced in protocol and etiquette. In fact what we are dealing with is for the most part an aggregation of simple but honest persons, unacquainted with the ways of government, not experienced in the conduct of it, threatened with anarchy as the result of their inexperience, who find themselves in their present situation largely because we have encouraged their democratic aspirations by our words and by our example, and because they have fought for three years, without the facilities for modern war possessed by the industrial nations of the west, thus rendering vital assistance to the cause of victory over autocratic Germany whatever may be their future course.

5: Act on the theory that Russia is entitled to sympathy not condemnation. She is passing through a dreadful experience in many ways unequalled in history. Under similar conditions no other nation might be expected to act otherwise.

If such a policy is not speedily adopted there will be no competition with Germany possible for the friendship of the Russian nation and the Russian people.

Russia will become practically a German colony and will be organized by Germany, long before this war is over, to render vitally needed assistance to the Central Powers, which will more than likely enable them to win the war. The probable cost to our country of a failure to adopt such a policy is then defeat; the death of hundreds of thousands of young Americans; tons of [supplies and] billions of debt; and a burden that will set us back a hundred years.

As Colonel Kerth, the second in rank of the Military Mission, is in agreement with its chief and to the contents of this communication, it has seemed reasonable that both should sign it.

Very respectfully,

DECEMBER 26, 1917
MEMORANDUM FOR THE AMBASSADOR:

With reference to my interview with Trotsky on Dec. 1st, and with special reference to your remarks on Dec. 22 and 23, concerning same, I have the honor to set forth the following facts:

Quotations from diary:—[88]

"Nov. 30: All day I have been talking with our Ambassador. . . ."

———

"Dec. 1: This morning I had an interview of about 40 minutes with Trotsky. . . ."

Quotation from my cable of Dec. 1, 1917.

"With assent Ambassador and emphasizing its non-official character I had long interview with Trotsky this morning. . . ."

I showed you my cable of Dec. 1, 1917, or read it to you on the day on which it was sent.

Armistice negotiations were to begin on December 2 between the Russians and the Central Powers. The Allies, including our own country, were vitally interested in the terms of this armistice if one should result. For several days I had been becoming more and more impatient to see what good I might accomplish in an interview with Trotsky, who would in my opinion control more or less completely the terms of the armistice. I talked to Mr. Wright and Mr. Sisson and both were convinced that it was worth while for me to have such an interview and agreed to recommend to you that I receive your consent.

You gave me to understand before I left you on the Morning of November 30 that you were practically convinced, but with some misgivings, that the interview should be arranged. I understood that you desired Riggs to go rather than me, for the reason per se that he was less important than I and also because if he suffered any rebuff it would be less embarrassing than if I was the chief of the Military Mission should have such an experience. I understood however that if Riggs were to make no satisfactory progress, or if he were to come to the conclusion that it would be well for me to join him or to visit Trotsky after him, I was to hold myself in readiness and continue the interview myself. It is to be remembered that our conversation was on Nov. 30. The interview was to be on Dec. 1, and the armistice negotiations were to begin on Dec. 2 at Brest Litovsk. Obviously there was not a moment to lose. Indeed the Commissioners might already have received their final instructions and it might already be too late. The extreme urgency of the matter I represented to you. I then went over precisely and carefully the matter I proposed to present to Trotsky. You then suggested that it might be explained that Kerth had of his own accord directed his protest to Dukhonin; that such was not by your instructions. To this of course I assented.

I then told you I was going to the British Embassy to dinner and would see there General Niessel and General Knox. I said I would talk the matter over with them and with the British Ambassador and would stop at the Embassy after dinner and let you know the result.

That evening I attempted to take several persons home after the dinner at the British Embassy. My automobile was taken possession of by the Red Guard and I was delayed about 2 hours so that it was about midnight when I stopped to see you. I found you still up, in your dining room, and, as always, ready to talk of the public business. I told you the result of my conversations at the British Embassy (See first quotation above). According to my best recollection, (and the whole matter is deeply impressed upon my memory) you then asked "Well what do you think about it now?"

I replied that I still thought I should go. And you said "Then go ahead."

Early next morning Mr. Sisson came in and as he and Robins had relations with Smolny[89] I asked him to arrange an interview for Riggs, explaining your desire that Riggs go first in any event, and that whether I should go later on or not would depend on circumstances. I then rehearsed with Riggs what he was to say, having carefully prepared some notes for my own guidance.

Sisson was gone for what seemed to me a long time, in view of the precious character of each remaining hour. He got back about noon and said he had only been able to arrange for an interview with me personally. Certainly there was nothing to do, in view of all the circumstances but to visit Smolny and interview Trotsky at once. This I did, and I had no idea or suspicion until three weeks later that you were at all of the opinion that I had not your entire consent and approval of the whole matter, although I knew that both of us were annoyed by certain press reports of the interview.

DECEMBER 26, 1917. DIARY

Robins was here today and went over the evidence relating to Trotsky's alleged relations with the German Staff. Robins first took this matter up in the days of Kerensky and found that then there was no evidence of such relations in the hands of the Minister of Justice or elsewhere in the possession of the government, although the press talked much about such evidence. He had made an analysis of the speeches and actions, and also had formed an opinion from many personal conversations. In Robins' judgment neither Lenin nor Trotsky are German agents but at present are most active in efforts to destroy the German Government and substitute therefore a government by the proletariat, devoted to peace and socialism. . . .

. . . The Peasants' Soviet has split into about even parts. The Bolshevik section has adjourned after denouncing the Bourgeoisie, demanding an immediate meeting of the Constitutional Assembly, which should be supported only so far as it works with the Soviet, etc. The right section formed an Executive Committee with Chernov at its head, condemned the action of the Bolsheviks with reference to the Ukraine, etc.[90]

The Council of People's Commissars has appropriated 2,000,000 roubles for the use of left internationalists of all countries.

DECEMBER 27, 1917. PARAPHRASE OF MESSAGE SENT WARCOLSTAFF WASHINGTON. NO. 210. HUNDRED FORTYEIGHT. 4 P.M.[91]

Our railway party should be held in order to await developments in Japan to which they have already started from Vladivostok according to the reports of the British.

I recommend that one division be prepared to start via Vladivostok since it is so certain to coincide with any plan in the future (i.e.) if break, *or if* [peace] plan [fails.]

The Russian people should not necessarily be held accountable for possible attacks by enemy prisoners or mobs on the Allied Military

Missions and Embassies and should such occur it is very important that they be considered by the United States as incited by German agents. . . .

. . . General peace failing the Russians will enter into separate negotiations with great anger at the Allies. Russia has practically been satisfied that a fair general peace will be made by the Central Powers. The enemy may induce hostile activities toward us during a long armistice or may persuade Russia to yield much to them in a separate peace. . . .

DECEMBER 27, 1917. DIARY

. . . The National City Bank was forcibly entered and closed today by the Red Guard, in connection with some general complaint against all of the banks.

The Ambassador has at last cabled home for authority to have intercourse with the Bolshevik Government. And to handle the matter of Trotsky's personal attack upon him and of the stoppage of our courier from Stockholm, he has authorized Robins and Stines "to go to Trotsky." If we could have had friendly intercourse before we might have accomplished much. Now it is perhaps too late. . . .

DECEMBER 28, 1917. PARAPHRASE OF MESSAGE SENT WARCOLSTAFF WASHINGTON. NO. 213. HUNDRED FORTYNINE. 3 P.M.[92]

Referring to our last cable, assent was given by the enemy to the proposal of the Russians against an economic boycott and a reply made to the Russian proposals. *The authority for the Ambassador to have intercourse with the Soviet Government has been cabled for following repeated recommendations from me, our Ambassador has cabled Washington for authority to have intercourse with Soviet Government. Referring to my recent cables, I advise that the Military Mission be included independently and that this authority be made as broad as possible. An attempt should be made to prevent the Germans from having the only friendly influence here but I fear that it is too late. German agents are already here openly undertaking commissions etc. and have a free hand of course.*

To understand Trotsky is very important. All the evidence has been studied by myself and Robins, the latter since the days of Kerensky. Apparently Trotsky is a pacifist, idealist, and internationalist, possessing his own controlling motives and apparently has never been under German direction. His pacifist activities suited the Germans and their propaganda was parallel until two months ago. He risked failure during the armistice negotiations in order to hold the enemy on this front and the fault is largely due to his Russian officer technical advisers if it was not completely accomplished. *As soon as he came into power his plans and those of the Germans completely diverged. The natural result based on human nature may come from continued non-intercourse, invitation to suspicion, and aloofness on the part of the Allies.*

Today the press publishes much against the Allies; reference to attempt to send armored cars to the Don by Americans was made, this refers to the already described Red Cross car incident; a deciphered intercepted telegram indicating French Military Mission activities in the Ukraine and against peace was published with drastic comments.

Operations hostile to Soviet plans cannot have Petrograd as a base. Bolsheviks in Ukraine have considerable numbers.

A week or two distant will see a real famine, apparently, due to interruptions in traffic on account of civil-war and other conditions.

Pershing cabled above message.

DECEMBER 28, 1917. DIARY

. . . Today we met at Gen. Poole's to select Committees of Finance Audit and Purchase, together with various sub-committees to handle purchases in Russia.

I took the position, and shall continue to do, that we should act openly and with the knowledge and consent of the government here; or that we should seek to have Russia prohibit the export of raw materials to all countries alike.

Have heard from Poole that our railway men have left Vladivostok for Japan, some 375 of them. Have wired home to hold them in Japan. Also to prepare one division of Americans ready to begin assisting Russians if peace fails and fighting is to be renewed against them.

DECEMBER 29, 1917. DIARY

Another long discussion today with Gen. Lavergne on policy. . . . We differ principally on Trotsky. I do not think him working under German direction, therefore I favor friendly relations.

Many German officers (50 or more already) are arriving here on various commissions. They pay many calls on Trotsky and the other Commissars of course.

DECEMBER 30, 1917. PARAPHRASE OF MESSAGE SENT
WARCOLSTAFF WASHINGTON. NO. 215.
HUNDRED FIFTY 3 P.M.[93]

A Central Executive Committee, which pretends to have assumed authority in the Ukraine, has been organized by the Bolsheviks in the Ukaraine after a conference of the local Soviets and a part of the Peasants' Council. They appeal to the troops of the Ukraine to oppose the bourgeoisie Rada and counter-revolution. In Kiev the strength of the Bolsheviks is not great and it is uncertain in the Ukraine.

It is reported by the press that the Ukrainian Rada Executive power, through Secretariat, announces that the Soviet peace negotiations are not recognized by the Ukraine; that a general peace on the same terms as the Bolsheviks is favored; and summons an international conference to enter into general peace negotiations and a Russian conference to arrange Russian representation.

According to the best information the Cossacks in their own country are generally unwilling to fight. The units made up of Russian officers etc. of whom many show monarchical tendencies appear to be the real fighting force. . . .

January 8th will be the date of the next peace conference at Brest, according to an announcement made by Trotsky.

Germany can supply many things that the Russians need and large commerce is indicated. Already there are here many officers of the enemy connected with the armistice and including trade questions.

An adroit move to completely alienate the sympathy of Russia for the Allies, if general peace fails, is included in the acceptance by the Central Powers of the Russian proposals as a basis of general peace. The Bolsheviks and probably the enemy, have started a strong propaganda to show that the failure to join the peace conference by the Allies proves that they are under capitalistic and imperialistic influences and that they have selfish aims of annexations, etc. The following is an example of the propaganda being quoted from the press as Krylenko's words: "Now when general peace is so near, if the Allies continue to preserve silence, when an end can be put to the world war by a single word from them, on the heads of these governments may the blood and curse of hundreds of thousands of men fall."

Direction has been given by Krylenko for "the necessary measures" against the Polish troops in view of the many complaints against them by the Bolsheviks and an order has been given to disarm them.

After five months spent all over Siberia the American Forester Commissioner, Simmons, reports that the peace sentiment is prevalent everywhere, and, although anarchy exists in spots, the Bolshevik authority is without important opposition. Nevertheless, the press reports that a Siberian Government has just been organized at Tomsk with all parties but the Bolsheviks represented. The former independent Siberian Government melted away.

Today there has been an immense peace parade.

It is estimated that the enemy divisions on the Baltic Sea-Black Sea front are as follows: Cavalry 25 to 22; infantry 110 to 95. Agency reports that troops are to be sent to the French front by Austria. The rumors of concentration by the enemy on the South West Front are not confirmed.

American passport control at the Swedish frontier has been abolished. The Swedes are not stopping many from entering Sweden, and all who have Smolny papers pass in either direction in so far as Russia is concerned.

Foregoing message has been cabled to General Pershing.

DECEMBER 30, 1917. DIARY

The next meeting of the peace conference, announced Trotsky in a speech last night, will be at Brest on Jan. 8.

. . . It may be gathered from the press that the Germans are telling what things they have [that] the Russians need, and that commerce between Germany and Russia will soon be reopened on a large scale satisfactory to both.

Much propaganda is being indulged in for peace and to alienate the Russians from the enemy [i.e., the Allies] by reason of their alleged unwillingness to consider terms of peace thought fair by Germans and Russians. Today there has been an enormous peace parade. Sisson estimates it at about 75,000.

. . . we read that a new Siberian government has been formed at Tomsk, with all parties except Bolsheviks represented. The last independant Siberian Government melted away. We have heard nothing of it except that it was created at Omsk.

DECEMBER 31, 1917. PARAPHRASE OF MESSAGE SENT
WARCOLSTAFF WASHINGTON. NO. 226.
HUNDRED FIFTY FOUR. 1 P.M.[94]

Don Cossacks have reelected Kaledin Hetman.

Again the Banks have been closed. A plan to nationalize them is being worked on by the Government.

According to a report American methods will be introduced by the Bolshevik Commissar of Railroads. In Russia now we have no railway men. As per my No. 117 [1 Dec. 1917, above] an opportunity might arise to arrange with the Soviet and any other Government concerned for work which was heretofore contemplated on the Trans-Siberian.

The most probable future course of events will be a prolonged armistice with a growing anti-Ally feeling which would afford soil for German propaganda, and to our increasing disadvantage, German commercial and other activities.

German intervention now would be welcomed by many elements, including monarchists, merchants, manufacturers and bankers.

Above cabled to Pershing.

DECEMBER 31, 1917. PARAPHRASE OF MESSAGE SENT
WARCOLSTAFF WASHINGTON. NO. 231.
HUNDRED FIFTY SIX. 5 P.M.[95]

Having just returned from seeing Trotsky, Robins reports that he *(Trotsky) is on the track of a German conspiracy and is on the point of a break in all negotiations. Trotsky asks, if a break should occur, what will the Americans do. Robins, as a result of a conference with the Ambassador and Judson, was authorized to inform Trotsky that the United States will assist to the utmost and will try to have the Allied Governments do the same.* There will be a meeting tomorrow morning at which a break is apprehended by Trotsky. I shall feel free, if this break occurs, to confer with Trotsky, Krylenko, etc. in the emergency, and to arrange for a meeting of the Allied military representatives to discuss immediate military plans and activities subsequent thereto.

The French and British Military Missions have been consulted and we are in agreement. The French and British Ambassadors are now being consulted by the Ambassador. Later: These Ambassadors are in agreement.

DECEMBER 31, 1917. DIARY

Today at about 3:30 Robins arrived directly from Smolny, with news that the peace negotiations were about to be broken off. . . . We hastened to the Embassy. After a short conference the Ambassador agreed that Robins should go to Trotsky and inform him that we would render all assistance possible; that the Ambassador would secure the concurrence of the Ambassadors (French and British) in the assurances we proposed to give. . . . Niessel and Knox were soon at my office. We agreed that immediate assurances should be given and that if a break came I should at once visit Trotsky and arrange for a "Council of War" between the Russians and us there to decide on immediate military measures and activities to follow. Robins had expected the break to come tonight, but later telephoned that the meeting at which it might be expected to occur had been deferred till tomorrow morning. He will come to me at 11.— Niessel came in at 11:30 tonight to learn the latest news.

A great fight has been going on at Irkutsk for eight days between Bolsheviks (troops and Red Guard) on the one side and cadets, Cossacks and civilians on the other. There may result a cutting of the Trans-Siberian at this front. . . .

. . . A meeting of prisoners of war occurred yesterday at the Circus Moderne at which Bolshevik resolutions were passed.

A great deal of friction exists among the railway men as to whether or no "Vikshel" (the Executive Committee) should rule. The situation is very confused. "Vikshel" is not pro-Bolshevik. There will be an All Russian conference of Railway men in a day or two—probably Bolshevik. The commissar for ways and communications (Bolshevik) has taken possession of the Ministry. . . .

. . . All of the Chiefs of Allied Military Missions to Russia have been withdrawn from Kiev to Petrograd.

JANUARY 1, 1918. PARAPHRASE OF MESSAGE SENT WARCOLSTAFF WASHINGTON. NO. 234. HUNDRED FIFTY SEVEN. 3 P.M.[96]

In my telegram No. 156, [31 Dec. 1917, above] the conspiracy referred to seems to be rather a German trick to interpret as an already established fact the self-definition of Poland, Courland, Lithuania etc. The placing of the White Sea route to Russia under practical German control, and the application of Russian inspection to movements of the enemy's troops on and from the front, as well as other acute differences, exist. This issue is now before Berlin where Kuhlmann and the German General Staff are in controversy. Although a break is not certain it is probable. The arrest of socialists recently in Germany is bitterly resented by the Bolsheviks.

Between the Bolsheviks and their opponents there is a long continued fight at Irkutsk. It is expected that the Trans-Siberian will be interrupted for an indefinite time.

The Military Mission Chiefs, who left for Kiev at the time Dukhonin was killed, have returned.

Frequent communication with Trotsky is had by the French and British officers.

A published controversy here between Trotsky and the Rumanian Minister indicates serious trouble between Rumanians and local Bolsheviks.

Many conflicts, mostly local, occur in Ukraine between the Ukrainians and the Bolsheviks. The Ukrainians generally are the winners but the Bolsheviks apparently hold Rovno, Kharkov, (together with the Railroad to the south of the latter) etc. The fighting is not very serious and truces occur locally. There is an entente against the Bolsheviks composed of Ukrainians and Cossacks.

A Bolshevik resolution has been passed here by enemy prisoners of war at a public meeting.

Amazement at the terrible breakdown in all directions is expressed by the Germans here, it is reported. They profess the fear that this is a world problem and that no single outside nation can cure it.

JANUARY 1, 1918. DIARY

The meeting at which Robins thought the break might occur was not held last night but tonight. According to Sisson, who was present, the meeting was of the Central Committee of the Soviet, together with the Petrograd Soviet, and was presided over by Trotsky. It was called to hear the report of the Russian Peace delegation. It seems that after the exchange of notes at meetings previously described there was another meeting at Brest-Litovsk at which the Germans presented a document placing certain German claims in concrete form. These claims were in substance that Poland, Lithuania, Kurland and part of Estland and Livland had already in effect expressed their desires as to what disposition should be made of them in the future; to which the Russians replied that no expressions of the kind considered, made while troops occupied the territory, were satisfactory. . . . Sisson left before the meeting was finished, leaving reporters behind and came to the Embassy where the Ambassador, Robins and I were in conference. Sisson reported that the speeches all indicated a spirit of readiness to resume the war if the Germans did not yield. Meantime it is understood that the matter is before Berlin where the General Staff opposes yielding while Kuhlmann might be willing to yield in some degree. We designed two papers for the Ambassador's action. One designed to indicate how far Robins could go in promising Trotsky the Ambassador's recommendation of support, to enable Trotsky to face a break with less apprehension; and the other a proposed cable to the Department requesting approval of the course he is proposing to take. . . .

. . . The Council of People's Commissars has agreed to recommend proposals to the Central Committee of the Soviet looking to consummating arrangements for an independent Finland. There are press reports of Cossack movement north toward Kharkov and of seizures by Cossacks of coal and provisions destined for Petrograd and Moscow.

At a private conference it was decided by members elected to the Constituent Assembly that the latter would commence its regular sessions when one third of all the members were present.

Tonight I have received a cable relieving me from duty here and ordering me to report to the Chief of Staff in Washington.

[A full month had passed, from Judson's meeting with Trotsky on 1 December 1917 to Judson's receipt of his recall orders, but the record indicates that the meeting led to the recall. Jane Weyant's analysis ably explains the complications:

Thus while Judson declined to comment upon his interview with Trotsky, reports of the event based upon Trotsky's version of the meeting were widely publicized. When it became apparent that the reaction to the meeting with Trotsky was largely unfavorable, the Department of State acted quickly to dispel the impression that the United States desired to open diplomatic relations with the Soviet government. First, although Secretary Lansing had received a cable from Francis affirming that Judson had seen Trotsky with embassy approval, the Secretary of State issued a press release stating that Judson had "acted without government instructions in presenting communication to the Bolshevist government." Hence, Francis's report was conveniently ignored so that the Wilson administration might disengage itself from Judson's action by asserting that he had acted completely on his own initiative.

The impact of Lansing's statement was not lost upon Ambassador Francis, who, perceiving that the Department of State had not included him in its disavowal of Judson's action, decided to extricate himself from complicity with Judson in planning the meeting with Trotsky. And so Francis, who had reported positively on December 1 that "Judson saw Trotsky today with my approval," cabled on December 2 that he had "consented that Judson should send subordinate to discuss armistice provisions only and was not aware that Judson had gone himself until after visit made." Then, a week later on 9 December, Francis advised Lansing that "Judson's personal call on Trotsky was without my knowledge or approval."][97]

JANUARY 2, 1918, PETROGRAD
SUGGESTED (BY ROBINS) **COMMUNICATION TO
THE COMMISSAR FOR FOREIGN AFFAIRS**
[FROM AMBASSADOR FRANCIS]

At the hour the Russian people shall require assistance from the United States to repel the aggressions of Germany and her Allies, you may be assured that I will recommend to the American Government that it render them all aid and assistance within its power. If upon the termination of the present armistice Russia fails to conclude a Democratic Peace through the fault of the Central Powers and is compelled to continue the war I shall urge upon my Government the fullest assistance to Russia possible, including the shipment of supplies and munitions for the Russian Armies, the extension of credits and the giving of such advice and technical assistance as may be welcome to the Russian people in the service of the common purpose to obtain through the defeat of the German autocracy the effective guarantee of a lasting and democratic peace.

I am not authorized to speak for my government on the question of recognition but that is a question which will of necessity be decided by actual future events. I may add however, that if the Russian armies now under command of the People's Commissars commence and seriously conduct hostilities against the forces of Germany and her Allies, I will recommend to my Government the formal recognition of the de facto government of the People's Commissars,

Respectfully,

I understand that Robins got the Amb. to initial this and retained it for his own information and guidance (to use it verbally and informally).[98]

JANUARY 2, 1918. PARAPHRASE OF MESSAGE SENT
WARCOLSTAFF WASHINGTON. NO. 236
HUNDRED FIFTY EIGHT 1 P.M.[99]

On account of probable break in negotiations for peace and the critical situation here the Ambassador says that he will not relieve me immediately though yesterday's cable from the Adjutant General orders me to Washington.[100]

The stand of the Russian peace delegation against the German concrete propositions for peace were endorsed by the Petrograd Soviet and the Central Committee Soviet last night in a combined meeting.[101] This was published this morning in full. The Council of People's Commissars had previously endorsed this stand.

The proposed treaty submitted by Germany . . . Second clause states that in accordance with the self-definition . . . principle, Livonia, Poland, Courland . . . have already declared themselves desirous of leaving Russia; apparently aimed to restrict trade relations between Russia and the Allies, the Germans make . . . provisions for trade between Russia and themselves; provision for exchange of prisoners. In reference to the merchantmen in the enemy's harbor at the outbreak of the war, they demand their return.

Ready resumption of war should a break take place was advocated in the speeches at the meeting.

Facilitating of separate peace is the only conceivable danger in promises of support to Trotsky in case of a break. Less advantageous terms to the enemy apparently desirable, might be the result even in case of a separate peace. In the case of a lengthy armistice or whatever happens it would make future relations with Russia to us more friendly. Above to Pershing.

JANUARY 2, 1918. DIARY

The meeting referred to in yesterday's diary endorsed the stand of the Russian peace delegation against the concrete German separate peace plans. . . . The delegation had refused to discuss the proposed draft after Clause 2 was read. The latter referred to the "self-definition" of Courland, Poland etc. . . .

It is said there is great excitement at Smolny today over the prospective break. The following appear in the evening papers. Krylenko is leaving for Stavka where a collegium will be formed of "better generals" to guide military operations . . . and a "declaration of war" is expected.

The prospects of a break are very great. It appears imminent.

JANUARY 3, 1918. DIARY

Trotsky has addressed a note to the French Military Mission accusing it of furnishing to the Press as information, false statements designed to incite Civil War, and calling upon the Mission to answer certain questions, including in substance the following: If the press correctly stated the French Military Mission to be the source of its information what steps has the Mission taken to punish its members who are guilty of spreading malicious lies? Does the Department of Propaganda function? Whence does it receive its cables and to whom does it furnish them? How many officers are attached to the French Mission to Russia and where are they? What does the Mission know of communications of its officers with Kaledin, Alekseev, the Rada, etc.?

The Soviet Government, recognizing the right of the Ukraine to independence, has proposed or accepted a proposal for a conference with a view to ending the conflict between the Ukraine and the Soviet. The sole condition appears to be that the Rada shall recognize Kaledin and his supporters as counter-revolutionists.

JANUARY 3, 1918. PARAPHRASE OF MESSAGE SENT
WARCOLSTAFF WASHINGTON. NO. 242
HUNDRED FIFTYNINE 3 P.M.[102]

Promotion of such harmonious action as is possible between all the elements confronting the enemy will be necessary in event of a break in the negotiations for peace, urging of military reforms and seeking a Holy-war proclamation by all the authorities possible including the Holy Synod, the Constituent Assembly, and the Bolsheviks, etc. . . . Every effort should be made to gain the cooperation of the Soviet Government when relations between them and ourselves are established.

In the event of resumption of hostilities it is to be expected that only short local advances . . . will take place for two months. . . .

. . . Soviet preparations for the beginning of hostilities are indicated by report of activities at Stavka. . . . It is further reported that Stavka will be the place of a conference between Russian generals and Krylenko, who is reported to be on his way there. . . .

. . . Incredible losses have been suffered by the Russians both in efficiency and in numbers since the first of November when there were 1,700,000 combatants and 6,000,000 ration strength, including the front depots. This estimate was for all the fronts. For the present strength the estimates vary within wide limits and losses continue through desertion, demobilization . . . , and the exodus of the Ukrainians. Today the probable strength, outside of figures, is 800,000 combatants with a ration strength of 4,000,000 of which one half is of good material.

Nearly all officers of the Staffs of fronts and other units have been reelected. These having suffered the least. There is some good material, though they are ignorant, among the officers elected largely from the soldiers of regiments and companies. Willingness to fight, morale, and discipline are absent. Germans or agents have bought some field guns from the soldiers.

(Above cabled to Pershing.)

JANUARY 4, 1918. PARAPHRASE OF MESSAGE SENT
WARCOLSTAFF WASHINGTON. NO. 244
HUNDRED SIXTY 1 P.M.[103]

. . . Agreement as to procedure, in case of a break [in Brest-Litovsk peace negotiations], has been made here by the British, French and American diplomatic and Military Missions.

Break may not formally occur for two weeks. Military and other plans should be made expecting break as practically certain in less time.

Harmony and not civil war in the Allies' interest is what the Chief of the British Military Mission, General Barter, agreed in conference with me.

The position of the French Military Mission is more equivocal except as to plans after a break, but such a position is becoming impossible. Information as to the activities of the French Mission has been demanded yesterday by Trotsky, also measures against certain of their propaganda and intelligence work was begun.

Approach of understanding is indicated by the interchanges between the Soviet Government and the Rada.[104]

If 400 are here, 18th January named as date of Constituent Assembly by the Soviet Government. Pershing cabled.

AMERICAN EMBASSY OFFICE OF THE MILITARY
ATTACHÉ, PETROGRAD
JANUARY 4, 1918

ORDERS   NO. 13.

To Lieutenant Colonel Monroe C. Kerth.

1: You will proceed to Mogilev as soon as practicable and put yourself in relations with Stavka. You will feel free to communicate in a
friendly and helpful way with all officials there, if opportunity arises
suggesting the necessity of immediate preparation in view of the contingency that has arisen that war may be soon renewed on the Russian front.

There should be encouragement extended as to recommendations
which may be expected from American representative here of Allied
support in case of a renewal of operations along lines with which you
are already familiar through conversations with the Ambassador and
with me.

2: It would be well to discuss Army reorganization plans, having in
view a volunteer paid Army and units based on nationalities (Polish
etc.). The importance of preserving what strength and efficiency the
Army now has should be pointed out, and the importance as well of
certain obvious reforms to make the exercise of command more certain
and to promote discipline. . . .

3: You will report to me upon the situation and upon activities at
Stavka as frequently as possible.
Note:
Original bears following
"Approved David R. Francis, Ambassador"

JANUARY 5, 1918. DIARY

General Niessel has replied to Trotsky's communication to the French
Military Mission, recently described in this diary [see 3 Jan. 1918,
above]. He explained the alleged "false statement: of news by attribut-
ing it to the indiscretion of a young officer; that he would guard against
repetitions of this occurrence; that the officers in South Russia reported

to Gen. Bertholot (of the Rumanian Mission) and are in contact with *de facto* authorities to insure the existence of the Army and civil population; that the French Mission had a right to be in contact with the various nationalities without participating in the civil war; that the General Staff had a list of the members of the Mission, and that the Mission has a wireless receiving outfit. Trotsky replies, closing the propaganda bureau; directing the indiscrete young officer immediately to leave Russia; ordering the removal of the wireless outfit; directing the immediate recall to Petrograd of French officers in the Civil War region, and requesting that he be advised of all measures taken by the mission in connection with Trotsky's letter. I hear informally tonight that the Mission has replied substantially that it is acting in accordance with the instructions of its government. The French rather expect to be obliged to leave Petrograd shortly. . . .

JANUARY 6, 1918. PARAPHRASE OF MESSAGE SENT
WARCOLSTAFF WASHINGTON. NO. 248
HUNDRED SIXTY TWO 4 P.M.[105]

That Siberia is apparently inclined to Bolsheviks is reported by Lt. Col. Ruggles, who has arrived in Petrograd. Best forecast in case of break in peace negotiations, which is probable, is indefinite extension of the armistice if it suits Germany, which is also probable, and the reference of the matter to the Constituent Assembly. The prospects of the actual resumption of war might be measured as say one in four or five. Resumption of war might be advocated by the Bolsheviks in assembly.

Three or four corps of Polish troops could be organized in case of break. Dissolution of the Polish troops might be prevented by representations now to the Soviet Government.

Enemy commissioners here, negotiating armistice details, have been prohibited from communicating with civilians or prisoners of war by the Soviet Government.

Since my cablegram No. 150, Dec. 30th, 3 P.M., no change in number of enemy divisions on Black Sea–Baltic Sea front has been reported. Continued movement is reported of smaller enemy infantry units from this front together with much artillery. In a controversy between Russians and the enemy, the latter claims armistice terms are being observed. According to several reports famine exists in Austria; also that supply of wheat to Germany and Austria is apparently refused by Hungary.

General Pershing has been cabled as above.

JANUARY 6, 1917. DIARY

Ruggles says that Siberia generally appeared Bolshevik as he came through. He saw many Chinese troops at Harbin, of which they had possession and where they were maintaining good order. . . .

Kerth has not been able to get away yet for Mogilev, trains being snow-bound. He goes, with the Ambassador's approval to get into relations with Stavka and advise them as to measures that we think should be taken to anticipate a break.

Trotsky left last night for Brest. Apparently after all the peace negotiations will be renewed there tomorrow.

JANUARY 8, 1918. PARAPHRASE OF MESSAGE SENT WARCOLSTAFF WASHINGTON. NO. 252 HUNDRED SIXTY FOUR 2 P.M.[106]

Correspondence between Trotsky and the Chief of the French Military Mission has resulted in the latter promising to discontinue wireless; send one offending officer home; denying they have a bureau of information, and saying that officers in the Ukraine etc. are attached to their Mission to Rumania. French Mission may soon have to go as Trotsky expresses continued dissatisfaction.

About 1,000 representatives of local workmen's and soldiers' soviets, peasants and soldiers of the Rumanian front, including about 300 Ukrainians, compose conference at Odessa which has disavowed Shcherbachev, endorsed the Bolshevik Government, etc. Bolsheviks here claim they now have Black Sea sailors as well as soldiers of Rumanian front and Odessa Military District. . . .

JANUARY 8, 1918. DIARY

Today is without news. The Russians celebrate Christmas for several days and this is the day after their Christmas. No newspapers are published.

JANUARY 9, 1918. PARAPHRASE OF CIPHER SENT
WARCOLSTAFF WASHINGTON. NO. 255
HUNDRED SIXTY SIX 4 P.M.[107]

Reported that there is underway a separatist movement including the eight North Eastern provinces of European Russia which includes the towns of Perm, Vologda, and Archangel. (Par[tial])

That the soldiers at the front cheered Trotsky saying that war must go on rather than to permit a disgraceful peace is reported; also reported that the Ukraine has been admitted to the peace conference and that the peace conference may adjourn to Berne or elsewhere.

Judson's Opposition to U.S. Policy toward Bolshevik Russia

"Recall for Consultations"

The decision that Judson be relieved of duty as military attaché at Petrograd and be recalled to the United States was made on or about 6 December 1917 by Secretary of State Lansing, apparently in response to Judson's meeting with Trotsky. The record strongly suggests that Lansing's intense anti-Bolshevik sentiment and Judson's evasion of the single specific instruction he had received—namely, that there was to be "no official contact with the Bolshevik government"—had led Lansing and Secretary of War Baker to order Judson recalled.

The Peace of Brest-Litovsk, the feared "separate peace" that finally ended the war between the Central Powers and Bolshevik Russia, was signed on the afternoon of Sunday, 3 March 1918. Since 8 November 1917, when the Bolshevik Revolution was less than twenty-four hours old and Lenin had issued his Decree on Peace, the United States and its allies were deeply concerned by the prospect that Russia would leave the war, ending the stalemate on the western front and allowing Germany to quickly win the war. In January 1918, no observer of the long war of attrition suggested that the U.S. entry in force on the western front, with or without Russia, would bring an end to the war in ten months. Throughout the four months from the Bolshevik Revolution to Brest-Litovsk, and even up to the Armistice on 11 November 1918, Judson and his allies attempted to reverse U.S. policy toward Russia.

Judson was convinced that the war hinged on developments on the eastern front. So he recommended plan after plan for U.S. cooperation with the Soviet leadership. Each was mutually beneficial, and each was detrimental to the German war effort and to Germany's territorial aggrandizement at Russia's expense. Judson ignored questions of the Bolsheviks' legitimacy, propaganda, diplomatic impropriety, debt cancellation, and reneging on war alliance commitments. He concerned himself only with pragmatic solutions for maintaining pressure on the Germans on the eastern front.

The president's message referred to in the 10 January 1918 diary entry was the "Fourteen Points Speech," which was to figure so prominently as a statement of U.S. war aims and postwar democratic commitments. The speech addressed the general Russian situation, and the Brest-Litovsk armistice negotiations in particular, giving encouragement to the Russians in their quest for an equitable peace. This is the portion of the speech that Judson hoped would serve propaganda purposes against Germany and bolster Russia's position at the negotiating table at Brest-Litovsk. The speech and its particular application to the Russian situation at this time is the subject of chapter 12 of Kennan's *Russia Leaves the War*. The term "en clair" refers to the message's having arrived without the use of cipher or code. Since the speech was intended as an international declaration for the widest possible dissemination, it was sent in plain English and immediately translated into many foreign languages.

JANUARY 10, 1918. DIARY

France and Sweden have recognized Finland, the Bolshevik government having previously done the same. France has appointed a representative (minister?) with the Ukraine.

The President's message delivered to Congress on Jan. 8 has just been received at the Embassy En Clair, except as to one or two sections. It is a splendid document from every point of view. It points the way to peace. It breathes freeness and unselfish purpose. It will encourage the Russians and it may bring the Germans to terms.

I hear Balfour has wired en clair that England will support Russia (the Russian Government?) if peace fails.

It is reported today that there was a recent battle in the South in which 400 Cossacks were killed; that a truce followed, and that now an understanding has been arrived at between the Cossacks and the Bolsheviks.

A few days ago there arrived en clair a long cable giving the results of the Paris Conference in the way of complete arrangements for cooperation between the Allies along lines military, naval, diplomatic, financial, alimentary, etc. This cable was evidently a prelude to the peace terms of today—designed to show Germany that something has occurred to offset her Russian and Italian gains.

JANUARY 11, 1918. PARAPHRASE OF MESSAGE
SENT WARCOLSTAFF WASHINGTON. NO. 263
HUNDRED SIXTY NINE 1 P.M.[1]

Situation here at present exactly suited by the President's message of the eighth of January. Excepting the now unimportant monarchistic element, etc. the expressions of sympathy will encourage, help harmonize, and please all classes. Should remove all chance of submission to a disgraceful peace by the Russians and convince them that the Allies' aims are just and reasonable.

January 23rd. expected date of departure from Petrograd, sailing from Norway about thirty first of January. A cable, if undertaken quickly, will be in time to suspend orders relieving me from duty here if change in the situation here and increased probability of renewed fighting make advisable. This suggestion which has the Ambassador's approval I am induced to give on account of my acquaintance with the situation and the peculiar military problems that may soon arise, and the fact that I have been given a good standing with the present authorities by past circumstances which standing might be useful. I might be useful home to explain needs and situation if, on the other hand, much is to be done by the U.S. for Russia.[2]

For several days the peace negotiations have been in progress at Brest with Trotsky present. There is no prospect of agreement and according to existing rumor there will be a postponement of a month with a continued armistice because of the international peace situation.

Finland's independence has been recognized by Sweden and France as well as Russia and Germany. Apparently the Ukraine is about to be recognized by France.

The formation of a volunteer paid army has been the subject of an appeal by Krylenko.

Pershing was cabled as above.

Polish and Czech units understood to be forming in the United States and complete information is requested.

Weekly receipt of all cables should be acknowledged.

JANUARY 11, 1918. DIARY

According to the press there has been much fighting in the Ukraine in the last few days in which the Bolsheviks have gotten the worst of it. The losses around Kharkov have been especially severe.

The Alekseev movement in the Cossack Country is amazing the Cossacks. The latter are for peace and order in their own country. The Alekseev movement is monarchistic.

In Sevastopol there was recently a wholesale murder of officers, about 200 being said to have been killed, including one general, three admirals and seven fleet captains.

Odessa is said to have declared itself a free city of the Russian Confederation.

There is much talk in the press of a joint Japanese-American occupation of Siberia.

Some members of the Central Executive Committee of the Soviet, including Lenin himself are said to differ with Trotsky on his peace program. Trotsky is said to demand too much of the Germans.

The President's message of Jan. 8, received Jan. 9 and 10 here, is marvelously well adapted to the situation. It states general peace terms in simple language; expresses sympathy for and understanding of Russia; and throughout breathes a lofty spirit of justice and humanity.

The Third Soviet Conference is postponed till the 25th of January.

The Austro-German delegations here on prisoners-of-war matters [are] about to leave. Their deliberations with the Russians were not entirely harmonious. They probably accomplished something however toward the amelioration of the condition of prisoners of war.

JANUARY 12, 1918. PARAPHRASE OF MESSAGE SENT
WARCOLSTAFF WASHINGTON. NO. 265
HUNDRED SEVENTY 1 P.M.[3]

It is reported that there has been much fighting in the Ukraine during the last few days, the success of the Ukrainians being general.

It is reported that dissensions occur in the Don Country between the Kaledin and Alekseev parties. Local peace and order only are desired by the Cossacks. The national anti-Bolshevik program favored by Alekseev apparently includes restoration of monarchy in Russia.

Some probably pro-German Bolsheviks criticize Trotsky, claiming that at the peace conference he is too unyielding.

On January 25th the third conference of Workmen's Soldiers' and Peasants' deputies is now called to convene.

Without accomplishing much the large Austro-German delegations which have been here on ameliorating conditions of prisoners of war, etc., as provided in armistice protocol, are leaving Russia. There is also arriving a similar Turkish delegation.

Above message has been cabled to General Pershing.

JANUARY 12, 1918.
FROM: THE CHIEF OF THE AMERICAN MILITARY MISSION, PETROGRAD
TO: THE CHIEF OF THE FRENCH MILITARY MISSION [NIESSEL], PETROGRAD
SUBJECT: RUSSIAN OFFICERS

1. I have received your letter of December 10/23, 1917, on the subject of the service of Russian Officers in the Allied and American armies.

2. The question has been the subject of several telegrams which I have sent to my Government. As yet the latter has not expressed itself as favorable to any arrangements looking to the utilization of the services of Russian officers.

3. I have heard from press reports of the formation of training units of Poles, Czechs, etc., in the United States, but I have never been informed officially of the exact status of such units. I have also cabled to my Government the proposition to send Polish officers to America for service with the Polish units there organizing. I have had no response to this cable but shall inform you as soon as one is received. . . .

JANUARY 12, 1918. DIARY

The Soviet News published a most responsive and appreciative comment on the President's message, which appears in its issue of today in full. The Pravda, in an article by a pro-German Editor, is sarcastic and says the U.S. wishes to make peace now to curb the ambitions of Japan and England.

A report from Brest was received at Smolny saying that before the world and before Germany, Russia has accepted the affirmative side of the unfair ultimatum of Germany that the negotiations go on at Brest or not at all. This report also denies that there is a French or British lobby back of the Russians.

JANUARY 13, 1918. PARAPHRASE OF MESSAGE SENT
WARCOLSTAFF WASHINGTON. NO. 267
HUNDRED SEVENTY ONE 2 P.M.

The document from the Russian Charge at Berne, which states on reliable authority . . . that Turkey would negotiate a separate peace with
Russia on conditions that straits would be opened and autonomy granted
to Armenia, is among secret archives published here. If no general peace
is concluded soon, this may indicate the possibility of a separate peace
with Turkey.

Very satisfactory appreciation of the President's message has been
published by Soviet News, which is the official organ; it is also reported
that comment in the same vein has been made by Lenin. General effect
of the message is very favorable. Some other press reports, perhaps influenced by political or pro-German leanings, were . . . critical.

Above message has been cabled to General Pershing.

JANUARY 13, 1918. DIARY

In an apparently inspired article [in the Russian press] the British, referring to my interview with Trotsky, which seems not to have been
well thought of at home, announce that the British Ambassador had
prior knowledge of my interview and gave it his approval and consent; this in the face of the fact that I have reason to believe that our Ambassador has disputed the fact that he assented in advance to this interview.

The Russians have refused to consent to demarcation lines in the
White Sea along lines proposed by the Germans. They say war conditions there are preferable and they will so endure during the armistice.

A "socialistic" army is to be organized on a liberal pay system. There
will be no army committee.

Diamandi, the Rumanian Minister, was arrested today at 9 P.M.

The Ambassador and I were at the Ballet where we were notified. The
Ambassador wished me to proceed with him at once to Diamandi's
house, to investigate, but I persuaded him to send Stalinisky (the Embassy interpreter) instead. We went from the Embassy to the French
Ambassador's. Mr. Noulens showed us a scrap of paper with a penciled

note, unsigned, in Diamandi's hand-writing, to the effect that he had been arrested with all his legation staff and was about to be taken to [the fortress-prison of] St. Peter and Paul. . . .

. . . We hear that the Rumanians have arrested several Austrian delegates to Commissions provided for in the Armistice protocols. Just why Diamandi has been arrested we do not know, but it is probably due to the arrest of the Austrians above mentioned. Tomorrow our Ambassador, who is doyen now that Sir George Buchanan is gone, has called a meeting of all the foreign missions for 12 noon.

JANUARY 14, 1918. PARAPHRASE OF MESSAGE SENT
WARCOLSTAFF WASHINGTON NO. 271
HUNDRED SEVENTY FOUR 2 P.M.[4]

The President's message continues to receive favorable comment generally.

In the local press appears a conciliatory article, apparently inspired in the British Embassy, containing the statement that the British Ambassador knew in advance and approved of my visit on Dec. 1st to Trotsky. It is implied in the same statement that the British Ambassador who is en route to London will report to his government that circumstances must logically lead to the recognition of the Bolshevik Government such recognition depending on the progress of Russian internal affairs.

Last night the Rumanian Minister [Count Constantine Diamandi] and part of his Staff were arrested and are reported to be confined in the Fortress of Peter and Paul.[5] It is reported that terrible conditions exist on the Rumanian front, the Russians being practically surrounded by hostile elements Rumanians, Ukrainians, etc. and without food. Serious incidents occur daily as the Russians ordered to retire are necessarily living on the country. Good fruit is not, and in my opinion, cannot be borne by a policy of fostering internal strife. The Austrian delegates to a Commission provided for in the Armistice protocol, have, it is reported, been arrested by the Rumanians. All anti-Bolshevik activities, I am afraid, are regarded as highly desirable by the Allied representatives in the South, which under present circumstances does not seem true.

On January 18 will occur an uprising here against the Bolsheviks, it is persistently rumored. The basic situation as to the allied interests will not improve although minor disagreeable incidents might be reduced in number if the Bolsheviks lose out.

The allies have not gained in the recent Cabinet disturbances in the Ukraine; the pro-Austrians probably have. Those who formerly possessed the hope that anything may be expected from the Ukraine are losing it. Peace is desired by the Ukrainians, and in demanding fair terms it is probable they would be more calculating and less firm than the Bolsheviks.

The above has been cabled to General Pershing.

JANUARY 14, 1918. PARAPHRASE OF TELEGRAM SENT
WARCOLSTAFF WASHINGTON. NO. 275
HUNDRED SEVENTY SEVEN 8 P.M.[6]

This afternoon for the purpose of demanding the immediate release of the Rumanian Minister [Diamandi] all diplomatic Missions called on Lenin.[7] A reply from the Council of Commissars will be given tonight. If Minister is not released some, including French and British say will ask for passports. Lenin dwelt on the impossible condition of several hundred thousand Russian troops on the Rumanian front who without food are surrounded by hostile Rumanians and Ukrainians. He said it was better to violate a precedent by imprisoning the Rumanian minister than to declare war. These people (the Bolsheviks) despise precedent and established usages and must be accepted as they are.

I urge as a measure of extreme military importance, should the present incident not prove fatal to all relations, *that the pressure of the Allies be brought to bear on all concerned, including Rumania and the Ukraine, to adopt a modus vivendi with the Bolsheviks in order to save from starvation the Russian troops now between the Ukraine and Rumania on the one hand and the army of Austria on the other*. Rumania will be guided by the Allies and perhaps Ukraine will also. *The trouble is they have probably thought to please the Allies by anti-Bolshevik activities.*

In my opinion it is of the first military importance that my recommendations contained herein be acted on without delay; also that there be discovered some way to avoid a break in diplomatic relations because of the imprisonment incident, which might result in turning the Russians over to Germany. The Ambassador has been advised in accordance with the foregoing.

LATER. It is now reported that the Rumanian Minister will be released. There is no modification in the urgency of the adoption of the policy recommended above.

The foregoing has been cabled to General Pershing.

JANUARY 14, 1918. DIARY

No newspapers today, as it is the Russian New Year's.

The diplomatic missions, neutral as well as Allied, met at our Embassy today at noon, at the call of our Ambassador, now dean of the Corps, to discuss the arrest of the Rumanian Minister. At four, by appointment, the entire Corps visited Lenin and presented a signed protest and demand for Diamandi's release. Lenin explained the cause of the arrest—the isolation of several hundred thousand starving Russian soldiers, hemmed in between the Austrian front on the one hand and the hostile Rumanians and Ukrainians on the other, trying to get back toward some base of supplies, necessarily living on the country, and harassed by the Rumanians in a manner that would ordinarily give cause for a declaration of war. But the Bolsheviks are opposed to war; they think it more logical to arrest a diplomat who will not secure the removal of a difficulty. . . . At eleven it was unofficially announced that Diamandi and his staff had been released.

Tonight the Ambassador said he would correct a misunderstanding by cabling home that he had authorized me to visit Trotsky.

I dined at Riggs' with Gen. Barter tonight. We are in thorough agreement on all important matters of policy. . . .

JANUARY 15, 1918

HON. DAVID R. FRANCIS,
AMERICAN AMBASSADOR, PETROGRAD.

Sir:

If you will direct me to undertake it I believe I can carry out the following program.

First. Go to Trotsky and secure his assent to the terms of a military modus vivendi between the Bolshevik Government on the one hand and the Ukraine and Rumania on the other.

These terms would involve substantially the following:

(A) The cessation of hostilities, at least temporarily, between the Ukraine and the Bolsheviks; the opportunity to purchase foodstuffs in the Ukraine by the Bolshevik Government for use either at the front or elsewhere, and the furnishing of facilities for the shipment of the foodstuffs purchased;

(B) The reestablishment of peaceful relations between Rumania and the Russian troops within the boundaries of Rumania; an immediate solution of the problem of feeding the Russian troops; . . . an agreement by the Rumanians to facilitate the passage from the Ukraine to the Russian troops of the food required.

Second. Go to Kiev and secure the assent of the Ukrainians to the modus vivendi.

Third. Go to Jassy and secure the assent of the Rumanians.

At Jassy the required information would be secured from General Shcherbachev,[8] who would be an important factor in the final working out of the details as to requirements and the satisfying of them.

It would be desirable that I be appointed a commissioner to the Ukraine and to Rumania for the special purpose in view. But it would not be necessary to wait on any such appointments.

I would take with me from here Major Emery and Captain Callahan for advice on economic and business questions; a Bolshevik special commissar with the highest powers, authorized to assent in the name of the Bolshevik Government to all arrangements made; a Russian railway official of high rank and proper qualification; a Bolshevik Commissioner with powers to purchase foodstuffs; and Captain [Eugene] Prince [aide to Judson in Petrograd], Lieutenant Bukowski and as aids, interpreters and clerks.

It would be necessary to cut out red tape and to give me as free a hand as possible. Of course I would keep you constantly advised and receive frequent counsel.

The direct results of such an undertaking would be far less valuable than the indirect ones. Real services would be done Russia and the Russian people in averting civil war; in supporting the Russian front, such as it is; and in promoting the possibility of harmonious action along the Russian front if war shall be renewed.

I urge, respectfully, that I be authorized to undertake this program at once. There is no time to be lost.

Very respectfully,

JANUARY 15, 1918. DIARY

Diamandi, the Rumanian Minister was released today together with his staff. Whether the diplomats will take any further action, and what if any, is not yet determined.

Kerth and Bukowski returned from Stavka on Jan. 12 at 4 A.M. Kerth had had a rather unsatisfactory interview with Krylenko. He [Krylenko] was unwilling to discuss details under present conditions.

8,000 Red Guards are said to have left Petrograd for the North Front yesterday.

Lenin was attacked in an automobile yesterday and one of his companions was slightly wounded.

There were meetings of the peace conference at Brest on Jan. 11 and 12. At the latter meeting Trotsky explained that there was no objection to the Rada delegates taking part independently, inasmuch as the Soviet recognized the right of Ukraine to "self-definition." He said further troubles between the Soviet government and the Ukraine had no relations to this question (of independence). . . .

. . . Trouble is expected Jan. 15 to 18, due to demonstrations in favor of the Constitutional Assembly.

JANUARY 16, 1918. PARAPHRASE OF TELEGRAM SENT
WARCOLSTAFF WASHINGTON. NO. 277
HUNDRED SEVENTY EIGHT 11 A.M.[9]

. . . A 24-hour ultimatum demanding the immediate release of the imprisoned Russian soldiers, guarantees for the future, etc., on penalty of decisive military measures has been submitted by the Soviet Government to the Rumanian Government.

Believing that it could be readily accomplished, would greatly serve the Russians in putting a stop to internal war and would be essential if there is to be ahead more fighting against the Central Powers, a plan has been submitted to the Ambassador by me to arrange a modus vivendi for military purposes between the Ukraine, Rumania and the Soviet Government.

The French now have a commissioner, a military officer, independent of other missions, representing them in the Ukraine. As was proven by their past experiences, an American commissioner is also required there, if we are to have proper representation.

It does not appear probable that in the near future arrangements will be effected for general commerce or for the exchange of ordinary prisoners. It is my understanding that the provision against the removal by the enemy of troops from this front will remain in force during the extension of the armistice. The movement of troops in violation of the armistice is denied by the German; nevertheless the departure of small units is continually reported. Though not completely effective, I believe the prohibition against operative transfers of troops is effective in a large measure.

With occasional interruptions the negotiations for peace continue at Brest. The spokesman for the Russians is Trotsky, who has refused to permit work on commercial provisions so long as the main issue of the self-definition of nationalities remains unsettled. But little progress is apparently being made. . . .

JANUARY 16, 1918.

LIEUTENANT COLONEL H. E. YATES,
MILITARY ATTACHÉ, AMERICAN LEGATION,
JASSY, [RUMANIA]

My dear Yates:—

I have thoroughly appreciated your tremendously difficult position, and I would have served you if I could. Two reasons have prevented. We could not have members of this Mission in the South without producing trouble, which in certain contingencies might be little less than disastrous.[10] The French found they couldn't and yet in trying they produced friction that was very embarrassing. There has been no connection for a long time between the French and British Military Missions here and the South of Russia. Again for a long time we have felt that the Germans would not consent to a peace that the Bolsheviks would accept. The latter may start fighting again. They seem more determined than any other element, at the present time, to renew the war if unfair terms are refused. If war is renewed it seems to me some modus vivendi, for military purposes, between all the contending Russian and Rumanian elements will be essential. The President's message displays a marked sympathy with the elements who are holding out at Brest against the Central Powers. It, although by implication more than anything else, has indicated a policy to us.

We have had so few instructions from home as to policy that I have no doubt we have both been eating our hearts out to see what was happening, without knowing just what we should try to do to combat it. Nevertheless the situation has been so confused and so desperate that we should not feel vexed that no one could see how to correct it. Events have moved with glacier-like irresistibility.

I hope that you may be guided by wisdom and have some feeling of satisfaction that you are doing the best you can.

Andrews is taking this.[11]

Yours very sincerely,

JANUARY 16, 1918. DIARY

The Pravda publishes an item that, by telephone, from an authentic source, just before the Commissars acted upon the demand of the foreign missions that Diamandi be released, there was received an assurance from the American Ambassador that, on Diamandi's release, he would go to Diamandi and demand a settlement of the difficulties in Rumania against which the arrest of Diamandi might be regarded as a protest. This was the main subject of discussion at a meeting of the Missions today. Diamandi said he'd go back to St. Peter and St. Paul unless our Ambassador denied the story. Then Francis said he would deny it in a letter to Diamandi which the latter could publish. . . .

. . . I am afraid the Ambassador has taken no action in the matter I have suggested to him of getting the Bolsheviks and Rumanians to compromise their difficulties. But the necessity of such action appeals to him.

Neither has the Ambassador yet sent a cable, as he promised me Monday night he would do, explaining that I had his authority to interview Trotsky. Sisson overheard him make the promise. This is "Water over the mill" but I wish the facts kept straight. Fortunately the Ambassador told Robins some weeks after the interview that it was had with his authority, and Sisson wired home long since that he "had secured from the Ambassador a wavering consent" to my interview.

It has been brought to the Ambassador from several sources that "the Bolsheviks are about to arrest the American representatives here." This seems absurd and is doubtless the work of those who would estrange still further the Allies and the Bolsheviks.

JANUARY 17, 1918. PARAPHRASE OF TELEGRAM SENT
WARCOLSTAFF WASHINGTON. NO. 277-181- 7 P.M.[12]

Ambassador says may desire me to stay Petrograd beyond January 23d depending on immediate developments. Have advised him he should cable if he proposes to detain me.

Central executive committee of Soviet on proposal of council of commissars has announced basic program for Constituent Assembly to be read at opening of latter and proposed to be adopted by assembly. This provides: the Russian republic of Soviets shall be a free union of free nations; principal aim, abolishment private ownership land; steps toward transfer to state of factories, railroads, et cetera, transfer of banks to state to prevent oppression by capital; democratic peace on Bolshevik terms; arming of laboring masses, with disarmament of wealthy classes; independence of Finland; cancellation of loans made by former government; governmental authority remain in present and succeeding Soviet governments; limitation of functions of Assembly to the arrangement of basic foundation and beginning Soviet republic, leaving (?) final decision and details to conference workmen and peasants. . . .

Disturbances in Petrograd expected tomorrow. Change in Ukrainian secretariat at Kiev giving majority social-revolutionists and left social-revolutionists. Rival Ukrainian Rada and secretariat at Kharkov mostly Bolsheviks.

Each Ukrainian government demands representation at Brest. Enemy and Russians disagree as to which to receive. . . .

JANUARY 17, 1918. DIARY

It is said that Smolny has issued orders for the arrest of the King of Rumania.

The Council of People's Commissars has proposed and the Central Executive Committee of the Soviet has ordained a program for the Constituent Assembly. . . . Briefly it provides for the following: a recognition of the Soviet as the supreme power, its own function having to do with basic principles only, subject apparently to ratification by the Soviet, although this is not clear; abolition of private ownership of land; transfer to state of banks, factories, mines, railways, etc; repudiation of foreign loans; requirement of universal labor; arming of laboring masses; a democratic peace.

I saw Diamandi today and asked him to convey to the queen my thanks for her picture. He had the Ambassador's letter alluded to in yesterday's diary.

I entertained officially, the heads of the Military Missions today, including Poole and Lavergne.

Andrews left yesterday for Rumania. I gave him a letter and memorandum for Yates.

JANUARY 18, 1918. PARAPHRASE OF MESSAGE SENT WARCOLSTAFF WASHINGTON. NO. 283 HUNDRED EIGHTY TWO 2 P.M.[13]

Precedents are despised by the Bolsheviks. They tried arresting the Rumanian Minister here rather than make war on the Rumanian people, and they are now reported to have ordered the arrest of the King of Rumania.

It is said by excellent non-Bolshevik authority (Verkhovsky) that the Bolsheviks are gaining in the Ukraine by occupation and propaganda. The Bolsheviks now have Kiev practically surrounded on a large circle including Kharkov, Ekaterinoslav, Zhmerinka, Bakhmatch and the railway junction 120 miles Northwest of Kiev. The Commissar Donetz coal basin is apparently held by them. About 6 divisions of Ukrainian troops have been organized like Bolshevik troops, without real officers. In Ukraine both important elements are radically socialistic: both favor Bolshevik peace and land programs: their principal difference is the extent of independence.

It is said by the same informant that the Cossacks have been impregnated with peace ideas. Alekseev's twelve officer regiments, which are pro-monarch, compose the principal fighting force in the Don country: a third regiment is forming, two regiments having already been formed.

Same informant says that the Bolsheviks will last for . . . many months and will yield only to economic pressure: also that any Allied movement against Siberia would encounter practically unanimous opposition.

As the Bolsheviks took great precautions, the disturbances which were expected today during the parade for the Constituent Assembly proved of a minor character.[14]

JANUARY 18, 1918. DIARY

This day was set for the opening of the Constituent Assembly. A demonstration was planned in honor of the occasion. The Bolsheviks anticipating an attempt at their own overturning, took great precautions, ordering all soldiers and workmen to stay in doors, etc., and stationing Red Guards and sailors in numbers of pickets about the city. A number of streets were barricaded. I walked out this morning with Ruggles and Prince but at the corner of Fourstadtskaya and Litanie was a picket firing down the Litanie and we turned back. There was much firing throughout the day in the street next south of us. My coachman did not show up and I was unable to keep an appointment with Poole. Obviously the shooting was to reduce the size of the hostile demonstration. As it was, the whole affair but revealed the strength of the Bolsheviks. They will certainly stay in for several or many months and until economic pressure, if it shall occur, drives their adherents to other allegiances.

Had a long talk with Gen. V. [Verkhovsky] today. He gave me the following information: the President's message was fine but too late by several months; any attempts against Siberia by Japs or others would find the population united against them; both parties in Ukraine are radically socialistic with programs not far apart except that the Kiev party is somewhat allied to the pro-Austrian element; the Bolsheviks surround Kiev. . . . The Ukrainians gave six divisions organized on Bolshevik principles; they have the same peace and land programs as the Bolsheviks, and they will not fight except Bolsheviks; the Cossacks are impregnated with Bolshevik peace doctrines and will only fight if at all to repel invasion; the officers' regiments of Alekseev are the only fighting force (2 regiments, 3rd organizing, pro-monarchy).

Trotsky has objected to the Ukrainian delegation at Brest and to their secret conference. the Central Powers have submitted arguments as to the correctness of their contention that Lithuanian, Courland, etc. have already expressed preferences and are in effect independent nations. In support of the contention they quote a decision of our Supreme Court (1808) holding the U.S.A. has been an independent nation since the Declaration of Independence.

JANUARY 19, 1918. PARAPHRASE OF MESSAGE SENT
WARCOLSTAFF WASHINGTON. NO. 286
HUNDRED EIGHTY THREE 2 P.M.[15]

Yesterday occurred the meeting of the Constituent Assembly, about 400 members being present. Chernov was elected temporary president by a vote of 244 Social Revolutionists to 153 Bolsheviks. As referred to in my No. 181, Jan. 1[7]th 7 P.M., program prepared by Soviet was read at the opening by a Soviet official and was subsequently rejected by a party vote. The Bolsheviks withdrew.

In the Assembly Chamber were present armed sailors and Red Guards; on the platform were the People's Commissars. In speeches by Social Revolutionists the Bolsheviks were reproached for keeping so many soldiers at the front; also the assertion was made that the program of the Social Revolutionists would lead to a speedier peace.

That Social Revolutionists will conduct sessions without a quorum until the third Soviet meets next week, when the Assembly may be dissolved, seems the best forecast.

About 12 were killed by Bolshevik pickets during the parades celebrating the opening of the Constituent Assembly. The parades were naturally of small proportions. Any plans to oppose force to Bolsheviks were abandoned. In the Neva were several Bolshevik cruisers, etc. No sufficient force appears to threaten the Bolshevik ascendancy in the near future, although several regiments are reported Anti-Bolshevik.

Russian anarchists and internationalists returning from Switzerland via Germany say the Germans are war-weary but military and civil discipline unaffected by the Russian revolution; also that living conditions in Germany are better than in Switzerland.

JANUARY 19, 1917. DIARY

The Constituent Assembly met yesterday at the Tauride Palace. . . . The Bolshevik program (see diary of Jan. 17) had been read at the opening of the meeting and after the election of Chernov it was taken up for consideration. Tseretelli spoke against it, urging the union of all the democratic elements. . . .

. . . The Japanese Embassy has denied the landing of troops at Vladivostok, and has replied to a demand by Trotsky that there be an explanation of the presence there of Japanese war ships by stating that it was an ordinary occurrence, without special significance, and that Japan had no idea of interfering in the internal affairs of Russia. Trotsky has made a similar demand upon England.

The Anarchists, in their special organ, make further threats against our Ambassador, in connection with their demands for the release of Berkman, Goldman, etc.[16]

Today at 1:30 P.M. the Central Executive Committee by decree dissolved the Constituent Assembly. The latter had previously published its program, which embraced an immediate general peace provision.

JANUARY 20, 1918. PARAPHRASE OF MESSAGE SENT
WARCOLSTAFF WASHINGTON. NO. 288
HUNDRED EIGHTY FOUR 3 P.M.[17]

Yesterday the Central Committee of the Soviet dissolved the Constituent Assembly. Immediate general peace was included in the announced program of the Social Revolutionists in the Assembly.

In reply to an urgent query by Trotsky, the Japanese Ambassador says that Japan has no intention to interfere in the internal affairs of Russia; also that the presence of Japanese cruisers at Vladivostok has no special significance.

It is now estimated that the enemy divisions on the Baltic-Sea–Black Sea front are as follows: cavalry 25 to 22; infantry 104 1/2 to 94. The continuance of the weakening of enemy forces by small units is reported.

According to an item of information reported by the Russian Intelligence Service quote Plan of German General Staff to transport to the west front, decided on Dec. 13th: Transportation, first, of a quantity of troops not yet decided upon, the drafts to be by battalions and companies, the reserves left on the Russian front to be held in the large towns of Vilna, Warsaw, Grodno, etc; Second, Field artillery, especially heavy artillery; Third, all munitions and all aero units. Shock formations to be transported to the French front; gas attacks to be made on a large scale (quote ends).[18]

General Pershing cabled as above.

JANUARY 20, 1918. DIARY

[F. F.] Kokoshkin and [A. I.] Shingarev, Kadet Ministers of the first Kerensky cabinet, who had recently been transferred to the Marinsky hospital from St. Peter and St. Paul, were killed last night by sailors. Chernov and Tseretelli are in hiding. . . .

JANUARY 21, 1918. PARAPHRASE OF MESSAGE SENT
WARCOLSTAFF WASHINGTON. NO. 291
HUNDRED EIGHTY FIVE 11 O'CLOCK THE MORNING.

Have received no answer to or acknowledgment of Nos. 135 Dec. 15th 4 P.M., 146 Dec. 25th 5 P.M., and 161 Jan. 5th 1 P.M.[19] The commercial organization has been perfected under control of the Committee consisting of the heads of the British, French and American Military Missions, and the British and French Governments have granted funds for this purpose. Actual purchases can begin at any time, but on the extent of American cooperation largely depends the action of our Allies. Can I have definite information promptly that funds will be provided or else instructions to state to the Allied Missions that we withdraw from the organization and that we are unable to cooperate? It is very embarrassing to block their activities further by the lack of definite instructions.

I should be promptly informed as to commodities available here which are especially needed at home if credit is granted and cooperation is authorized. Glycerine, sugar-beet seed, manganese, and hides are among goods on which immediate action is suggested by Allies. If they can be shipped, are any of these wanted in the United States?

For exchange purposes, will the Government of the United States allow the export of such goods as shoes, cheap cottons, and canton flannels?

JANUARY 21, 1918. PARAPHRASE OF MESSAGE SENT
WARCOLSTAFF WASHINGTON. NO. 292 4 P.M.[20]

Two members of the first Kerensky Ministry, Kokoshkin and Shingarev, have been assassinated.

It is reported that peace negotiations have been suspended for 10 days.

It is also reported that the Bolsheviks are gaining rapidly in Ukraine; and that the Kiev Rada has requested Austrian assistance against them.

[Handwritten diary on separate sheets]

January 22, 1918
My last day at Petrograd. Lunched with Barter; Dinner at Niessel's with all chiefs of Missions. (Sunday Night the Ambassador gave me as guest of honor a farewell party. Supper cards and dancing.)

At 3 P.M. meeting of Military Missions, called by Niessel, to send an irritating note to Bolsheviks (through Chief of Staff) subject: removal of enemy Missions from this front. I objected to offensive tone—held out to end (3 hours) and secured a polite letter sending information and making a query. Ambassador had previously agreed that some such letter should be sent—

We heard today that Germans still demand annexations from the Russians. There is a 10 day halt in the negotiations and it is reported that Trotsky will not return to Brest but will put matter before Soviet (3d—new [the third Soviet], meets on 25th [January]) advocating no peace. Belgian minister thinks we should now make promise to support to influence Soviet.

JANUARY 23, 1917 WARCOLSTAFF, 296 188.[21] LEFT THIS MORNING 7:40 FOR STOCKHOLM. . . .

[Handwritten diary on separate sheets]

January 24. Arrived Torneo 5:30 P.M. Bolsheviks still running passport control but Finns talk of taking over in 1 week. 8:30 started across Torneo in sledges—2 stages 1 to customs 1 to station. Left Haparanda at about 10 P.M.

January 25. En route to Stockholm. Suggestion for cable to sum up Russian situation. Bolshevik government will probably endure several months, perhaps 6, and until economic conditions become such as to drive away adherents—In the meantime there will probably be a disintegration of the recuperation power of the country, through the weakening of the landed, industrial and manufacturing commercial classes due to the socialistic regime. (Today there are no returns on investment except in small mercantile enterprises which uncertain though sometimes large profits.)

JANUARY 27, 1918. FROM STOCKHOLM TO W[AR] C[OLLEGE] STAFF,

On leaving Russia it seems a duty to attempt to forecast the future based on most careful consideration of tendencies and conditions.

The government of the Bolsheviks will last several, probably six, months until the collapse of transportation and the country's economic life. We may lose many chances to serve our own interests and thwart the enemy and our representatives may soon have to quit Russia unless we have friendly intercourse with the Bolsheviks, not involving recognition. As their leaders will not compromise, the Bolsheviks are the only Russian element likely to be at all hostile to the Central Powers. There are very many Russians who would welcome Germans to end socialistic regime and to preserve private interests. The recuperative power of Russia through possible efforts of well-to-do educated classes experienced in affairs is departing due to the drastic nature of the socialistic regime. These classes are on the verge of enduring great distress and becoming submerged. Local reigns of terror, especially in Petrograd, are likely to accompany the breakup of the Bolsheviks.

An increased disintegration may be expected, smaller local communities, often mutually hostile, forming for local protection, following the above. Many elements will actively seek German and Austrian assistance.

It is probable there will be a great shock to civilization in Russia and the accompanying incidents may be of catastrophic nature.

Russia's restoration will be an enormous world problem but till the Bolsheviks have run their course it cannot be fully entered upon. To pursue opportunist policy, doing everything to show friendliness and sympathy for all Russian elements is the most important thing now, in order to lay foundations for future helpfulness and not let the Russians feel they must turn to Germany for assistance.

After reference of the peace question by Trotsky to the Soviet, if military operations should be renewed they will be on small scale and in the nature of a forlorn hope, but as holding of enemy troops on the east front will be worth more than cost, they should be assisted.

[Handwritten diary on separate sheets]

January 29. Left Stockholm evening of January 27 arrived here (Christiania [Oslo]) 11:30 A.M. January 28. Hotel Victoria—Found Bergensfjord would sail from here on February 7. This seems quickest way to reach U.S. and at the same time keeps me in touch here longer if Ambassador does what he said he might do; i.e. have me intercepted from Washington and ordered back to Petrograd in certain contingency. . . .

February 7. Left Christiania by Bergensfjord for New York through fjords hugged coast till 5 P.M. on 8th then made course north of Orkneys.
February 12. News by wireless that Russians have refused to sign peace treaty but declared peace exists on all fronts and army ordered demobilized. Is this true? Couldn't we have prevented it?
February 17. Off Long Island—due in New York tomorrow morning. Our propaganda in Russia is rotten. [H]ide the patronizing film about Uncle Sam patronizing Ivan, which our YMCA workers say disgusts and the real Ivan, who is not so unsophisticated as people think—We need real radicals in Russia for propaganda work with the Bolsheviks against our enemy—along lines where the said radicals' honest purposes would run parallel to the purposes of our government. . . .

Example of German propaganda. Boldly drawn cartoon in colors representing John Bull lashing Ivan into the gates of war where the gate of peace stands open (both gates appropriately illustrated), Uncle Sam pats John Bull on back and says, "Go to it John, you will save our men on the western front."
February 18.—landed—till 2 or 3 in process . . .

Germans and Austrians trying now to hold us quiet while they despoil Russia—Greatest chance they have ever had to become a supernation, we must act quickly.

Austro-German [?] talk quiet on western front etc. is camouflage behind which Central Powers are making one of the greatest conquests of history. Either we must get busy with an eastern front or make peace at expense of Russia and let Germany be a supernation.
February 20. Arrived Washington and reported Warcolstaff.

JANUARY 30, 1918. PARAPHRASE CIPHER TELEGRAM
TO DEPARTMENT OF STATE. 6 P.M. SECSTATE
WASHINGTON. NO. 497.[22]

The following message is transmitted on behalf of General Judson and is intended for the War College:
"In case the American Military Mission is obliged to leave Russia, it is suggested that Martin and Bukovski be assigned to Copenhagen, Denmark, Kliefoth to Stockholm, Sweden and Stine and Ruggles to Christiania, Norway. It would be desirable to keep Major Totten at Christiania until their arrival if they come soon. The War College could use Prince

very advantageously, as he is a good compiler of information and knows, besides the English language, French, Russian and German.

"If a general peace is being delayed by Germany, the aspect of the situation from the point of view afforded in Scandinavia and Russia indicates both the possibility and the military urgency of attempting, by a separate peace with the Allies, to detach from Germany the Allies of the latter power namely, Bulgaria, the Ottoman Empire and Austria-Hungary. The best way to approach these powers might be through military agents, perhaps by way of Russia, with the probability that such agents might be assisted by the Bolsheviki. These military agents might subsequently be disavowed, should this become advisable later. Were this done quickly, it might be possible to save Rumania from the apparently inevitable fate that would otherwise befall her of being forced to conclude a separate peace. The success of the plan referred to would have the effect of isolating and defeating Germany and at the same time bring about contact with Russia along the Black Sea front, thus avoiding the Germanization of Russia.

"I plan to leave on the 7th of February by the s/s Bergensfjord which sails for the United States."

Schmedeman

FEBRUARY 26, 1918.
MEMORANDUM. TO: ACTING CHIEF OF STAFF.
SUBJECT: ACTION IN RUSSIA. URGENT.[23]

The wreck that has occurred of Russian military, political and economic functions appears to be so complete and so disheartening that the Allies seem to have abandoned themselves to expressions of resentment against Russia and to complete despair as to what may happen on the eastern front.

This seems to me to be very unfortunate and very dangerous. It is as though, after a severe defeat in battle, no effort were made to check the panic, rally the retreating forces and occupy a new line.

There is still an enormous margin in the Russian situation. For example, let us contemplate the worst, and then the best sequence of future events, viewed from our own standpoint, which it would be within the bounds of reason to anticipate.

The worst might involve the following: the speedy formation of independent (?) states, very friendly to the Central Powers, in the Ukraine, Poland, Rumania, Lithuania, the Baltic Provinces, Finland, and possibly, in the Don Cossack region. . . . ; to the eastward of these regions the complete absence of opposition to the Central Powers. . . . ; a great readiness throughout Russia to furnish all kinds of supplies (food, fodder ((forage)), copper, manganese, guns, munitions, etc.); the release for active service of some 1,600,000 war prisoners held by the Russians; the retention by Germany of many former Russian war prisoners as laborers on a wage basis, and the employment of many additional Russians in the same manner; the addition to the fighting strength of the Central Powers of great numbers of . . . volunteers from the newly created and friendly "buffer states"; at home, among the Central Powers, a feeling of exultation at enormous successes achieved; a growth in strength of the morale of the people, of the imperialistic instinct, and of the dominance of the military parties.

On the other hand, the best possible sequence of future events, from our standpoint, might be somewhat as follows: the military occupation by the Central Powers of the Russian territory lying along their borders, in the face of the continued hostility of a large part of the population, i.e., that part which is now radically socialistic or Bolshevik; a hostile Russia to the east of the occupied territory; continued resistance, if not of an orthodox military character . . . ; no trade with Russia east of the occupied region; no systematic release of prisoners; compulsion placed upon the Central Powers to maintain large numbers of troops along the eastern border of the occupied territory . . . ; relative weakness of Germany upon the western front, due to the retention of troops in Russia. . . .

Instead of laying down our cards and "cussing" Russia, it seems to me we should consider quickly and deeply whether there are not some things we can do which will make the worst that can happen less probable and the best more so.

A very careful but frank attitude of sympathy and friendliness to Russia and all anti-German Russians must accompany the inspiration of such hopes, and such sympathy and friendliness must not be withheld from any element, even because it is Bolshevik and thus to many Americans anathema.

From those withdrawing before the German advance, and from those joining from Siberia and from southwest Russia, could be found the manpower for a great organized resistance along a line far more disadvantageously located, for the Central Powers, than was the line of 1917.

It would not be long under such conditions before some government stronger and better than the Bolshevik could establish itself, which would doubtless give us great satisfaction. Even a temporary military dictator would be acceptable.

To have a reasonable chance of success we should of course be sure in advance of a friendly reception. A week ago this might have been brought about by unofficial negotiations with the Bolsheviks. A week hence possibly some other element or elements must be looked to for an invitation. Besides administering the railways and paying and supplying troops, we would have to send over some American troops to show our good faith. . . . The number of such troops should be at least 50,000. The knowledge that we were going to act as proposed would cause resistance to the enemy to form long before our assistance could become effective.

As to the lessening of our efforts upon the western front, the following observations are in order: 50,000 men placed upon the western front simply neutralize, it is fair to say, 50,000 enemy troops, while 50,000 men placed somewhere west of the Urals, inducing the active pressure of say 1,000,000 other men, might neutralize more than 1,000,000 enemy troops.

The plan suggested would restore to Russia, perhaps, her historical role of conquering by the circumstance of her magnificent distances. The Kaiser might be overcome by the same weapon that destroyed the power of Napoleon and of Charles the Twelfth.[24] There can be little doubt that the adoption of no other plan of action or of inaction would be so unwelcome to the Germans.

I suggest the immediate issuance of a statement such as the following:

"If to the renewed attack of the imperialistic German Government upon free Russia it shall be determined by Russia to continue armed opposition, even if the final lines of resistance shall be far in the interior of Great Russia, and even if thus heroic sacrifices shall be demanded of the Russian people in the cause of liberty, the United States of America assures Russia that it will spare no effort in any direction to support her and to help defend her liberty. In this proffering assistance the United States makes no condition other than that of cooperation and seeks no end other than the satisfaction that follows its own efforts to promote international justice and to defend freedom."

On account of the immediate importance of the Russian situation, I hasten to submit this preliminary recommendation dealing with general policy.

MARCH 4, 1918. MEMORANDUM.
TO: ACTING CHIEF OF STAFF.
SUBJECT: ACTION IN RUSSIA. URGENT.

On February 26, 1918, I submitted to the Acting Chief of Staff a memorandum on the subject "Action in Russia, Urgent." This memorandum was subsequently returned to me with notation by the Secretary of War that "The Secretary of State has charge of this." In the meantime the Secretary of State had requested from me a copy of the memorandum, which was furnished him on the morning of March 1.

The present memorandum is supplementary to that of February 26, 1918, and it is suggested that the original or a copy be immediately furnished the State Department.

Having been in Petrograd until January 23, 1918, and having kept in close touch there with recent Russian opinions of all shades, I feel that I am quite sure of my facts in stating that the effect of Japanese intervention in Siberia would be as follows:

(1) The creation of a feeling almost universal in Russia, that the former allies of Russia, in rage at her defection, have adopted a policy of revenge and have decided upon punitive measures.

(2) Complete despair in Russia as it becomes evident that she lies prostrate between two military autocracies, each apparently free to work its will upon her. The democratic element will believe that similar elements among the former allies of Russia have rejected her through fear and displeasure at the forms adopted and the action taken by the Russian democracy or by the radicals who have been most recently in power. The moderate and the conservative elements will feel that Russia is completely isolated and that no action on their part can restore her to respectability among her former allies.

(3) Thinking that they have no other choice but between two imperialistic powers, each bent upon despoiling them, but feeling that the Germans have already done their worst, Russia will choose the white rather than the yellow peril. The Russian people as a whole will feel that no path lies open to them but to cultivate friendly relations with a power ready, by reason of its own needs, to appreciate such relations. Certainly if Japan intervenes on a large scale and if she intervenes alone, European Russia will fall into the lap of Germany. No number of enemy troops will be detained in Russia. The "buffer" states now in

process of creation will be thoroughly pro-German. The remainder of European Russia will probably soon accept the control of a military dictator friendly to Germany and bent upon the restoration of monarchy. Russia will go to work raising food; mining coal, copper, platinum, iron and manganese ores, and manufacturing munitions, all for Germany. Many will seek service in the German Army.

Russia is the greatest reservoir in the world of supplies and man-power not today serving the interest of ourselves or our enemies. Nothing is more certain than that Japanese intervention in Siberia will place that reservoir at the disposal of Germany, and the Russians would not be merely passive in the matter, but would lend aid to Germany to almost the maximum of their ability.

Japan would find no friendly element in Siberia, welcoming her as a deliverer. We might hear of some individual Cossack commander with little if any following who would welcome the approach of the Japanese to relieve him of some present embarrassment, but this is unlikely and unimportant outside of press reports.[25] The Siberians would destroy the railways to the greatest extent practicable before the Japanese advance and would make common cause with their fellow Russians west of the Urals. The Japanese would probably not get west of Lake Baikal. They would never get in touch with German or Austrian fighting men. They would never disturb German plans. In producing a pro-German feeling in European Russia they would in fact serve Germany's interests to the utmost. All that Germany needs can be secured, not only west of Lake Baikal but west even of the whole of Siberia.

In this connection, I would again recall certain revelations in the secret documents recently published by the Bolsheviks:

(1) The secret treaty between Japan and the old Russia Government evidently hostile to the United States.

(2) The apprehension in Japan that differences may arise between Japan and the United States over interpretations that may be placed upon the terms of the recent United States-Japanese Entente.

(3) Indications that Japan is of the opinion that, with Russia out of the war, the outcome of the war may be entirely altered.

Japan does not go to war for reasons of sentiment. Her occupation of Siberia east of Lake Baikal would place that lake and the northerly projection of the Gobi desert between her and any military power to the westward, affording her a strong frontier for possessions in Manchuria, the Amur valley and the Ussuri region, the latter of enormous value by reason of its mineral resources.

Under all of the circumstances it seems worthy of consideration whether the proposed large-scale intervention by Japan in Siberia is dictated by a desire to serve any purpose of the Allies as a whole, or merely the purposes of Japan her-

self. And it is even to be considered whether the fact that such intervention would in a large degree serve the interest of Germany is not at this time present in the minds of Japan.

If Japan, having war ships present at Vladivostock, undertakes merely the custody of the freight (nearly 700,000 tons) lying on and about the wharves at that place, if necessary landing marines as a part of this operation, it might possibly be made evident to the Russian people that Japan has no large and hostile ends in view.

If Japan does attempt to occupy large portions of Siberia, it is possible but not certain that participation in the movement by the United States would palliate the offense in the minds of the Russian people. If there were a joint occupation, the share and purposes of the United States should be emphasized as much as possible.

Intervention on a relatively small scale by the United States alone would do most to excite resistance to Germany on the part of the Russians themselves, and, after all, unless the Russians do themselves resist there can be no real obstacle to Germany in all of European Russia.

Even American intervention, as proposed, should not be undertaken unless and until it is made evident that it is acceptable generally to the Russian people.

Any allied forces operating west of Vladivostock must seem to be deliverers and not conquerors.

I submit this memorandum with a deep sense of the vast and immediate importance of the subject and of my duty, by reason of my recent presence in Russia, to make report upon it.

I enclose a memorandum by Lt. Col. Sherman Miles, General Staff, who recently served in Russia as Military Attaché, upon the subject of the proposed Japanese intervention I believe that his conclusions are thoroughly sound. . . .

MARCH 8, 1918.
MEMORANDUM. FOR ACTING CHIEF OF STAFF.
SUBJECT: ACTION IN RUSSIA

Our ambassador, according to press reports, has just issued a statement at Vologda, promising if war shall continue to urge his government to extend all possible assistance. This statement could be backed up from Washington now to the greatest advantage.

An invasion of Siberia by Japan would seem a hostile act to practically every Russian and would in effect throw European Russia into the arms of Germany. . . . And yet I would not send a man to Russia or spend a dollar there

unless, acting as acknowledged friends and deliverers, not seeming to impose
our will upon the Russian people or any element of them, we shall see a reason-
able chance . . . to array in opposition to the Germans a force of Russians say
twenty times as numerous as the forces we may send to cooperate with them.

I suggest that a military mission be sent to Russia, via Siberia, at once,
with ample funds and personnel and with broad discretionary powers, to assist
in stirring up and organizing opposition to German activities. The personnel I
had with me in Petrograd would form a nucleus for such a mission and by
reason of my personal acquaintance with the situation and with many of the
Russian leaders I think it would be in the public interest if I were assigned to
the mission. In 1904–5 during the Russo-Japanese War I lived for about a year
upon the Trans-Siberian or its far eastern extension, and for the past nine
months I have been in Western Russia, nearly all of that time as Chief of the
American Military Mission.

MARCH 14, 1918. MEMORANDUM.
TO: ACTING CHIEF OF STAFF.
SUBJECT: INSTRUCTIONS ETC. TO MILITARY ATTACHÉS ET AL.

From July 9, 1917 to January 23, 1918, by virtue of an order signed by
the Chief of Staff and approved by the Secretary of War, I acted as Military Attaché at Petrograd. . . .

Under these circumstances I of course had occasion to send very
many cables, containing information, requests for information, recommendations and advice.

During this period it may be noted that the French and British Military Missions were able to count upon replies to their important cables
within a few days time.

To practically none of my communications did I ever receive response, nor were any instructions sent for my general guidance. The
only significant actions taken [were] instructions through the Embassy,
in December 1917, that neither I nor Kerth were to have direct intercourse with the Bolshevik authorities, the latter being in fact at the time
in complete control of the Russian Army and the military destinies of
our great Ally.[26]

[The following is an abridgement of Judson's forty-eight page final re-
port on Russia, excluding technical and repetitious sections.[27] It is Jud-
son's most comprehensive report on Russia, the World War, the Provi-

sional Government, Bolshevik power, and U.S. and Allied relations with both regimes. It expresses his dismay at receiving no responses to his hundreds of reports and recommendations, usually not even an acknowledgment of their receipt. Finally, Judson provides seven pages of "quotations" that he considered the most important excerpts from the extensive body of his reports, recommendations, and predictions. This latter body of evidence is submitted to the Acting Chief of Staff of the U.S. Army, not only to justify his past work as Military Attaché and Chief of the American Military Mission, but to support his case (made in the memoranda of 26 February and 8 March), that he be sent back to Russia to head a mission that would support anti-German forces in Siberia.]

MARCH 16, 1918. MEMORANDUM.
TO: CHIEF OF INTELLIGENCE SECTION, GENERAL STAFF.
SUBJECT: RUSSIAN SITUATION[28]

On May 15, 1917, I left Washington for Russia as Military Attaché to the Root Mission and remained on that Duty in Russia until July 9, 1917, when I was relieved by General Scott, Chief of Staff, then in Petrograd as a member of the Root Mission, and assigned to duty as Chief of the American Military Mission to Russia and Military Attaché to the American Embassy at Petrograd. The order signed by General Scott in this connection was confirmed by cable by the Secretary of War.

Having been relieved from duty as Military Attaché in Petrograd by cable from the Adjutant General dated December 29, 1917, I left Petrograd on January 23rd, returned to the United States via Norway and reported to Chief of Staff on February 20, 1918.

An account of events in Russia following the revolution which overturned the Government of the Czar, and an interpretation of such events, are necessary accompaniments of any effort to describe present conditions in Russia and to attempt forecast of the future. Such an account is, from an Allied standpoint, a painful one from start to finish; and if it is critical of the Russian policies and activities in Russia of ourselves and our Allies, such criticism is necessary for historical accuracy and to facilitate an understanding of present and future conditions.

In the first place it is necessary to describe certain circumstances connected with the revolution of March, 1917, which were not at all well understood at the time . . . nor for some time thereafter.

Generally speaking, two elements were at work to bring that revolution about, which may for convenience be termed respectively the left and the right of the opposition to the autocratic government. The left represented of course the radical elements, many of whose adherents later became well-known as Bolsheviks. The right centered about the Kadet, Octobrist and conservative socialist leaders of the Duma, including Rodzianko,[29] Guchkov and Miliukov. Of course a more complete analysis would include a center, having as leaders Kerensky, Tseretelli??, Tereschenko and others, but in the interest of a ready comprehension of the revolution itself the simpler division is preferable.

The left embraced the less intelligent elements and had great strength among the peasants, soldiers and sailors. Toward the creation of this left there had been directed much German propaganda.

The left stood upon the platform of an immediate peace, distribution of the land among the peasants and the control of industry by the workmen.

The right wished for a continuance of the old social and economic regime but under a liberal government of democratic tendencies. . . . The right had for the most part no strongly held views upon the continuance of the war, but seemed quite willing to go on with it as a matter of course. It recognized the obligations of Russia's treaties and attributed to the moral and physical support of the Allies a very great importance, perhaps an undue importance so far as concerned its own political security in Russia.

The rapid growth of the left is better appreciated by the right than by any other Russian element outside of the left itself, and was not at all appreciated by Russia's allies.

The left was not well organized. It was bound together by a community of ideas. The right was very well organized indeed but its program was not very popular among the masses of the people and its adherents were not numerous although it embraced most elements which we in America are accustomed to think of as politically efficient.

It was evidence furnished for the most part by the activities of the left which indicated that the regime of the czar was without the support of the Russian people. The right alone was prepared to take advantage of the situation and organize a government. The interests of the right and of the left ran parallel to a very slight extent. But the left, in its impotence permitted the right to take the lead.

It is but fair to say that before the storm broke the right had not . . . created organization and developed a program. In this sense the revolution was premature, but Russia through its ignorant myriads was moving with the irresistibility of an avalanche and the right accepted its responsibilities when they were placed upon it.

When the revolution occurred we had little conception in America of the influences that had brought it about. Some important persons thought that the more honest and conscientious Russians, who of course were assumed to be democrats like ourselves, had seized the power not only to be rid of monarchical institutions but also to stop the machinations of those who were plotting for a peace: On the contrary, the most active cause of the revolution, guarding it from suppression by the army, was the very desire for peace, especially widespread among the soldiers and peasants. The Russian peasants are not a warlike people, as I had occasion to remark in my report on the Manchurian War. They prefer peace to war, and their longings for peace had been fostered not only by the hardships and terrors of modern war but also by long-continued absence from their villages and by assiduous socialistic and German propaganda.

It is a peculiarity of the Russian peasant that his patriotism is more of the village than of the nation, and it is characteristic of all Russians to attach more importance to Russian internal affairs than to the relations of Russia to other nations. For example, during the Manchurian War I heard many Russian officers say they hoped their own side would lose. They were afraid a victorious Russia would be a reactionary Russia, which would neither demand nor receive a constitution and a Duma.

If it had been realized that Russia intensely desired peace and if the nature of the Russian people had been better understood, the Allies would early have stated their peace aims in such fair, simple and concrete terms as to convince the Russians that they were not being asked to fight to gratify the imperialistic instincts of any of their Allies, nor yet to crush the German people, but that the world could have peace as soon as Germany was willing to be fair and just. Under such conditions the Russians would probably have fought on.

On August 7, 1917, I embodied the following in a cable to the War College: "At least an even chance that Russia will go out of war within few months. Our larger war plans should be made accordingly. . . ."[30]

Nevertheless some representatives of the Allies in Petrograd persisted in reporting from March to December, 1917, that Russia would surely stay in the war and devoted much thought to preventing a statement of peace aims.

They would even have abandoned or postponed the Paris confer- ence[31] which began in November lest opportunity be afforded there for an expression of the universal Russian demand for such a statement. This was mistake No. 1.

Mistake No. 2 was a failure in some quarters to understand that only discipline will make an army fight, certainly if that army be composed of Russian peasants and those peasants be war-weary. . . .

Mistake No. 3, in my opinion, lay in our failure to send troops to Russia. We observe that when the situation on any enemy front threat- ens to be bad, the Germans rush there a few divisions of their own to stiffen up the line, afford example to their Allies and make them realize they are not fighting alone. A few American troops in Russia beginning to arrive in June or July, would have made the Russians know that their sister democracy was willing to share their hardships, and would have afforded concrete proof that Russia was fighting in a common cause with other allied nations. . . . The Bolsheviks would not have lifted up their heads and Russia would still have been in the war. . . . I am still of the opinion that circumstances may arise under which we should send several divisions to a new Russian front. . . .

Mistake No. 4 was a very natural one and involved a failure of the Allies to understand, in June, that the Russian Army, by reason of disor- ganization and lack of discipline, was already incapable of conducting a great offensive. Our reiterated suggestions that we desired and counted upon an early offensive caused the Provisional Government to under- take one against the opinion of many competent Russian officers, who held that there must be a restoration of discipline before any offensive could be successfully conducted. The offensive which was attempted ended in disaster. . . .

There was until the advent to power of the Bolsheviks a great uncer- tainty as to what body was the real repository of authority in Russia. A much stronger argument on legal grounds could be made for the Provi- sional Government than for the Soviet. But the people were behind the Soviet and if strictly legal and not revolutionary grounds were sought to justify the existence of authority Russia indeed remained a monarchy. The Allies never realized the strength of the Soviet with the Russian people.

The First Soviet or its Central Executive Committee endured until the Second (Bolshevik) Soviet assembled in November at the call of the Soviet of Petrograd and a number of other cities. In the interim these local Soviets had become Bolshevik and complained that their delegates in the First Soviet no longer correctly represented them. . . .

[Judson continues with an account of the relationship between the Provisional Government and the Soviets, with special emphasis on Kerensky's efforts to retain their support through the successive crises of his regime. It is an account which is noteworthy in its evenhandedness, narrative accuracy, and detachment—even on 16 March 1918, so soon after the Bolshevik Revolution.]

The Moscow Conference was called together in August by the Provisional Government. . . . This conference seemed to strengthen the hand of the Provisional Government, and it afforded a forum for the presentation of a number of plans for the regeneration of the army.

The Democratic Assembly met toward the end of September and was called together by the Soviet after the ill-fated Kornilov movement, hereafter to be described, had given the country an added impulse toward extreme radicalism. . . . Tereschenko always told the allied diplomats what he thought they wished to hear and the diplomats always believed what Tereschenko told them. Thus some of us lived in a fool's paradise until the early days of November 1917.

The Kornilov movement, September 8 to 12, 1917, has already been described by me in a report to the War College. . . . [Military note of 11 September 1917, above.] Kerensky used the Red Guard of Petrograd, an armed agency of the Bolsheviks, to resist the approaching troops of Kornilov. I cabled at the time that, having used the Red Guard to defeat the troops, Kerensky would not be able later to use troops to defeat the Red Guard. In other words Kerensky on this occasion, made it very probable that later he would be overthrown by the Bolsheviks.

Following the Kornilov episode Kerensky became Commander-in-Chief as well as Minister President. . . . His theory was that he could govern almost solely by persuasion. Trying to please everybody, he pleased no one. He would take advice from no one. He agreed "in principle" with Kornilov and later with Verkhovsky, that the army should be reorganized and redisciplined, but by his speeches and his inaction he permitted discipline to be destroyed.

During the summer and fall of 1917 the extreme radical element assembled under the Bolshevik banner grew continually stronger. The social revolutionists . . . probably represented the majority of the people until well into October. Certainly many of their adherents swung over to the Bolsheviks after the latter came into power and it is probable that a majority of the Russian people had become Bolshevik by December if not before.

Lenin had fled from Russia during the old regime. I never saw him and know of him only by report, but he seems to be a man of great learning in the literature of socialism, able to write and reason well, possessed of great personal magnetism, impressing favorably all he comes in contact with, something of a philosopher and probably a sincere pacifist and internationalist, whom his own extreme theories and not the German General Staff furnished with rules of conduct. I was always much less certain of Lenin however than of Trotsky.

Trotsky, . . . [Lenin's] principal lieutenant, was for a short time in custody after the July disorders. Following his release Trotsky became very active in the Petrograd Soviet. That body became Bolshevik soon after the Kornilov episode and Trotsky became its president.

[Judson continues with a sound history of the Russian Social Democratic Party and its ideological and tactical, Menshevik and Bolshevik factions. He continues, focusing on the Bolsheviks.]

Being fanatical, extreme and uncompromising, the Bolsheviks can not be used to further the interests of any second party except under circumstances where their own interest and that of the second party run parallel. The Bolsheviks are the friends of the proletariat of all countries and the foes of all classes and of all governments which in their opinion oppress or exploit the proletariat. But they do not disapprove equally of all governments other than their own. For example their hatred of the German government is extreme, while their condemnation of our government is not severe, for they believe that the German government is the greatest foe in existence to the interest of their favorite class not only in Germany itself but in Russia and elsewhere, while under our scheme of government they recognize that it is the fault of our proletariat itself if it does not take over the government at a general election and revise our constitution and laws at its own pleasure.

In describing the Bolsheviks as a whole I have in large part described Trotsky.

In my judgment Trotsky has been and is as far from being under the control of the German government or the German General Staff as is Marshall Joffre.[32] I have not doubt that the hatred of Trotsky for these two German agencies is, and long has been, as bitter and as implacable as one can possibly imagine. . . . It is to be remembered that the Bolsheviks are internationalists. Trotsky and Lenin cared very little more for the Russian than for the French or the Italian or even the German proletariat. They conceived that they were working for the proletariat of all the world. . . . No mere separate peace between Russia and the Central Powers would at all have satisfied their ambitions. Even today, if they have indeed been forced to conclude a separate peace, their regret doubtless is not especially that Russia has suffered, but that they have failed to force upon the world a general peace, for these leaders do not count patriotism a virtue. . . .

I have no doubt of the sincerity of Trotsky or of his personal honesty. And in the face of his apparent failure today [the terrible provisions of the Treaty of Brest-Litovsk] I am convinced that he is a man of practical ability in some directions, of remarkable force and a natural leader of men. His activities have apparently been most unfortunate for the allied cause.

With the greatest regret and apprehension I watched his ascent to and establishment in power. But when the power was his I thought we should recognize the inevitable and try to guide his exercise of that power along lines most in our own interest, although I knew that we could accomplish nothing in that direction except where it could be shown to Trotsky that our interest and the interest of the "proletariat" ran parallel. . . .

During the first two or three weeks of its existence very few who were not Bolsheviks themselves supposed that the Bolshevik Government would endure more than for a few days or a few weeks. . . . I knew the weakness of Kerensky with the army but I did not give up hope of his restoration to power until about November 13th. By that time it was evident that he had found only a few half-hearted Cossacks to approach Petrograd with him and that these Cossacks were fraternizing with the Bolshevik forces. A day or two later Kerensky disguised as a sailor, fled from the Cossacks, who were about to turn him over to the Bolsheviks, and thereafter Kerensky had no party and practically no friends in all of Russia.

Potential resistance to the Bolsheviks now crystallized into two groups. One, resorting to the Don Cossack country, included certain military chiefs, among them Alekseev, Kornilov, and Kaledin; and a number of the leaders of the old right, such as Rodzianko, Miliukov and Guch-kov. Of this group very little hope was to be entertained.

The other group centered about Stavka, the headquarters of the grand army, at Mogilev. Here gathered many of the leaders of the Mensheviks and social revolutionists, such as Chernov, Avksentiev, and Tseretelli; Verkhovsky, the former Minister of War; Stankevitch, the chairman of the Army Committee; and here also were the military chiefs who re-mained loyal, not indeed to Kerensky, but to the old Provisional Gov-ernment, including Dukhonin, the Chief of Staff. . . . Under the leader-ship of the Mogilev group there was great hope for a time that the Bolsheviks could be suppressed.

. . . I began at this time to seek the approval of our Ambassador to an interview with Trotsky so that I might attempt to exercise an influence favorable to our interests upon the course of the armistice negotiations which were about to be inaugurated. . . .

[Here Judson examines the circumstances and repercussions of his fateful meeting with Trotsky. Most of the details have already been given in his 26 December 1917 Memorandum to Ambassador Francis in chapter 4.]

I am confident that my interview with Trotsky produced the following excellent results:

(1) It made more certain the embodiment in the armistice protocol of a provision designed to detain the enemy troops upon the Russian front. This provision was probably violated by the enemy, but never-theless it retained many troops which otherwise would have been moved to our great detriment.

(2) It induced Trotsky to send able technical advisers with the Bolshe-vik parliamentaries, so that it would be more difficult for the Germans to accomplish their ends by verbal subterfuges.

(3) It tended to make Trotsky adopt a more uncompromising course during the negotiations, thus increasing the chance of a break.

(4) It had some effect probably in limiting for a time the interchange of goods and the release of prisoners.

(5) According to Colonel Robins, who subsequently had much inter-course with Trotsky, it served to establish me somewhat in Trotsky's confidence so that if necessary or advisable later he might have been willing to listen to my suggestions and advice. I always had it in mind that I might be able to induce Trotsky to keep the army as much in hand

as possible, in anticipation of a possible break; and I thought also that if a break occurred much could be done by me, if I had Trotsky's ear, to assist in impeding the activities of the Germans by appropriate suggestions and advice.

My interview with Trotsky was reported in the American press without regard to the facts. I have not seen any of these reports and can only speak of them from hearsay. In advance the danger of misrepresentation in the press was quite apparent, but the risk appeared to be more personal to myself than to any public interest, and certainly the risk seemed small in comparison with the very great results that might be secured.

After my interview with Trotsky, following instructions, there was no further direct intercourse on the part of our Embassy or Military Mission either with Trotsky or with other members of the Bolshevik Government. For the next two or three months, however the ablest Germans and Austrians were in the closest association with them at Brest-Litovsk and Petrograd.

During the months of November, December and January, while our Embassy and Military Mission in Petrograd were practically out of communication with the de facto government of Russia, some touch was maintained with Lenin, Trotsky and other leaders by Colonel Raymond Robins, head of the American Red Cross. Colonel Robins performed his part circumspectly and with the greatest skill and his sympathetic, friendly and helpful attitude had much to do with the fact that the American and other allied missions were permitted to remain at Petrograd very long after the middle of November. But for his contact with the Bolshevik leaders the Russians, desiring peace as they did, would have been led by the Germans to believe, long before the present time, that the Allies were opposed to any general peace on fair terms and were bent upon imperialistic ends, in contrast to the Germans and the Russians who desired only a democratic general peace. The effect of such a belief might long before this have brought about a situation where Germany could have removed her troops from the Russian front, having gained by less drastic methods much more than has actually come into her hands of Russia. . . .

It is not so simple to attempt now to discount the effects upon distracted Russia of the German occupation, the Japanese threat and the terrible economic, transportation and financial conditions. Certainly the Bolsheviks will tend to lose strength because the old peace issue has died a more or less ignominious death. It is probable that there will soon be an extension of membership in the Soviet to all socialistic factions and that such a broader soviet [will retain power], without surrendering for a time to some [would-be] dictator, perhaps Verkhovsky, or to a small directory. This is more apt to be the case if the Japanese do not become a factor. If they do, however, there is likely to be a short struggle between a weakened soviet and some would-be dictator, perhaps Alekseev, in which the latter, supported by German influence and by many Russians of the land-owning and other superior classes, will soon prevail. I mention Verkhovsky and Alekseev merely as types. . . .

[Judson then reports on Bolshevik domestic economic policy, including strategically important railroad operations, and on Russian military manpower.]

The following table shows the number of effectives in the Russian Army at different periods:

<u>Effectives</u>

Before Mobilization	1,300,000
After Mobilization	4,300,000
May 1, 1916	7,650,000
July 15, 1916	8,500,000
June 20, 1917, at least	10,000,000

The losses to June 20, 1917 (from Russian and French estimates) were as follows:

Killed or died of wounds	1,375,000
Wounded beyond recovery for further military service	2,025,000
Prisoners	2,250,000
Total	5,650,000

On June 20, 1917, the whereabouts of the effectives was approximately as follows:

235 divisions of infantry	2,700,000
50 divisions of cavalry	200,000
Services and works at front (Not in divisions)	2,200,000
Effectives in the Interior (depot b[ar]ns., etc.)	3,400,000
In a state of desertion	1,500,000
Total	10,000,000

By November 1, 1917, as the result of losses by desertion and at the hands of the enemy the ration strength had fallen from 8,500,000 on June 20th to about 6,000,000; and the number in divisions from 2,700,000 to about 1,700,000. On January 1, 1918, the ration strength was estimated at 4,000,000, and the numbers in divisions at 800,000, but the soldiers were leaving their units as fast as they could remove themselves by rail, on foot or otherwise.

[Following a brief account of the growing troop strength of the Red Guards in Petrograd, Judson provides a detailed analysis of the breakdown of discipline in the Russian army from the time of the February Uprising of 1917 to his departure from Russia in February 1918.]

The lot of the Russian officer has been the most pathetic imaginable. It is to be remembered too that before the domestic difficulties of these officers began they had lost far greater numbers at the hands of the enemy than have yet the Germans, French or English.

During my tour of duty in Russia . . . I was always painfully conscious of the facts that the political drift was constantly toward the more radical and less competent elements; that the peace program was rapidly spreading; that discipline was departing from the army; and that general disintegration was setting in along economic lines.

[Here Judson includes four single-spaced pages of quotations on developments in Russia from twenty of his communications to his superiors in both Petrograd and Washington.][33]

Referring to the items quoted above, I would say that I received no response to any of them; nor during my entire tour of duty did I receive instructions of any character except as to several unimporant matters and except also, through the Embassy, after my interview with Trotsky, instructions to have no further direct intercourse with the Bolshevik Government.

When I left Petrograd on January 23, 1918, there seemed a reasonable probability that no agreement would be reached in the peace negotiations and that an armistice would continue indefinitely between Russia and the Central Powers. It seemed likely that Rumania would be compelled to make a separate peace on terms onerous to herself; that the Ukraine, already pro-Austrian, would gladly come to terms with the Central Powers; that Finland would seek German aid in expelling the

Bolsheviks and establishing her independence; and that hunger and economic distress would finally wear out the Bolshevik Government. Since then Germany has advanced into the Estonian Peninsula, and to the East of Pskov, Vitebsk, Mogilev and Kiev, and has terrorized and starved the Petrograd Government into a peace treaty which is as yet subject to the approval of a Soviet which will meet in Moscow, it is reported, on March 12th, many local soviets have announced themselves against the peace, and many social revolutionists oppose it.

Whether this peace treaty be approved or not some Russians will in some fashion continue to oppose the Germans, while, others, including many land-owners, manufacturers, bankers and the like, will support them. . . .

If the Japanese invade Siberia, European Russia and Western Siberia as well will in all probability fall into the lap of Germany. It is of course preposterous to believe that the Japanese will ever establish military contact with the Germans. They would find practically all Russians their enemies and their operations would not extend far west of Lake Baikal.

On the other hand if now, while all elements in Russia are distracted between one plan and another to govern their future conduct, the United States could extend a helping hand, many of these elements could be encouraged to continue resistance, a weak line of resistance could be formed east of the region of German occupation, Germany could be restricted in her commercial operations to the region she may actually occupy and many German troops could be contained on a new Russian front. I have discussed at length the effect of a Japanese occupation of a part of Siberia in a memorandum to the Acting Chief of Staff dated March 4, 1918 [above], which I quote below in full.

On February 26, 1918, I submitted a memorandum [above] to the Acting Secretary of War, recommending the immediate issuance of a statement designed to afford information and encouragement to the Russians, who are in groups now planning for the future and who are about to vote at Moscow upon the question of approval of a peace treaty. I further recommend that, if we could arrange to appear on the scenes as deliverers, we send a small force to Russia as quickly as possible, to serve as a nucleus, a visible evidence of our support, and an example of disciplined troops in the service of a free government. This memorandum also I quote below in full:

In this report now submitted I have not alluded to technical military operations. Since March, 1917, political events in Russia have not only overshadowed all others, but have in fact controlled them. Students of military psychology, but not students of the military art in other branches, would find interest in an account of the operations of the Russian Army during the period to which this report refers. I hope to find time later for a supplementary report which will be devoted to this subject. In the meantime this report seems to contain in brief most that seems necessary for an estimate of the present situation in connection with any decision as to what should now be done in Russia. Very many additional facts could be presented now, but the importance of an immediate decision is so great that I do not feel justified in taking now the time to embody them in this report.

JULY 6, 1918

POST MASTER GENERAL,
A. S. BURLESON, WASHINGTON, D.C.

My Dear Mr. Burleson:—

According to the newspapers we seem to be about to send another Mission to Russia. I may soon be in France. There is one bit of information I had about happenings in Petrograd which I hoped I would never have to dwell upon, but the possibility of a new Mission and my early probable departure have made me set it all down and I enclose it as a memo to you. When I hear from you about it I will send it in formally to the Intelligence Department of the General Staff.[34]

I also enclose the letter I told you of but which I never delivered to you, from your former constituent, the tall youth whose name I have forgotten, who acted for a time as the Ambassador's Secretary at Petrograd.[35] I think his letter relates to Madame de Cram but only from a brief account he gave me as he handed me the letter. If Mr. Francis had come home I'd feel at liberty still, as I did in February, to lock these sordid [tales?] in my own memory and burden no one with them.

I believe Butler Wright is about the State Department and may be able to report whether Madame de C is still dangerously present in Russia.

If you are decidedly of the opinion I should keep my mouth shut in this matter, please let me know, and also as to whether Mr. "Tall Constituent's" letter does not confirm the very remarkable story in the memorandum.

I liked Mr. Francis and we were close friends except where Madame de C was concerned. By reason of her he did me some injustice for a time, but I forgave him for it and hate to mention his name in connection with the incidents. I wouldn't to save my right arm, were it not for the possible public importance of the whole matter.

Yours faithfully,

PROGRAM.

Brought to Washington by W. V. J. July 8, 1918 when we were about to send troops to Vladivostock. This was of course before the Great War ended.[36]

1. Rejuvenate the railroad of Siberia and the trunk lines extending into European Russia (say to the Volga).

2. Furnish the Russians with certain necessities, through the media of trade and gift, as far as the Volga, on assumption that this would not benefit the enemies of mankind (the Germans) while enabling us to assist those now the most unfortunate of people. Such necessities would include medicines and medical attention; clothes; tools and machinery; agricultural implements.

3. Preach internal peace; "love one another"; the ultimate efficacy and fairness of a universal ballot; the importance of order.

4. Propose the reorganization of Siberia, on ultra-democratic lines, as a part of Russia, the restoration of order and the growth of efficiency to follow.
Note: Nothing in the constitution of Siberia hostile to the rest of Russia, or to its development, political and economic, as it may see fit: a continued union with Russia never lost sight of.

5. Purpose of United States, in so far as it is not inspired by the heart, to prevent the gradual subjugation of Russia by the principle remaining forces of autocracy; to retain thus more of the power of the world in the hands of the people of the world. The United States has no economic theory which it would champion, and it has no propaganda directed merely toward the form of things, but it does believe that justice everywhere demands the rule of the people and it fears that the rule of any other force within some strong nations, but especially the exercise of arbitrary power by certain autocratically ruled governments upon the free people of other lands for national profiteering, will lead to the death of justice and the resumptions everywhere of conditions designed to benefit the few at the expense of the many.

6. Ultimately, when this war shall have demonstrated that at last the old order has changed and the people cannot be overcome, it will be possible for the world to have a new birth and for its people, in their governments to seek in reality the greatest good of the greatest number. But never can the "greatest number" protect its interests except it remain on guard with the political weapon of democracy always ready.

AUGUST 21, 1918. WASHINGTON, D. C.
MEMORANDUM FOR THE CHIEF OF STAFF:

Russians who have been absent from their country during the past year are incompetent witnesses as to conditions and tendencies in Russia. Their experiences during this year have left indelible impressions upon individuals and parties actually present in Russia which can not be fully comprehended and weighed, even by Russians themselves who have been at a distance.

Russia is by no means lacking in men competent to organize and lead; but political management, of course, demands intercommunication between leaders and the formulation of plans and platforms resulting from the attrition of minds and the adoption of compromises.

Since November, 1917, it has been impossible for two decently patriotic and politically competent Russians to meet together for an interchange of views.

It occurs to me that only in some other and hospitable land could a small group of competent Russians be gathered, away from the terror surrounding them at home, to formulate a reasonable policy to extricate their country from its present state of deadly anarchy.

The events of the past year have created the possibility of a great solidarity among all non-Bolshevik elements; have demonstrated the need of discipline among all elements of the Russian people; and doubtless have produced a willingness to compromise among all reasonable Russian elements.

Among the wise and patriotic Russians whose services today are not at the disposal of their country, nor of the Allies, who are groping about so eagerly, but so blindly, to find a way to save Russia, are the following:

Guchkov;[37] I name him first because of his completely patriotic and unselfish purposes, his great ability and his unequalled and educating experiences in important Russian affairs. In 1904–5 he was at the head of the Russian Red Cross during the Manchurian War; and in Russia the

Red Cross attends to many functions performed in our country by the Army Medical Department, in addition to those we commonly understand as Red Cross functions. Later he was the head of the Octobrist Party, which stood between the radicals and the conservatives and made the Second Duma the first practical Russian legislative body and for years Guchkov presided over that Duma, refusing Cabinet office because he thought the greatest task for Russians was to learn parliamentary government. For several years Guchkov was president of the Council of National Defense. Following 1914, when Russia found herself at such a disadvantage in modern war because she was not an industrial nation, Guchkov became the head of a committee similar to our War Industries Board, which by the spring of 1917, had wrought miracles in the munitions productivity of Russia. When the revolution approached Guchkov was the leader among those who tried to have ready for the inevitable occasion an organization capable of assuming the reins of government. Knowing that the czar must fall it was Guchkov who presented to Nicholas the document, by signing which he abdicated, but by changing which, before signature (because he was too weak to permit his son to rule with his brother as regent), Nicholas defeated the plans so carefully prepared to give Russia a democracy while retaining, as seems to so many necessary, a figure head to be a symbol of authority to the Russian peasant. Then Guchkov was Minister of War and of Marine in the Lvov Cabinet which the growing tide of radicalism soon submerged. I have reason to believe that Mr. Guchkov was the only Russian who had the courage, the honesty and the prescience to tell Mr. Root, in June, 1917, exactly what the future had in store for Russia. And so I mention Mr. Guchkov first and describe him at length because I believe him to be the greatest and wisest of Russians.

Tseretelli; a social revolutionist, but a wise and reasonable man, of excellent courage and judgment; a man who almost alone held back the forces of extreme radicalism in the fall of 1917, when the so called Democratic Convention was called to eject the more moderate from office; a sort of Russian Henry Clay, eloquent, idolized by his followers, and almost universally respected; wonderfully able in inventing compromises and harmonizing seemingly irreconcilable conflicts.

Verkhovsky; the last secretary of War under Kerensky, strong and able but sacrificed because he wished to rediscipline the Army, although another reason for his dismissal was given by Kerensky.

Alekseev and Brusilov; great soldiers and leaders of men, patriotic and wise, both of them.[38]

I have mentioned but four or five. There are doubtless a few others such as Savinkov, Avksentiev, Rodzianko, Chaikovsky, Vostrotin, Kolchak, all men whose action, taken after common counsel, would insure to the Russian people that only purity of purpose and comprehending wisdom were directing any action they might take together.[39]

By reason of the conditions which prevent these statesmen now from serving Russia; because they know Russia and could better than any others, work out a plan for her salvation; because their recommendations would be so completely acceptable in Russia, except to the irreconcilable Bolsheviks; and because we so lack the data to estimate the situation and therefore to suggest the remedy, I recommend that a number from among the men above mentioned be invited in a discrete way to come to America to offer suggestions and advice.

There can be no Constitutional Convention now in Russia, but the suggestions of these great Russians would have among their own countrymen almost the force and effect of the resolutions of a Constitutional Convention.

The almost inevitable immediate future of Russia is Civil War, one side supported by the Germans and the other side by the Entente. We must do what we can to insure that on our side are as many Russians as possible and I know no surer way to advance our interests in this matter than in the manner suggested herein.

Our adopted policy toward Russia, apparently involving a complete break with the Bolsheviks, is already in process of execution. If we have indeed broken irrevocably with the Bolshevik government, which may not be in as weak a state as current information would indicate, it is, of course necessary to make strenuous efforts to win the other elements, which have already shown some tendencies toward a pro-German "orientation".

WAR DEPARTMENT
OFFICE OF THE CHIEF OF STAFF, WASHINGTON
NOVEMBER 8, 1918

BRIGADIER GENERAL WILLIAM P. [sic] JUDSON
PORT OF EMBARKATION,
HOBOKEN, N.J.

My dear Judson:

A Number of representatives of new nations, the Czechs and others, are going to have a dinner in New York in the near future and have asked the War Department if there was any objection to inviting an Army officer to be present and your name has been suggested to them.

There is no objection to your accepting and making a speech, if it is desired and you care to, but the Secretary wants you to be warned not to make any remarks which might be regarded by them as committing the Nation to any policy at all with reference to these nations.

Sincerely,
[signed] Peyton C. March
General, Chief of Staff

PERSONAL   NOVEMBER 17, 1918
MAJOR GENERAL GEORGE W. GOETHALS,
DIRECTOR, PURCHASE, STORAGE & TRAFFIC,
WAR DEPARTMENT, WASHINGTON, D.C.

My dear Goethals:

I encountered a tragedy the other day. I had been feeling like the devil for the past month, or since the time I seem to have had the influenza, which is over a month, and latterly have been postponing a thorough physical examination by the doctors only until the armistice might be signed after which I considered it less important as to what might happen to me.

Last Wednesday a very good doctor, temporarily in the service, went over me and found what he described as a very serious condition of the heart. He said that unless I began a complete rest immediately my period of usefulness would be very short indeed. . . . In any event, assuming the diagnosis will be confirmed, it would seem necessary that I ask to be relieved from my present duties. . . . I shall submit something official which, I suppose, should be addressed to The Adjutant General. I am writing March a line today and am enclosing him a copy of this letter to you. . . .

. . . Was it not a complete and sudden lay-down in Central Europe? Doubtless Bolshevism had a tremendous amount to do with the whole result, and God knows what will happen before the antics of Bolshevism cease. It is not impossible that Bolshevism will so run through the Italian and French armies as to render them imperfect instruments for combatting disorder in Central Europe. It is even possible that internal disorders will arise in Italy and France sympathetic with disorders in Central Europe. We may find ourselves in a devil of a fix without much support from former Allies if we are placed in the roll of restorers of order.

I certainly feel distressed at my physical condition. The doctor says the trouble with my heart is dilation, but what that is I do not know. I hope very much that it will work out so that, at the worst after a considerable rest, I may get on my feet again.

Yours faithfully,

Roosevelt Hospital

N.Y. City—February 14, 1919

Col. Robert R. McCormick
Tribune Bldg. Chicago, Ill.

My Dear McCormick:

I expect to break out of the hospital within a day or two, and after a sickleave of a month or two return to duty.

With reference to the clipping you sent me (of Dec. 4, 1917, Chicago Tribune) I wish that good old paper, in the interest of truth and justice, could publish something that would include the following as to the accuracy of which I assure you. As the Bolsheviki are still diplomatically important, I cannot of course tell you all about my experiences in Russia—nor even publish anything over my own name.

My suggestion for the Tribune is something as follows;

"On Dec. 4, 1917 we published certain references to alleged intercourse between two of our military officers at Petrograd on the one hand and Bolshevik or other Russian authorities or pretended authorities on the other. We now are aware that our article contained certain important inaccuracies, which we desire to point out at this time in the interest of truth and of justice. The two American officers referred to were Brigadier General Judson and Colonel Kerth. The former was Chief of the American Military Mission and Military Attaché. The latter was General Judson's assistant.

"The article of Dec. 4, 1917 made it appear that these two officers were working at cross purposes whereas Col. Kerth's action was throughout precisely as directed by General Judson. Our article made General Judson (whom we described as Lt. Col. Judson) state in a letter 'to the Bolsheviki Chief of Staff' that America felt Russia was quite right to raise the question of a general peace. We really might have felt sure that no American officer should have made such a statement to anybody, any where, at any time. And we know now that General Judson made such a statement at no time and least of all 'to a Bolshevik Chief of Staff,' who did not exist at that time.

"A day or two later we published another article to the effect that there was rejoicing in Germany over the observed intercourse between our military officers and the Bolsheviks at Petrograd. We are afraid now that this 'information,' which had its origin in Copenhagen, was simply German propaganda. At the time hundreds of German officers and diplomatic officials were [The unfinished letter ends here.][40]

LEXINGTON, KENTUCKY
APRIL 10, 1919

ALBERT SYDNEY BURLESON,
POSTMASTER GENERAL

Dear Mr. Burleson:

. . . When the Bolsheviks finally got in, in November 1917, we who alone, among all the Allied representatives and agents, had done anything of real moment to keep the Bolsheviks out, recognized that they were in fact firmly established for the vital period of the war; and we alone seemed to realize that if the peace negotiations, which were at once undertaken at Brest-Litovsk, were to be prevented or delayed, or other-wise affected in our interest, it would be necessary to deal quickly and wisely with the Bolshevik leaders. For this task Raymond Robins was rarely fitted, through possession of the very qualities, perhaps, that make him so many enemies here and now. He is a great idealist and a man of almost too broad human sympathies, if you understand what I mean. Thus there lay in him some strong appeal to Lenin and Trotsky, fanatical idealists as they are, even although these leaders knew on his own confession, that Robins had worked hard, with Thompson's million dollars and the Breshkovsky Committee, to keep them out of power, and did not believe in their governmental or economic theories. Robins saw Lenin and Trotsky every day, and every bit of influence he possibly could develop, he used to sow dissension between the Germans and the Russians at Brest-Litovsk. When I was ordered home he even made himself and the Russians think I was being sent for to explain to President Wilson how best he could help the Bolsheviks, if they refused to sign a peace with Germany.

My own interview with Trotsky, which was greatly misrepresented in America on information set afloat, for very obvious reasons, by German propagandists, who wished all intercourse with the Bolsheviks to be limited to German agents, did its part in stiffening up Russian reluctance to sign the peace.

Now, think for a minute what it meant in a military way; first to delay the advent of Bolshevik power in Russia for at least a month prior to November 7th, 1917; second, to make trouble between Germans and Russians while engaged in treaty negotiations at Brest-Litovsk, effectively heartening the Bolsheviks there to resistance of German terms by near-promise which we hoped were not without proper justification, and thus delaying for several months, until the middle of March, the signing of a peace that was really scarcely a peace at all.

I think there is no question that but for the work done by certain Americans in Russia and recited in the preceding paragraph, the Germans would have had nearly a million more men in their 1918 spring drive against the channel ports and Paris. As it was, the result of that drive hung long in the balance. In all probability a few more fighting men from the Russian front would have tipped the beam to the side of the Hun. And so it seems reasonable to believe that the work done by the Americans in Petrograd was an absolutely essential element in the winning of the war. Those who did this work seem now, most unfairly, to be receiving only obloquy.

The membership of the American Red Cross Mission to Russia was very distinguished as to ability and patriotism. Under all the circumstances it need not excite hostile comment that members of this mission engaged in Actions outside of its very limited essential functions. It must be remembered that the current of events seemed to set toward a most terrible anarchy and complete disorder, which would imperil the allied cause, perhaps bring disaster upon our country, and certainly cause famine and catastrophe in Russia. It must also be remembered that nearly every American at the time officially present in Petrograd, whether connected with the Embassy, the Military Mission or the Red Cross Mission, suspected that one Madame de Cram, too influential at the Embassy, was a German agent. This naturally led to the taking of initiative, greater than might otherwise have been expected, by such Americans as composed the Red Cross Mission.

I am naturally of a cheerful disposition, as you know, but if I do not live to see this injustice corrected, I shall believe, not only that Republics are indeed ungrateful, but also, with a certain cynical historian, that "History is a pack of lies agreed upon."

Some day when the dangers of Bolshevism are past and the truth is more safely to be told than now, I think I shall submit a belated report as Chief of the Military Mission to Russia, recommending the D.S.M. [Distinguished Service Medal] for the principal members of that very admirable but unfortunate Red Cross Mission.

Well, when I started to write this letter I had no idea that I was going to make it so long or put so much in it. Indeed I was only intending to say that, although my heart is no longer a normal organ, I hope it will not prevent years of future usefulness, and if it confines its evils to an eventual sudden and final action, I shall have no complaints to make.

Clay is in Paris, hearing law lectures at the Sorbonne. I suppose he will soon be coming home and entering an office in Chicago. It was for that reason principally that I asked Black to send me there for station. Clay seems well and happy.

Mrs. Judson was recently in an automobile accident, which resulted in breaking of her collar bone. She is all right again now.

We both send our love to all of the Burlesons.

Yours faithfully,

JUNE 18, 1919. <u>SECRET</u>

FROM: COL. W. V. JUDSON, CORPS OF ENGINEERS, FORMERLY CHIEF AMERICAN MILITARY MISSION TO RUSSIA.
TO: THE SECRETARY OF WAR.
SUBJECT: REPORT OF CERTAIN EVENTS IN RUSSIA, 1917–1918, INCLUDING CERTAIN RECOMMENDATIONS FOR DISTINGUISHED SERVICE MEDALS AND CROSS.

1. This belated official report is submitted directly to the Secretary of War by his permission, conveyed to me in a personal letter by the Chief of Staff. It is submitted in the interest of justice to certain Americans

who were in Petrograd during the troubled days of 1917–18, and as a truthful contribution to the history of those days, which seems in some danger of becoming but a "pack of lies agreed upon."

2. The growing menace of Bolshevism, which threatened to take Russia out of the war, was appreciated outside the American Embassy as early as August 7, 1917, when I cabled the War Department as follows:

"It is at least an even chance that coming events may take Russia out of the war within the next few months. Our larger war plans should be made accordingly."

3. During August and September, 1917, I devoted my efforts, unsuccessfully, toward inducing our Ambassador, in conjunction with the diplomatic representatives of our allies, to force upon Kerensky the policy of redisciplining the Russian Army and cooperating with Kornilov. It seemed to me the last chance to stand off Bolshevism and defeatism and for a time, as Military Attaché to the Embassy, I submitted a daily memorandum on the subject to our Ambassador urging him to take the initiative in this matter before it was everlastingly too late. If all of the diplomatic representatives of the allies had joined in a demand upon Kerensky, the story of Russia might have been different. Unfortunately our Ambassador and Kerensky thought too nearly along the same lines upon this subject of discipline. What our Ambassador replied to me was always in substance as follows:

"Why, Judson, I can understand how soldiers feel on this subject, but an old politician like me understands human nature much better and I can assure you that the Russian Army will never quit but will fight like lions, inspired by a sense of freedom newly won," etc.

4. It was sickening and it was terrible, for before we knew how rapidly troops could be transported to France, it looked as though the issue of the war might depend on Russia's course, and that depended at one time entirely on the state of discipline in the Russian army.

5. Our Red Cross Mission to Russia contained a number of very able and patriotic men who in the terrible emergency that existed did not see fit to confine their thoughts and efforts to very narrow limits. During the two critical months of August and September these gentlemen were orienting themselves, studying the political situation and forming opinion as to what should be done in the interest of America. I do not think that they attached any particular importance to redisciplining the Army. I know they regarded the Kornilov movement, which I fervently wished might succeed, as but an unfortunate flash in the pan tending to weaken

Kerensky and predestined to failure. As to who was right up to this point is not now a matter of great importance as in any event there was no accomplishment by any of us in these matters.[41]

6. Toward the end of September it became increasingly evident that the Bolsheviks were going to make a strong play to seize the state and that if they succeeded Russia would go out of the war.

7. But one thing remained to be done and the gentlemen of our Red Cross Mission, and especially Colonel William B. Thompson, its Chief and Colonel Raymond Robins, his principal Assistant, set about doing it to the utmost of their ability. This last remaining resort was propaganda upon an enormous and effective scale, such propaganda as might be likened for example to the operations of a heated political campaign in New York City during days just preceding a most important election.

8. Thompson and Robins had both had experience in such campaigns. It was estimated that the advent of Bolshevism could be put off indefinitely with an expenditure of about $3,000,000 per month. I cabled to Washington a hearty indorsement of these plans. A Russian committee was organized consisting of Madam Breshkovsky as the figure-head chairman; Tchaikovsky (now the head of the Archangel Russian government); and Soskice (Kerensky's very able executive secretary) being among the five members.[42] We did the best we could to advise them in America of the money requirements. In the mean time Colonel Thompson went into his own pocket and put up $1,000,000. He thus has the honor of being the only one among all the persons or nations of the allies to do anything really substantial to delay the advent of Bolshevism. Through the acumen in practical politics of Thompson and Robins, these gentlemen, collaborating with the Russian Committee I have already mentioned, and with a proper distribution of Thompson's $1,000,000, set back the advent of Bolshevism from one month to six weeks, during the critical period of the meeting of the so-called "Democratic Convention" which had been hand-picked and carefully assembled to vote Kerensky out and the more radical element in. It was almost incomprehensible, except to those who knew about Thompson's $1,000,000, why the Bolsheviks did not come in about October 1, instead of, as actually happened, about November 7, 1917. The effect of this hitch and delay in Bolshevik plans if it set back everything that followed, including the Brest-Litovsk treaty, for a similar period of time as it seems fair to assume, was of incalculable value.

9. It proved impossible to get funds from America on the large scale which would have been necessary to continue the political campaign

against Bolshevism, and Colonel Thompson naturally enough could not go on with his personal expenditures indefinitely. The campaign was necessarily brought to a close and it was almost simultaneous with its close that the Bolsheviks seized the state. At this time Colonel Thompson came to my quarters and remained quietly there until there was an opportunity for him safely to leave Petrograd and Russia.

10. When the Bolsheviks did get in it became necessary as quickly as possible to estimate the situation, with a view to preventing if possible, or postponing, the making of a separate peace. Were the Bolsheviks going to stay in power during the critical period of the war? Nothing could well be done until the question was answered, and it was quickly and correctly answered in the affirmative, largely through the agency of the very efficient secret service organization which Thompson and Robins had formed a month or two earlier, with Colonel Thompson's money, to combat the Bolsheviks.

11. Fortunate it now was for America and the allies that Robins was in Petrograd and that he was exactly the kind of a man he is. His enemies say he is a socialist. I know he speaks the truth when he says he is not, but I do not care in the least whether he is or not. He is certainly a man of very broad human sympathies and very tolerant of people whose theories he can not agree with. At any rate he soon became the principal liaison between Lenin and Trotsky and the active Anti-German elements in Petrograd; and he used all of the great influence which he developed with those two, in almost daily intercourse, to defeat the purpose of the Germans to make a quick treaty favorable to their own interests. In perfect sincerity, so far as concerned his own convictions, he convinced the Bolshevik leaders that the Germans were asking too much; that the Bolsheviks could get better terms the longer they waited; and that the United States would probably assist the Bolsheviks if they came to a final falling out with the Germans.

12. I have already reported that during these days I also saw Trotsky and assisted to sow dissensions between the Russians and the Germans, and I have already reported what advantage apparently resulted from my interviews.

13. As a result of reports sent from Russia and neighboring neutral counties by German agents there were widely published in American Newspapers, as I discovered long afterward on my return to America, entirely false accounts of my intercourse with the Russian General Staff in November and with Trotsky on December 1. It was even made to appear that I, "Lieut. Col." Judson (I was then Brig. General) was having

a great controversy with Colonel Kerth "the Military Attaché" (I was Military Attaché), and that while Kerth was sending a splendid protest to the Russians against a separate peace, I was in correspondence rather approving of what was going on! Now Kerth was my very efficient and loyal assistant; the protest he made was formulated by me and submitted by my direction at a time when I still hoped that the Military Chiefs could suppress the Bolshevik uprising; and my letters which appeared to be inconsistent with "Kerth's" (my) protest were directed toward a new condition that subsequently arose, and were maliciously distorted in words and meaning. At this time Robins and I were the only Americans who were maintaining any touch, unofficial of course, with those who actually ruled Russia and who had the power to take her out of the war. Hundreds of German agents were in the closest relations with these Russians and they used every device to cut off all communication between the Russians and ourselves and allies.

14. When I was recalled to America, leaving Petrograd on January 23, 1918, Robins used my departure cleverly to induce Lenin and Trotsky to believe I had gone to make arrangements for assistance to the Russians in case they failed to come to terms with the Germans. And Robins was perfectly sincere as well as clever in this matter. For on February 26, 1918, I did submit to the Acting Chief of Staff a memorandum containing certain recommendations looking to encouragement of the Bolsheviks while they were still at war with the Germans, which, if they could have been adopted, would no doubt have prevented ratification of the treaty of Brest-Litovsk. The Soviet, before it ratified that treaty, marked time for days while it awaited some word from America which would indicate it might expect support if it broke with the Germans.

15. I have no complaint to make as to any injustice which may have resulted to myself through my recall from Russia, whether such recall was a result of false publications in the American press which might readily have been denied on information furnished by my own cables to Washington, or whether such recall was due to other cause or circumstance. When an officer is called upon to suffer humiliation, he must often assume that the public interest will be best served if he suffer in silence. But in the cases of Colonel Thompson and of Colonel Robins the rule is different. It seems unfair and unnecessary for the Government to abandon them when their services to the Government have been as great as they have been misunderstood, and when such misunderstanding has fostered the widespread and monstrous belief

that these two gentlemen have been self-seeking mischief-makers with Bolshevistick tendencies.

16. It is impossible for me to reread what I have written above without perceiving the necessity of explaining why there now exist, apparent to the public, certain evidences of friction between the Red Cross Mission to Russia and the American Ambassador. How can be explained the actions in Russia of Colonels Thompson and Robins, so largely conducted without consultation with and the guidance of the American Ambassador? Certainly without sufficient explanation the charge of meddling brought against these gentlemen appears to be a plausible one. And yet such explanation I would rather cut off my own right arm than make, did I not feel that it need be circulated only to a limited extent and as may be necessary in the interest of justice.

17. On _____, 1916, [March] our newly appointed ambassador sailed from America for Petrograd via Sweden.

18. There was presented to him on the dock one Madame de Cram, who claimed to be a Russian returning to Petrograd. This woman had previously learned from Mr. Ben Yoakum, a friend of Mr. Francis, the ship on which Mr. Francis would sail and some of his personal characteristics, Mr. Yoakum of course being entirely ignorant of the use that would be made of this information. There was evidence in the secret records of the Interallied Passport Bureau and of the French Counter-Espionage Bureau at Petrograd that Madame de C. had previously arrived in America in company with a Russian woman who was well identified as an important Central Powers spy and conspirator. The circumstance of this arrival has been mentioned in American newspapers which have described the plots of the Russian woman Madame de C. accompanied. It was long after I arrived in Petrograd, probably in October or November, 1917, that the secret service dossier on Madame de C. came to my attention.

19. Madame de C. and Mr. Francis crossed on the same steamer and arrived in Petrograd by the same train. Thereafter they became the most intimate of friends. Sometimes he spoke of her as his French teacher. For a long time she spent nearly every evening at the Embassy. I was frequently present at their tete-a-tetes and was able to study the woman and her influence over the Ambassador.

20. She was an exceedingly bright and attractive person about forty, but seemingly much younger. Her influence over the Ambassador in all directions seemed vastly greater than that of all the Embassy Staff and

Military Mission combined. He made it a practice to talk over the public business with her. She knew the contents of many if not most of his cables. Much information of this character came to me just as I was leaving Petrograd, from a man who acted for a time as the Ambassador's private secretary. I do not remember this man's name, but do remember that he had formerly been prosecuting attorney in his home town in Texas, and said that his experience in connection with criminals enabled him to pass judgment on the de Cram woman; that she was a German agent; that by reason of her relations with the Ambassador American interests were suffering extremely; and that in his opinion the highest American authorities would be invoked at once to stop what was going on.[43]

21. Through some agency known to Mr. Wright the State Department was advised as to Madame de Cram and a cable was sent the Ambassador warning him to avoid the woman.

23[sic]. Mr. Wright told me in advance that he expected such a message to arrive. When it came the Ambassador had Wright decode it, remarked that he would "get the _____ who had caused it to be sent," and received Mr. Wright's diplomatic, and, I will not say, inexcusable denial that he knew anything of it. I am quite sure this message did not have the desired effect.

24. Mr. Sisson of our Public Information service, I understand, sent a warning message to Washington.

25. I personally appealed to the Ambassador to see Madame de C. no more, and I showed him the dossier relative to her which Captain Riggs borrowed from the Interallied Passport Bureau. Thus I was the only one who personally approached the Ambassador on the subject of Madame de C. Doubtless for a month or more thereafter he erroneously attributed to me the submission to Washington of some despatches with unfriendly references to myself or to my official conduct as Chief of the American Military Mission. Later, and not long before my departure from Petrograd (which occurred on January 23, 1918) I think the Ambassador came to suspect others and to believe that it was not I who had reported the de C. matter to the State Department.

26. At this point it is but fair to myself to say that there was a time when I would have felt it incumbent upon me to make my suspicions known in Washington had I not been aware that others had already acted in the matter. I felt that all I could do, and all that was left to be done, was to speak on the subject to the Ambassador himself, and do

my best to get along with him under very difficult conditions, the issue of which no one could certainly foresee except that they might be well nigh disastrous to the interests of our country.

27. When I was ordered home I suspected that I was not in favor with the State Department. I attributed this to the probable tone of the Ambassador's despatches as well as to certain American press reports of my informal intercourse with Trotsky, etc., seemingly of German origin, as above reported, and manufactured largely out of whole cloth in order to prevent us from having any influence over the Trotsky regime during the time the Germans would be negotiating with it.

28. It is quite certain that during this period when I might have expected to be upheld by our Ambassador, having acted always with his approval and consent, the latter was laboring under the impression that it was probably I who had made report to Washington about him and Madame de C.

29. When I arrived in Washington (February 20, 1918) the importance of the de Cram matter had become apparently wholly historical. When I submitted my final report it looked as though Russia was out of the war and the Ambassador practically on his way home. Consequently I brought up none of these matters, as they seemed at this time to bear principally upon my own personal experiences and fortunes, which seemed of very little relative importance in the spring of 1918. Even it might have seemed I was seeking revenge upon our Ambassador, or trying in some way to magnify the service I had rendered or seemed almost able to render, through getting in touch with the then existing Russian Government and assisting to bolster Trotsky up against German diplomacy and the intrigue at Brest-Litovsk. It is by no means beyond the bounds of possibility, indeed it is even very probable, that Baron Mirbach, who, while Russia was at war, attended to Russian affairs for the German Foreign Office, controlled the activities of Madame de Cram and through her influenced the theories and opinions of our Ambassador from the time we entered the war until Russia retired from the war.

30. Thus it may well be true that our diplomacy with regard to Russia was in large degree guided from Berlin by the crafty Mirbach himself.

31. Now suspicions of these remarkable and terrible possibilities were rife, as I have said, at the Embassy, and among the members of the Red Cross and Military Missions. It has been necessary to describe these possibilities so that there may be a clear understanding of why in those days when the fate of the world was at stake, some persons may

have seemed to be working, in certain details, without complete Ambassadorial sanction.

32. I understand that the Ambassador has now convinced himself that the Germans tried to reach him through a woman, but that he soon discovered and thwarted their plot! No such discovery had been made by the Ambassador prior to my departure from Petrograd on January 23, 1918, nor apparently prior to the departure of Colonel Kerth, a few weeks later, for Colonel Kerth has written me of a stormy scene he passed through with the Ambassador, regarding the de Cram woman, just before he, Kerth, left Petrograd.

33. The Brest-Litovsk treaty was not approved by the Russians until the middle of March, 1918. If this treaty had been consummated several months earlier and with less friction than was developed between negotiating parties, the Germans would have had from five to six hundred thousand more men in their spring drive against the channel ports and Paris. Considering how the issue hung in the balance it is difficult to believe that this additional force might not have changed the result. Among those most responsible for this result, as I have pointed out above, were Colonels Thompson and Robins, and certain other members of our Red Cross Mission to Russia who have had much obloquy cast upon them by persons who themselves should have done something to prevent the Russian debacle but did not. Justice seems to demand that the services in particular of Colonel William B. Thompson and of Colonel Raymond Robins should be now pointed out by someone who was officially on the ground, who knew the history of those days, and who has no motive now to misrepresent their services.

34. To sum the matter up I desire to point out that the services of Colonel Thompson and Colonel Robins were essential elements in the winning of the war. If William B. Thompson had not had a million dollars to give and the willingness to give it to delay the advent of Bolshevism in Russia; and if Raymond Robins had not been a man of just his own unique personality, which made him influential with Lenin and Trotsky for the great good of America, in all probability the Germans, with 500,000 or 600,000 more men in the spring drive of 1918, would have won the war.

35. In recognition of these services I recommend that Distinguished Service Medals be awarded to Colonel William B. Thompson and Colonel Raymond Robins, each formerly head of the American Red Cross Mission to Russia.

36. And for his most faithful, intelligent and loyal services to the United States during as difficult and critical days as perhaps the world has ever seen, while serving as my principal assistant during the time I was Chief of the American Military Mission to Russia, I recommend that the Distinguished Service Cross be awarded to Colonel Monroe C. Kerth, General Staff. In pursuance of his duties, assigned him by me, Colonel Kerth was frequently under fire, where of course he acquitted himself as an American officer should.

37. If, in this communication I have mingled with commendatory remarks upon the services of others many references to my own experiences, I hope nevertheless it will be understood that my principal motive has not been a selfish one. The threads of my own story and of the stories of some others are in many respects inseparably interwoven, and besides one yields readily to the temptation to explain his own part in events which have been wretchedly misunderstood.

38. I deeply appreciate the action of the Secretary of War in permitting me to submit this report.

ADDRESS BEFORE THE MEMBERS OF THE CITY CLUB OF MILWAUKEE, THURSDAY, OCTOBER 30, 1919.[44]

Ladies and Gentlemen of the City Club of Milwaukee:

I found myself stationed in Milwaukee in the year 1905 and here I spent four of the pleasantest years of my life. Soon after I arrived, at the University Club I spoke to a Milwaukee audience of my experiences in Manchuria with the Russian Army during the Russo-Japanese War, the year preceding my arrival among you. In the course of my previous talk I told you how I had come to have an affection for the Russian people. I even ventured to say that they were more like ourselves than were any other Europeans whom I had encountered. I have not had occasion to change my mind in this matter although I am afraid that many of the Russian people who were most like ourselves a few years ago have disappeared from the face of the earth today, or through the most horrible sufferings have found themselves changed and utterly submerged. . . .

During the early part of the great war, before we entered it, naturally my interest largely centered itself upon the doings of the Russians. During the first year of the war you may remember the Russians under Nicholas advanced into Galicia and were almost successful in occupying the European plain through the passes of the Carpathians. In this movement Russia threatened to put Austria out of the war. Before this great military campaign, however, had reached its height, further to the north the Russians had given evidence of unequalled chivalry, when Samsonov with an army of several hundred thousand, reckless of all military precedents and precautions and regardless of the safety of his Army had plunged from Poland westward into East Prussia to create a diversion which might save the French upon the Marne by distracting from the German forces confronting them. Samsonov I had the pleasure of knowing in Manchuria where he commanded the Cavalry upon the Russian left. He was a soldier without fear and without reproach. He accomplished the purpose for which he was sent, he enabled the French to win the Battle of the Marne, but at Tannenberg his Army was literally destroyed and he himself and his Chief of Staff were killed by the German hordes which, but for his movement, would have been upon the Western Front.

Thus the first period of the war brought great glory to my friends the Russians.

The second period brought them terrible reverses. In 1915 in order to save to herself [and] her ally Austria, Germany began a great campaign against the Russians in Galicia and Poland. These were the days of which you have read when the Russian Divisions retreated without ammunition; when men joined the colors in great numbers to replace the frightful losses without rifles; when there wasn't a chance for these brave men, even though skillfully led, to resist the terrible onslaughts that were being made upon them.

Grand Duke Nicholaés[45] has won as great military distinction for his success in withdrawing this almost unarmed army as he had previously won in his remarkable advance into the Carpathians, and for the fact that these armies were unarmed Sukhomlinov, the Minister of War, was tried and, I believe, executed. In my judgment, however, it was not the treason of Sukhomlinov which caused the terrible debacle of the second period. Rather it was the circumstance that the character of modern warfare, changed somewhat during the course of the great war, resolved itself into a frightful competition as to which of the opposing sides could manufacture and direct into the lines of its enemies the greater number of projectiles. Manufacturing nations like Germany, France and England could meet the new condition. Russia, because she was not a manufacturing nation, could not. At the beginning Russia was as well prepared for war as France and better prepared for war than England, but she was not a manufacturing nation and could not take an equal part in the competition of production that began to mark the war during the second period.

Incidentally I may say that Sukhomlinov was tried for treason while I was in Petrograd and I heard some of the evidence given at his trial. One interesting piece of evidence was as follows: Just before the war began late in July, 1914, the Czar and the Kaiser were said to have been in close conference by telephone. The Kaiser told the Czar that war could be averted only if he would stop the mobilization of his troops which had just begun. The Czar sent for Sukhomlinov, the Minister of War, and told him to stop the mobilization of his troops at once. Sukhomlinov informed the Czar, according to evidence, that this could not be done. The machinery that has been devised and provided permitted the inauguration of the mobilization but provided no way for checking it once it had begun. The Czar was utterly unable to induce Sukhomlinov to admit that there was any way to stop the mobilization, and it was this guilt in the eyes of the Kerensky Court rather than the lack of preparation of Russia that led to Sukhomlinov's conviction.

I might repeat also what I heard many times in Russia and from many persons, but which I can not myself vouch for. Grand Duke Nicholas was said to have been at the head of a party which expected to profit by the war to the extent of being able as an incident to it to put the Czar off the throne and replace him with Nicholas himself. Sukhomlinov was said to have belonged to this party of the Grand Duke and some said that it was by reason of this affiliation that he did not desire to stop the mobilization. This bit of gossip, however, may have been entirely propaganda in its nature—and even German propaganda. It was very hard in Russia to sift one kind of propaganda from another.

When I was in Russia in 1904 and 1905 the most remarkable man whom I met was Alexander Guchkov. I had the good fortune to be on the train with him from Petrograd to Mukden—a three weeks journey at that time—and I came to know him very well. He educated me in matters Russian. . . .[46] In a way I knew from Guchkov that a sort of race was on between these two revolutionary elements to see which should control the State when czarism disappeared. Afterward I knew that this race endured until the day that the Czar abdicated—indeed it endured a year longer than that until the Reds, the Bolsheviks, won the race at least for a time in the winter of 1917–1918. Before I started for Russia with the Root Mission in the spring of 1917 I was, of course, tremendously interested to know that my friend Guchkov who, since I had first known him, had become successively the leader of a political party, the Octobrists; the President of the Duma; Chairman of the Committee of National Defense; the head of the Red Cross; and finally the Minister of War in the revolutionary cabinet. He had been the very man who placed before the Czar the document, signing which he abdicated. He was among the leaders of the conservative revolutionists, and there was desperate anxiety among the latter for years lest the Russian people, so many of them ignorant, should fall under the radical leadership of such as now control in Moscow and Petrograd. These men did not desire that the Romanov family should be lost to Russia. Their plan was that the Czar should abdicate for himself and that his son should rule with a regent of the Royal Family. This plan the Czar refused to follow. He resigned in behalf of himself and his son as well. Probably if he had been a strong man, seeing the highest interests of his country, and possibly of his family, he would have yielded to the urging of Guchkov and Russia might have become a limited monarchy. Probably in such event the Reds might have been successfully withstood; for such classes as the officers of the Army and of the Navy, landholders and most of the educated classes would have had a rallying point. When the Czar failed, then it seemed quite certain to men like Guchkov that the radicals would eventually gain possession of the State.

When I arrived in Russia with the Root Mission, one of the first things I did was to bring Guchkov and Mr. Root together. Guchkov had recently lost his portfolio to Kerensky and Mr. Root, who did not know Guchkov as I did, suspected that a natural disappointment might have had something to do with his pessimistic views. I thought I knew better, for I knew Guchkov to be a patriot of the loftiest type who could submerge himself and his own ambitions in planning for his country. I am sorry to say that not all of the Russians who saw Mr. Root were of this type. Only a few weeks in Russia, with his visitors necessarily picked out largely by Kerensky and Tereshchenko, the Minister of Foreign Affairs, Mr. Root naturally enough heard much that was favorable to Kerensky, to his political sagacity, to the probable long endurance of his Government and to the advisability of loaning money to the Russians as a steadfast and dependable ally. Certainly the words of Guchkov in the spring and early summer of 1917 were remarkably prophetic. I know not where he is today or whether he be dead or alive, but if I could hear now from Guchkov what may be expected in the future for this once great country, I should confidently assume tonight the role of prophet.

I do not mean to say that Kerensky and Tereshchenko, the two leading figures of the summer and fall of 1917, were willfully weak or willfully deceptive. You have read much of Kerensky, and of Tereshchenko too I suppose, so I shall describe them but briefly. . . .[47]

. . . When we first came into the war, perhaps we might have saved the situation in Russia by sending a few divisions to the Russian front. Certainly we would have lessened the force of the propaganda which said that the British and the Americans were but utilizing the poor Russian soldiers to pull their chestnuts out of the fire, that they themselves were furnishing money but doing very little fighting anywhere. When we let that chance go by perhaps the situation might have been saved if the allied diplomats, with the great influence which they had over Kerensky and Tereshchenko, had compelled these latter to permit such men as Kornilov to sustain and restore the discipline of the Army. When Kerensky witnessed without action the departure of discipline, it became evident to many of us in Russia that very little chance remained that Russia would stay in the war.

As early as on August 7, 1917, I cabled home: "It is at least an even chance that coming events may take Russia out of the war within the next few months. Our larger war plans should be made accordingly."[48]

Following the unfortunate Kornilov episode, when a very brave and patriotic general, [?] seeing the inevitable advent of Bolshevism unless strong Government could be introduced, attempted unsuccessfully to seize the power, the strength of the Bolsheviks waxed greater and greater. Perhaps you do not know what the Bolsheviks are, notwithstanding all that has been written about them. Originally they constituted a faction of the Social Democratic Party which differed from the Menshevik faction principally as to the speed with which it sought to introduce a Marxian socialistic regime. Its members were internationalists of the most uncompromising type, and being internationalists they were naturally pacifists where international wars were concerned. The Bolsheviks go the whole way. They seek at once to confiscate all land and industry to the State. They would require all persons to labor, seeking thus to abolish what they call parasites. They believe that only the proletariat can be trusted to make and administer the laws,—but they would abolish all classes except the proletariat—thus promoting, as they claim, both economic and political justice. They think much more of economic equality, however, than of political justice and regard the latter as a means to the former as an end. They would prefer a Bolshevik dictator to a democratic form of government. But if the proletariat were organized, class conscious and politically supreme, they would be willing to employ democratic practices to attain their ends, provided so-called parasites were debarred from voting. They are ruthless in their methods and [act] regardless of human suffering. While pacifists in theory, they do not condemn the use of force if employed to secure the supremacy of the proletariat. They regard patriotism as a weakness and would engage in no international war unless one purpose of the other side was to suppress or oppose their own regime or their own theories. Being fanatical, extreme and uncompromising, the Bolsheviks can not be used to further the interest of any second party except under circumstances where their own interest and that of the second partly run parallel.

I never knew as much about Lenin as I felt I did about Trotsky. In my judgment Trotsky was never under the control of the German Government or the German General Staff. I have no doubt that the hatred of Trotsky for such German agencies was as bitter and implacable as one can possibly imagine. Upon the other hand I have no doubt that Trotsky and some of his associates that came back to Russia in 1917 were in frequent communication with German socialists and would-be revolutionists, and that the subsequent conduct of the Bolsheviks in Russia was to a large extent influenced by these communications. Doubtless the German revolutionists believed that the course later pursued by the Bolsheviks in Russia would promote revolution in Germany.[49]

The most important communication I had with Trotsky was in an interview the day before he sent representatives to Brest-Litovsk to negotiate with the Germans for an armistice prior to a peace. . . .[50] I tried to show him how history would regard him if he, who had so much to do now with the de facto Government of a country which had been our friend and ally for years, should turn upon us so unnecessarily.

In the course of this interview I assured Trotsky that if Russia should find herself again engaged in active hostilities with the Central Powers, it was very probable that Russia would receive assistance in large measure from the allies. Trotsky seemed to be very receptive to my representations. He promised that no arrangements would be made which would not detain the Germans and Austrians upon the Eastern front during the period of the armistice. He promised to send experts with his representatives to Brest-Litovsk and he told me that I might assure my Government that these things would be done and in all matters the interests of the allies would be protected in so far as such protection did not conflict with his intentions to bring about a peace. To give the devil his due, I must say that Trotsky did all in his power to carry out these promises. I am sure that my interview with Trotsky and other influences that were brought to bear upon the Bolshevik Government led to a prolongation of proceedings at Brest-Litovsk for many months. During this time, until the middle of March, 1918, the Central Powers were obliged to keep their forces upon the Eastern front unavailable for their spring drives in France.

During August and September, 1917, we military men in Russia, of America and of all the allied powers, devoted our efforts, unsuccessfully, toward securing measures for the restoration of discipline in the Russian Army. It was perhaps natural that men like Kerensky and even men like the diplomatic representatives of the Allies in Russia, should think discipline a much less important matter than did we soldiers. Our lack of success in these efforts was sickening and terrible, for before we knew how rapidly troops could be transported to France it looked as though the issue of the war might depend upon Russia's course and that depended entirely upon the state of discipline in the Russian Army. . . .[51]

When the Bolsheviks did get in it became necessary as quickly as possible to estimate the situation, with a view to preventing if possible, or postponing, the making of a separate peace. Were the Bolsheviks going to stay in power during the critical period of the war? Nothing could well be done until this question was answered, and it was quickly and correctly answered in the affirmative, largely through the agency of the very efficient secret service organization which Thompson and Robins had formed a month or two earlier, with Thompson's money, to combat the Bolsheviks. . . .

The Brest-Litovsk treaty was not approved by the Russians until the middle of March, 1918. If this treaty had been consummated several months earlier and with less friction than developed between the negotiating parties, the Germans would have had from five to six hundred thousand more men in their spring drive against the channel ports and Paris. Considering how the issue hung in the balance, it is difficult to believe that this additional force might not have changed the result. (Among those most responsible for this result, as I have pointed out above, were Colonels Thompson and Robins and certain other members of our Red Cross Mission to Russia, who have had much obloquy cast upon them by persons who themselves should have done something to prevent the Russian debacle but did not. Justice seems to demand that the services in particular of Colonel William B. Thompson and of Colonel Raymond Robins should be now pointed out by someone who was officially on the ground, who knew the history of those days, and who has no motive now to misrepresent their services.)[52]

I have arrived at the end of my talk and yet I have told you but a small fraction of what I would like to feel that all Americans should know about the Russian situation. In closing I beg of you not to lose all patience with the Russian people. Some day they will work out their own salvation. For the most part their troubles have arisen through an excess of idealism engendered perhaps by the vast solitudes of their steppes and forests. They did not know, as we more practical Americans know, what I saw this afternoon so well expressed in one of our most popular periodicals.

"The need of the country is not more idealism, but more pragmatism; not communism, but common sense. Radical idealism is always promising more than it can pay and then defaulting. It is always going to make good sixty days after date and then stepping out from under. . . .

In the end, common sense always has to straighten out the messes and pay the notes of radical idealists; to feed the starving and bury the dead of the reds. Common sense not only means well, but does well. Though its best is not perfection, it is pretty good and getting better."[53]

PERSONAL
MAY 20, 1920

MR. E. L. PACKER,
DEPARTMENT OF STATE, WASHINGTON, D.C.

My dear Packer:

I have received your letter of May 6, 1920 and the several publications of the State Department relating to the Far Eastern question forwarded by you in separate package.

There have been several times in the past when I have thought that something might be done to ameliorate the Russian situation at reasonable cost. Today I am in very great doubt as to whether anything can be accomplished until there is some change in the situation. The following, however, are facts which I think we must start with in any solution of the problem:

(1) The Japanese have but one purpose in connection with their presence in Siberia and Manchuria. They doubtless intend to take possession of and to retain under one pretext or another the whole of Manchuria, of Mongolia, of all Siberia and of Lake Baikal. Lake Baikal and the northeasterly projection of the Gobi Desert would form an excellent frontier for their continental possessions making it easy for them to protect themselves against any assailants from the West. There is no limit to Japanese ambition and hardly any limit to the cunning with which they pursue such ambition. I am not blaming the Japanese either. Nations as such are rarely blameworthy and in any event, it is idle to blame nations. They, like trees, possess instincts for growth and, like trees, they blossom and they wither. Within the Japanese today lies the greatest impetus for growth that is resident in any nation. They will dominate Eastern Asia within the next 20 years and perhaps they will be satisfied with such domination. The Russians, however, will constantly fear that the Japanese will not be satisfied with Lake Baikal as a frontier, but will desire to penetrate always further westward until they reach the Urals. At any rate, we may always know that the Russians will fear and dislike the Japanese and if the latter are to be limited in their westward course, it probably must be by a strong Russia.

(2) On the other side of Russia lies Poland with probably almost as great an imperial instinct as Japan, Poland, of course, being pushed along in her contest with Russia by France.

(3) The Russians are very amenable to expressions of sincere sentiment. The 14 points of the President, if they had happened to be stated two months earlier than they were, would probably have kept Russia together and in the War. Russia can still be influenced by honest expressions of good will which, in themselves, must demonstrate a lofty idealism. For example, I think it would be possible in connection with such an expression by our President to guide the Russian people toward a Constitutional Convention even though the Bolsheviks remain in power until such Convention is held. It would be necessary, in such a Message as I have in mind, for the President to point out the value of democratic institutions to the lower classes. In no way except by democratic processes can the proletariat retain with certainty what they may possess, or secure modifications in government in their own interests. It may take time to educate people to an ability to take effective part in

government under democratic institutions, but there is no other safety for them in the long run.

Starting with the above statements of fact, tentatively, I would propose the following program, which is by no means satisfactory, but which seems to be the only one at this time:

1. By diplomatic methods limit as much as possible the Japanese seizure in Siberia. Possibly it may be necessary to let them take certain parts under agreement to take no more, but this latter should not be done until, in some way, there is assent by Russia to such a course. It might be possible to retain the friendship of Japan and of Russia while acting as intermediary in this matter.

2. Stop the war being waged by Poland, if it is possible to do so, through representations by our own Country and by England addressed to France and to Poland.

3. Open the gates to trade between Russia and the outside world and bring influence to bear upon Russia by such expressions as I have referred to herein-before to secure unity among the different elements of the Russian people through the agency of a Constitutional Convention.

The above program does not look very promising, or very definite, and the time may come when our best course there may be more readily pointed out than today. We have made some tremendous mistakes with regard to Russia, and by we I mean the rest of the world and not alone America, but I believe that if we follow the policy above outlined, at least for the moment, we will be making no further mistake.

Yours faithfully,[54]

SEPTEMBER 20, 1920
CONFIDENTIAL

MR. E. L. PARKER,
DEPARTMENT OF STATE,
WASHINGTON, D. C.

My dear Mr. Parker:—

I have received your interesting letter of July 22, 1920, in which you invite me, speaking for your Chief and yourself, to write again on Russian matters. I was delighted when the President found opportunity for his recent statement on the Polish-Russian situation. There doesn't seem any immediate step worth taking, at least on the basis of any facts known to me, although consideration following may be suggested of a line of honest propaganda, directed at influencing <u>every element</u> of an idealistic, sentimental and relatively simple people. In what follows I have tried to use expressions and lines of thought which in my opinion would be most appealing to the Russian people as a whole.

Without being either hypocritical or dishonest I think America can express herself in accordance with the loftiest formulae, and thus accomplish most. We must preach, for Russia, internal peace; the importance of order for efficiency in government as well as in production and distribution; the ultimate efficiency and fairness of a universal ballot; "love one another". The Russians love to be preached to, if the preacher be sincere and actuated by lofty motives. We should lose no opportunity thus to appeal to Russia. Our President knows how to find occasion and words for such propaganda, if indeed it be fair to apply to such honest teaching a word that commonly is applied to specious lying. Besides preaching I think we should continue to give practical evidence as we have begun to do, that we are on the side of the Russian people when it comes to encroachments upon their land, whether by Japanese or Poles, and that we are willing to engage in peaceful trade with them.

The <u>purpose</u> of the United States in Russian matters is largely inspired by the heart. We see a great people with whom we are related by extraordinary ties of past friendship and by bonds of similarity in individual disposition and national environment. We see such a great people cruelly suffering and our purpose and ambition in Russian matters extend no further than to alleviate that suffering. Our single desire is to see the Russian people restored to a state of peace, prosperity and happiness. . . .

. . . Being thus long and whole-heartedly devoted to the principles of democracy we are embarrassed at present in our contact with the Russian people by the circumstance that today it seems to be among the policies of those governing Russia, by force and propaganda to attempt the destruction of our system of government by the majority. We frankly are unwilling to risk the security and the future of our own people, as the great majority of us see it, but within that limitation we stand ready in so far as in us lies to alleviate the distress of our Russian friends.

We should continue to announce our position that, however our theories of government or the theories of other nations may differ from those of any Russian element, nevertheless it would be wrong through force of arms to interfere with internal affairs in Russia; that Russia in this time of her travail should not be despoiled of her lands; and that the world should trade with the Russian people.

I cannot help thinking that the time may come, not indeed when we can fully recognize the Bolshevik government (unless bolshevism be indorsed by a fairly chosen constitutional assembly which in my opinion is well nigh impossible), but when by a sort of careful intercourse we can induce it to lessen the number of its follies and atrocities and perhaps assist in persuading it to such an act of renunciation as the calling of a constitutional assembly. Only perhaps after inaugurating some such intercourse can we know best how we can help in the most terrible situation the world has ever seen, and possibly constitute ourselves an important element in its amelioration.

Certainly we would not profit by the presence in Russia of any diplomat camouflaged or otherwise, of the decayed and selfish politician type.

You know and I know that the Stevens Railway Mission never really accomplished anything in Russia. During 1917 it was only a laughing stock to our allies and a continual source of their reproaches. Any real help rendered in railway matters would be otherwise than an operating or directing force. Perhaps one big, philosophic, statesmanlike railway man as an adviser might some day be both helpful and appreciated.

Military men can go anywhere and have intercourse with anybody without committing their governments. So can Red Cross agents. So, less certainly, can commercial agents. I do not doubt that German and British agents of these descriptions are over-running Russia now, probably performing no services of value to Russia and certainly none to ourselves. I may be all wrong but I think perhaps I might go to Russia without exciting the suspicion of any element there that I would interfere in internal political affairs or have any purpose [except] to help along lines as to which all elements would approve, and to report home how America might help in not too costly fashion. I have been twice in Russia and I know all kinds of Russians and have more hope for them and a better opinion of them than most. In mentioning myself in this connection I remember that General March, Chief of Staff, told me once that if ever the time seemed to me to come when I could serve my country well in Russia, he would desire to send me there. In this connection I may say I am still only slowly recuperating from a heart attack following the influenza, and if I went to Russia at this time I should not be very hopeful of returning.

Mr. Thomas Thacher, who was on the last Red Cross Mission to Petrograd, would head a new mission to Russia with great intelligence and success, in my opinion. Perhaps the time has not yet come thus to get in touch with Russia, but I cannot help thinking very earnestly that it has.

Yours, sincerely,

NOVEMBER 1, 1920

TO: CHIEF OF MILITARY INTELLIGENCE DIVISION,
GENERAL STAFF, U.S.A. WASHINGTON, D.C.
SUBJECT: SERVICES IN RUSSIA DURING THE WAR.

I understand that certain Military Attachés have received the Distinguished Service Medal for services abroad during the war. As I was both Military Attaché and Chief of Military Mission in Russia during the war, I desire to present my case to you in the event of my being considered for the Distinguished Service Medal.

There are certain facts in my case that perhaps are not known to you, some of which might indicate "meritorious service," some that my duty in Russia was "of great responsibility," and others that my service in Russia might fairly be held to have been rendered "with the Army of the United States."

When I was detached from the "Root" Mission and left behind in Russia, in July, 1917, it was in pursuance of an order, signed by the Chief of Staff, General Scott, who was present in Petrograd, of which copy is enclosed herewith. It will be observed that I was appointed Chief of the American Military Mission to Russia, as well as Military Attaché with the American Embassy, etc. The order long subsequently issued relieving me from duty in Petrograd simply relieved me as Military attaché. For this and various other reasons I am constrained to believe that certain War Department records are defective, indicating that my services were limited to those of an Attaché with an Embassy. While in Russia, however, subsequent to July 9, 1917, the date of the enclosed order, I was recognized by all of the representatives of our allies; by the Russians, and by myself as well, as possessing far greater responsibilities than those of Military Attaché, —to wit those of General Officer serving in time of war as Chief of the Military Mission of my country to an allied nation, the importance of whose military forces and the uncertainty of whose conduct lent the greatest importance to my actions and judgment, and especially to the correctness of the information I obtained and sent home, and in effect charged me with very great responsibilities indeed.

As Chief of the American Military Mission to Russia, I had a group of American Officers under my command, and I was the chief liaison officer between the Russian Army and the Army of the United States. Certainly the Army of the United States had necessarily to furnish a small (very small) fraction of itself to perform this liaison function. It was an army function, and while performing it I was certainly serving "with the Army of the United States" as much as was a liaison officer serving with a British or a French Army, Corps or Division. This fact has been established by the award to me of a clasp for Russia on my Victory Medal.

In accordance with the order of which copy is enclosed, I sat upon the allied Commission which passed upon all questions of manufacturing and tonnage priority for articles of military or other vital necessity required by Russia from beyond the seas.

Among the items of vitally important information sent home by me was one in a cablegram dated August 7, 1917, to the effect that —

> "It is at least an even chance that coming events may take Russia out of the war within the next few months. Our larger war plans should be made accordingly."

Our Ambassador, at this time and long subsequent thereto, was, I have every reason to believe, informing our Government that Russia would stay in the war "as long as we would." It is to be noted that as Chief of the Military Mission I was in a sense independent of the Ambassador and responsible to the War Department. It was of course important that I "get along" with the Ambassador, but not of course to the extent of sending in erroneous or false information.

Attention is also invited to the following extracts from reports of mine to the War Department:

September 3, 1917 —

November 14, 1917 —[55]

It will be noted that in my cablegram of November 14, 1917, I suggested "the fourteen point" pronouncement of the President, which, as propaganda, had a great deal to do with winning the war. I do not maintain that the President acted on my suggestion, although I have no doubt it was before him when he acted, inasmuch as I appended to my cablegram a request which should have insured such a result. I do know this, however,—that subsequent to its despatch I discussed my cablegram with the gentleman in Petrograd who was our "publicity agent," representing Mr. Creel's bureau, who, after seeing my cablegram, although some time thereafter, sent a similar recommendation to Washington, which is reported in the press to have resulted in the vitally important "fourteen point" statement of the President.[56] If the President could have been sufficiently advised at a period early enough to have issued this statement in November instead of in January, it is quite possible that the pro-war Russians might have suppressed the Bolshevik uprising early in its course.[57]

In another cablegram sent shortly subsequent to the one first mentioned above, in response to a message from the War Department directing me to report whether Rumania could be relied upon to stay in the war, I was able to convey the correct information that Rumania, although well disposed herself, would be obliged to withdraw from the war when Russia did, and that the latter action was to be expected. I have reason to believe that a long time elapsed before reports from other sources ceased to contradict the correct information I was able to furnish.

The general purport of my cables, after the Bolshevik ascendancy began, was to the effect that the latter would endure during the period of the war (this contrary to the cabled views of our Embassy).

On December 1, 1917 (with the assent of our Ambassador and after discussing the matter with the British Ambassador with the knowledge and approval of our Ambassador) I had a long interview with Trotsky the day before he departed for Brest-Litovsk to begin negotiations for an armistice with representatives of the Central Powers, with results which I duly reported, and which, not wishing to exaggerate my services, I can nevertheless fairly assert were at least in some small degree influential in setting Trotsky's mind in opposition to the minds of our Enemies, so that in the Armistice protocol he required that the Central Power troops remain in position on the Eastern front and so that he subsequently refused to conclude a peace at Brest-Litovsk, broke off negotiations with representatives of the Central Powers, and in March, 1918, opposed peace before the Soviet at Moscow, in opposition to Lenin, although Lenin had his way.

Considering that the German drives beginning in March, 1918, were so alarming in their threats of defeat to the allied arms before the Americans were present in sufficient numbers to do their share, I cannot but think in all modesty that anyone who did anything, however little, to lessen the number of men the Germans were able to bring to bear on the Western Front in March, 1918, may be entitled to be among the many who are recognized as having performed "meritorious service."

My dear old Fellow:[58]

What wonderful weather we're having! I never saw so glorious a climate, although I'm troubled much by our world.

Your mother has gone to dine (lunch?) with the Pines—from Chicago—who live about 20 miles from here. They have 7,000 acres and—a place at Lake Forest so you may know them. I declined but took a nice motor ride with Mr. Potter. Mr. and Mrs. Forgan took your mother with them, and the other evening we dined with the Forgans, who were entertaining the Pines here. You know how I like old people—well, Mr. Potter is my present favorite I have a standing invitation to lunch with him.

I enclose an orange blossom.

Some Harvard men dropped in here the other day—a Percy Howe of my class and a Mr. Wood of 1885, who had a son in your class.

> Love to all—
> Faithfully,

. . . I'm reviewing Haig's book for the *Nation*.
If I only had a house now I might be able to write "my book."[59]

Epilogue

Judson's book on his mission in Russia was never written. His death in 1923 came too soon. But Judson's narrative and analysis of this important subject can readily be surmised. On the basis of his personal papers and official reports, the contemporary reader can gain an appreciation for his astute observations of a most complex situation. Responding to the spirit of his father's wishes, Clay Judson put his father's papers in the public domain. It was an act of courage in the late 1940s, when cold war hysteria and McCarthyism demanded a high price from anyone who chose to look at Soviet Russia and the U.S.-Soviet relationship dispassionately and objectively.

It is hoped that this collection of Judson's papers, hitherto seen by only a dozen individuals in their archival home, will help draw renewed attention to this subject and further our understanding of the Russian-American relationship.

Notes

INTRODUCTION

Editor's note: "WCD" represents the papers of the War College Division/Staff or Warcolstaff in Judson's correspondence, which are contained in RG 120 and 165 in the National Archives, Washington, D.C.

1. The Root Mission, under the leadership of Elihu Root, the former secretary of state (and secretary of war between 1899 and 1904, at the time Judson was military attaché and observer of the Russo-Japanese War), was one of several such delegations of U.S. men sent to Russia within weeks of the United States' entry into the war to solidify the U.S.-Russian military alliance.

2. The following documents the "Military Record of William V. Judson," prepared on or about 6 June 1911 (WJP).

> Military History.—Kadet at the Military Academy, June 15, 1884, to June 11, 1888, when he was graduated third in his class and promoted in the Army to
> Add. Second Lieut., Corps of Engineers, June 11, 1888
> Second Lieut., Corps of Engineers, July 23, 1888.
> Served: with Battalion of Engineers at Willet's Point, N.Y., since Sept. 30, 1888 and under instruction at the Engineer School of Application; on Special duty as Aide-de-Camp to the President of the United States [Benjamin Harrison], Apr. 28, to May 2, 1889. . . .
> Captain, Corps of Engineers, July 5, 1898
> Chief Engineer, Department of Puerto Rico, and President of Board of Public Works, Puerto Rico, July, 1889 to Aug. 1900; in charge of river and harbor improvements and fortification construction, gulf coast and Alabama and Georgia, Aug. 1900 to Nov. 1901; Instructor, U.S. Engineer School, member of River and Harbor Board, Chief Engineer, Department of the East, Assistant to the Chief of Engineers, etc., Nov., 1901 to March, 1904; Military Attaché, U.S. Embassy, Russia, and with Russian Army in Russo-Japanese War, March, 1904 to July, 1905; in charge of harbor improvements, west shore of Lake Michigan, etc., Lighthouse Engineer, Lake Michigan, and member of various Boards, July 1905 to March, 1909;
> Major, Corps of Engineers, March 2, 1906
> Engineer Commissioner, District of Columbia, since March 15, 1909, (one of the three Commissioners charged with the government of the District of Columbia.)

The following "Statement of the Military Service of William V. Judson" was prepared on 23 May 1924 in the Adjutant General's Office of the War Department in Washington, D.C. by L. Wahl, Brigadier General, Acting Adjutant General (WJP, box 6).

Cadet, M.A.	June 15, 1884
Add'l 2nd Lieut., Engrs.	June 11, 1888
2nd Lieut.	July 23, 1893
1st Lieut.	May 18, 1893
Captain	July 5, 1898
Major	March 2, 1906
Lieut. Colonel	March 2, 1912
Colonel	May 15, 1917
Retired	Aug. 31, 1922

In Federal Service Other Than the Permanent Establishment:

Brig. Gen., N.A.	Aug. 5, 1917
Accepted	Aug. 31, 1917
Honorably discharged	Feb. 5, 1919

Graduate, Engr. School of Application, 1891. A.M. Harvard, 1911.

3. William V. Judson, "Strategic Value of Her West Indian Possessions to the United States," *Annals of the American Academy of Political and Social Sciences* 19 (Jan.–May 1902): 383–91. Published version in WJP.

4. See, for example, a portion of Judson's letter to Ambassador McCormick in Petersburg, 26 July 1904, written from this post.

5. Judson to Robert McCormick, 26 July 1904 (WJP, box 1), also in Weyant, "General William V. Judson" (15).

6. William V. Judson, "Report of Captain William V. Judson, Corps of Engineers, Observer with the Russian Forces in Manchuria," *Reports of Military Observers Attached to the Armies in Manchuria during the Russo-Japanese War,* part 5, no. 8 (Washington, D.C.: Government Printing Office, 1907). Published version in WJP.

7. In a 10 April 1919 letter to Burleson, a close family friend and steady correspondent, Judson wrote, "because you had something—or everything—to do with my going to Russia, I am going to put modesty aside and tell you what I really think some of us accomplished at Petrograd. . . ." See the Dramatis Personae for more information on Burleson.

8. U.S. ambassador to Russia, David Francis, to Lansing, telegram, 10 July 1917, no. 1483, WCD 10166-1, RG 165/NA. Scott to Sec. of War Baker, 10 July 1917, WCD 10166-1.

9. John F. Stevens, see the Dramatis Personae.

10. Judson documented the size and distribution of responsibilities of the British and French diplomatic and military missions in his telegram of 19 July 1917. ("The British have more than sixty officers, and the French more than half as many.") See the full text in chapter 2.

11. Newton D. Baker, Secretary of War, to Robert Lansing, Secretary of State, 24 December 1917, relieving Judson as military attaché. This and subsequent communications ordering Judson back to Washington made no mention of his additional title and responsibilities as chief of the U.S. Military Mission to Russia. WCD 10166-27, RG/165.

12. See the "Statement of the Military Service of William V. Judson" (23 May 1924) in note 2 above.

13. Judson's official orders included his appointment as military attaché to the United States' embassy at Petrograd as well as "chief of the American Military Mis-

sion to Russia, observer in connection with military operations in which Russia is engaged, and the military representative of the United States Government in all matters connected with the supply to Russia of materials and personnel for use during the war." Gen. Scott to Judson, 9 July 1917; Judson to Chief, War College Division, General Staff, 19 July 1917, no 1175 (WJP, box 4).

14. See Kennan, *Decision to Intervene;* Kennan, *Russia Leaves the War;* McFadden, *Alternative Paths;* Salzman, *Reform and Revolution;* Ullman, *Anglo-Soviet Relations;* Unterberger, *American Intervention;* Weyant, "General William V. Judson"; Williams, William Appleman, *American-Russian Relations;* Williams, William Appleman, "Raymond Robbins and Russian-American Relations."

15. William A. Williams to Clay Judson, 18 Sept. 1953; "Uncatalogued Material Recently Added to the Judson Papers by Judson's Granddaughter Alice Ryerson Hayes" (WJP). Plans for such a study were first broached by Williams in a letter to Clay Judson on 4 August 1950, at the time Williams had just completed his doctoral dissertation on Raymond Robins. Williams's plans to write a full Judson biography were abandoned, as were his similar plans for a study of Robins's life. Williams chose larger canvases to paint.

CHAPTER 1

1. This report was published in *Annals of the American Academy of Political and Social Sciences* 19 (Jan.–May 1902): 383–91.

2. This letter was written by Clay Judson, William V. Judson's only child. He became a lawyer after the completion of his military service. As executor of his father's estate, he was responsible for placing his father's letters and papers in the Manuscripts Division of the Newberry Library in Chicago.

3. Robert S. McCormick, United States Ambassador to Russia.

4. Thus begins page ten of Judson's letter. The first nine pages deal with logistics, troop numbers, and their transport on both the Japanese and Russian sides— essentially a technical discussion.

5. These *x*es are Judson's notation for a break in the narrative.

6. Surrounding with troops to prevent escape or entry.

7. This speech appears to have been delivered in Milwaukee, Wisconsin, and is dated 20 December 1905 in Judson's handwriting. The excerpt here follows a long analysis of the role and responsibilities of the professional soldier.

8. This ninety-nine-page report was published on 1 March 1907 as the "Report of Captain William V. Judson, Corps of Engineers, Observer with the Russian Forces in Manchuria," in *Reports of Military Observers Attached to the Armies in Manchuria During the Russo-Japanese War.* Most of the report focuses on technicalities of trench construction and distribution and other matters of military engineering. Only the introductory two pages of the typescript and the concluding paragraph are reproduced here.

9. A speech to the Society of Colonial Dames, circa 1906. This Russo-Japanese War eyewitness account, so reminiscent of the western front of World War I, was the basis of Judson's warnings about the war-of-attrition nature of modern defensive battle. The typescript for the speech is incomplete in the William V. Judson Papers. It begins as quoted here on a page numbered 11 (in pencil) and continues for six pages. Judson's title, as given here, appears on the second page. Judson's handwritten corrections appear throughout. The 1906 date, with which I concur, is the suggestion of the archivist of the Judson Papers.

10. This forty-two-page paper, which was prepared in 1914 after the outbreak of war in Europe, was used by Judson, in abbreviated form, as the basis for a number of his public addresses. One such address was given on 12 May 1914 at the Union League Club of Chicago, the text of which is in the William V. Judson Papers.

In a 4 November 1921 letter to William B. Thompson, who headed the American Red Cross Commission to Russia, Judson wrote of this preparedness article:

> I have endeavored to show that as a result of the adoption of such a military policy as I have outlined above we should lessen the chance of war through the provision of defensive without aggressive strength. No one would care to attack us, while we should be unable to proceed across the sea to attack others.
>
> Finally I have tried to show that, as the result of the adoption of such a policy, we would not lessen our ability to secure justice through diplomatic negotiations.

11. This is a reference to the boundary dispute between British Guiana and Venezuela in which the Cleveland administration—particularly Secretary of State Richard L. Olney—intervened. Claiming that "the United States is practically sovereign on this continent" on the basis of the Monroe Doctrine, the United States acted in the very arrogant and bellicose manner, spurred on by partisan party politics, that concerned Judson. But, since the United States had not yet become embroiled in overseas possessions, acquired in the Spanish-American War, and the associated imperial rivalries, war was not a serious concern in spite of the diplomatic affront.

CHAPTER 2

1. On U.S. Ambassador David Francis's and U.S. Consul General in Moscow Maddin Summers's objections to the Root Mission, see Kennan, *Russia Leaves the War*, chapters 1, 2, 5, and 7. On their objections and opposition to the political role of the American Red Cross Commission, see Salzman, *Reform and Revolution*, chapters 10–18.

2. Another brief report on Guchkov was prepared by Judson on 21 August 1918, for the U.S. Army chief of staff. This second report (to be found in chapter 5), prepared after Judson's return from revolutionary Russia, should be compared with the first report, provided here.

3. President Wilson gave his message to Congress requesting a declaration of war on 2 April 1917. Judson learned of his appointment as military attaché to the Root Mission on or about 15 April, and departed from Washington for Petrograd on 15 May 1917. It was in connection with his appointment, and before his departure for Russia, that Judson wished to inform his superiors of the details of his personal connection to a high-ranking minister of the Provisional Government.

4. The island was entirely in Russian hands after 1875 and until 1905, when the southern half was ceded to Japan in the Peace of Portsmouth, which ended the Russo-Japanese War. In 1945, in the closing days of World War II, it was reoccupied by the Red Army of Soviet Russia.

5. The zemstvo assemblies were popularly elected representative bodies, divided according to social and class status and created through the constitutional initiatives of Czar Alexander II in the 1870s. Supporters of the zemstvos hoped for constitutional monarchy and for the reforms promised by such evolutionary methods.

6. Judson was traveling to the west coast from Washington, D.C., en route, via Japan and Vladivostok, to Petrograd. He was serving as military attaché and was traveling with his Root Mission colleagues.

7. Here and elsewhere, only individuals not listed in the Dramatis Personae are identified in the notes. James H. Glennon was a rear admiral in the U.S. Navy. The "medical doctor" is Surgeon Holton C. Curl, U.S. Navy.

8. Judson's official title while in service on the Root Mission to Russia. So reads his calling card used during the mission.

9. Clay Judson.

10. Nearly all of Judson's letters to his wife, Alice, written from Russia, bear this salutation.

11. Because his appointment prolonged the separation from his wife, Judson restrained expression of his excitement and satisfaction at having been chosen for this post. In a letter to his mother, dated 23 July 1917, Judson's son, Clay, wrote: "Isn't it great to get this news from Father? and isn't it fine that he got his wish to stay over after the [Root] mission came back!" (WJP).

12. In the three months that followed, Judson did all he could in terms of requests for financial support and military aid for the Romanian cause. Aid was not forthcoming. When the Romanian capitulation to the Central Powers finally occurred in December 1917, Judson was convinced that the U.S. failure to provide that support was significantly to blame.

CHAPTER 3

1. The "July Uprising," as these "present disorders" of 17 July 1917 came to be called, resulted in the toppling of the first Provisional Government, of Prince George E. Lvov. It was replaced on 7 August by the regime of Alexander Kerensky. This more radical, second Provisional Government consisted of four Kadet, six Socialist Revolutionary, and six Menshevik ministers, who were approved by the Executive Committee of the Petrograd Soviet.

2. The island fortress of St. Peter and St. Paul on the Neva River, opposite the Winter Palace.

3. WCD 10166-15, RG 165/NA.

4. Weyant, "General William V. Judson," citing volume 2 of John J. Pershing's *My Experience in the World War* (New York: Frederick A. Stokes, 1931), 110–11, 119, points out that in July 1917, General Pershing and Allied leaders had agreed to "concentrate all possible forces on the Western Front." Hope for Russia and the eastern front as a viable military theater was relegated to a "purely defensive" position.

5. The "Michelson Commission" was the name that Judson consistently used to refer to the Russian Supply Commission, which was chaired by Gen. Michelson of the Russian general staff.

6. The persons referred to here are radical socialists, like Trotsky, who were returning to Russia from America in significant numbers to overthrow the Provisional Government.

7. As noted in the Kennan epigraph to the Introduction, as chief of the American Military Mission to Russia, Judson had responsibility to report directly to his superiors in Washington as he saw fit. Since he also served as military attaché to the American ambassador, he often shared his reports with Ambassador Francis, though

usually after they had been dispatched to the War College. Judson would often convey his Washington communications to Francis in an abbreviated form, as illustrated by this paraphrase of the previous document (WCD 10166-15, RG 165/NA).

8. See WCD 10166-5, RG 165/NA.

9. "Legation U.S.S.R. General Correspondence 1912–19," file 800, RG 84/NA.

10. Judson and other Americans in Petrograd who recommended an active American support of the Provisional Government often cited this telegram and its prescient warning. Ambassador Francis, on the other hand, refused to give credence to the reports of difficulties bordering on crisis in Russia's war-fighting capability. Judson, along with William Boyce Thompson and Raymond Robins, also warned of the influence of the soviets and the Bolsheviks and of the possibility of their revolutionary seizure of power from Kerensky's government.

11. Judson was convinced that the Russian military situation could be improved by the symbolic presence of even a small U.S. Army contingent, fighting alongside Russian soldiers. For the same reason, and because of the efficacy of airplanes along the long length of the eastern front, Judson pressed his case for the sending of some aerial units. Finally, on 3 November 1917, four days before the Bolshevik seizure of power, P. D. Lochridge of the War Department, notified Judson that planes would be sent to Russia "if there existed a government favorable to the Allies." Box 74, RG 120/NA.

12. Original cable uses the word "stop." Here, a period is used instead.

13. This note should be read in conjunction with Judson's 16 March 1918 final report (see chapter 5). Both attempt a categorization of the wide spectrum of political parties in revolutionary Russia. A notation in Judson's handwriting on the typescript reads: "Forwarded as corrected as incl. 'A' to letter #1241 to WCD [War College Department?] 11/15/17."

14. Judson's brief military note of 27 August 1917, with alternative spelling of the general's name, reads: "General Litchitsky does not yet command the North Front. There is some trouble about his appointment and meantime the command is vacant."

15. Please see Judson's 10 and 11 September additions to his 1 September letter to his wife in which he refers to the Kornilov Uprising and the prospects of civil war in Russia. This "Military Note," with its convolutions and cautious language supports Kornilov, or at least a "compromise" government of military dictatorship—a self-contradiction. Judson was not alone in that support. Nearly all Allied chiefs of military missions supported Kornilov's seizure, especially General Knox, who headed the British Mission. See discussion of this support in Salzman, *Reform and Revolution*, 192–95, 200–202. Also see chapter 5, here, for Judson's reflections on his support for Kornilov.

16. Judson has added in a note here "bad paraphrase."

17. The "Wild Division" was a nationalist, pro-czarist contingent.

18. The same information was conveyed to the War College Staff in a telegram on 21 September 1917, see WCD 10220-D-1, RG 165/NA, to which Judson added this final paragraph: "From reports I have received from secret agency, the offensive undertaken by the Germans in the North has come to a halt because of the demands of the Austrian Government that the Rumanian campaign be completed. The same reports state that the latter campaign may be resumed in Northern Moldavia and in the vicinity of Focsani, and across the Danube into Bessarabia."

19. WCD 10166-24, RG 165/NA.

20. There follows three pages of detailed discussion of supplies warehoused at Russian ports and of the organization of the Allied system of supply to Russia and the problems in the U.S. role in that system. The "recapitulation" here is on page 4.

21. WCD 10220-D-2, RG 165/NA.

22. WCD 10220-D-3, RG 165/NA.

23. Judson met with the leaders of the American Red Cross Commission to Russia on 9 August 1917, only two days after its arrival in Petrograd. William Boyce Thompson, who soon took on formal leadership of the commission, and his successor to that post, Raymond Robins, soon drew close to Judson on almost every important political issue in Russia of concern to the American community in Petrograd. It was this mutual trust that Judson reflected in his request to his superiors to put his military code and telegraphic facilities at the disposal of the Red Cross.

24. The Committee on Civic Education in Free Russia (also known as the "Breshkovsky Committee") was chaired by Catherine Breshkovsky, "Grandmother of the Russian Revolution," and contained these members: Nicholas Chaikovski, leader of the peasant cooperatives; George Lazarov, who headed a Russian revolutionary underground station in Switzerland until his return with the formation of the Provisional Government in February 1917; General Neslouchovsky, of Kerensky's own staff; and David Soskice, Kerensky's private secretary.

25. The Breshkovsky Committee.

26. WCD 10220-D-4, RG 165/NA.

27. This is the first of Judson's "Monthly Resumés." The earlier one referred to here is not in the Judson Papers.

28. WCD 10220-D-5 with correction, RG 165/NA.

29. WCD 10220-D-6, RG 165/NA. At the War Industries Board, Council of National Defense, a memo was prepared for the War College Division by Col. Palmer E. Pierce, on 2 November 1917, in response to Judson's request. Pierce was "of the opinion that no steps are necessary by our military authorities. . . . I recommend that a cablegram be sent to read substantially as follows: '. . . The purchase of supplies for foreign countries must be made through this Board. The Russian Commission know the methods that are necessary to secure the clothing asked for. It is considered advisable that in the future request for supplies come through the Russian Purchasing Commission.'" The established channels did not address the serious mistakes and problems surrounding the shipment of unnecessary goods, while desperately needed material was not sent. WCD 10220-D-60, RG 165/NA.

30. WCD 10220-D-7, RG 165/NA.

31. It is assumed that Brialmont adhered to traditional nineteenth-century strategy.

32. The sheet referred to does not appear to be in the Judson Papers, nor in the appropriate file in the National Archives. However, see the next document for a description of the Petrograd defenses.

33. WCD 10220-D-10, RG 165/NA.

34. WCD 10220-D-11 [with omissions due to transmission problems], RG 165/NA.

35. Mott's letter was dated 25 September 1917. It is archived in the William V. Judson Papers. See also the epigraph to chapter 4.

36. WCD 10220-D-12, RG 165/NA.

37. Generally, "battalions of death" were volunteer offensive formations sent into the most dangerous situations.

1. See Judson's response to Mott in his 3 November 1917 letter, included in chapter 3. Mott's letter is archived in the William V. Judson Papers.

2. Judson paginated and collected the diary entries in batches, each batch individually dispatched to the War College Staff. Selections from daily entries in the diary will be included here in chronological order, along with the telegrams and memoranda for a given day.

3. WCD 10220-D-13, RG 165/NA.

4. WCD 10220-D-21, "Dated November 8, 1917, Received (Warcolstaf) November 21, 11 A.M.," RG 165/NA.

5. This monthly resumé is organized under several headings, many military and technical, that are not reproduced here. The heading subdivisions are as follows: *Military Events, Discipline of Army, Verkhovsky's Resignation, Railway Matters, Political, Russia as an Ally, Finland, The State Duma, The Ukraine, Paris Conference, Some Pressing Needs, Food Supply, Finance,* and, *Later.* The final heading, "Later," with subdivisions for each day from 7 November through 13 November, was written after the Bolshevik seizure of power. Judson wrote this summary of one week's revolutionary events while he was awaiting the delayed departure of the diplomatic pouch.

6. This last sentence was added to the resumé typescript in Judson's handwriting.

7. This sentence was added to the resumé typescript in handwriting.

8. Judson is referring to the Inter-Allied Conference, that finally convened in Paris on 29 November 1917. The conference, consisting of high-ranking representatives of all eighteen Allied combatants, was called to unify their war effort and to determine war priorities and commitments. The failure of a Russian summer offensive under Kerensky's government, followed by the late-October defeat of Italian forces, lent urgency to the Allied need for greater cooperation, as reflected in Judson's diary. The Bolshevik Revolution only exacerbated the situation, and even before its impact was known or understood, a supreme war council was agreed upon by the British, French, and Italians.

9. This sentence was added to the typescript in Judson's handwriting.

10. Judson is referring to the February (March) Revolution. It should be noted that Judson is suggesting sending Allied troops to Russia *with the sanction and approval of the Russian government*. This communication should not be misconstrued as Judson's recommendation for an Allied intervention hostile to any *de facto* or *de jure* government in power.

11. WCD 10220-D-14, "dated November 9, 1917 and received in Washington on November 17, 9:00 A.M.," RG 165/NA.

12. WCD 10220-D-17, RG 165/NA.

13. On this day, Judson composed and dated a Western Union cablegram to Warcolstaff, Washington (no. 85), and noted the time as 5 P.M. He reiterated the developments of both 12 and 13 November, which are repeated in this and other communications included here. WCD 10220-D-16, RG 165/NA.

14. WCD 10220-D-16 "second half of cable," RG 165/NA. The National Archives copy of this document has the complete number identification sequence. It also indicates a 5 P.M., rather than an 11 A.M., time. The cablegram was received at Washington on 19 November at 9 A.M., and copies were distributed to the chief of staff and several other officers.

15. A handwritten note by Judson indicates that the diary entries for 14–19 November were dispatched together—one copy sent via the Pacific route (see no. 1244 of 20 November 1917), the other sent via the Atlantic (see no. 1246 of 23 November 1917).

16. WCD 10220-D-15, RG 165/NA.

17. This note was added to the typescript in Judson's handwriting.

18. WCD 10220-D-19, RG 165/NA.

19. This was one of several such interviews by Judson or his subordinates.

20. WCD 10220-D-20, RG 165/NA.

21. The Smolny Institute was a school for the daughters of the czarist aristocracy until the revolutionary days of 1917. In the summer of 1917 it became the headquarters of the Petrograd Soviet and, with the October (November) Revolution, housed the offices of Lenin and the Bolshevik Party. It was, therefore, for a time the seat of the revolutionary government of Russia.

22. WCD 10220-D-22 "received Nov. 22, 12 Noon," RG 165/NA. The speed of cable communication had returned to near normal.

23. WCD 10220-D-23, RG 165/NA.

24. WCD 10220-D-26 "dated Nov. 21, and Nov. 22, 1917," RG 165/NA.

25. WCD 10220-D-24, RG 165/NA.

26. Ensign Nikolai V. Krylenko, along with Lenin and Stalin, made this phone call which began at 2 A.M., lasted two and a half hours, and concluded with Dukhonin's dismissal. A "verbatim" record of the conversation was published in *Rabochy i Soldat* (*Worker and Soldier*), which may have been Judson's source of information for this diary entry. The account may also be found in Lenin, *Collected Works*, 26: 309–10.

27. Judson's handwritten note follows: "Diary to here sent via Atlantic #1246—November 23, 1917."

28. WCD 10220-D-27, RG 165/NA.

29. WCD 10220-D-28, RG 165/NA.

30. WCD 10220-D-29, RG 165/NA.

31. General V. V. Marushevski.

32. *New York Times*, 21 November 1917.

33. This letter, quoted in full in Kennan, *Russia Leaves the War*, 102–3, also appears in Cumming and Pettit, *Russian-American Relations* (47–48), and U.S. Department of State, *Papers Relating to the Foreign Relations of the United States; 1918, Russia*, 266–67. Kennan concludes that "In this curious manner the *New York Times* correspondent in Washington became the author of the first statement of United States policy made to the Soviet Government." And Judson's letter in response, that legitimated that statement, and that was forwarded to the highest levels in the Bolshevik government, constitutes the first direct official communication between the U.S. and that government.

34. See preceding letter.

35. WCD 10220-D-30, RG 165/NA.

36. Monroe C. Kerth, as Judson's immediate subordinate, was carrying out the mission specified by Judson and his superior, Ambassador Francis, including the very language of this important communication. See Judson's mention of this mission in his paraphrase of 26 November 1917, no. 112, above.

37. General V. V. Marushevski.

38. There are two copies of this letter in the Judson Papers. At the bottom of one of them, in the handwriting of Ambassador David R. Francis, is the following note:

"No objection to M. Attaché writing this letter in explanation of his letter of November 12/25th 17. DRF."

39. This diary entry repeats Judson's telegram of 27 November 1917, no. 115, 102. See the Judson Papers and WCD 10220-D-31, RG 165/NA.

40. WCD 10220-D-32, RG 165/NA.

41. WCD 10220-D-34, RG 165/NA.

42. Member of either the British Military Mission or the ambassador's staff.

43. This paragraph, and the five which follow, were bracketed in dark pencil by Judson in the characteristic way that he used to identify selections from his communications to be included in his "quotations." While these paragraphs were not included, according to the archival record, their importance for Judson's fateful decision to meet with Trotsky and to the genesis of American-Soviet relations is self-evident.

44. C. Butler Wright, counselor of the American embassy, Petrograd. The substance of this diary entry had been cabled Warcolstaff on 29 November 1917. See WCD 10220-D-36, RG 165/NA.

45. WCD 10220-D-40, RG 165/NA.

46. WCD 10220-D-39, RG 165/NA.

47. Weyant, "General William V. Judson," astutely points out the vagaries of Ambassador Francis's communications to the State Department on the issue of Judson's 1 December interview with Trotsky. See editor's comment to follow at end of Judson's diary entry of 1 January 1918.

48. These are Judson's handwritten brackets in the typed text.

49. Italicized portions of this telegram appear in a February 1918 collection of important quotations assembled by Judson. They do not appear in his final report of 16 March 1918.

50. WCD 10220-D-37 "dated Dec. 4," RG 165/NA.

51. The English translation of the text of the article was cabled by Ambassador Francis to Secretary of State Lansing on 2 December 1917, in part as a rebuke to Judson's initiative:

> . . . General Judson, chief of the American Military Mission, visited Comrade Trotsky in Smolny. General Judson informed Comrade Trotsky that at present he has no opportunity of speaking in the name of the American Government since recognition of Soviet authority is not yet an accomplished fact, but he appeared for the purpose of establishing relations, elucidate certain circumstances and dispel misunderstandings. General Judson inquired whether the new government is seeking to terminate the war jointly with the Allies, which according to the words of the General can hardly participate in the negotiations taking place on December 2. Comrade Trotsky in short words explained to the General the policies of the Soviet government in the matter of a struggle for general peace. The paramount circumstance which the People's Commissar specially emphasized is the fact that all negotiations will be openly conducted. The Allies will be able to follow the progress of the negotiations and can therefore join the Russians at any later stage of the proceedings.
>
> General Judson asked for permission to cable this information to his Government and in conclusion stated that "the time for protests and threats is over, if it ever existed." The General asked whether the People's Commissar insists upon explanations on the subjects of various incidents that have taken place (statements of protest of members of the American Military Mission). Comrade Trotsky stated that

the formal side of the matter is not interesting and the incident may be considered closed with the General's statement that the time for threats and protests is over.
U.S. Department of State, Papers Relating to the Foreign Relations of the United States, Russia, 1918, I, 282–83.

52. This is in Judson's handwriting across the bottom of the typewritten page.

53. WCD 10220-D-43, RG 165/NA.

54. WCD 10220-D-41, RG 165/NA.

55. This is one of several early expressions by Judson of his concern about, and opposition to, the often recommended option of an uninvited Allied intervention in Bolshevik Russia. Regardless of the justifications set forth by a number of senior military and political figures, Judson was convinced that such an enterprise was doomed to failure since it would lack the support of the overwhelming majority of the Russian population, both Bolshevik and anti-Bolshevik. See the telegram of 3 December, no. 140, 114, for Judson's complete rationale.

56. In Judson's handwriting: "Diary from Nov. 23–Dec. 4, inclusive forwarded via Atlantic despatch No. 1250, Dec. 5, 1917."

57. WCD 10220-D-63, received 25 December 1917 at 11 A.M., after a request for repeat of message cabled to Judson from the War Department on 19 December. WCD 10220-D-68, RG 165/NA.

58. V. D. Bonch-Bruyevich also served as chief of Chancery of the Soviet of People's Commissars.

59. In Judson's handwriting on typewritten page.

60. WCD [10220-D-48], RG 165/NA.

61. This is a typewritten paragraph, in parenthesis, with Judson's handwritten comment.

62. WCD 10220-D-44, RG 165/NA.

63. WCD 10220-D-45, RG 165/NA.

64. Arthur Bullard, a moderate socialist in the United States, served as an unofficial listening post for Colonel House, President Wilson's key foreign policy advisor, and continued in that capacity while undertaking the new responsibilities described here.

65. WCD 10220-D-47, RG 165/NA.

66. WCD 10220-D-46, RG 165/NA.

67. WCD 10220-D-49 "received Dec. 14, 9 a.m., numbers given: Serv. No. 162, no. 124," RG 165/NA.

68. WCD 10220-D-50, RG 165/NA.

69. A central issue in the American diplomatic and military community in Petrograd at this time was the status of the American Red Cross Commission to Russia and its new head, Raymond Robins. Did President Wilson's injunction against official communication with the Bolshevik Government apply to the American Red Cross, which was a quasi-private humanitarian organization? Robins asserted—and the American ambassador sustained him in most instances—that the injunction did not, or should not, apply to him and his organization. What was the Wilson administration's answer? Like many questions in this unprecedented situation, it was most complicated, with often contradictory answers provided by both Ambassador Francis and Secretary of State Lansing. Robins did, however, meet with Trotsky on nearly a daily basis, and also met with Lenin on at least six separate occasions.

70. WCD 10220-D-53, RG 165/NA.

71. WCD 10220-D-55 "14 December Service No. 177, no. 132 [10220-D-51] cast doubts on optimistic Bolsheviki reports south Russia. . . . Reported that majority Black Sea fleet opposed to civil war and refuses support either side," RG 165/NA.

72. WCD 10220-D-52 of 13 December, no.172, 130, to Warcolstaff is reiterated in diary for 14 December 1917.

73. See Ullman, *Anglo-Soviet Relations*,131–32, for details on these released Bolsheviks.

74. WCD 10220-D-54, RG 165/NA.

75. WCD 10220-D-57, RG 165/NA.

76. Correction from RG 165/NA copy.

77. WCD 10220-D-58, RG 165/NA.

78. In Judson's handwriting at the conclusion of the diary entry for 17 December: "Note. Diary forwarded to War College (& to Pershing) 5–17 Dec. inc. with despatch #1262, 17 December 1917."

79. WCD 10220-D-59, RG 165/NA.

80. WCD 10220-D-60, RG 165/NA, of 19 December 1917, no. 193, 141, to Warcolstaff contains the same information in less detail as this diary.

81. WCD 10220-D-61 "duplicate telegram and cablegram," RG 165/NA.

82. WCD 10220-D-62, RG 165/NA, of 22 December 1917, no. 200, 143, communicates the information in this diary entry in shorter format.

83. WCD 10220-D-65, RG 165/NA.

84. The five "general principles" of U.S. policy in Russia that follow in this first draft are almost exactly the same as those in the final 26 December draft (see below).

85. The following diary entry is nearly identical to the memorandum sent by Judson and Kerth to Francis on 26 December (see below). At the end of this diary entry, in Judson's handwriting, is a note indicating that the 26 December draft should replace that of 23 December.

86. WCD 10220-D-66, RG 165/NA.

87. Judson is referring here to Ambassador Francis's support of the policy of nonintercourse with the Bolshevik regime.

88. Please see the diary entries of 30 November and 1 December and the cable of 1 December 1917, no. 133, 110 (all above). Those passages quoted or paraphrased here are in italics. The 1 December cable is again quoted by Judson in his "important quotations" section of his final report of 16 March 1918.

89. See Salzman, *Reform and Revolution,* and Sisson, *One Hundred Red Days,* for accounts of this meeting.

90. In mid-December, the Council of People's Commissars arrested the Petrograd Rada the Ukrainian council in Petrograd. Constitutionalists, from the Kiev Rada, to Chernov, vehemently protested these arrests, even sending an ultimatum threatening war against Russia in the case of the Ukrainian Rada.

91. WCD 10220-D-67, RG 165/NA.

92. WCD 10220-D-69, RG 165/NA.

93. WCD 10220-D-75, RG 165/NA.

94. WCD 10220-D-82, RG 165/NA.

95. WCD 10220-D-73, RG 165/NA.

96. WCD 10220-D-72, RG 165/NA.

97. Weyant, "General William V. Judson," 213–15. The formal order of recall came in a "Memorandum for the Adjutant General of the Army," prepared by Maj. Gen. John Biddle, Acting Chief of Staff of the War Department, on 26 December 1917

(WCD 10166-27. RG 165/NA). Paragraph 1 states: "The Secretary of War directs that Brigadier General William V. Judson, General Staff, be relieved from duty as military attaché to the American Embassy at Petrograd, Russia by cable and directed to return to the United States and report to the Chief of Staff." Nowhere in the memorandum is mention made of Judson's additional post as chief of the American Military Mission to Russia. The memo also directs Lt. Col. Monroe C. Kerth to "report to the American Ambassador at Petrograd, Russia for such service under his supervision as may be assigned to him by the War Department." No longer would there be an independent voice from a military mission to Russia. The ambassador was to be in complete charge.

98. This is a notation in Judson's handwriting.

99. WCD 10220-D-74, RG 165/NA.

100. Secretary of State Lansing's desk diaries for 6–7 December 1917 (see reel 2, Lansing Papers, Library of Congress Manuscript Division Microfilm) refer to meetings with Secretary of War Baker and, on 7 December, with President Wilson on "Judson's conduct in Petrograd." Judson had met with Trotsky on 1 December. Judson's recall orders were not dispatched from Washington until 29 December (WCD 10166-27, RG 165/NA). Specific memoranda regarding his recall were not composed until 24 December, when Baker wrote to Lansing: "I have the honor to inform you that owing to the exigencies of the service, it has been found necessary to relieve Brigadier General William V. Judson, National Army, from duty as Military Attaché to the American Embassy at Petrograd, Russia, and that orders to this effect have been cabled" (WCD 10166-27, RG 165/NA).

101. This position, put forward and endorsed by Trotsky, and supported by a majority of both bodies, was strongly opposed by Lenin and a minority, who feared that Germany would not hesitate to resume hostilities. Lenin's opposition was so strong that he submitted his resignation in protest. The Trotsky "no war no peace" strategy, as it came to be called, did result in renewed fighting and even more punitive conditions in the final peace settlement that removed Soviet Russia from the World War.

102. WCD 10220-D-77, RG 165/NA.

103. WCD 10220-D-76, RG 165/NA.

104. The Ukrainian Rada, or central council, had declared the Ukraine a sovereign republic after the fall of the Provisional Government in Petrograd, and it was recognized by the Soviet Government. In the months that followed, a sequence of complex events transpired, including Red Army overthrow of the Rada, German takeover, White Army takeover under General Denikin, and final Soviet control after deposing Denikin in the fall of 1919.

105. WCD 10220-D-90, RG 165/NA.

106. WCD 10220-D-81, RG 165/NA.

107. WCD 10220-D-80, RG 165/NA.

CHAPTER 5

1. WCD 10020-D-84, RG 165/NA.

2. Judson, while always attempting to mask his anger and disappointment, considered his recall ill advised and unjustified and to be an unwarranted reprimand. Here he expressed his hope for a reversal of that decision.

3. WCD 10220-D-86, RG 165/NA.

4. WCD 10220-D-88, RG 165/NA.

5. "The Diamandi Incident," as this arrest, diplomatic intervention, and release has been called, is most thoroughly detailed in an entire chapter, by the same name, in Kennan, *Russia Leaves the War*.

6. WCD 10220-D-89, RG 165/ NA.

7. This meeting of Lenin with the entire diplomatic community present in Petrograd (at 4 P.M. in Lenin's office, Room 81, the Smolny Institute) was the one and only face-to-face meeting between the Bolshevik leader and most of the members of the diplomatic corps, including the American ambassador. Judson was not present, nor did he ever meet Lenin.

8. General Shcherbachev commanded the Russian forces on the Romanian front that became disaffected and mutinied against their commanders in December 1917, supported in that action by Bolshevik propaganda and agents. The general accepted the help of Romanian forces in disarming and expelling his mutinous forces into nearby Russian territory.

9. WCD 10220-D-91, RG 165/ NA.

10. Yates's request for an American Military Mission representative in the "South" is a suggestion for official U.S. presence in the camp of anti-Bolshevik forces then assembling for the purpose of opposition, both political and military, to the Lenin government. Judson and many other Allied officials considered such representation an encouragement to civil war and a complete detriment to any positive relations with the Bolshevik government. The French effort to afford such representation in the South led to a serious rift in Franco-Russian (Bolshevik) relations, as suggested further on in Judson's letter to Yates.

11. Andrews served as courier for this letter.

12. This telegram is missing from the Judson Papers at the Newberry Library. WCD 10220-D-93, RG 165/NA.

13. WCD 10220-D-95, RG 165/NA.

14. The Constituent (or constitutional) Assembly had been scheduled for 25 November 1917 under the Provisional Government. Its opening was then postponed to 18 January 1918, in the aftermath of the Bolshevik seizure of power. Elections for the Assembly took place after the Bolshevik Revolution and found Bolshevik representation in the minority. Only 9,800,000 votes of 41,700,000 were cast for the Bolsheviks, and only 168 Bolshevik deputies were elected of the 703 in the Assembly. On 19 January 1918, the Central Executive Committee dissolved the Constituent Assembly under orders from Lenin and his party.

15. WCD 10220-D-96, RG 165/NA.

16. Anarchists Alexander Berkman and Emma Goldman were then under arrest in the United States for seditious opposition to U.S. participation in the World War.

17. WCD 10220-D-92, RG 165/NA.

18. The last sentence and parenthetical comment are written in Judson's handwriting.

19. The first two telegrams are paraphrased above. The last, not included in this book, can be found paraphrased at WCD 10220-D-87, RG 165/NA.

20. WCD 10020-D-97, RG 165/NA.

21. WCD 10220-D-98, RG 165/NA.

22. WCD 10166-31, RG 165/NA. Schmedeman was U.S. attaché in Oslow.

23. This statement is the first prepared by Judson after his return to Washington on 20 February, six days earlier, and is of special significance for that reason alone. It

should be compared with his report to the secretary of state for 30 January 1918 (above). He included it in his comprehensive 16 March 1918 "Russian Situation" report.

24. Sweden's Charles XII fought against Peter the Great in the Great Northern War and nearly defeated the Russians.

25. Judson may be referring to Gregory Semenov, a cossack commander of Transbaikalia, who, with the backing of the Japanese, controlled portions of eastern Siberia. "Sensational" press coverage, in Judson's opinion, seriously overstated the importance of both the counterrevolutionary and Japanese dimensions of this development.

26. Judson's desperation at receiving neither specific responses nor requested information and instructions—other than the proscription from any contact with the Bolshevik authorities—is the most telling evidence of the sad, if not tragic state of the conduct of U.S. foreign policy. Judson's personal suffering of this disadvantage must be seen in the context of a far more serious detrimental impact on the national interest and on the lives of soldiers put in jeopardy.

27. Not included here are Judson's six enclosures, including cable excerpts and copies of complete memoranda and official letters, many of which have been reproduced earlier in this volume.

28. This report should be read in conjunction with Judson's 23 August 1917 "Military Note" on "Political Parties in Russia," which was his first effort to describe the political spectrum in revolutionary Russia before the Bolshevik seizure of power.

29. The Octobrists accepted the October Manifesto of 1905 of Czar Nicholas II as a legitimate basis for Russian constitutional monarchy. The Kadets (Constitutional Democratic Party) considered the Manifesto merely as a first step toward Russian constitutionalism.

30. Judson goes on to quote from his cable of 14 November 1917. See that cable in its entirety in chapter 4.

31. The Inter-Allied Conference that finally convened in Paris on 29 November 1917 is discussed at length in Judson's 8 November 1917 memorandum and "Monthly Resumé" under the heading "Paris Conference."

32. Trotsky and Lenin were accused of being under control of the German government or the German General Staff from well before the Bolshevik Revolution. By March 1918—being particularly under the influence of the counterfeit documents championed by and soon named for Edgar Sisson, the COMPUB (Committee on Public Information) representative in Petrograd—many Washington decision makers had concluded that the Bolshevik leaders were German agents. The gravity of such a mistake of judgment became a major concern of Judson and his allies.

33. The quotations consist of the italicized portions from the documents of dated 7 August 1917; 3 September 1917; 14, 28 November 1917; 1, 2, 6, 11, 14, 15, 17, 21, 23, 27, 28, 31 December 1917; and 14, 16 January 1918, 4, 8 March 1918.

34. Judson is referring to what would become his full report on the de Cram affair and "certain other events in Russia, 1917–18," which was finally prepared and submitted to Secretary of War Newton D. Baker on 18 June 1919.

35. Probably Norman Armour, Second Secretary of the American Embassy, Petrograd.

36. This penciled paragraph is in Judson's handwriting in the top margin.

37. Compare this statement to the document of 21 April 1917, prepared prior to Judson's departure to Russia with the Root Mission.

38. See Judson's cable of 15 September 1917, regarding Alekseev's problems in the throes of revolutionary Russia.

39. Vostrotin has not been identified. The others are detailed in the Dramatis Personae.

40. The situation that had led to the paper's inaccurate reporting occurred at the time Kerth was sent to the headquarters of the Russian Chief of Staff (Stavka) at Mogilev to register U.S. objection to the Russian unilateral call for an armistice. See the appropriate documents for the period from 28 November to 3 December 1917.

Judson wrote this letter on his stationery as commanding general at the Headquarters Port of Embarkation, Hoboken, New Jersey.

41. Throughout Judson's communications and reporting while in Russia, nowhere did he openly express such a "fervent wish." His concern for the "redisciplining of the Russian army" remained a major concern and preoccupation, and he expressed his conviction that Kornilov could accomplish that goal (if anyone could), but, perhaps because of the diplomatic impropriety, Judson never used any such language of his personal support in his official or personal correspondence.

42. See Judson's telegram on the "Breshkovsky Committee" of 28 September 1917.

43. Judson appears to be referring to Norman Armour, Second Secretary of the American Embassy, Petrograd.

44. A typescript of the speech is in the Judson Papers along with a newspaper clipping from the *Milwaukee Journal* of Sunday, 2 November 1919, 10, that provides a verbatim reproduction of the speech. Judson's handwritten corrections are marked in the clipping.

45. Grand Duke Nikolai Nikolaevich served as vice regent of the Caucasian front during the World War.

46. See the various memoranda and reports relating to Judson's relationship with Guchkov, particularly his "Military Note" of 23 August 1917 and his memorandum of 21 April 1917.

47. The accounts that follow in the speech, but omitted here, are very close to those in several of Judson's reports and memoranda. See for example his "Military Note" of 23 August 1917 and his memorandum of 21 April 1917.

48. See this date for the complete communication.

49. At this point, after the speech had been delivered and appeared in the *Milwaukee Journal*, Judson made a number of editorial changes in the typescript, reversing the sequence of a few paragraphs.

50. All of the details of this portion of the speech duplicate Judson's memoranda to the ambassador and telegrams to the War College Staff. See the documents of 1–10 December 1917.

51. The four paragraphs that follow duplicate Judson's account in the "secret" document of 18 June 1919, above, and have not been repeated here. Also not duplicated is the paragraph detaling the Robine-Thompson role.

52. The concluding segment of this paragraph, in parentheses, was struck from the typescript. It does not appear in the newspaper version of the speech, but there is no way to know whether it nevertheless was in the speech's actual presentation and struck thereafter. Judson's second thoughts about publishing this poorly veiled accusation of Ambassador David Francis, and perhaps of others in the War and State Departments, came in the aftermath of the U.S. Senate hearings on Bolshevik propaganda, cited in the bibliography. These hearings, under the auspices of the Senate Committee on the Judiciary, were held in March 1919, eight months before this

speech. Testifying at the hearings, Ambassador Francis made accusations against Thompson. Judson considered them unfair and untrue and was attempting here to right that wrong. The record of Judson's communications throughout his tenure in Russia never wavered from a staunch appreciation for Thompson and his work with the American Red Cross Commission.

53. There is no indication of the source of the quotation. Judson had clipped it and stapled it to the typescript of the speech.

54. It should be noted that in this letter Judson signs his name under the title "Colonel, Corps of Engineers." His promotion to brigadier general was in the "National Army" during wartime; after resuming his prewar duties, he was returned to his previous rank.

On 27 August 1920, Judson penciled in the following note on the carbon copy of this letter in his files: "Since this was written [Cerhan ?] tried to influence Japan and Poland (as proposed); have opened the doors to trade, and the President has made a pre[?] designed to lead the Russians toward a Constitutional Convention."

55. See the documents under these dates. Text that is quoted in this memorandum and elsewhere by Judson are in italics.

56. Judson is referring to Edgar Sisson of COMPUB.

57. In chapter 12, "The Fourteen Points," in his *Russia Leaves the War*, George Kennan cites the many individuals, including Judson, who laid claim to having influenced Wilson to issue the famous "Fourteen Points Speech" in a message to Congress on 8 January 1918. Here Judson attempts to rule out the claims of Edgar Sisson.

58. Judson died on 29 March 1923 of further complications of his heart condition. This may well be his last letter to his son, Clay.

59. Judson's review never appeared in the *Nation*, nor are any notes for a review extant in the Judson papers. We can only assume that Judson was referring to J. C. Haig's *Socialism Put to the Test* (London: F. Griffith, 1923).

Bibliography

PRIMARY AND SECONDARY SOURCES ON THE INCEPTION OF
U.S.-SOVIET RELATIONS RELEVANT TO GENERAL WILLIAM V. JUDSON

MANUSCRIPTS

The Newberry Library, Chicago
   William V. Judson Papers (WJP)
State Historical Society of Wisconsin, Madison
   George Gibbs Papers (GAP)
   Alexander Gumberg Papers (AG)
   DeWitt Clinton Poole Papers (DPP)
   Edward A. Ross Papers (ARP)
   Raymond Robins Papers (RAP)
Collections in the Library of the University of Florida, Gainesville
   Margaret Dreier Robins Papers (MRP)
   Raymond Robins Papers (RAG)
Collections in the Fales Library of New York University
   Elizabeth Robins Papers (ER)
Collections in the Library of Congress
   William E. Borah Papers (WP)
   George B. Creel Papers (GAP)
   Harold Ickes Papers (HIP)
   Robert M. La Follette Papers (BLIP)
   Robert Lansing Papers (RAP)
   Theodore Roosevelt Papers (TAP)
   William Boyce Thompson-Herman Hagedorn Papers (WP)
   William A. White Papers (WARP)
   Woodrow Wilson Papers (WAC)
Collections in the New York Public Library
   Thomas D. Thatcher Papers (TAN)
Collections in the Butler Library, Columbia University, New York
   Oral History Research Office, transcript of recorded reminiscences of
      DeWitt Clinton Poole (DO) and Allen Wardwell (ADO)

Bakhmeteff Archive
  Charles R. Crane Papers (CRCP)
  E. Francis Riggs Papers (FRP)
  Lincoln Steffens Papers (LAP)
  Thomas D. Thacher Papers (TIC)
  Allen O. Wardwell Papers (ALP)
Collection in the Library of Princeton University
  Arthur Bullard Papers (ABA)

UNPUBLISHED DOCUMENTS

National Archives. General Records of the Department of State. RG 59.
"Records of the Department of State Relating to the Internal Affairs of Russia and the Soviet Union, 1910–1929."
National Archives. Records of the Foreign Service Posts of the Department of State. RG 84.
National Archives. Records of the Adjutant General's Office. RG 94.
National Archives. Records of the American Expeditionary Forces (WW I). RG 120. "Records of Chief of American Military Mission to Russia, 1917–19."
National Archives. Records of the War Department General and Special Staffs. RG 165.

PUBLISHED SOURCES

Bailey, Thomas A. *America Faces Russia: Russian American Relations from Early Times to Our Day*. Ithaca, N.Y.: Cornell Univ. Press, 1950.
Baker, Ray Stannard. *Woodrow Wilson: Life and Letters*. 8 vols. New York: Doubleday Doran, 1939.
Beatty, Bessie. "The Fall of the Winter Palace." *The Century Magazine* 96 (August 1918): 523–32.
———. "Gold and Fool's Gold, Col. Thompson Stakes His Faith on the Russian People." *Asia* (August 1918): 665–66.
———. *The Red Heart of Russia*. New York: The Century Pub., 1919.
Bennett, Edward M. *Franklin D. Roosevelt and the Search for Security: American-Soviet Relations, 1933–1939*. Wilmington, Del.: Scholarly Resources, 1985.
———. *Recognition of Russia: An American Foreign Policy Dilemma*. Waltham, Mass.: Blaisdell, 1970.
Berle, Beatrice Bishop, and Travis Beal Jacobs, eds. *Navigating the Rapids, 1918–1971: From the Papers of Adolf A. Berle*. New York: Harcourt, Brace Jovanovich, 1973.
Borah, William E. "The Threat of Bolshevism in America—How to Meet It." *Current Opinion* 66 (March 1919): 152–53.
———. "Senator Borah Pleads for Recognition of Soviet Russia." *Current Opinion* 74 (February 1923): 215–16.

————. "Shall We Abandon Russia." *New York Times Magazine* (2 December 1917).

Bradley, John. *Allied Intervention in Russia.* Latham, Md.: University Press of America, 1984.

Browder, Robert. *The Origins of Soviet-American Diplomacy.* Princeton, N.J.: Princeton Univ. Press, 1953.

Bryant, Louise. *Six Red Months in Russia, an Observer's Account of Russia Before and During the Proletarian Dictatorship.* New York: George H. Doran, 1918.

Bullard, Arthur. *The Russian Pendulum: Autocracy—Democracy—Bolshevism.* New York: Macmillan, 1919.

Bullitt, William C. *The Bullitt Mission to Russia: Testimony before the Committee on Foreign Relations, United States Senate of William C. Bullitt.* New York: B. W. Huebsch, 1919.

Bunyan, James, ed. *Intervention, Civil War and Communism in Russia, April–December, 1918, Documents and Materials.* Baltimore: Johns Hopkins Univ. Press, 1936.

Bunyan, James, and H. H. Fisher, eds. *The Bolshevik Revolution, 1917–1918: Documents and Materials.* Stanford: Stanford Univ. Press, 1934.

Calhoun, Frederick S. *Power and Principle: Armed Intervention in Wilsonian Foreign Policy.* Kent, Ohio: Kent State Univ. Press, 1986.

Carr, Edward Hallett. *A History of Soviet Russia: The Bolshevik Revolution, 1917–1923.* 3 vols. New York: Macmillan, 1950–54.

Chicherin, George. *Two Years of Foreign Policy: The Relations of the R.S.F.S.R. with Foreign Nations, from November 7, 1917 to November 7, 1919.* New York: Russian Government Bureau, 1920.

A chronicler [John Cudahy]. *Archangel: The American War with Russia.* Chicago: A. C. McClurg, 1924.

Coates, William Peyton, and Zelda Kahan. *Allied Intervention in Russia, 1918–1922.* London: Victor Gollancz, 1935.

Cooper, John Milton. *The Warrior and the Priest: Woodrow Wilson and Theodore Roosevelt.* Cambridge, Mass.: Harvard Univ. Press, 1983.

Cumming, C. K., and Walter W. Pettit, eds. *Russian-American Relations, March, 1917–March, 1920: Documents and Papers.* New York: Harcourt Brace and Howe, 1920.

Davison, Henry P. *The American Red Cross in the Great War.* New York: Macmillan, 1920.

————. *The Work of the American Red Cross During the War.* Washington, D.C.: The American Red Cross, 1919.

Davison, Joan Doverspike. "Raymond Robins and United States Foreign Policy Toward Revolutionary Russia." Ph.D. diss., Notre Dame University, 1984.

Degras, Jane, ed. *Soviet Documents on Foreign Policy.* Vol. 1, *1917–1924.* Oxford: Oxford Univ. Press for the Royal Institute of International Affairs, 1951.

Destler, Chester McArthur. *American Radicalism, 1865–1901*. New York: Octagon Books, 1972.

Deutscher, Isaac. *The Prophet Armed, Trotsky, 1879–1921*. Oxford: Oxford Univ. Press, 1954.

Dobrjansky, A. N. "The Tragedy of Russia." 2 pages; and "Vital Reasons for the Recognition of the Omsk Government." 2 pages. New York: privately printed and distributed by author, 1919. [To be found in the New York Public Library catalogue under "Russian Pamphlets *CC p.v. 18 (1919)"— and perhaps nowhere else.]

Ferrell, Robert H. *Woodrow Wilson and World War I, 1917–1921*. New York: Harper and Row, 1985.

Fischer, Louis. *The Life of Lenin*. New York: Harper and Row, 1964.

Francis, David R. *Dollars and Diplomacy: Ambassador David Rowland Francis and the Fall of Tsarism, 1916–1917*. Ed. Jamie H. Cockfield. Durham, N.C.: Duke Univ. Press, 1981.

———. *Russia From the American Embassy: April, 1916–November, 1918*. New York: Charles Scribner's Sons, 1921.

Frost, Stanley. "Raymond Robins, Practical Reformer." *The New York Tribune* (19 April 1919).

Gelb, Barbara. *So Short a Time: A Biography of John Reed and Louise Bryant*. New York: Norton, 1973.

The German-Bolshevik Conspiracy. War Information Series, no. 20. Washington, D.C.: Committee on Public Information, 1918.

Golder, Frank. *War, Revolution, and Peace in Russia: The Passages of Frank Golder, 1914–1927*. Ed. Terence Emmons and Bertrand M. Patenaude. Stanford, Calif.: Hoover Institute Press, 1992.

Graves, William S. *America's Siberian Adventure, 1918–1920*. New York: Jonathan Cape and Harrison Smith, 1931.

Hagedorn, Herman. *The Magnate, William Boyce Thompson and His Time, 1869–1930*. New York: The John Day Co., 1935.

Hard, William. "Anti-Bolsheviks: Mr. Lansing." *The New Republic* 19, no. 243 (2 July 1919).

———. *Raymond Robins' Own Story*. New York: Harper and Bros., 1920. [First serialized in the *Chicago Daily News* (July 1919).]

———. "The Testimony of Raymond Robins." *The New Republic* 18, no. 230 (29 March 1919): 261–63.

Harper, Paul V., ed. *The Russia I Believe in: The Memoirs of Samuel N. Harper, 1902–1941*. Chicago: Univ. of Chicago Press, 1945.

Hicks, Granville. *John Reed: The Making of a Revolutionary*. New York: Macmillan, 1936.

Jordan, Philip. "Letters from Russia, 1917–1919." *Missouri Historical Society Bulletin 14* (January 1958): 139–66.

Judson, William V. "Report of Captain William V. Judson, Corps of Engineers, Observer with the Russian Forces in Manchuria," *Reports of Mili-*

tary Observers Attached to the Armies in Manchuria during the Russo-Japanese War, part 5, no. 8 (Washington, D.C.: Govt. Printing Office, 1907).

———. "Strategic Value of Her West Indian Possessions to the United States," *Annals of the American Academy of Political and Social Sciences* 19 (January–May 1902): 383–91.

Kennan, George F. *The Decision to Intervene.* Vol. 2 of *Soviet-American Relations, 1917–1920.* Princeton, N.J.: Princeton Univ. Press, 1958.

———. *Russia and the West under Lenin and Stalin.* London: Hutchinson, 1961.

———. *Russia Leaves the War.* Vol. 1 of *Soviet-American Relations, 1917–1920.* Princeton, N.J.: Princeton Univ. Press, 1956.

———. "Soviet Historiography and America's Role in the Intervention." *The American Historical Review* 64 (January 1960): 302.

Kerensky, Alexander. *The Catastrophy: Kerensky's Own Story of the Russian Revolution.* New York: D. Appleton, 1927.

———. *The Crucifiction of Liberty.* New York: John Day, 1934.

———. *The Prelude to Bolshevism: The Kornilov Rising.* New York: Haskell House, 1927.

Kettle, Michael. *Russia and the Allies 1917–1920.* Vol. 1, *The Allies and the Russian Collapse.* Vol. 2, *The Road to Intervention.* New York: Routledge, Chapman and Hall, 1986–88.

King, David. *Trotsky: A Photographic Biography.* New York: B. Blackwell, 1986.

Knox, Alfred. *With the Russian Army, 1914–1917: Being Chiefly Extracts from the Diary of a Military Attaché.* 2 vols. London: Hutchinson, 1921.

Lasch, Christopher. *The American Liberals and The Russian Revolution.* New York and London: Columbia Univ. Press, 1962.

———. *The Agony of the American Left.* New York and London: Alfred A. Knopf, 1969.

———. *The New Radicalism in America.* New York: Alfred A. Knopf, 1965.

Lenin, V. I. *Collected Works.* 36 vols. London and Moscow: Lawrence and Wishart and Progress Publishers, 1965.

Levin, N. Gordon. *Woodrow Wilson and World Politics.* New York: Oxford Univ. Press, 1968.

Libbey, James K. *Alexander Gumberg and Soviet-American Relations, 1917–1933.* Lexington: Univ. of Kentucky Press, 1977.

Link, Arthur S. *Woodrow Wilson and the Progressive Era, 1910–1917.* New York: Harper and Bros., 1954.

———, ed. *Woodrow Wilson and a Revolutionary World, 1913–1921.* Chapel Hill: Univ. of North Carolina Press, 1982.

Link, Arthur S., and William M. Leary, Jr. *The Progressive Era and the Great War, 1896–1920.* New York: Appleton Century-Crofts, 1969.

Lockhart, Robert H. Bruce. *The Diaries of Sir Robert Bruce Lockhart: 1915–1938, 1939–1965.* Ed. Kenneth Young. 2 vols. London: St. Martin's Press, 1973–80.

————. "L. D. Trotsky: A Pen Portrait." *The Fortnightly Review* 239 (April 1923): 295–311.

————. "Lenin, the Man and His Achievement." *The Edinburgh Review* 239 (April 1923): 295–311.

————. *Memoirs of a British Agent, Being an Account of the Author's Early Life in Many Lands and of His Official Mission to Moscow in 1918*. London: Putnam, 1932.

————. *Retreat from Glory*. London: Putnam, 1934.

————. *The Two Revolutions, an Eye-Witness Study of Russia, 1917*. London: Phoenix House, 1957.

Maddux, Thomas R. *Years of Estrangement, American Relations with the Soviet Union, 1933–1941*. Gainesville: Univ. Presses of Florida, 1980.

Manning, Clarence Augustus. *The Siberian Fiasco*. New York: Library Publishers, 1952.

Mayer, Arno J. *Political Origins of the New Diplomacy*. New Haven, Conn.: Yale Univ. Press, 1959.

McFadden, David W. *Alternative Paths: Soviets and Americans, 1917–1920*. New York: Oxford Univ. Press, 1993.

McKenna, Marian C. *Borah*. Ann Arbor: Univ. of Michigan Press, 1961.

Meiburger, Sister Anne Vincent. *Efforts of Raymond Robins Toward the Recognition of Soviet Russia and the Outlawry of War, 1917–1933*. Washington, D.C.: Catholic Univ. of America Press, 1958.

Mock, James R., and Cedric Larson. *Words That Won the War: The Story of the Committee on Public Information, 1917–1919*. Princeton, N.J.: Princeton Univ. Press, 1939.

Noulens, Joseph. *Mon Ambassade en Ruisse Sovietique, 1917–1919*. 2 vols. Paris: Librarie Plon, 1933.

O'Connor, Richard, and Dale L. Walker. *The Lost Revolutionary: A Biography of John Reed*. New York: Harcourt Brace and World, 1967.

Payne, Robert. *The Life and Death of Lenin*. New York: Simon and Schuster, 1964.

Proceedings of the Brest-Litovsk Peace Conference: The Peace Negotiations Between Russia and the Central Powers, 21 November, 1917–3 March, 1918. Washington, D.C.: GPO, 1918.

Pusey, Merlo J. *Charles Evans Hughes*. 2 vols. New York: Macmillan, 1907.

Ransome, Arthur. *Russia in 1919*. New York: B. W. Huebsch, 1919.

Reed, John. *Ten Days That Shook The World*. New York: Boni and Liveright, 1919.

Robins, Raymond. *An American Prophet Speaks: A Historic Interview with Premier Stalin on the Eve of U.S. Recognition of the U.S.S.R. by President Roosevelt in 1933*. Foreword and ed. Cedric Belfarge. New York: Boni and Gaer, 1952.

————. "Social Control in Russia Today." *The Annals of the American Academy of Political and Social Sciences* 84, no. 3 (July 1919): 127–44.

————. "Soviet Russia after Fifteen Years." Address delivered over the National Broadcasting Company Network, 26 July 1933. *The Congressional Record.* Appendix. 2 June 1943.

————. "United States Recognition of Soviet Russia Essential to World Peace and Stabilization." *Annals of the American Academy of Political and Social Sciences* 126, no. 215 (July 1926): 100–104, 110–16.

"Robins on Russia." *The Survey* 41, no. 26 (29 March 1919): 962.

Rosenstone, Robert A. *Romantic Revolutionary: A Biography of John Reed.* New York: Alfred A. Knopf, 1975.

Ross, Edward A. *The Russian Bolshevik Revolution.* New York: Century, 1921.

————. *The Russian Soviet Republic.* New York: Century, 1923.

Ruddy, T. Michael. *The Cautious Diplomat, Charles E. Bohlen and the Soviet Union, 1919–1969.* Kent, Ohio: Kent State Univ. Press, 1986.

Sadoul, Jacques. *Naissance de l'U.R.S.S.* Vol. 1. Paris: Charlot, 1946.

————. *Notes sur la Revolution Bolchevique.* Paris: Editions de la Sirene, 1920.

————. *Quarante Lettres de Jacques Sadoul.* Paris: Editions de la Librarie Humanité, 1922.

————. *The Socialist Soviet Republic of Russia, Its Rise and Organization.* London: People's Russian Information Bureau, 1918.

Salzman, Neil V. *Reform and Revolution: The Life and Times of Raymond Robins.* Kent, Ohio: Kent State Univ. Press, 1991.

Sayers, Michael, and Albert E. Kahn. *The Great Conspiracy Against Russia.* New York: Boni and Gaer, 1946.

Schlesinger, Arthur M., and Fred L. Israel, eds. *The State of the Union Messages of the Presidents, 1790–1966.* New York: Chelsea House, 1966.

Schuman, Frederick Lewis. *American Policy Toward Russia Since 1917.* New York: International Publishers, 1928.

Seymour, Charles. *The Intimate Papers of Colonel House.* Vol. 3., *Into the World War, April 1917–June 1918.* New York: Houghton Mifflin, 1928.

Shelton, Brenda K. *President Wilson and the Russian Revolution.* Vol. 23, no. 3 of *Monographs in History,* Buffalo, N.Y.: The State University of New York, Buffalo, 1957.

Silverlight, John. *The Victors' Dilemma: Allied Intervention in the Russian Civil War.* London: Barrie and Jenkins, 1970.

Sisson, Edgar. *One Hundred Red Days: A Personal Chronicle of the Bolshevik Revolution.* New Haven, Conn.: Yale Univ. Press, 1931.

Soskice, Victor. "A Message to Kerensky." *Metropolitan Magazine* (September 1918): 29–31.

————. "The Red Guard Takes a Hand." *Metropolitan Magazine* (August 1918): 21–22.

Steffens, Lincoln. *Autobiography.* New York: Harcourt Brace, 1931.

Strakhovsky, Leonid Ivan. *Intervention at Archangel: The Story of Allied Intervention and Russian Counter-Revolution in North Russia, 1918–1920.* Princeton, N.J.: Princeton Univ. Press, 1944.

————. *The Origins of American Intervention in North Russia, 1918*. Princeton, N.J.: Princeton Univ. Press, 1937.

Thacher, Thomas D. "Economic Force and the Russian Problem." *The Annals of the American Academy of Political and Social Science* (Philadelphia) 84 (July 1919).

————. "Russia and the War." 14 pages. New York: privately printed and distributed, 4 June 1918.

Trotsky, Leon. *From October to Brest-Litovsk*. London: Allen and Unwin, 1919.

————. *The History of the Russian Revolution*. 3 vols. New York: Simon and Schuster, 1932.

————. *Lenin*. London: Minton Balch, 1925.

————. *My Life*. New York: Charles Scribner's Sons, 1930.

Ullman, Richard H. *Anglo-Soviet Relations, 1917–1921*. Vol. 1., *Intervention and the War*. Princeton, N.J.: Princeton Univ. Press, 1971.

Unterberger, Betty Miller. *American Intervention in the Russian Civil War*. Lexington, Mass.: D.C. Heath, 1969.

U.S. Department of State. *Papers Relating to the Foreign Relations of the United States: The Lansing Papers, 1914–1920*. 2 vols. Washington, D.C.: 1939–40.

————. *Papers Relating to the Foreign Relations of the United States: 1918, Russia*. 3 vols. Washington, D.C.: 1931–32.

————. *Papers Relating to the Foreign Relations of the United States: 1919, Russia*. Washington, D.C.: 1937.

U.S. Senate. *Bolshevik Propaganda, Hearings before a Subcommittee of the Committee on the Judiciary*. 65th Cong. 3rd Sess. 1919.

————. *Recognition of Russia, Hearings before a Subcommittee on Foreign Relation*. 65th Cong. 3rd Sess., 1919.

————. *Relations with Russia, Hearings before the Committe on Foreign Relations*. 66th Cong. 3rd Sess., 1921.

Varneck, E., and Harold H. Fisher, eds. *The Testimony of Kolchak and Other Siberia Materials*. Stanford: Stanford Univ. Press, 1935.

Volkogonov, Dmitri. *Lenin: A New Biography*. New York: The Free Press, 1994.

Ward, John. *With the "Die-Hards" in Siberia*. New York: George H. Doran, 1920.

Warth, Robert D. *The Allies and the Russian Revolution*. Durham, N.C.: Duke Univ. Press, 1954.

Weyant, Jane Gilmer. "The Life and Career of General William V. Judson, 1865–1923." Ph.D. diss., Georgia State University, 1981.

Wheeler-Bennett, John W. *The Forgotten Peace: Brest-Litovsk, March, 1918*. New York: William Morrow, 1939.

Whelpley, J. D. "Russia's Soviet Government." *Fortnightly Review* (October 1925).

White, John Albert. *The Siberian Intervention*. Princeton, N.J.: Princeton Univ. Press, 1950.

Williams, Albert Rhys. *Journey into Revolution, Petrograd, 1917–1918*. Chicago: Quadrangle Books, 1969.

———. *Lenin: The Man and His Work and the Impressions of Colonel Raymond Robins and Arthur Ransome*. New York: Scott and Seltzer, 1919.

———. *The Soviets*. New York: Harcourt Brace, 1937.

———. *Through the Russian Revolution*. New York: Boni and Liveright, 1921.

Williams, William Appleman. *American-Russian Relations, 1781–1947*. New York: Rinehart, 1952.

———. "The Outdoor Mind." *The Nation* 179 (30 October 1954): 384–85.

———. "Raymond Robins and Russian-American Relations, 1917–1938." Ph.D. diss., University of Wisconsin, Madison, 1950.

Young, Kenneth, ed. *The Diaries of Sir Robert Bruce Lockhart: 1915–1938, 1939–1965*. 2 vols. London: St. Martin's Press, 1973–80.

Index

Abdication, 38; and Bolshevik program, 110; on behalf of Michael Romanov, 53

"Action in Russia" (memo), 234–40

Air raids, 91

Airplanes, 45–46, 57; U.S. construction, 60; use on Eastern front, 294n.11

Aland Islands, 118, 131, 132

Alekseev, Mikhail V., 77, 79, 80, 81, 256; and anti-Bolshevik forces, 176, 206, 215, 227, 247; as Chief of Staff, 84; and dissension with Kaledin, 215; resignation, 85

Alexander II (czar of Russia): and Wilhelm II (kaiser of Germany), 273; and zemstvo assemblies, 292n.4

"All power to the soviets," 109

All-Russian Committee for the Salvation of the Fatherland and Revolution, 118, 126; and civil war, 127

All-Russian Congress of Soviets of Workers' Deputies, 110; and new government, 112

Allies (Entente Powers), 188, 290n.10, 296n.8; and alternative Allied-Bolshevik policy, 208; ambassadors and Kornilov Uprising, 76, 79, 81, 294n.15; and blame on Russia, 234; and contact with anti-Bolshevik forces, 180; and impending Romanian defeat, 79; and Michelson Commission and supplies, 44, 230, 295n.20; and negotiations with Bolsheviks, 9, 111; and non-intercourse with Bolshevik leaders, 188; and non-interference in internal affairs in Russia, 185, 218; and peace terms, 127, 243; and

Provisional Government, 41; representatives seen as "Bolshevik enemies to be killed," 100; and response to Bolshevik Revolution, 110; responses if peace fails, 181, 187, 200–201, 207; and revision of war aims, 165–66; and Russian Army discipline, 67, 72; Russian opinion on peace issue, 162; Russian role critical, 30; and Russian treaty violations, 147, 154, 159; and safety in Bolshevik Russia, 111, 160; and separate peace, 41–42; and splitting Central Power allies from Germany, 234; and supplies in Russia, 8; and supplies falling into enemy hands, 190; troops and assistance to Russia, 122, 124, 276, 296n.10

Alternative Paths: Soviets and Americans, 1917–1920, 13

American Embassy, 45

American Military Mission, 8, 43–44

American National Red Cross, 91

American Railway Commission, 141

American Red Cross Commission to Romania, 185

American Red Cross Commission to Russia, 7, 30, 70, 90, 100, 128, 292n.10; and delaying of Brest peace, 261; Judson's first meeting with, 295n.23; and Kalpashnikov affair vis-à-vis Romania, 185; personnel, 58; and propaganda work, 170, 264–66; and railroad advisors, 141; under Robins's leadership, 9, 11; and Thompson's support, 92; and Thacher, 282

American troops to Russia, 122, 124; at Bolshevik invitation, 166–67, 197

Amur Valley, 238

Anarchists, 46–47; and Bolshevik program, 99; demands for release of Berkman and Goldman, 228, 302n.16; and February Revolution, 53

Anarchy: after Kornilov Uprising, 82, 94; after Revolution, 121, 124, 128; and July Uprising, 42; on eve of Bolshevik Revolution, 109, 114; and opposition to Bolshevik Revolution, 120

Anderson, H. W., 185

Annexations, 123, 177; and German demands, 231

Anti-Americanism, 95

Anti-Bolshevik forces, 112, 121; among army units, 152, 161; and groupings within, 176; and impact of "Peace, Land, and Bread" slogan, 139

Archangel, 8, 136, 159–60; and separatist movement, 21; and supplies, 189

Armenia, 217

Armenians, 87, 92

Armistice, 8, 110; and Allied contingency plans if it fails, 166, 174; and German terms, 158; and immobility of German troops during negotiations, 154, 167; and Judson meeting with Trotsky, 156; and negotiations with Germany, 152–53; of 11 November 1918, 212; and propaganda, 157; proposed by Bolsheviks, 123, 147; terms, 167, 171–73, 181, 205; and Trotsky invitation to Allies to participate, 168

Armour, Norman, 303nn.35, 43

Army Chief of Staff (U.S.), 105–6

Army Corps of Engineers, 2, 11

Atrocities, 92

Austria-Hungary: army and trapped Russian troops, 220; and separate peace, 41; and surrender at Tarnopol, 55

Avksentiev, Nicholai D., 127, 248, 257

Baker, Newton D., 1, 105, 290n.11; and Judson's final reports, 234–40, 303n.34; and Judson's recall, 212,

300–301n.97; and war matériel, 59–60

Bakhmatch, and Bolshevik supremacy, 226

Balfour, Alfred, 213

Baltic Fleet, 82

Baltic provinces, 235

Baltic Sea, 21, 90, 115; and armistice terms, 181; German activity, 95, 108, 132, 147, 158, 171, 179; and prisoner of war negotiations, 169, 181; Russian fleet, 105

Baltic Sea–Black Sea front, 199, 209, 229

Barter, General, 147, 207, 220, 230

"Battalions of death," 295n.37

Battle of the Marne, 272

Bay of Tavlagakhta, 101

Beabodsky, Countess, 84

Beach, W. D., 21

Beatty, Bessy, 164

Belgium, 49, 190

Bering Sea, 35

Berkman, Alexander, 184, 302n.16

Berlin, 202

Berne, 211, 217

Bertholot, General, 209

Bertron, Samuel R., 34, 87–88

Bessarabia, 294n.18

Billings, Frank, 58, 100

Black Sea, 108, 115, 132, 147; and armistice terms, 181; and Cossack claims of support, 178; and German activity, 158, 171, 179; and prisoner of war negotiations, 169, 181; and support for Bolsheviks, 300n.71

Blair, Colonel (British attaché), 82, 85, 92

Blockade, 15

Boer War, 33

Bolshevik Government: and Allied promises, 181; and allocation for "left internationalists," 195; and armistice, 175, 205; and Bolshevik ideology, 143; and Bolshevization of German army, 152; and Bolshevik-Ukrainian-Romanian modus vivendi, 220–21; and centrality of peace for political power, 184; and Commission of

People's Commissars, 117, 123; and
Constituent Assembly, 153, 225,
228–30, 302n.14; and evaluation of
strength, 176, 183, 187, 199, 231, 281;
and general program and policies,
225; and peace negotiations, 142; and
recognition of Finland, 214; and
relationship with German
government, 181; and response
to Japanese intervention, 237–38;
and Russian peace delegation, 162;
and split on membership, 133;
and war supplies, 8. *See also* Soviet
(Council/Committee) of Workers'
and Soldiers' Deputies
Bolshevik Party: as menace, 263; and
breakdown of army discipline, 70;
and counterfeit documents, 303n.32;
growing power after Kornilov, 82,
246, 294n.10; in service of the German
government, 54, 151–52, 173, 195, 247;
and Judson, 9; and July Uprising,
42–43, 46–47; and Kornilov Uprising,
75; and Provisional Government, 1,
40, 54, 61, 80, 107, 113, 246;
revolutionary program, 94, 117; and
vote in Constituent Assembly, 179
Bolshevik Revolution, 9, 11–13, 110;
first reports of, 107, 111, 115; first
suggestions of, 80, 102, 114
Bolshevik Propaganda Hearings, 304n.52
Bonaparte, Napoleon, 236
Bonch-Bruyevich, Vladimir D., 164
Bothnia, 138
Bourgeois, 107, 109, 113, 195; after
Bolshevik Revolution, 129;
Tereshchenko labeled, 116
Breshkovsky, Catherine, 295n.24
Breshkovsky Committee, 91, 295n.24;
and anti-Soviet propaganda, 114, 170,
304n.42
Brest-Litovsk Peace Treaty, 168, 194, 212,
214, 222, 285; and Allied aid in the
event of failure, 276–77; and German
annexation demands, 231; and
German "ultimatum," 216; and
negotiation issues, 222, 227; and
reported signing, 232; Robins's

delaying of signing, 260–61, 270; and
Wilson's "Fourteen Points," 213
Brialmont, General, 103, 295n.31
Britain: and Allied treaty violations,
147; and Ambassador to Russia, 76;
and arrest and release of socialists in
England, 158–59, 178; and general
peace, 154; military attaché on
Kornilov, 79; and Russia, 16
British Guiana, 292n.11
Brody, 72
Browne, Louis Edgar, 164, 173
Brusilov, Aleksei Alekseeivich, 37, 51,
56, 95, 256
Buchanan, Sir George, 120–21, 147; and
communication with Trotsky, 155;
and Judson's meeting with Trotsky,
217–18; and revision of war aims of
allies, 165
Bukovina, 72
Bukowski, Lieutenant, 131, 221–22, 233
Bullard, Arthur: 170, 299n.64; and
propaganda, 172
Burgess, Professor, 28
Burleson, Albert, 7, 125, 253, 260, 290n.7

Cadets (military), 126
Callahan, Captain, 221
Canada, 15, 75
Capital punishment, 54, 81
Capitalism, 95, 142
Carpathians, 272
Caucasian front, 92, 115, 147, 162, 170
Caucasus, 58, 159, 161
Central Army Committee (at Stavka),
142–43
Central Powers, 30; and armistice
expansion, 183, 196; and 1917
counteroffensive, 55; and Romanian
capitulation, 293n.12; and separate
peace, 10, 12; and supplies, 8; and
winning old Russia's territory, 235
Chaikovski, Nicholas, 257, 295n.24
Chamansky, 169
Charles (prince of Sweden), 169
Charles XII (king of Sweden), 236,
303n.24
Cherimetseif, General, 85

Finland (*cont.*)

lines, 77; and revolution, 130, 138; and separate government, 137, 176

Fleurot (newsperson), 164

Fokshany (Focsani), 64, 159, 294n.18

"Fourteen Points," 213, 214, 215, 279, 305n.57; and Soviet press reports, 216

France: and Allied treaty violations, 147; and apology to Trotsky, 208; and aviation mission, 57; and contact with anti-Bolshevik forces in the Ukraine, 197, 302n.10; and intervention in Soviet Russia, 2; military attaché attitude on Kornilov Uprising, 79; and Monroe Doctrine, 15; and recognition of Finland, 213, 214; and representation in Ukraine, 222; and Trotsky accusations of anti-Bolshevik activity, 206, 207

Francis, David, 40, 59, 290n.8; and alternative U.S.-Bolshevik policy, 208; and anti-German propaganda, 93; and authorization for Robins to consult with Trotsky, 196, 298n.51; and auto permit from Bolshevik authorities, 161; and Diamandi arrest, 217–18, 224, 302n.7; exhausted under strain, 165; and financing American Military Mission, 46–47; and Japanese intervention, 240; and Madame Matilda de Cram, 253, 267–70; and opposition to sending American troops, 124; and Kalpashnikov affair, 186; and Provisional Government weakness, 294n.10; and Root and American Red Cross Missions, 30, 292n.1; and Tereyoki, 48; and U.S. aid if armistice fails, 204

Francis and Judson: and ban on communication with Bolsheviks, 10, 135–36, 138, 300n.87; communications, 110, 129, 160, 293n.7; Judson suspected of de Cram accusations, 269; Judson's recall, 203, 300–301n.97; Judson's "Report on Events in Russia," 263–71; meeting with Trotsky, 156, 159, 168, 224

Franco-Prussian War, 7

Friederichstadt, 96

Front in modern war, 23–25

Galicia, 50, 72, 271, 272

Gatchina, 131

General strikes, 94

General William V. Judson, 300–301n.97

George III (king of England), 8

Georgia, 289n.2

Germany, 2; action in Dvina and Jacobstadt, 89; and Allied supplies in Russia, 189, 192; and armistice talks for all fronts, 153, 205; as "supernation," 233; and Baltic–Black Sea front forces, 179; "Decree on Peace" and victory in the war, 212; and democracy, 68; and Finland, 73, 81–82, 138, 214; hatred for, 35; and impact of civil war in Russia, 174; and impact of Bolshevik Revolution, 130; major Riga offensive, 80, 81; and Monroe Doctrine, 15; and non-movement of troops during armistice, 167, 179, 182; and Northern front, 82, 90, 101, 103, 109, 294n.18; and peace negotiations, 131; and Petrograd 57, 96, 198; and relations with Bolshevik government, 181; and reported offensive on Macedonia and Mesopotamian fronts, 144; and revolution, 276; and Riga, 96, 104; and Romanian front, 73; and separate peace, 12, 41; and threat of colonization of Russia, 192; wartime civilian conditions, 228; and western front buildup, 229

Gobi desert, 238, 279

Goethals, George W., 258

Goldman, Emma, 302n.16

Golievsky, Colonel, 131

Great Britain, 7; and intervention in Soviet Russia, 2

Grodno, 229

Guchkov, Alexandr, 62, 242, 247, 255, 273–74, 292n.2; arrest, 80; and Bolshevik Revolution, 123; and Czar's abdication, 38, 53; and Judson, 7, 37, 53; Judson's report on, 31, 304n.46; and July Uprising, 43; and

Kornilov Uprising, 77, 79; and mass peace demand in Russia, 161–62; resignation, 9, 53
Gulf of Finland, 90, 104, 138, 160
Gulf of Neva, 77
Gulf of Riga, 96, 103, 104, 171
Gulf of Tartary, 34
Gurko, General, 63

Hagood, Lieutenant, 47–48, 108
The Hague, 32
Haig, J. C., 286, 305n.59
Haparanda, 231
Harbin, 20, 36
Harper, Samuel, 42
Harvard College, 2, 286
Havard, Col. Valery, 6
Hayes, Alice Ryerson, 291n.15
Heart condition, 11
Helsingfors, 104, 138
Hoboken, New Jersey, 11
Hoffmann, Max, 171, 173
Hogard, 57
Holy Synod, 206
Horne, Henry J., 141, 167
House, Edward M., 92

Illinois, 37
Imperialism: German, 235; Judson's outlook, 2–3, 7, 27; U.S. new, 14, 27–29
India, 16; and Lenin urging Muslim revolt, 169
Indianapolis, 2
Influenza epidemic, 11
"Instructions to Military Attachés," 240
Inter-Allied Conference in Paris, 296n.8. See also Paris Conference
International organization, 27
Intervention in Russia: first warnings against, 163, 299n.55; Japanese in Siberia, 237
Ireshti, 159
Italy, 75, 85; and Allied treaty violations, 147

Jacobstadt, 89, 90, 96
Janin, General, 85

Japan: and Allied treaty violations, 147; attaché in Russia in 1917, 85; and conquest of east Asia, 279–80; and landing at Vladivostok, 228, 237; and occupation of Siberia, 215, 252, 303n.25; and secret treaties with Russia on China, 184; siege of Mukden, 6; and Trotsky invitation to Allies to participate in armistice, 168
Jarvie, 58
Jassy, 49, 71, 167, 185; and proposed modus vivendi with Bolsheviks, 221
Jews, 172
Jingoism, 5, 28
Joffre, Joseph Jacques, 247
Judson, Clay (son), 262, 291n.15, 292n.2; and the Judson papers, 287; and military assignment, 65, 83
Judson, William V.: "Action in Russia" memo, 234–40; and American Red Cross, 295n.20; and American troops to Russia, 122, 244; as prisoner of war, 6; biography of, 12, 291n.15, 305n.58; and Bolshevik power, evaluation of, 191; and Bolshevik Propaganda Hearings, 304n.52; and Bolshevik-Ukrainian-Romanian modus vivendi, 220–21; career in engineering and the military, 2–3, 14, 289n.2; and Constituent Assembly, 227; departure from Russia, 214, 224, 230, 232; and Diamandi arrest, 217; and Distinguished Service Medal, 283–85; early reports, speeches, and letters, 2, 5; early years, 2–3; and final evaluation of Russia, 232; final report, "Russian Situation," 240–53; and Francis, 10, 110, 144, 146, 165, 167, 194, 224; and Gen. Alexander Guchkov, 7, 9, 255–56; influenza and heart condition, 11, 258–59; and "Instructions to Military Attachés," 240; and January 1 order to Washington, 205, 300–301n.97; lack of staff as attaché, 106; and the language of his reports, 304n.41; and Madame Matilda de Cram, 253; meeting with Trotsky, 9–10, 12, 156–59, 192–95, 217–18, 248, 285, 298n.51; and

Judson, William V. (*cont.*)
non-intercourse with Bolsheviks, 138, 144, 146, 155, 173, 178, 186, 191, 240; of restoration of Kerensky, 115; on Minister of War Verkhovsky, 88; on Romanian front conditions, 78; on Russo-Japanese War, 6, 18–25; on U.S.-Soviet Relations, 2, 5, 9, 212; and opposition to U.S. policy on Bolshevik Russia, 212, 254; outlook on U.S. foreign policy and imperialism, 2, 4–5, 9, 23–29, 292nn.10–11; and polarization among Russians in U.S., 255; and postwar evaluation of Bolsheviks, 258; and President Wilson, 2, 11; "Program" memo, 254–55; promotion to brigadier general, 59, 65, 69–70, 305n.54; and recall to U.S., 2, 5, 10–11, 203–4, 212, 292n.2, 301n.2; recommendation to Wilson, 125; reflection on Russian responsibilities, 241, 283–85; "Report of Certain Events in Russia, 1917–1918," 262–71; responsibilities in Russia, 1–2, 7–8, 10, 12, 14, 30, 34, 290nn.11, 13; return to Russia, 240–41; and Robins, 2, 183, 249; and Root Mission, 35–37, 292n.3; and Russian army, 1, 7–8, 30, 39, 42, 50–55, 64, 87, 102, 104, 244; and self-determination as a hitch in negotiations, 203; and separate peace, 150; and shock at Bolshevik Revolution, 89, 120; and support for Kornilov, 294n.15; title and George Kennan, 293n.7; and Trotsky and German government, 195, 247; Trotsky and Lenin, 164, 196–97, 247; and a unified Allied policy in Russia, 188; and U.S. aid if armistice fails, 204; and Wilson's "Fourteen Points," 213, 285
July Uprising, 41–42, 46–48, 293n.1; and role of the Bolsheviks, 54

Kadets. *See* Constitutional Democratic Party
Kaledin, Aleksei M., 82, 119, 247; and activity in the Don, 139, 142, 174; and Allied contact, 182; and armed opposition to Bolsheviks, 126, 131, 176, 180, 206; and dissension with Alekseev, 215 and joint front with Ukraine and Romania, 163; seeking Allied support, 176; and Ukrainian opposition, 132
Kalpashnikov, Andrei, 185–86
Kaluga, 178
Kalushch (Kaloutch), 72, 98
Keller, Count and Countess, 59, 70, 80, 84, 92
Kemp, Admiral, 159
Kennan, George, 1, 10, 13, 187, 292n.1, 293n.7; and *Russia Leaves the War*, 213
Kerensky, Alexander, 242; as Commander-in-Chief, 84; as dictator, 57; and Cossack support, 65; flight from Petrograd, 107, 111, 115, 117; and General Lechitsky; government reshuffle, 80; and Judson meeting, 59; and July Uprising, 43; and Kornilov Uprising, 75, 80, 97–98, 245; and new coalition government, 101; request for Allied non-recognition of Bolsheviks, 112, 115; and rising power of Bolsheviks, 82; and Second Provisional Government, 1, 41, 57, 264, 274; with Northern front troops, 112, 115, 117, 247; with Savinkov after Bolshevik Revolution, 118, 123
Kerth, Monroe C., 8, 39, 45, 48, 84, 108, 266; and alternative U.S.-Bolshevik policy, 187–88, 191–93, 208; and armistice, 147, 149, 158, 167; at Stavka, 140, 142, 159; and danger at Mogilev, 161; and delayed return to Mogilev, 210; and Distinguished Service Medal, 270; and Judson's recall, 203, 300–301n.97; and Krylenko interview, 222; and protest of Russian armistice, 168, 259, 297n.36, 304n.40
Kharkov, 202; and Bolshevik battle reverses, 214; and Bolshevik supremacy, 226
Kiev, 163, 164, 175, 178, 198, 252; and Bolshevik government arrest of Ukrainian Rada, 300n.90; and proposed modus vivendi with

Bolsheviks, 221; and Rada request for Austrian help, 230
Klembovsky, General, 63, 75, 77, 98
Klieforth, 233
Knox, Alfred, 147, 154, 294n.16; and aid for Russia if peace fails, 200; and Allied troops to Russia, 121, 122; and Allied-Bolshevik relations, 163–64, 194; and general peace, 155; and propaganda, 172; and Trotsky invitation to Allies to participate in armistice, 168, 170
Kokoshkin, F. F., 229
Kolchak, Alexander V., 257
Kornilov, Lavar G., 56–57, 247, 275; and armed opposition to Bolshevik government, 175, 176, 178; and Cossacks, 65, 75; and escape, 163; and restoration of army discipline, 70; and Romanian front, 64; and Savinkov and Kerensky, 63; surrender-resignation, 79–80, 96; uprising, 98–99
Kornilov Uprising, 1, 72–79, 98–99, 245; aftermath demoralization, 97; first news, 71; and Kerensky, 75
Kovel, 159
Krimov, General, 81
Kronstadt, 42, 105
Krylenko, Nikolai, V., 141; and anti-German alliance, 206–7; and armistice negotiations with Germany, 152; and control of Stavka, 162, 164; and Dukhonin's dismissal, 296n.26; and military response if armistice fails, 205–6; and volunteer paid army, 214
Kuban Cossacks, 176
Kuhlman, Richard von, 202
Kumanski Cossacks, 77
Kurile Islands, 16
Kuropatkin, A. N., 6, 18, 32, 103

La Lonne, Count, 92
Lake Baikal, 33, 238, 252, 279
Lake Michigan, 289n.2
Lansing, Robert, 105; and ban on communication with Bolsheviks, 10; and Judson's final reports, 234–40;

and Judson's recall, 203–4, 212. 298n.51, 300–301n.97
Laverne, General, 85, 121, 154, 197, 225
Lazarov, George, 295n.24
Lechitsky (Litchitsky), General, 63, 294n.14
Lemberg, 55
Lenin, Vladimir Ilyich Ulyanov, 10–11, 246, 265, 275; attacked, 222; and Constituent Assembly, 173, 302n.14; and counterfeit Sisson documents, 303n.32; "Decree on Peace," 110; and dictatorial powers, 133, 136, 137; and diplomatic missions and Diamandi affair, 219–20, 302n.7; and Dukhonin's dismissal, 296n.26; ending titles and civilian ranks, 145; forming new government, 112; Judson's impressions of, 164; and July Uprising, 43; and Robins, 299n.69; and separate peace, 12
Letts, 180
Lexington, Kentucky, 3, 17, 65, 93
Liaoyang, Manchuria, 6, 17, 32
Likomsky, 77
"The Life and Career of General William V. Judson, 1865–1923," 131
Liteyni Bridge, 43
Lithuanians, 87, 235; and self-determination, 201
Lochridge, P. D., 294n.11
Long, Mr. (at Department of State), 35
Looting, 172–73
Luga, 134
Lvov, Prince George E., 9, 41, 293n.1
Lvov, Vladimir N., 77, 80, 98–99
Lynching Russian officers, 95, 97

McCarthyism, 287
McCormick, Cyrus, 34
McCormick, Robert R., 259
McCormick, Robert S., 5–6, 17, 19, 290nn.4–5
McCully, Newton, 18
Macedonia, 144
McFadden, David, 13
McKinley, William, 5
Mahan, Alfred, 7

for peace after Russo-Japanese War, 32; and U.S., 8

Niessel, Gen. Henri, 92, 141, 154, 165, 230–31; and aid for Russia if peace fails, 201; and armistice, 170, 194; and propaganda, 172

Noe, Mademoiselle, 107

Non-interference, Allied commitment, 185

Northern Front, 63–64, 77, 80, 82, 90, 96; and armistice negotiations with Germany, 152; and Austria, 294n.18; and famine, 140, 142; to the Bolsheviks, 118, 152

Norway, 241

Noulens, Joseph, 183; and Diamandi arrest, 217–18;

Novocherkask, 140, 181

Novoye Vremya, 79

Oconee, 156

October Manifesto, 62, 303n.29

Octobrists, 9, 62, 242, 303n.29

Odessa, 166, 180; claimed by Bolsheviks, 210, 215

Offensive strength, 15

Okna, 64

Olney, Richard L., 292n.11

Omsk, 199

One Hundred Red Days, 300n.89

Orenburg Cossacks, 176

Oslo, 232, 233

Packer, E. L., 278, 280

Panama Canal, 16, 27; the price of its defense, 28

Paris Conference (of WWI Allies), 101, 116, 213, 244, 296n.8, 303n.31

Parker, Francis L., 8, 39, 45, 48, 56, 61, 65, 84

Peace, 94, 99, 249; and Allied contingency plans, 166; and Allies, 155; and Bolshevik program, 108; and Kerensky appeal, 100; conference, 110; "Decree on Peace," 110; and Judson meeting with Trotsky, 156; and Judson's recommendation to Wilson, 125; and mass demand in Russia, 161–62, 174, 243; or civil war,

106; and Russian army initiatives, 141; and self-determination as a hitch in negotiations, 185, 202–3; and terms with Germany, 158, 252; and Trotsky "no war no peace" position, 301n.101

Peasant's Soviet, 153–54

Peking, 36

Perm, and separatism, 211

Pershing, John J., 60, 77, 102, 125, 293n.41

Persia, 171, 181

Peter and Paul Fortress, 43, 293n.2; and Diamandi arrest, 217–18; in Revolution, 115

Peterhoff, 77, 123

Petrograd, 5, 7, 34, 64, 77; as center of most Russian munitions, 97; defense of, 104, 295n.32; and deteriorating civilian conditions, 139; and "disorders" (July Uprising), 41–42; Food Commission resignation, 43; garrison, 105, 115; in Bolshevik Revolution, 112, 124; vulnerable to German bombardment, 96. *See also* St. Petersburg

Petrograd Duma, 118

Petrograd Soviet, 102; and Menshevik representatives, 293n.1

Philippines, 3; and U.S.-Japanese Relations, 28

Pierce, Palmer E., 295n.29

Pogroms, 87, 172

Poland, 235, 272, 279; self-determination, 201

Poles, 87, 109, 174; and loyalty only to Poland, 187

Polish National Committee, 186, 187

Polish troops: and peace talks break, 209; units forming in U.S., 214, 216

Polovtsev Palace, 37

Poltava, 178

Poole, Maj. Gen. F. C., 106, 141, 163, 197, 225

Port Arthur, 17, 18

Potopov, Q. M., 81, 171

Pravda, 178, 216

Preparedness, 20, 25, 292n.10

Preparliament. *See* Democratic Council

182; non-intercourse with Bolshevik leadership, 189, 196; and Provisional Government weakness, 294n.10; and self-determination as a hitch in negotiations, 203; and Trotsky and Bolshevik propaganda, 151–52; and Trotsky in service of the German government, 195

Rodzianko, Mikhail V., 62, 77, 176, 242, 247

Romania, 37, 39, 174, 293n.12; and Allied treaty violations, 147; ambassador to Russia, 105; and anti-Bolshevik alliance, 163; and armistice provisions, 175; and arrest of Austrian delegates to Brest talks, 218; asylum for king of, 49; Bolshevik orders to arrest King, 225–26; and Bolshevik-Ukrainian-Romanian modus vivendi, 20–21; to Central Powers camp, 235; claimed by Bolsheviks, 210; and Diamandi re. Bolshevik soldiers surrounded, 218; front, 49; Judson memo on military situation, 78; and Kalpashnikov affair, 185; 1916 defeat, 51, 56, 60, 63, 130; separate peace, 49

Romanian front, 63, 152, 167; King in command, 63, 92

Romanov, Michael, 53

Romanovski, Gen.Vladimir Z., 82, 90

Roosevelt, Franklin Delano, 13

Roosevelt, Theodore, 5

Root, Elihu, 30, 34, 122; and financing American Military Mission, 46–47; meeting with Guchkov, 9, 38; and opposition to sending American troops, 124

Root Mission to Russia, 30, 36, 87, 273–75, 292n.1; en route, 34, 293n.6; Judson's role, 2, 7–9, 14, 241, 289n.1, 293n.11

Rostov, 178, 181, 185

Rovno, 202

Ruggles, James A., 233; and Bolshevik power in Siberia, 209, 210; and Constituent Assembly, 227

Russell, Charles E., 34

Russia: and Monroe Doctrine, 15; and Allied relations, 1; as slave of Germany, 74–75; and "breakup," 134, 176, 211; and constitutionalism, 32; and democratic government, 1, 8, 32, 68; and Judson's final report, 240–53; leaving the war, 174; and mass demand for peace, 161–62, 174; and obligations to Allies, 157; and sea power, 16; and secret treaties with Japan on China, 184; supplies urgently needed, 190; and territorial expansion, 22–23; and transport system, 39–40, 93; under the Czars, 22, 32–33; and U.S. relations, 1; and upper classes, 39

Russian army: at Tarnapol, 48; and Bolshevik influence, 95; and discipline breakdown, 244, 251, 277; and election of officers, 54; in crisis in Romania, 219–20; Judson's memos on discipline, 66, 71–74; organization, battle readiness, and discipline, 1, 7–8, 30, 39, 42, 50–55, 64, 104; manpower, 250; and 1915 failures, 50; and 1917 offensive, 39, 55, 244; and organization under the Bolsheviks, 133, 180; and peasant soldiers as slaves, 32, 66; and railroads, 8; reorganization after Kornilov Uprising, 85–86; retreat, 72; and sea power, 33; and separate peace, 42; and strength estimates 1 January 1918, 207; and supplies to Germany, 189

Russian Commission, 40

Russian Daily News, 131

Russian finances, 116

Russian General Headquarters. *See* Stavka

Russian military manufacturing, 51–52

Russian navy, 123

Russian officers, and service in U.S. army, 216

Russian political parties, 61–63, 242–43, 294n.13

Russian Purchasing Commission, 295n.29. *See also* Michelson Commission

Bolshevik government, 127, 130;
parties, 62, 113; parties supporting
the Bolshevik government, 146
Society of Colonial Dames, 291n.9
Soldatenko, and mass peace demand in
Russia, 161–62
South Africa, 33
South-Western front, 63–64, 80, 85,
90, 167, 134; and German strength,
199; and opposition to Bolsheviks,
152, 218
Sovereignty, 5
Soviet-American Relations, 1917–1920, 13
Soviet of Petrograd. *See* Petrograd
Soviet
Soviet (Council/Committee) of
Workers' and Soldiers' Deputies: and
Bolshevik ideology, 143; Bolshevik
membership, 99; election of Lenin
and Trotsky, 122; and July Uprising,
42; and Kerensky, 81–83, 94; and
Kornilov Uprising, 99; militia, 81; and
Paris Conference, 116; and parties of
opposition, 113; role in Provisional
Government, 1, 36, 41, 245; role in
second Provisional Government, 54;
and support among masses, 244
Soviet Union, end, 12. *See also* Bolshevik
Government
Spanish-American War, 3, 7, 14
Spring Offensives of 1918, 8
Spying, 267–70
Stalin, Joseph Dzhugashvili, and
Dukhonin's dismissal, 296n.26
Stalinisky, (American embassy
interpreter), 217
Stanislaus, 55
Stankevitch, Commissar, 161, 248; and
mass peace demand in Russia,
161–62
State Bank of Russia, 134, 136, 142
State Department, 29
Stavka (Russian General Headquarters),
39, 45, 48, 65, 103; and Kornilov
Uprising, 76, 80; and offensive failure,
56; and Romania, 61
Steppes, 37
Stevens Railroad Advisory
Commission, 7–8, 30, 105, 282

Stines, 196, 233
Stockholm, 121, 231, 232, 233
"Strategic Value of Her West Indian
Possessions to the United States,"
14–16
Strikes, 98, 127–28, 136; railroad, 102,
119
Suicide of Russian officers, 90
Sukhomlinov, Vladimir A., 272–73
Sweden, 81, 82, 199; and recognition of
Finland, 213; and prisoner of war
negotiations, 169
Swift, Harold, 58
Switzerland, 228, 295n.24

Tannenberg, 272
Tarnapol, 48, 55, 72–73; commune,
95, 98
Tekuci, 159
Telephone exchange in Petrograd
during Bolshevik Revolution, 119,
126
Tereschenko, Mikhail I., 43, 107, 162,
242, 274–75; as proposed delegate to
the Paris Conference, 116; and
Kornilov Uprising, 76, 77, 79;
Kornilov aftermath, 81, 82, 108
Tereyoki (Finland), 48, 59
Terrorism, 63, 116
Thacher, Thomas D., 141, 186, 282
Thompson, William B., 11, 90, 264–67,
277–78, 292n.10; as Head of the
American Red Cross Commission, 91,
295n.20; and *Bolshevik Propaganda
Hearings*, 304n.52; and delayed Brest
peace, 270; and financial contribution
to the American Military Mission, 58;
financial support democratic
propaganda, 93, 100–101, 105, 109,
150, 170, 264; and Provisional
Government weakness, 294n.10
Thornhill, Major, 172
Tokyo, 6, 17, 184
Tomsk, 199
The Torch, 184
Torneo, 132, 136, 231
Totten, Major, 233
Trachtenberg, 131
Transbaikalia, 303n.25

Ural Cossacks, 176
Urals, 237
Ussuri, 18, 238

Velitchko, General, 103, 113
Venezuela, 28, 292n.11
Verdun-Nancy sector, 171
Verkhovsky, Aleksandr I., 84, 248, 250, 256; as minister of war, 87, 104, 105; and "Fourteen Points" and general outlook, 227; and mass peace demand in Russia, 161–62; and opposition to Bolshevik Revolution, 127, 129, 131; reorganization of army after Kornilov Uprising, 85–86, 113, 245; and resignation, 108, 113
Viborg, 104
Vilna, 179, 229
Vinaver, Maksim M., 145
Vitebsk, 252
Vladivostok, 34, 35, 36, 195; and Japanese landing, 228, 239; and Judson during Russo-Japanese War, 6, 18; and supplies in, 189
Volodchenko, General, 90
Vologda, 77, 160, 239; and separatist movement, 211
Von Meck, 32
Vopica, Minister, 185
Vostrotin, 257, 303n.39
Vyrubov, 119

Wahl, L., 289n.2
Wallace, William, Jr., 91
War, modern, 7, 15, 19–20, 23–25, 50, 291n.9
War College Division (Warcolstaff), 9, 289; and creation of a Russian section, 46; and organization of Military Attaché office, 43, 46
War Department, 6
War Industries Board, 295n.29
War weariness in Russia, 243
Warsaw, 229
Washington, D.C.: and Judson as Engineer Commissioner, 289n.2; and Judson's recall, 5
West Indies, 14–16

West Point (U.S. Military Academy), 2, 19, 21, 108, 289n.2
Western front, 8, 285, 291n.9, 293n.4; and armistice, 168; and the "Decree on Peace," 212; and German concentration, 171, 229; and Russian command, 63; and separate peace, 41; and support by preoccupying Germany in the east, 236
Weyant, Jane, 13, 293n.4; and recall to U.S. from Soviet Russia, 203, 298n.47, 300n.97
White Army, 301n.104
White Sea, 201, 217
Whitehouse, 154
"Wild Division," 77, 134, 163, 294n.17
Wilhelm II (kaiser of Germany), 236, 273
Wilkie, John, 49
Williams, Albert Rhys, 110
Williams, William Appleman, 12–13, 187, 291n.15
Wilson, Gen.J. M., 3
Wilson, Woodrow: and "Fourteen Points Speech," 213, 305n.57; and Judson's recall, 203–4; 300–301n.97; and non-intercourse instructions after Bolshevik Revolution, 111, 173; and relations with Judson, 2; and response to Bolshevik Revolution, 125; and U.S.-Soviet relations, 11; and U.S. intervention in Soviet Russia, 2; war message to Congress, 178, 292n.3
Winter Palace, 36, 37, 43, 117, 172
Winter Park, Florida, 11
Witte, Sergei, 15, 33
Women's battalion, 89
Wood, 286
"Workers of the world," 177
"World empire," 27
World War I, 8, 109, 152, 166; Allied concerns about Russia, 2; and impact of U.S. entry in the war, 212; prolonged, 67, 2; Russia's role, 1–2, 41
World War II, 13
Wright, Butler, 70, 155, 193, 253, 268

RUSSIA IN WAR AND REVOLUTION
was composed in 10/13.5 Palatino
on a Power Macintosh using QuarkXPress; at The Book Page; printed by sheet-fed offset
on 50-pound Lions Falls Turin Book Natural stock
(an acid-free, totally chlorine-free paper),
Smyth sewn and bound over binder's boards
in ICG Arrestox B cloth,
and wrapped with dust jackets printed in 3 colors on 100-pound enamel stock
by Thomson-Shore, Inc.;
designed by Diana Dickson; published by
THE KENT STATE UNIVERSITY PRESS
Kent, Ohio 44242